ROGER D

Roger Domeneghetti is a senior lecturer in journalism at Northumbria University. His first book,
*From the Back Page to the Front Room: Foot-
ball's Journey Through the English Media*, was
shortlisted for the 2015 Lord Aberdare Literary
Prize for Sports History, and received widespread
critical praise.

Prior to this, he worked as a journalist for more
than twenty years in both print and new media.
He continues to work as a freelancer for a variety of publications including the *Blizzard*, *New
European*, *BBC History Magazine*, *Times Literary Supplement* and *Wisden Cricket Monthly*.

ALSO BY ROGER DOMENEGHETTI

*From the Back Page to the Front Room: Football's
Journey Through the English Media*

ROGER DOMENEGHETTI

Everybody Wants to Rule the World

Britain, Sport and the 1980s

VINTAGE

1 3 5 7 9 10 8 6 4 2

Vintage is part of the Penguin Random House group of companies
whose addresses can be found at global.penguinrandomhouse.com

First published in Vintage in 2024
First published in hardback by Yellow Jersey in 2023

Copyright © Roger Domeneghetti 2024

Roger Domeneghetti has asserted his right to be identified as the author of this
Work in accordance with the Copyright, Designs and Patents Act 1988

Tony Harrison, 'V.' (Bloodaxe Books, 1985)
www.bloodaxebooks.com

penguin.co.uk/vintage

Printed and bound in Great Britain by Clays Ltd, Elcograf S.p.A.

The authorised representative in the EEA is Penguin Random House Ireland,
Morrison Chambers, 32 Nassau Street, Dublin D02 YH68

A CIP catalogue record for this book is available from the British Library

ISBN 9781529114843

Penguin Random House is committed to a sustainable future
for our business, our readers and our planet. This book is made
from Forest Stewardship Council® certified paper.

For Amy, Lucy and Kes,
with love

CONTENTS

INTRODUCTION

The Name of the Game

FOR Britain, the 1980s arguably began when Margaret Thatcher became prime minister and entered Downing Street on 4 May 1979 and ended when she left tearfully on 28 November 1990. The country was a very different place when her time in office finished than it had been at the start. Whatever your politics, it is hard to argue that any other twentieth-century prime minister, outside of wartime, had such an impact on the country. The phrase for which she is perhaps best known is 'There is no such thing as society'. It is actually a slight misquote, but it resonated because it neatly summed up the core tenet of Thatcherism, her political ideology, which rejected the post-war consensus and mixed aggressive free-market capitalism with a strong emphasis on law and order and a disdain for civil liberties. Her attitudes towards the welfare state, labour relations, the economy, race and sexuality were all infused with this philosophy. And, in various ways, we're still living with the effects of Thatcher's legacy today, one reason the 1980s still seem so close.

Yet we all experience these epochs differently, dependent on where we live, who we live with and how much money we have to live on. The high points of most decades pass the majority of people by. For how many did the twenties really roar or the sixties really swing? Despite this, there is a temptation to imagine a shared collective experience: 'the eighties'. In part that's because, thanks to television, we were increasingly sharing communal experiences. Only 80,000 people were present at Wembley for the Live Aid concert in 1985, but millions more, billions more around the world, watched on television. It was because of TV that sport also became a regular communal event during the 1980s. Major sporting events began to draw large television audiences in the 1950s − the 1966 World Cup final is still the most watched television event in British history − but it wasn't until the 1980s that television companies in Britain really began to understand the true value of sport as content and the amount of sport we could watch grew. Throughout the decade we gathered in our millions, separate but together, to cheer on as cricketers put the Aussies to the sword, snooker players duked it out to the last black of the last frame, ice skaters executed perfect routines and middle-distance runners pushed each other to their limits.

Yet one wonders how often the woman who defined the decade was watching. Margaret Thatcher seemed curiously divorced from all of this. Although her husband Denis was a keen golfer and a rugby referee and her son took part in the 1982 Paris–Dakar rally, famously getting lost for six days, Thatcher had little interest in sport. Her successor, John Major, suggested that 'She tried occasionally to show an interest and dutifully turned up to watch great sporting events, but always looked rather out of place.'[1] Her most active involvement, both publicly and politically, came at moments of controversy or crisis. Her time in power was bookended by two major sporting incidents. Within nine months of her first entering No. 10, the Soviet Union invaded Afghanistan. It was a chance for Thatcher to flex her muscles on the international stage and demonstrate her anti-Soviet credentials and led to her government, ultimately unsuccessfully, exerting significant pressure on British athletes not to attend the Moscow Olympics in 1980. Eighteen months before she left office, ninety-five Liverpool fans died in a crush during an FA Cup semi-final against Nottingham Forest at Hillsborough (over the following decades the death toll would grow to ninety-seven).

It's perhaps because of Thatcher's disinterest in sport that too often historians seem to divorce it from the rest of 1980s society. If it's there, it's either relegated to its own chapter, or reduced to anecdote, an unloved footnote to supposedly more important events. In either case, the deep connections between sport and the rest of society tend to go unrecognised or ignored. It's easy, for example, to suggest that hooliganism was football's problem and had nothing to do with wider society. But was that really the case when the country was also beset by numerous inner-city riots and the violence of the miners' strike? Likewise, the stadium disasters at Valley Parade in Bradford and Hillsborough in Sheffield: were they indicative only of the way football was run, or a mirror of the litany of public-service disasters that beset the country in the latter half of the decade?

A more nuanced understanding would acknowledge that modern sport is a microcosm of society beyond the field of play. It tells us something fundamental about the era in which it takes place, reflecting the cultural trends, contested identities and areas of conflict of the time. As such, sport is the key to understanding what really happened to Britain in the 1980s, one of the most dramatic, turbulent, divisive and colourful decades of the twentieth century. By examining key sports events, performances and personalities and setting them in the context of a period of major social, political and cultural change, I endeavour to show not only that sport is a mirror of society but also what its reflection tells us about Britain during that decade.

I also believe that many aspects of the way we live today have been shaped by trends which developed around sport in the 1980s.

In all aspects of life during those years, sport challenged and changed Britain. It was a transitional decade which saw sport and society become highly mediatised, hyper-commercialised and commodified and during which sport became truly part of the national conversation, something that we now take for granted and only appreciate when it is taken away from us, such as during the first coronavirus lockdown. The 1980s also saw the growth of identity politics and the start of a culture war which, although not always having been labelled as such, is constantly being fought, at certain times more aggressively, such as now, post-Brexit. The 1980s was another such period, the sporting arena being a battle-field on which these identities were expressed and contested.

These themes are explored in the book's four sections. The first, *Culture*, charts the pivotal relationship between sport and the media and the rising impact of television in what were also the last years before sport was repackaged, and in many cases priva-tised, made available only to those willing to pay to watch. It shows how this helped define modern celebrity and accelerate the Americanisation of British culture. The second section, *Identity*, looks at how successful black sportsmen and women – the chil-dren of the Windrush generation – began challenging the negative narratives about young black Britons, while still facing very high levels of racism. It explores the increasing prominence of wom-en's sport despite continued antagonism towards female athletes, and how the demonisation of the gay community, particularly during the moral panic around AIDS, affected gay and bi-sexual sportsmen and women. The third section argues that the 1980s was a decade of *Conflict* played out to a backdrop of the Falklands War, the Troubles in Northern Ireland, industrial disputes such as the miners' strike, and riots across the country. This violence spilled into the sporting arena, particularly the football terraces. The final section, *Politics*, suggests that although Thatcher had little interest in sport, it was never far from her in-tray, be it the Moscow Olympics, the anti-apartheid boycotts or the horrific tragedies that beset football, a game that embraced her financial policies.

I hope you enjoy revisiting, or visiting for the first time, the sporting landscape of the decade. I also hope that the book shows that sport is inextricably linked to, and can help us understand, the society and culture in which it takes place. As such, the legacy of 1980s sport has much to tell us about ourselves, for it was during that decade that we began to see the outline of what we might call twenty-first-century Britain develop.

AUTHOR'S NOTE

This book gives an overview of a decade in which racism, sexism and homophobia were endemic and overt in British culture and society. To that end, language which some will find shocking, and most will (and all should) find unacceptable has, at times, been retained. This has not been done to offend, but to offer a true picture of the prejudices of the 1980s. It was, sadly, the grim reality of the era and that cannot and should not be erased. History is not always pleasant to re-examine, not least because doing so sometimes makes us realise how little has changed, but that does not mean we should pretend it did not happen.

PART I:

CULTURE

CHAPTER 1

The Sun Always Shines on TV

I

AT JUST past midnight on the last Sunday of April 1985, Steve Davis, then the best snooker player in the world, watched in disbelief as his hopes of a third successive world title slipped through his fingers. 'The Golden Nugget', as he was known by his fans, held a comfortable 8−0 lead after the first frame of the second session. However, his opponent Dennis Taylor had doggedly clung on, eventually squaring the match 17−17 to set up a winner-takes-all final frame. Even then, Davis had led 62−44 with four coloured balls remaining; he needed just one, his opponent all four. Taylor potted the brown, the blue and the pink to take the score to 62−59 but missed the black. After nearly fifteen hours at the table over two days, it all came down to the final ball. The players traded safety shots and missed pots before Taylor, having never been ahead in the match, finally sunk the black to take the crown. As the Northern Irishman pumped the air in triumph with his cue, Davis could only look on, forlorn. Despite the late hour, some 18.5 million people stayed awake to see Taylor's victory. Yet those inside Sheffield's Crucible Theatre were unaware that nearly a third of the population of the country were glued to their sets watching the drama unfold. 'We were in the goldfish bowl,' says Barry Hearn, Davis' manager.[1] 'It wasn't until the Monday or Tuesday that we saw the figures and thought "Fuck!". Great sport evolves. It was like Agatha Christie's best ever book and you didn't know who did it until the last page. That's a very special one-off.'

The iconic final was BBC2's most watched programme of the year and had the largest viewing figures for any programme extending beyond midnight.[2] That the audience was so vast was indicative not just of the appeal of sport but also that in the 1980s watching television was still a communal, national experience. Viewers had yet to fracture across numerous satellite and cable channels. The internet, social media and streaming services did not exist. In 1981 20.3 million households in Britain, approximately 97.6 per cent, had at least one television set,[3] and yet often there hardly seemed anything worth watching. At the start of the decade there were just three channels: BBC1, BBC2 and ITV. Prior to midday, content had a decidedly beige feel and was aimed at Open University students and schoolchildren. The two BBC channels regularly shut down for an hour or so at lunchtime. Broadcasts ended before midnight with the news, weather, a brief look at the next day's schedule and a polite reminder to turn off your set after the national anthem. Then the screen went blank and, for those who hadn't been paying attention, began to emit a high-pitched whine as one last prompt to hit the 'off' button.

By the end of the 1980s, the TV landscape had changed beyond all recognition. Channel 4 made its debut in November 1982 (although, initially it didn't start until 5 p.m. and around 13 per cent of households couldn't access it). Two months later, in January 1983, the BBC launched the country's first breakfast television show. Its commercial rival TV-am started a fortnight later. Satellite dishes and 'squarials' began appearing on houses in 1989, the now-defunct British Satellite Broadcasting company and its rival Sky Television giving a glimpse of the even more diverse future to come. Suddenly the schedules opened up and there were hours of time to fill. Viewers had a choice, the watchword of the free-market Thatcherite ethos built on individual and personal freedom. Content became slicker and more professional. Soap operas, dramas and quiz shows, even an advertisement for Gold Blend coffee, could pull in tens of millions of viewers. The BBC launched a gameshow, *Telly Addicts*, hosted by Noel Edmonds, to celebrate the growing national obsession with the box.

Coverage of sport also changed significantly during the decade. At the turn of the 1980s, sport accounted for around 12 per cent of the BBC's output and just slightly less for ITV.[4] Both broadcasters had long acknowledged that some events – for example, the football World Cup and the Olympics – had huge pulling power which they were willing to rip up their schedules to accommodate. These competitions, and a select few others, were also deemed to be central to a supposed shared national culture, in large part determined by the Oxbridge, amateur ethos that pervaded both sports administration and the BBC at the time. Back in 1956, a like-minded Conservative government, unwilling to allow these sports to be sullied by commercialisation, had stepped in to mitigate the effects of the free market by creating so-called 'listed' sports: the 'crown jewels'.* At face value this benefited both broadcasters as they could each show the events at the same time. However, in essence it decreased their value to ITV, which needed exclusivity to court lucrative advertising deals, thereby effectively giving the BBC a monopoly. Beyond this, most other

---

* The events were: the football World Cup, the Olympics, the Commonwealth Games when held in the UK, the FA Cup final, Wimbledon, Test match cricket, the Derby, the Grand National and the Oxford vs Cambridge Boat Race.

sports were seen as cheap programming, filler to offset the cost of more expensive dramas, and thus coverage consisted mainly of highlights, or magazine shows which offered a veritable smorgasbord. Take, for example, the global menu on offer from Grandstand on Saturday 26 January 1980. There was half an hour of *Football Focus*, followed by boxing from London's Royal Albert Hall. Soon viewers were in Chamonix, France, for World Cup skiing, before they were transported to Gothenburg, Sweden, for the European Figure Skating Championships. Then it was back to the UK for coverage of the national basketball final in Sheffield, national indoor athletics from RAF Cosford and the opening game of rugby league's European Championship between Wales and France in Widnes. Then it was down to Adelaide for highlights of the third Test between Australia and the West Indies before, finally, the football results. All this was interspersed with racing from Cheltenham.[5]

Yet the growing need to compete for viewers in increasingly crowded schedules meant broadcasters moved away from the likes of *Grandstand,* and its ITV rival *World of Sport,* in favour of live events. This was particularly important for the commercial ITV network which relied on revenue from advertisers, who were in turn attracted by the programmes that could deliver large viewing figures but also, and crucially, viewers with high disposable incomes. This process was accelerated with the advent of satellite TV, where sport could be used not just to pull in audiences for specific events and timeslots but also to promote subscription to entire channels. The listed sports aside, suddenly everything was up for grabs to the highest bidder and battles for broadcast rights became increasingly common. At the same time, the need for live events plus the competition for them also saw broadcasters look beyond the narrow range that had dominated coverage to that point. Sports that had received little coverage were suddenly thrust into the spotlight.

II

When Taylor beat Davis at the Crucible in Sheffield in 1985, colour TV had been available in Britain for less than twenty years, the service having made its debut on BBC2 with coverage of the 1967 Wimbledon Championships. By 1972 about 1.5 million people had a colour TV licence. Within six years that number had risen to eleven million,[6] accounting for more than half of all licences. To avoid simply using imported programmes and repeats, home-produced colour content was needed and the channel again looked to sport. In the black and white era snooker made little sense on television. The World Championship had received some brief coverage of highlights in the 1950s but watching players potting balls of various shades of grey on a light grey table was confusing and not particularly entertaining viewing. In reality, it could be a vibrant sport thanks to the green baize of the table and twenty-two balls of eight different colours, perfect for the new medium. To capitalise on this, in 1969 *Pot Black*, a non-ranking competition featuring the world's best eight players in quick-fire, knockout rounds, was commissioned. Initially the coverage had to accommodate viewers without the benefit of colour sets, leading to the memorable occasion when commentator 'Whispering' Ted Lowe explained: 'Steve is going for the pink ball; and for those of you who are watching in black and white, the pink is next to the green'.[7] No one had particularly high expectations for the show, which was fundamentally designed to promote colour TV, not snooker, yet *Pot Black* defied expectations, quickly becoming one of BBC2's most popular programmes.

The Welsh amateur champion Ray Reardon was the first to win the small gold *Pot Black* trophy and pocket the £1,000 prize money. Seeing him and other former and future world champions inspired some youngsters who would go on to dominate the sport in the 1980s. Steve Davis, reminiscing about watching *Pot Black* with his father, called the show 'a breath of fresh air' because 'it was really the first time you could watch snooker on television'.[8] It wasn't until 1980 that the BBC first broadcast live coverage of the World Championship, held at Sheffield's Crucible Theatre, from the opening day of the tournament and they also planned to broadcast complete coverage of the final, split between BBC1 and BBC2. The match was a close affair between Alex Higgins, who had won the World Championship eight years earlier, and Canada's Cliff Thorburn, who would eventually win the title. Higgins played an uncharacteristically measured game to establish leads of 7–3 and 9–5; however, his usual flamboyance crept back in, and the pair were tied 9–9 at the end of the first day. Over the course of the next day, they traded frames, neither at any point being more than two ahead. Those watching were engrossed, yet just as the match was entering its tense, final stages, at 7.23 p.m. on the Monday evening, the BBC cut away to footage of the SAS storming the Iranian Embassy in London (in most people's memories it is 'live' but in reality it was slightly delayed). The embassy had been taken over six days earlier by dissident Iranians opposed to Ayatollah Khomeini, demanding the release of Iranian Arabs in their homeland. At the same time, they had taken twenty-six hostages. The raid was over within seventeen minutes. When the smoke had cleared, the SAS had burnished its reputation as the world's most elite military unit. Margaret Thatcher, just three days into her second year as prime minister, had established the hallmarks of her hardline approach to terrorism. Despite the gravity of the situation in London, the BBC was inundated with complaints from snooker fans who wanted to stay with the match. Some even rang the stage door of the Crucible Theatre to complain.[9] If the 1985 final was 'the high watermark of snooker's appeal',[10] then the 1980 final was when the sport first demonstrated the full extent of its popularity. 'The fact that they went back and forwards between the siege and the snooker was incredibly complimentary to snooker,' says Hearn. 'And the fact that some people said: "Who gives a shit about the siege, you've taken off my snooker" was a statement about the size of snooker at that time.'

Commentator Ted Lowe had calmly segued from coverage of the final to coverage of the siege with another immortal line: 'And now from one Embassy to another.'[11] The World Championships had quickly become synonymous with the cigarette brand Embassy, highlighting the growing attraction of televised sports to sponsors. For tobacco companies, this attraction had been heightened in 1965 when the government banned the advertising of their products on TV. Prior to the ban, sports sponsorship in Britain was worth less than £1 million. By 1970 this had more than doubled to £2.5 million. By 1980, the figure stood at £46 million and it hit £100 million in 1983.[12] At the end of the decade it was estimated that sponsorship was worth between £200 and £275 million to sport, with support spending worth as much again.[13] While not all sponsorship came from cigarette companies, by 1986 five of the top six events measured by the amount of coverage were tobacco-sponsored, with Rothmans, John Player and Benson and Hedges leading the way. Embassy had offered £24,000 in total prize money for the 1978 World Snooker Championships. That had risen to £300,000 by 1985. On top of that, the company were spending about £250,000 behind the scenes on sets, hospitality and accommodating journalists. However, they saw this as 'the media buy of the century'.[14] For an outlay of around £500,000 they were getting the equivalent of advertising worth £75 million. All this on the supposedly advertisement-free BBC.

In 1982, Higgins finally regained the world title that he craved. Having beaten Ray Reardon in the final, the emotion became too much for the new champion. Tears of joy – and perhaps relief – streamed down his face. Victory showed that he wasn't just was a great player; it also suggested that things hadn't spiralled too far out of control for this mercurial character. Higgins beckoned to his wife Lynn in the crowd to bring their eighteenth-month-old daughter, Lauren, to him. The familial tableau became an iconic image, and Hearn is in no doubt it gave snooker a further boost. 'Tears are always important if you're growing things,' he says. 'Tessa Sanderson winning the gold medal [at the 1984 Olympics], Gascoigne at Italia '90. There's nothing like a tear. Great moments in all sport – they live with you forever.' It is of no small significance that the rise of televised snooker in the 1980s came at a time when there was very little live coverage of football. Only internationals, domestic cup finals and some European games involving British teams were deemed worthy of coverage. The first, and for more than two decades, only, live broadcast of the English Football League had come on an autumnal Friday night in September 1960 when the second half of Bolton's 1–0 win away at Blackpool was shown by ABC, one of the then-ITV networks. The League had only allowed coverage after half-time because it believed that TV coverage would divert fans from turning up. Over the years, it rebuffed various offers for live rights for this reason and when the attendance at Bloomfield Road was lower than average, their fears were seemingly confirmed. Plans to cover other games on a similar basis were dropped. Somewhat astonishingly given today's saturation coverage, television was seen as a novelty which would not significantly benefit the game's finances.

This view had undergone a dramatic re-evaluation across mainland Europe during the 1970s. Taking their cue from the development of TV sport in the USA a decade earlier, and increasingly sophisticated advertising research that showed that domestic football could deliver large, high-value audiences (that is, free-spending young men), the football authorities in Italy, Germany, Spain, and France realised that the future of the game was intertwined with the small screen. Furthermore, they understood that the game itself would become more valuable to television companies. In tandem, the amount of coverage increased, and the leagues demanded higher rights fees. However, in Britain, there was, beyond a few exceptions, such as Robert Maxwell, the chairman of Oxford United, and David Dein and Irving Scholar, at Arsenal and Tottenham respectively, continued hesitancy. The English Football League bowed to the increasingly inevitable and agreed a deal worth £5.2 million to show twenty live games during the 1983/84 and 1984/85 seasons.[15] Scotland would not see a league game broadcast live until 1986.

The first live game broadcast, in October 1983, saw Spurs play Nottingham Forest at White Hart Lane. Before the match, there were concerns that fans, used only to edited highlights, would be bored by the coverage of an entire game, which included the 'dull' parts as well. However, such fears proved unfounded. The broadcasts regularly pulled in more than ten million viewers, a revelation given Sunday afternoons had previously been considered a dead slot. The attendances of games were unaffected. There was little analysis focused on the match at White Hart Lane. Instead host Jim Rosenthal, pundit Jimmy Greaves and Spurs chairman Douglas Alexiou discussed the coverage. 'As far as you're concerned, football and television can live quite happily together this season?' Rosenthal asked Alexiou. 'I think we got on quite well today,' replied the Spurs chairman.[16]

Such bonhomie didn't last long. Despite being rivals, when it came to football the BBC and ITV effectively operated a cartel, acting as the sole purchaser of football rights. Thus, when they came to renegotiate their deal with the League ahead of the 1985/86 season, they were able to present a united front and play hardball. They offered a four-year deal worth £3.8 million a year for the rights to cover sixteen League games, two League Cup semi-finals legs and the League Cup final. The League rejected the offer and, in response, the TV companies left their offer on the table but walked away from negotiations. Jonathan Martin, the BBC's Head of Sport, said, simply, that he would continue to show snooker instead; it was cheaper and more popular. 'Soccer is no longer at the heart of the TV schedules,' he said matter-of-factly, 'and is never likely to be again.'[17]

As we shall see in Chapter 10, at the time football was beset by hooliganism and suffering a crisis that some considered to be existential. The month before Taylor beat Davis at the Crucible, Luton and Millwall fans fought running battles with each other and the police during an FA Cup quarter-final. Eighty-one people were injured, mostly police, and thirty-one arrested. Within a fort-night of Taylor's triumph, fifty-six died as fire consumed a stand at Bradford's Valley Parade ground. On the same day, a teenager died after a wall collapsed during fighting at Birmingham's St Andrew's. Before the end of the month, thirty-nine more people were killed after Liverpool and Juventus fans rioted at the European Cup final at the Heysel Stadium in Brussels. The *Sunday Times* branded football 'a slum sport played in slum stadiums increasingly watched by slum people, who deter decent folk from turning up'.[18] While the derogatory language unfairly tarred all football fans with the same brush, failing to acknowledge that the overwhelming majority were in fact themselves 'decent people', the newspaper had a point about the effect on attendance figures. In the 1984/85 football season, just 17.8 million people went through the turnstiles in all four divisions of the Football League,[19] fewer than were still awake watching when Taylor beat Davis. It was the lowest combined attendance figure since the Second World War. In the 1986/87 season it would fall again, to 16.4 million. Not only were there fewer fans present, but the stalemate between the League and the broadcasters meant there were no television cameras present either. Even *Match of the Day* was off the air. In December 1984 the League caved in and signed a deal worth £1.5 million for the remainder of the season and the following July they signed a two-year deal worth £3.1 million. Both were on worse terms than they had initially been offered. It was a salutary lesson for the League. In the mid-1980s, football was not yet the thoroughbred that would come to dominate the TV landscape; it was just one of many sports jockeying for position.

III

Darts was one of those other sports. The 1972 final of the *News of the World* Darts Championship attracted some seven million viewers, popularity that led to the creation of *The Indoor League* which featured darts and other saloon bar sports such as bar skittles, arm wrestling, shove ha'penny and billiards. For all its success, the programme had an unashamedly rudimentary feel. It wasn't until darts got regular coverage with the production values afforded to other sports that it really took off. This came with the creation of the Embassy World Darts Championships, the inaugural tournament being held at Nottingham's Heart of the Midlands club in 1978. There were just thirteen entrants, indicative of the relatively early stage of darts' development as a professional sport. The BBC broadcast the final live with highlights from the other rounds.

By 1980, the tournament had moved to Jollees Cabaret Venue

in Stoke-on-Trent and the BBC devoted live coverage to all rounds of the tournament. The final, which was played between two of the game's most flamboyant characters, Bobby George and Eric Bristow, took the popularity of the sport to another level. 'Eric used to say to me, we changed the darts completely,' George tells me.[20] 'We made it more entertaining. It all snowballed from there.' George had only started playing darts seriously in 1976, but he took to the sport easily. He knew Bristow, twelve years his junior, well, the pair having played doubles and exhibition matches together. They knew each other's game and the final was close-fought. George made the early running, but the younger man eventually asserted his dominance in the seventh and eighth sets. After Bristow hit a double ten to take the match five sets to three, he planted a victorious kiss on the cheek of his vanquished friend.

Bristow's celebration was in keeping with the showmanship and entertainment the pair brought to the sport. Unlike their con-temporaries, both players had nicknames — Bristow was 'the Crafty Cockney', George was known as 'Bobby Dazzler' — some-thing which is commonplace nowadays. Each crafted an on-stage image, which also translated well onto television. Bristow dressed all in red, his nickname emblazoned above a Union Jack on the back of his shirt. George wore all black, his shirt embroidered with gold sequins and 'B' and 'G' on the lapels. 'I took the idea for the shirts from the ice skaters,' says George. 'I thought it would make the sport more entertaining and that whatever happened, people would remember me. If I played badly, they'd say, "Did you see that idiot Bobby George all dressed up in the sequins?" Because I had all the glitter, and I looked like Liberace, two tour-nament officials gave me a candelabra all lit up as I walked on the stage. I thought, "Oh well, here you go you'll look a pratt," but the audience all got their lighters out. Over the week, the crowd got louder and louder, chanting our names. By the end, I noticed two or three guys in the audience in sequinned shirts. I thought, "Bloody hell! That didn't take long."'

By the time of the tournament, the now familiar split-screen technique, which showed the board on one side and a close-up of the thrower's face on the other, had become a staple of the coverage. Pioneered during the inaugural World Championship in 1978, it was as revolutionary as the introduction of colour television had been for snooker just a decade earlier. 'Sport is only as good as the presentation and the technology,' George says. 'Darts is a fast game to actually cover on television. They couldn't switch from the camera on the player to the camera on the board quickly enough. But when they split the screen, they could see the player's action and the board at the same time.' Not only were those watching at home able to soak up the heightened atmosphere, but thanks to the innovative production technique they were able to see the rollercoaster of emotions that the competitors experienced. 'Darts could have been invented especially for television,' opined *The Times* in a preview of the tournament. 'The close-up comes into its own – the tense hand, the gleaming eye, the dampness on the brow, the aborted grin, the gnawed lip. This is a man under pressure, without artifice.'[21] Split screen also helped make the players more recognisable to the public. 'Having a focus on your face – that's how everyone knew you,' says George.

To the delight of the BBC, the organisers and sponsors, eight million people tuned in to see Bristow's win. By the middle of the 1980s, the number of tournaments being organised by the British Darts Organisation (BDO) had increased significantly, with as many as sixteen receiving regular coverage on both the BBC and ITV. The players, too, were enjoying increased exposure. Soon, Bristow was on *Punchlines* and *Celebrity Squares*; he even played the drums to 'I Shot the Sheriff' on *The Leo Sayer Variety Show*. George also became an entertainment show regular. 'I was on all sorts,' he says. 'I was on *Rod Hull and Emu*, *Saturday Superstore*, *Juke Box Jury*. Television makes you. I became a celebrity without throwing darts.'

IV

Very quicky the popularity of both darts and snooker spilled over into wider popular culture. In 1984, a pre-Live Aid Bob Geldof starred in the film *Number One* as an amateur snooker player pressured to play professionally by a local gangster. *The Last Election*, a 1986 novel by Pete Davies, told the story of a dystopian near-future London, where a cable TV channel called *147* broadcast snooker to the unemployed masses twenty-four hours a day, 365 days a year. Three years later darts played a central role in Martin Amis' *London Fields*. Perhaps the peak was reached when Dexys Midnight Runners performed 'Jackie Wilson Said', an ode to the soul singer, on *Top of the Pops* in front of a huge photo of Jocky Wilson, then world darts champion. Long believed to be an error, Dexys lead singer Kevin Rowland revealed the band had requested the photo as a laugh.[22] This was indicative of a wider fusion of sport and entertainment, which was central to a range of TV shows such as *Superstars*, *Pro-Celebrity Golf* and even, to a certain extent, the garish, rowdy *It's A Knockout*. The relaxed quiz show *A Question of Sport* brought sports stars into living rooms every week, peaking in the ratings in 1987 when Princess Anne, a European gold medallist in eventing and former BBC Sports Personality of the Year, appeared on the show. A fortnight earlier ex-Liverpool player Emlyn Hughes, one of the regular team captains, had mis-identified a photo of the princess, albeit covered in mud after a horse race, as the jockey John Reid. When told who it actually was, Hughes was mortified, exclaiming, 'they'll hang me'. His horror was further compounded when host David Coleman told him that the princess was due to be a guest a fortnight later. It set her appearance up nicely and some nineteen million viewers tuned in to see her good-natured banter with Hughes.

A pseudo gameshow, *A Question of Sport* benefited from the fast-growing popularity of the genre with an increasingly aspirational population. This, coupled with their low cost relative to sitcoms and drama, saw gameshows, which had been around since the 1950s, fill up the schedules. *3-2-1*, hosted by Ted Rodgers and Dusty Bin, led the way, having first been broadcast in 1978, but the boom really began with *Play Your Cards Right* and *Family Fortunes*. Hosted by Bruce Forsyth and Bob Monkhouse respectively, the shows both made their debuts in 1980. Other versions of the genre ranged from cerebral offerings such as *Blockbusters* and *Countdown* to the unashamedly materialist *The Price Is Right*. One of the most popular was *Bullseye*, which combined general knowledge with skill at the oche. The show was hosted by Lancastrian stand-up comic Jim Bowen, who had made his name on the club circuit before gaining national exposure on ITV's *The Comedians*. He was aided by professional darts referee Tony Green counting the scores, and Bully, an overweight, anthropomorphic cartoon bull. Bowen was not a slick host by modern standards, often fluffing his lines or appearing to mishear contestants, especially when they were talking about themselves. But his avuncular charm and catchphrases such as 'Super, smashing, great!', 'You can't beat a bit of bully!' and, agonisingly, 'Here's what you would have won,' made him an engaging and popular host. It was a ratings winner, pulling in more than seventeen million viewers in 1982.[23] The format was so successful it was subsequently applied to snooker, first with *Pot the Question*, which lasted just one series in 1984, and then more successfully in the 1990s with *Big Break*.

Bullseye was still regularly getting ten million viewers when it was cancelled in 1995,[24] its popularity further demonstrating the mass appeal of a sport that a little more than a decade earlier had been merely a competitive, pub pastime. Yet not all the attention darts got was positive. In a reflection of the sport's roots, many of the players drank beer and smoked during the games. The satirical *Not the Nine O'Clock News* lampooned such behaviour in a sketch featuring Mel Smith and Griff Rhys Jones with pillows stuffed up their shirts as two stereotypical overweight players, Dai 'Fat Belly' Gutbucket and Tommy 'Even Fatter Belly' Belcher. The pair took turns to down drinks, not throw darts, with a referee calling out what was required of the competitors: 'Fat Belly, you require three triple Bacardis.' The sketch aired a few weeks after George had played Bristow in the 1980 final. 'I thought that was good,' George tells me. 'Everyone else complained, but I thought that was really funny. If they're taking the piss out of the sport, then it's recognised. When they're not taking the piss, that means no one knows about it.' However, he doesn't think the stereotype the sketch fed off was an entirely accurate depiction. 'I never had a beer gut, Eric never had a beer gut, John Lowe never had a beer gut. There was Leighton Reece – he had two beer guts – but that image of big bellies and swilling beer was all that some people thought of the sport and that wasn't fair.' The representation was demonstrative of a condescending attitude from some towards what was fundamentally a working-class sport. These negative experiences showed that despite the popularity, the glitz and the glamour, darts couldn't shed its saloon-bar image.

V

Yet, thanks to the BBC's coverage, sports like darts and snooker gained a measure of respectability and credibility they would not otherwise have had. 'The BBC had the power to make any change,' says Hearn. 'They were omnipotent. They always had the arrogance of being the state broadcaster, a bit of monopoly, an air of "we can do it better than anyone else". But they did have power because if the BBC put it on screen, it meant it was real. It was almost "by royal approval".' Yet Hearn believes that, while the BBC helped create the modern market for live televised sport, they were quickly left behind by the technological and particularly financial transformation their coverage triggered. 'They did the protected, listed events,' he says, 'but when the money came, they couldn't afford to play the game. The BBC had all the trappings but no money and no desire to change the status quo. While they were stuck in their ways, you had ITV with younger people, trying to be a bit more creative.'

One of those younger people was Greg Dyke, who became director of programmes of London Weekend Television (LWT) in 1987. Dyke made his name in the early 1980s as the saviour of the ailing TV-am before moving on to TVS, the ITV franchise covering the South and South East. Three years later, in 1987, he was back in the capital. LWT was faced with a fall in viewers and Dyke quickly identified the problem, saying that the schedules had 'a very old look' and were increasingly reminiscent of the Co-op in an era when people shopped at Sainsbury's.[25] 'One of my major aims was for ITV to lose that fifties reputation it had,' says Dyke.[26] 'It didn't recognise the British working class was in decline, a whole generation of people were coming through who had been to university. You could see that comparing the figures then to the figures a decade or two decades earlier. Britain had moved upmarket, and ITV hadn't.' Out went traditional variety shows such as *Live From . . . The Palladium* and *Cannon and Ball*. In came dramas like *London's Burning* and *Poirot*. Dyke was also increasingly unwilling to schedule the sport acquired and produced centrally by ITV. So, he successfully pushed to become chairman of the ITV Sport committee.

It wasn't just the viewers who were changing; so, too, was the television marketplace. Margaret Thatcher's Conservative government was determined to introduce more competition. ITV franchises were, from 1991, to be given to the highest bidder and, as part of a wider policy of deregulation, British Satellite Broadcasting (BSB) was awarded the right to broadcast in Britain. On the periphery was Rupert Murdoch's rival Europe-based satellite service Sky Television which, although it did not have a licence, was still able to broadcast to British homes. Dyke was acutely aware of the threat posed by BSB, although he now feels he took the wrong approach in tackling them. 'We still had the rather simplistic view that if we took away their access to the best sport and movies – I also ran another campaign on ITV 'movies are free on ITV' – that we could stop them,' he says. 'We were living in cuckoo land. I would have done far better to have spent my time looking at how we could compete with them, as opposed to how we could defeat them. In other words, we should have gone into pay television much earlier.'

Backed by the likes of Pearson, Granada and Virgin, BSB had a significant war chest. They seemed to be in a position to shake up the stuffy world of television, just as Thatcher wanted. In 1988, they made their first move: an audacious bid for the rights to broadcast the Football League over the next ten years at a guaranteed minimum of £9 million a year. This led to the collapse of the BBC/ITV cartel. All bets were off, and a competitive process began. Dyke knew that losing football to BSB would be hugely detrimental to ITV. He also knew that if he could win the rights, he could deliver a blow to BSB before they had even started broadcasting. He offered £11 million a year for eighteen League games plus the League Cup semi-finals and final. Before the bids could be put to a vote, BSB withdrew.

Dyke discussed his strategy at the Edinburgh Television

Festival later in 1988, the first time that the importance of sport for the medium had been acknowledged at the festival, signifying its increasing value to broadcasters. Dyke accepted that he had overpaid for the football rights, but he also warned that other sports should not expect such largesse. Arguing that sport was 'the last totally uncontrolled area of television', he claimed that there were only a few sports guaranteed to provide the audiences needed to generate high rights fees. Furthermore, to pay for the football, he said, other sports such as bowls, gymnastics, wrestling and even darts would be gone from the ITV schedules by the end of the year.[27] Not only was darts suffering because of the image of beer-swilling players, but it was also experiencing overkill. The huge increase in the number of tournaments broadcast meant viewers were being fed a televised diet with little variation. As quickly as darts had begun to appear on the television schedules, so it disappeared. By 1988 all that was left on the BBC was the Embassy World Championship, while ITV had followed through on Dyke's threat and axed its entire coverage.[28] In his biography, John Lowe argued that 'this wasn't a small decrease; it was the darts world's equivalent of the Wall Street crash'.[29] BDO chief Olly Croft was unconcerned as he was still overseeing around 800 amateur tournaments annually. However, the top professionals suddenly found the lifeblood of the elite sport gone. Without the exposure that television had given them, their main source of income was destroyed, instigating a bruising period for the sport. Sixteen of the top players broke away from the BDO, to form the rival World Darts Council (WDC). The new organisation was willing to embrace the requirements of television, employ marketing and public relations strategies and package the sport in a way that Croft was not. They set about organising their own tournaments and tying up separate TV deals with the newly formed Sky TV. Ultimately darts survived. Other sports weren't so lucky.

At the start of the 1980s wrestling had a TV audience on a par with both snooker and darts. Although it was not a sport in the traditional sense, its fights and their outcomes being choreographed, it had a regular slot on ITV's Saturday afternoon magazine show *World of Sport* between 4.00 and 4.45 p.m., just before the football results. In June 1981 two of the sport's biggest stars (literally and figuratively) took to the ring in front of a sell-out Wembley Arena crowd. In one corner was Big Daddy, a living John Bull Toby jug who stood 6ft 6in. tall and weighed in at 26 stone. Shirley Crabtree, to give him his real name, wore a costume adorned with the Union Jack and was the people's champion. He was adored by children and grannies alike who would chant 'Easy! Easy!' as he entered the fray and dispatched opponents with, well, ease. Despite retiring in the early 1990s, Big Daddy remains one of the most well-known figures in British wrestling. In the other corner was Giant Haystacks, real name Martin Ruane. Big Daddy's arch enemy, Haystacks was 6ft 11in. tall and tipped the scales at a massive 40 stone. The bout is reputed to have been watched by eighteen million people, although that seems apocryphal. Whatever the reality, it was a disappointment, Big Daddy taking less than three minutes to overcome his opponent. It was also wrestling's last hurrah.

Over the second part of the decade the sport was beset by a string of negative publicity. Tony 'Banger' Walsh, Big Daddy's former tag-team partner, gave a tell-all interview to the *Sun*, under the headline 'EXCLUSIVE: Wrestler reveals truth about fake world of grunt 'n' groan'.[30] Walsh not only suggested that the sport was a sham, but so was Big Daddy's child-loving image. Then in 1987 during a bout in Great Yarmouth, Big Daddy pinned his opponent Mal 'King Kong' Kirk to the canvas with his trademark 'splash'. Kirk never regained consciousness and was pronounced dead on arrival at hospital. The resulting inquest found that the fifty-one-year-old had died as a result of an unknown heart condition, attributing no blame to Big Daddy. However, it left a cloud over the sport. By this time, wrestling had lost its fixed spot in the schedules when in 1985 ITV cancelled *World of Sport*. Wrestling continued with its own show but, unloved, this bounced around the schedules without promotion and was often aired in early, lunchtime slots. Only ardent fans knew when the sport would be shown, and in an era when many working-class people, who made up the majority of the sport's audience, still put in half a day on a Saturday, the viewing figures plummeted. This all put wrestling on Dyke's hit list. In December 1988, when the sport's contract with ITV came to an end, it was counted out for the final time. 'It was old-style ITV; it was ripe for axing,' says Dyke. 'It wasn't a proper sport, nobody won or lost, but I got a lot of flak for it, a lot of people wrote and complained. I still get people today saying, "You're the bloke who took wrestling off." It was forty years ago!'

The following year, wrestling returned to British screens, at least those that were attached to a satellite dish. However, it wasn't the likes of Big Daddy, Giant Haystacks and Kendo Nagasaki in front of the cameras but Hulk Hogan, Randy Savage and Ultimate Warrior from the World Wrestling Federation (WWF). American wrestling had been effectively relaunched by Vince McMahon, WWF's owner, in 1985 with the first WrestleMania, a pay-per-view event. WWF highlights had been broadcast on Sky Television since its early days. McMahon could offer it as cheap content, having already recouped his costs and more in its home market. He used the increased exposure as an opportunity to expand into a new market. By 1992 the WWF had become so popular in Britain that its fifth annual SummerSlam event was held at Wembley Stadium with more than 80,000 fans in attendance, to date still the largest WWF event outside the USA.

It's hard not to wonder whether British wrestling might have won a reprieve if ITV's contractual commitment to the sport had lasted a year or two longer, or if the WWF boom on Sky had begun a couple of years earlier. Would the glitz and glamour of their US cousins have rubbed off on Big Daddy and his peers? Perhaps, but it would have taken more than just that. The WWF aggressively courted a younger audience through links with MTV and singers such as Cyndi Lauper. It had a roster of compelling characters involved in soap opera-style storylines which played out in weekly pre-recorded shows before culminating in huge pay-per-view bouts. By contrast, British wrestling had been operating the same business model since the 1950s and its focus on Big Daddy had become stale. Its demise reflected the need for sports to be packaged in a way that appealed to the audience that television, advertisers and sponsors wanted, a characteristic that is so commonplace today it is all but unnoticeable. This was a crucial development for televised sport in the 1980s – it became increasingly merged with entertainment, and entertainment needed stars.

CHAPTER 2

When Will I Be Famous?

I

ON a bright autumn afternoon in 1985, ITV sports reporter Martin Tyler took to London's Waterloo Bridge to film a segment for the football show *Saint and Greavsie*. Over the course of an hour or so, he asked various passers-by what they thought of the West Ham striker Frank McAvennie. Unsurprisingly, the response was overwhelmingly positive, as McAvennie was scoring goals for fun in the English First Division. Then Tyler asked if they knew who the young man with bleached-blond hair standing next to him was. Few did, and they were surprised to discover it was McAvennie himself. While many people had heard about the Scot's exploits on the pitch, following a £340,000 move that summer from St Mirren in Scotland to West Ham, very few had actually seen them (or him). The television blackout caused by a breakdown in negotiations between the Football League and ITV and the BBC meant that just nine of the twenty-eight goals McAvennie scored in his explosive debut season at Upton Park were caught on camera. Manchester United fans also missed their team's imperious start. Looking to build on their FA Cup triumph the previous season, when they beat Everton 1–0, the team managed by 'Big Ron' Atkinson romped to victory in their first ten League games and were unbeaten in their first fifteen, a run which took them nine points clear of Liverpool and thirteen clear of champions Everton.

It was perhaps fitting that after the League eventually capitulated and agreed a deal with the broadcasters in December 1985, West Ham's third round FA Cup tie at Charlton early in the New Year was the first game broadcast. The public at large finally got to see McAvennie in action and he delivered, lobbing the goalkeeper from just inside the area before his strike partner Tony Cottee beat an onrushing defender to poke home the only goal of the game. Over the course of the season, the pair racked up fifty-four goals between them as the Hammers reached the FA Cup quarter-finals and finished third – the club's best finish to date – behind the Merseyside duo Liverpool and Everton. Manchester United had been unable to keep up their early season form, winning just five of their final seventeen games. They were bystanders as Liverpool accrued thirty-four points from a possible thirty-six in the run-in, romping to the first part of a historic double in Kenny Dalglish's first season as manager.

McAvennie finished second in the race for the Golden Boot, behind Everton's Gary Lineker, but he was the undisputed star of the season. Although the lack of television exposure meant that, initially, few recognised him, it took just one chat-show appearance for the Scot to gain celebrity status. *Wogan* went out three times a week, and thanks to host Terry Wogan's easy-going self-deprecation and gentle mocking of his guests, it regularly gained viewing figures in excess of ten million.[1] Suddenly McAvennie's name had a face. 'People with no interest in football knew who I was,' he later told the *Irish Post*. 'I went to meet my mum for lunch the next day and people were asking me for autographs at the airport. I was at Stringfellows on the Saturday night and the press were waiting on me.'[2]

McAvennie's sudden ascent to fame was indicative of the power of television in the 1980s and there was one sportsman who stood astride the decade like a colossus. Ian Botham had burst into the England cricket team as a twenty-one-year-old in 1977 just as their football counterparts were in the process of failing to qualify for a second successive World Cup. His powers began to wane in the early 1990s around the time Paul Gascoigne was wiping the tears from his eyes. During the summers of the 1980s Botham filled a vacuum, showcasing his talents on TV for days at a time when football had barely any live coverage. In the process he transcended both cricket, and sport in general, to become a cultural icon.

II

Botham's England debut came in the shadow of Kerry Packer's World Series Cricket revolution. Rebuffed in his attempts to buy the rights to the Australian home Test series for his Channel 9 TV station, Packer launched his own competition. He signed up seventy of the world's best players, including most of the top Australian and West Indies players, and staged sixteen so-called 'Supertests' and thirty-eight one-day matches. After two seasons of innovative floodlit day/night matches, white balls, coloured kits, even players wearing helmets, a truce was called. The Australian Cricket Board caved in and gave Packer the rights he wanted.

The involvement of Tony Greig, England's captain and established all-rounder, in Packer's venture effectively opened up a spot in the England setup for Botham. Greig, along with Australia's Ian Chappell, played a key role in recruiting players for Packer, something for which he was never forgiven by the Test and County Cricket Board (TCCB). He was immediately stripped of the

England captaincy, and although he maintained his place in the team in the short term, by the end of the home Ashes series of 1977 he had played his last Test.

Greig was only thirty at the time, so it's likely that, but for his involvement with Packer, he would have played on for another five years or so. In the two Tests he played with Botham, in the summer of 1977, Greig was the all-rounder, batting at number five, the younger man a strike bowler, batting at number eight. It's not unreasonable to assume that had they continued to play together those roles would have been maintained. Thus, for the first few years of his England career at least, Botham would have been known as a bowler who could bat a bit, not a swashbuckling all-rounder knocking opposing bowlers around the field for fun. It's unlikely he would have established himself as a mainstay of the England team as soon as he did and in the manner he did.

Botham also benefited off the field from Packer's revolutionary mixture of private capital and televised spectacle. By 1976, the TCCB had begun looking for sponsors for Test match cricket. However, because of what *The Times* cricket correspondent John Woodcock suggested was a 'need, universally accepted, to prevent Mr Packer from continuing to filch the game's best players',[3] this became an imperative when the Australian launched his assault on the game. A deal with Cornhill Insurance worth £1 million over five years was quickly agreed. Botham, like other players, reaped the financial rewards. During the 1977 Ashes series, the Test fee for England players increased from £210 to £350, with a £100 bonus for matches won. By 1978 the fee had risen again to £1,000. By 1983 it was £1,500 and by the end of the decade it was £2,400. Fees for touring were also increased in 1977, from £3,000 to £5,000, with option contracts introduced for players willing to make themselves available for future England tours, and thus unavailable for Packer.[4]

The partnership with Cornhill was an acceleration of a commercialisation process which had begun in the 1960s. Despite an image of men in blazers drawn largely from public school, Oxbridge backgrounds, cricket's administrators proved surprisingly receptive to television. The game had long been underpinned by an amateur ethos and a split between 'gentlemen' (who played for fun) and 'players' (who played for a living). The first professional captain of the England team, Len Hutton, was only appointed in 1952. It was another ten years before the practice of differentiating the status of players on scorecards by placing an amateur's initials before their surname and a professional's initials after was discontinued. Yet as crowds at County Championship games dwindled in the 1960s, those running the game used their links with the men in blazers at the BBC to promote the sport. Understanding the need for cricket to be packaged for television, they dropped their resistance to the one-day form of the game. They also embraced sponsorship and a more commercial future in the shape of first the Gillette Cup and then the John Player League. By the 1980s, therefore, thanks to the coverage of home Test series and the one-day competitions for county sides, cricket was regularly receiving more TV coverage than any other ball sport. Only snooker came close. The stage was set. There was a willing audience. It was just the right time for Botham to take on the role of leading man.

III

Although he made his debut in 1977, Botham didn't secure a regular place in the team until the following year, after which he enjoyed a scintillating run of form with Mike Brearley as his captain. Despite question marks over his batting, Brearley, who went on to have a post-cricket career as a psychoanalyst, was recognised as an out-standing leader. According to Australia's Rodney Hogg, he had 'a degree in people'[5] and he understood how to get the best out of England's new young star. Between June 1978 and February 1980, Botham, marshalled by Brearley, played twenty Tests across six series, scored 1,099 runs and took 112 wickets. England won twelve of the matches, losing just four. They also won five of the six series they played. Botham was instrumental throughout. When in early 1980 Brearley declined to tour again (he offered to captain England in home Tests if and when required) a heated debate ensued about who his replacement should be. Geoff Boycott was perhaps the obvious choice having stood in for Brearley on occasion. But Boycott was a divisive figure and, at thirty-nine, his best years were behind him. The rest of the contenders could be split into two groups: those who had strong captaincy credentials but little Test-playing experience, and those who were Test regulars but had little or no experience leading a team. Botham fell into the latter category but, because of his dominance with bat and ball, and thanks to a recommendation from Brearley, he got the nod.

It proved to be a disastrous decision. In his last appearance for England before he was made captain, the Golden Jubilee Test against India in Mumbai in February 1980, Botham became the first player ever to take ten wickets and score 100 in a Test match. Once he had the added responsibility of leading the team, however, his form collapsed. In twelve Tests he averaged thirteen with the bat and thirty-three with the ball. England too looked a shadow of the team that Brearley had led. Botham's first ten games in charge, six of which were at home, produced no victories and three defeats. As the 1981 home Ashes series loomed, his captaincy became the subject of national debate. The first Test did little to improve matters, Australia winning a low-scoring game thanks largely to England's poor fielding. Bad weather played its part in the second Test at Lord's, which ended in a draw. *Wisden* described it as a 'morbid' affair,[6] and it was most notable for Botham recording the only pair of his Test career. As he walked back to the pavilion having recorded his second duck, he was met by silence from the members in the MCC enclosure. None met his eye. He had reached the point of no return as captain and resigned before his inevitable sacking. The selectors turned to Brearley in his stead. Former skipper Ray Illingworth wrote in the *Sunday Mirror* that Botham was 'overrated, overweight and overpaid. He should be dropped from the team.'[7] He was not the only one who thought this, but Brearley insisted that Botham retain his place.

Thus it was that England limped to Headingley, tucked away among the red-brick terraced houses on the outskirts of Leeds, for the third Test. Although there was no real hint during the first four days of what was to come, the pressure had clearly been lifted from Botham. Australia won the toss and elected to bat. They were cruising at 335-4 before Botham stepped up and took five wickets for thirty-five after tea on the second day. The tourists were still able to declare on 401-9, a total which looked even better after England collapsed to 174 all out on day three. Botham, slowly recovering his form, had top scored with fifty off fifty-four balls. Australia enforced the follow-on, but bad light meant only three more overs were possible, in which England lost Graham Gooch. As the crowd waited for a resumption that never came, the stadium's new electronic scoreboard outlined the enormity of England's task. Ladbrokes' odds for the match were flashed up. The hosts were 500/1 outsiders. They looked to have called it about right as England lost wickets with metronomic regularity the next day. Reduced to 135-7, Brearley's team were still ninety-two runs behind. Botham had toiled to thirty-nine in eighty-seven uncharacteristically ponderous minutes when he was joined in the middle by pace bowler Graham Dilley. There were just three wickets left. With nothing to lose, the pair decided to have fun. They cut loose.

It was agricultural, village-green stuff with more than a little luck involved. By the time Dilley was out eighty minutes after coming to the crease, he had scored fifty-six: his maiden Test half-century. Botham motored past a hundred thanks to fourteen fours, a single and a six which, according to Richie Benaud's famous commentary, went 'straight into the confectionery stall and out again'. He was all smiles as he knocked the ball around the ground with carefree abandon. Joy had returned to Botham's game and with it his seemingly superhuman abilities. By the time England were all out, he stood unbeaten on 149 and the hosts, astonishingly, had a lead of 129. Australia were still the favourites to win and, at fifty-six without loss, victory seemed all but assured. Bob Willis had other ideas. Like Botham, he had been subjected to intense media scrutiny prior to the match with his place in the team being questioned. Unlike Botham, he drew on barely concealed rage, not love of the game, to prove his critics wrong. With an expression of thunderous menace etched on his face, he tore in from the Kirkstall Lane End and reduced the tourists to 75-8. After a mini revival took them to 110, Willis polished off the final two wickets to finish with career-best figures of 8-43. Somehow England had won by eighteen runs and Botham was named man of the match. If his *Boy's Own* heroics had been made for television, they couldn't have been scripted better than this. The melodrama provided a perfect redemption arc for the fallen hero. Botham's performance was made all the greater because of the decline that immediately preceded it. The presence of the cameras served to amplify it further. His second innings batting performance was watched by only a few thousand people in the stands but by millions at home.

Eight days later, on 29 July 1981, they were back in front of their TVs for the wedding of Prince Charles, the Prince of Wales, to Lady Diana Spencer. As 3,500 guests gathered at St Paul's Cathedral, 28.4 million were watching at home. A further 750 million were watching in seventy-four countries worldwide. Trestle tables overflowed with sandwiches, orange squash and beer as Britain enjoyed a giant street party. If the Headingley Test provided the country with a swashbuckling hero, the royal wedding gave it a virginal princess. 'Here is the stuff of which fairy tales are made,' said the Archbishop of Canterbury, Robert Runcie, who was presiding over the wedding. The media devoured the image, as did much of the public, although many failed to heed Runcie's portentous caveat, 'but fairy tales usually end at this point with the simple phrase: "They lived happily ever after." This may be because fairy stories regard marriage as an anti-climax after the romance of courtship.'[8]

The Headingley Test and the royal wedding are figuratively married in the national memory of that summer. In a way it was 1953 redux. Then it was the FA Cup final, labelled 'the Matthews Final', in which a thirty-eight-year-old Stanley Matthews lifted the trophy at the third attempt, and Queen Elizabeth II's coronation. Sales of television sets sky-rocketed in the run-up to the events which became intertwined with a sense of modernity and technological progress that the new young queen represented. But that summer, which heralded the dawn of a New Elizabethan era, symbolised a nation united. In 1981, England's Botham-inspired comeback victory and Charles and Diana's wedding became emblems of a patriotic, Union Flag-waving Britain – or more accurately perhaps England: the two were, and continue to be, conflated. But not everyone was celebrating in what was a deeply divided country enduring a tumultuous period. In May 1981, Bobby Sands, the IRA member, had died after sixty-six days of hunger strike in the Maze Prison. Just over two weeks later Peter

Sutcliffe, 'the Yorkshire Ripper', was found guilty of the murder of thirteen women and the attempted murder of seven others. Rising unemployment and racial tension sparked riots across the country. A week before the Headingley Test, police in riot gear clashed with a 200-strong group of youths in the Chapeltown area of Leeds just two miles from the ground. Cars and a police van were overturned. Shops were looted and petrol-bombed. Police even claimed to have come under fire from a sniper with an air rifle.[9]

Over time, Botham's performances in the summer of 1981 have been replayed and mythologised to such an extent that legend and reality have blurred into one. It's easy to forget that Botham's explosive innings at Headingley lasted barely two hours out of the five days of play (one of which *Wisden* described as 'pedestrian in the extreme'[10]). It was arguably Willis' performance which won the match, Botham having wrenched it back into the balance. Botham was man of the match again in the fourth Test, taking 5-1 in twenty-eight balls at Edgbaston, as England won by twenty-nine runs. Yet who remembers that spinner John Emburey took more wickets and scored more runs? England retained the Ashes with a 103-run victory at Old Trafford and Botham was named man of the match for a third time, thanks to a second innings knock of 118. Yet Chris Taveré's two dogged half-centuries were the foundation on which England's score was built. This is not to denigrate Botham's achievement, nor to suggest these weren't his Ashes, but to acknowledge that our collective memory of sporting events, and those who take part in them, is shaped and framed into drama by the narrative constructed around them. Similarly, the royal wedding was a moment caught in time and shaped for consumption. As the country would soon discover through the couple's bitter divorce, they did not live happily ever after.

IV

Journalists had always been interested in stories about sports stars and royalty. However, in the early part of the twentieth century that was trumped by a sense of deference. Edward VIII's relationship with the American divorcée Wallis Simpson gained considerable coverage in Europe and the USA, but Fleet Street's editors demurred to print it. The British public knew nothing of the story until nine days before the king abdicated in 1937. Sportsmen (and at this point it was mainly men) were also afforded a measure of privacy, despite their popularity. It was widely known among journalists that inter-war cricketer Wally Hammond enjoyed a playboy lifestyle. Considered to be England's best batsman of the era, Hammond contracted syphilis while the side toured the West Indies during the winter of 1925/26.[11] In a time before antibiotics, he became gravely ill, nearly losing a leg. He was forced to miss the following season as he recovered from the infection. Publicly his absence was blamed on malaria. After the Second World War, journalists began to test the bounds of acceptability and newspaper coverage began to become more intrusive. Princess Margaret's relationship with Group Captain Peter Townsend became one of the biggest stories in the early 1950s, but the coverage was still reverential. By the end of the 1960s, George Best – labelled the 'Fifth Beatle' – had burst onto the scene. His hedonistic lifestyle, lubricated by champagne and involving a string of Miss Worlds, was never far from the back pages. Yet, the Manchester United star was still granted licence to behave with little condemnation.

By the summer of 1981 that had changed. The tabloids were on the cusp of a circulation war. In 1980, the combined readership of the *Sun* and the *Daily Mirror* was around twenty-two million.[12] Sport and celebrity news were fundamental to both. Botham, like Princess Diana, was a dream come true for journalists. At the time, the *Sun* was devoting about 27 per cent of its space to sport and 17 per cent to celebrity news, the *Mirror* slightly more: 29 per cent to sport and 19 per cent to celebrity. By 1986, both were allocating more than 50 per cent of their space to sports news and celebrity stories combined.[13] This was in part due to the threat posed by the young upstart *Daily Star*. Announcing its arrival in 1978 with a front-page story, 'JIMMY GREAVES: My Life on the Booze',[14] the new title aimed to lure readers from the more established titles with a cheaper, even more downmarket product. At the time, the paper's editorial director Derek Jameson was quoted as saying the new paper's ethos was 'Tits, bums, QPR and roll-your-own fags'. He denied this, even complaining to the *Sun*, which had printed the story. The paper duly issued an apology: 'Sorry, Derek, but it did sound like you.'[15] Whatever the truth, the *Star*'s formula was working and by 1980 it was selling around a million copies a day. The *Sun* was hit hardest, its circulation falling from over four million in 1978 to 3.6 million in 1981.[16]

In an attempt to stop the rot, Rupert Murdoch, who had bought the paper as the *Daily Herald* in 1964 and renamed and relaunched it, cut the *Sun*'s cover price, started giving away huge cash prizes in 'bingo' competitions and in 1981 appointed Kelvin MacKenzie as editor. The new editor unashamedly embraced Thatcherism, giving the paper a hard right-wing edge and taking it aggressively downmarket. He demanded that his staff 'SHOCK AND AMAZE ON EVERY PAGE'[17] and that they 'monster' the subjects of their stories and 'piss all over them'.[18] There is a risk in overstating the influence of any one individual, but such was the *Sun*'s impact under MacKenzie's editorship that Tom Baistow, the respected elder statesman of the profession, was moved to lament in his critique of the British press that the paper's rise in the 1980s

corresponded with the 'metamorphosis of relatively healthy popular journalism into the junk food of the mass mind market'.[19]
MacKenzie himself would later say that his tenure at the *Sun* had
had a 'positively downhill' effect on British journalism.[20]

Infused with its editor's self-confidence, and with people watching television in ever-increasing numbers, the *Sun* staff began to
focus their attention on showbiz news. In particular, they latched
onto the booming interest in soap operas, championing *EastEnders*
in its rivalry with *Coronation Street*. As the paper's biographers Peter
Chippendale and Chris Horrie wrote: '*The Street*, with its ageing
audience, had always been essentially the property of the *Mirror*.
But *EastEnders* was young, southern and rough – just like *The Sun*.'[21]
US imports like *Dallas*, its spinoff *Knots Landing* and rivals *Dynasty*
and *Falcon Crest*, were aspirational, focusing on the trials and tribula-
tions of the wealthy. By contrast, their British cousins were working
class and built on the established tradition of kitchen-sink dramas
of the 1960s. Just before *EastEnders* first aired on BBC1 in 1985, its
co-creator Tony Holland wrote in the *Radio Times* that 'gossip,
intrigue and scandal are high on the list of daily events'[22] for the
residents of Albert Square, where the show was set. Mary Whitehouse, who as the founder and first president of the National
Viewers' and Listeners' Association was the self-appointed watch-
dog of the nation's moral standards, wanted the programme
banned, complaining about 'its verbal aggression and its atmosphere of physical violence, its homosexuals, its blackmailing pimp
and its prostitute, its lies and deceits and its bad language'.[23] Despite
her protestations, *EastEnders* was a huge success, topping the TV
ratings charts for 165 out of 167 weeks from October 1985.[24] It
reached its apex on Christmas Day 1986, when approximately thirty
million people[25] – more than half the country – gathered to watch
'Dirty Den' Watts hand divorce papers to his estranged wife Angie.

Thanks to a mole inside the show's production team, the *Sun* was able to print numerous stories about both the show's plot and the off-screen lives of its cast members. Many of the latter were rooted in the paper's increasing fascination with 'bonk journalism' – stories about celebrities' sex lives. Gameshows such as *Blankety Blank*, *Celebrity Squares* and *Give Us A Clue* gave minor celebrities greater exposure, helping them become famous simply for being on TV, expanding both the definition of celebrity and the pool of people subject to tabloid kiss 'n' tell exposés. Writing in 1994, the music journalist Tom Hibbert, who had spent much of the 1980s gently mocking celebrity culture in his column 'Who The Hell Do They Think They Are?' for *Q* magazine, opined that 'In 1986 Britain was awash with celebrities like never before, under threat from the famous only famous for being famous, the famously awful turning the soul of a once-brave country to mush.'[26] By the end of the 1980s, battle had been joined by magazines such as *Hello!*, *Chat*, *Bella*, *Best* and *Now*. The competition for stories about the private lives of the famous intensified further, a process that would continue through the 1990s and into the early twenty-first century with the advent of reality TV shows such as *Big Brother* and *I'm A Celebrity . . . Get Me Out of Here!*

It was against this backdrop that Lady Diana married Prince Charles. Glamorous and media-friendly, she became the ultimate tabloid catch, despite pleas from Buckingham Palace for sensitive treatment. After it was announced she was pregnant in 1982, both the *Sun* and the *Daily Star* printed long-lens shots of her relaxing in the Caribbean on a private holiday in a bikini, her bump visible. The *Sun* responded to criticism from the queen, with a half-hearted apology. It also printed the photos again and declared its 'legitimate interest in the Royal family not merely as symbols, but as living, breathing people'.[27] The paper's message was clear: the royals would be treated like any other celebrities. They were the ultimate soap-opera family.

Ian Botham was one of the leading members of the wider cast of this story that was playing out in the pages of the tabloids. Even Wimbledon, a bastion of establishment respectability, was embroiled in the drama. In the American John McEnroe, tennis had a player whose ability and personality rivalled Botham's. He first became known to British fans when he reached the semi-finals of the 1977 tournament as an eighteen-year-old qualifier. Two years later, McEnroe claimed his first Grand Slam title at the US Open and this was followed by defeat at the hands of the Swede Björn Borg in the 1980 Wimbledon final. The epic five-set affair, in which McEnroe won a fourth-set tie-break 18–16, was widely regarded at the time to be the greatest tennis match ever played. McEnroe exacted his revenge at the US Open later in the year. When the pair met again on Centre Court at SW19 in the 1981 final, their rivalry was at its peak. Borg was looking for his sixth straight Wimbledon title, his younger opponent his first.

Thanks to McEnroe's numerous infamous on-court tantrums, the British tabloids had long since been referring to him by a range of uncomplimentary names such as the 'SuperBrat', the 'Incredible Sulk' and 'McTantrum'. His semi-final victory against Australian Rod Frawley ran true to form. McEnroe disputed numerous line calls, at one point yelling, 'I'm screwed because of the umpires in this place.' When he was heckled by members of the crowd he responded in kind, calling them 'vultures'. Eventually he was penalised for saying, 'You're a disgrace to mankind', a remark that umpire Wing Commander George Grimes took to be directed at him. McEnroe claimed he was talking about himself.[28] All this played out in front of Lady Diana Spencer less than four weeks before her wedding.

The presence of the royal bride-to-be only served to heighten the media's interest, as did the rumour that McEnroe and his girlfriend Stacey Margolin, a fellow tennis player, had separated. 'I can remember the clamour just to get into the room and be part of the press conference after the match was intense,' says former sports journalist Simon O'Hagan,[29] who worked for several national newspapers but was then in his first job for the *Kent Messenger*. 'Wimbledon had a small subterranean room in the bowels of Centre Court where we would go and talk to the players. By the time the press conference started the place was absolutely crammed, you could barely move there were so many people.'

When he arrived, McEnroe was wary. The first few questions were routine, focused on the match and the player's game. However, the tone changed when he was asked about his private life. In an indication of the blurring of the lines between sport and entertainment, the incendiary question came not from a sports reporter but from James Whitaker, the *Daily Star*'s royal correspondent. 'Whitaker was huge and not to say notorious on the tabloid scene,' says O'Hagan. 'He made it his business to get every exclusive going that he could, mainly about Lady Di in the run-up to the royal wedding. The news reporters were known as the Rotters, and he was the "king of the Rotters". He lit the blue touch paper when he interjected after a pause. I remember his very words were "John, have you and Stacey split up?"'

McEnroe was incensed. 'It's none of your damn business,' he responded. 'Wimbledon being Wimbledon, people are as much interested in your private life as in your tennis,' continued Whitaker. 'You're a disgrace to the press,' replied the exasperated player. 'You ought to be ashamed of yourself, mister. Go stick your head in the sand. That's where it belongs.'[30] At that he flung back his chair and stormed out. The anger was true to character but for once there was some justification. The American sports writers were equally incensed. 'There was a heated discussion among the press,' says O'Hagan, 'with Whittaker being basically accused of having ruined this press conference for everyone with this highly

incendiary, extremely tactless interjection. There was a lot of pushing and shoving and chairs being knocked over.' One of Whitaker's
most vociferous critics was Charlie Steiner of RKO Radio who
was in turn confronted by Nigel Clarke, a tennis writer for the *Daily
Mirror,* who nonetheless supported Whitaker's right to ask whatever questions he saw fit. 'Clarke punched Steiner. I don't know if
blows were exchanged, but at least one blow was delivered.'

Eventually peace was restored although, thanks to the presence of an American camera crew which had breached protocol
by attending, footage of the scuffle made it onto the BBC News,
magnifying its significance. 'It became this international incident,'
said Steiner years later.[31] Along with Clarke, he was ordered to the
office of the All England Club chairman, for a polite dressing
down. O'Hagan says the fight was about more than a disagreement over how to cover tennis. 'It was an extraordinary moment
and anyone who was in the room at the time will never forget it. It
was slightly shaming of the press and how they were carrying on,
but I think in a way it marked the end of the age of deference.
Until then I just don't think anybody would have dared say to
McEnroe what Whitaker said. It was a hugely intrusive personal
question but as far as Whitaker was concerned that was his job;
that's what he was there to find out because "McEnroe and Stacey
in bust-up" would sell a huge number of papers and that was the
only criterion. Sport became a soap opera and McEnroe was a
leading plotline, there's no doubt about that.'

Peter Roebuck, who replaced Botham as captain of their
county Somerset, recognised how the England star fitted into all
of this, writing, 'He is not so much a creation of the Press, not so
much a Frankenstein, as a man prone to outrage whose name can
sell newspapers, and who is seized upon for that purpose.'[32] This
was also symptomatic of a shift in the coverage of sport that
occurred during Botham's career. 'In the 1970s the cricket

correspondents didn't necessarily want to write about what was happening off the field,' says Simon Wilde, the *Sunday Times*' cricket correspondent and author of a biography of Botham.[33] 'If a player got into some sort of high jinks, the journalists might say "maybe you shouldn't be doing this", but they'd be their friends first and reporters second. That was how it was when Botham started touring. But partly because of Botham's celebrity, and the circulation war, the rules of engagement changed, and cricket correspondents were required to write about the news as well as the cricket. So, five or six years into Botham's career, he finds that the people he trusts – his mates and friends – had either been replaced by other people who were newsier or were under pressure from their editors to write about off-the-field incidents. That made life more complicated for him.'

When the *Sun* was relaunched by Rupert Murdoch in 1964, the sports editor Frank Nicklin proudly declared that its coverage would have 'four rows of teeth'.[34] He had signed Botham as a columnist for the paper for £100 per article before the player earned his first England cap. This seemed like an absolute bargain when Botham was appointed England captain in 1980, but increasingly like a mistake when his and England's form deteriorated. MacKenzie joined the paper just weeks before the 1981 Ashes series began and when the team capitulated in the first Test at Trent Bridge, he stormed round the office shouting: 'Who's the cunt who signed this useless cunt Botham?'[35] Nicklin, with whom MacKenzie never saw eye-to-eye, was gone by the end of the following week, Botham remained with the paper until 1988. By then, its aggressive shift in mentality under MacKenzie saw Nicklin's successor David Balmforth boasting that its sports coverage now had 'eight rows of teeth'.[36] As its star columnist, Botham was, initially at least, protected from the worst of the paper's bite, but the relationship made him a target for the *Sun*'s rivals. 'For him to be engaged in the thick of the circulation war himself didn't help,' says Wilde. 'I remember Ted Corbett, who wrote for the *Star*, telling me that he had to write about Botham, but he didn't have any access to him because he worked for the opposition. So, Ted's strategy was to criticise Botham every step of the way; to take up the opposite point of view because that was the only one available to him.' Eventually, as Botham acknowledged, 'The *Sun* felt impelled to join in as well, trying to outdo the more sensational stories of their rivals.'[37]

Sex and drugs were never far from the centre of these revelations. In early 1984 England lost a series to New Zealand for the first time. The shambolic tour, which saw the players regularly socialising with Elton John, who was touring the country at the same time, reached a low point when the visitors were bowled out for eighty-two and ninety-three in Christchurch. There were allegations that the players had smoked pot in the dressing room and that Botham and Allan Lamb had snorted cocaine with a couple of women in their room.[38] The *Mail on Sunday*, a recent entrant to the tabloid battlefield, having been launched in 1982, was the worst offender and Botham sued. The incident also changed his attitude to future tours, making him more reclusive, his room becoming known as the 'bat cave'.[39] Botham made himself unavailable for the tour to Sri Lanka the following winter, but that afforded him little respite. On New Year's Eve 1984, police raided his house in Epworth, Lincolnshire, and found a small amount of cannabis, worth less than £4, in a bag at the bottom of a drawer in an upstairs bedroom. He was fined £100 for possession.[40] More revelations were to come. During England's tour of the West Indies in the winter of 1985/86, Botham met Lindy Field, a former Miss Barbados, at a party hosted by the Rolling Stones' Mick Jagger. The *News of the World* subsequently published her claims, for which they had reportedly paid £25,000,[41] that the pair had snorted cocaine; however, the detail in her story that captured most attention was that the pair had supposedly broken the bed while having sex.[42] Again, Botham denied the allegations but despite the presence of his father-in-law as a witness he could do little to dampen the furore.

Botham was never going to satiate the tabloids' prurience on his own. The soap opera needed a wider cast and Botham's teammates also found themselves subject to the papers' attention; most notoriously, Mike Gatting who was sacked as England captain two days after the first Test against the West Indies at Trent Bridge in 1988 following allegations published in the *Sun* – which Gatting denied – that he had had sex with a barmaid at the team's hotel.[43] By this time Botham had withdrawn his libel suit against the *Mail on Sunday* with an admission that he had smoked dope,[44] which led to a two-month ban from the game. He chose not to sue the *News of the World* over Lindy Field's claims as his pockets were not deep enough to take them on in the libel courts.[45] Furthermore, he had concluded: 'It doesn't matter what I say, they print what they choose.'[46]

V

If the *Sun* embraced the spirit of Thatcherism in the 1980s, Botham embodied it. 'He was completely into her agenda,' says Wilde. 'He fitted it perfectly and would have been proud to have been identified with it.' Here was a man who had left school at fifteen with no qualifications to speak of but who, through sheer talent and hard work, reached the pinnacle of a sport dominated by the public school-educated, Oxbridge old-boy network. Botham espoused his ethos on the BBC show *Open to Question* in which he received an uncomfortable grilling from Scottish teenagers on a wide range of topics from his drug use and love of hunting to his attitudes on parenting. 'I do believe in free enter-prise,' said Botham. 'I do believe that if a guy gets off his backside and wants to go out and try and make something of his life, he should have that opportunity.'[47] And make something of his life he did with deals from a range of products including Shredded Wheat and Volvo. He was represented by Reg Hayter, a former cricket journalist who had left the Press Association in 1955 to set up his own agency. Hayter was innovative – the sports media agency he set up is still in business and still bears his name – and soon diversified, becoming an agent for several sportsmen includ-ing Basil D'Oliveira, Henry Cooper and Bob Wilson. However, in the early 1980s, he was in his seventies and, although he had no intention of retiring, he was inevitably slowing down. Consequently, Botham felt he was missing out on financial opportunities.[48]

Unhappy with his lot, Botham became friends with Tim Hud-son, who held celebrity charity cricket matches at his mansion in Cheshire. Referring to himself as 'Lord Tim', Hudson had made his fortune in America as a property developer, DJ and small-time band manager. He convinced Botham that he could earn just as much as comparable sports stars across the Atlantic, which was probably true, and that he could help the player cash in, which was probably not. Botham parted company with Hayter and employed Hudson as his manager, embracing his radical ideas such as marketing a range of 'country-house cricket' clothing – mainly striped blazers in Rastafarian red, gold and green and jumpers with matching trims. Hudson also convinced Botham he could have a movie career. In a much-publicised trip to Holly-wood, the pair met Israeli producer Menahem Golan, who had founded the Cannon production company. Botham, Golan sug-gested, had 'the looks, the build and the accent to be the next James Bond'[49] but also needed acting lessons, which, because of the player's commitment to a forthcoming tour of the West Indies, he would be unable to undertake. The meeting came to nothing.

The gloss was wearing off the relationship with Hudson and others in the Botham camp, including his wife Kath who had always been sceptical, eventually convinced him to part company with his new manager. Botham later wrote that he was 'embarrassed' to admit he had been taken in by Hudson.[50] Yet although Hudson could not deliver on his promises, his ideas were in many respects ahead of their time. What might have seemed ludicrous then is commonplace now. Numerous athletes from Serena Williams to Cristiano Ronaldo have their own clothing range, while many others including Eric Cantona, Dwayne Johnson and even Vinny Jones have converted sporting success into box-office success. What Hudson realised was that Botham was more than just a sportsman, he was a brand.

Another person who realised that sports stars could be brands was Barry Hearn. A self-declared 'ducker and diver',[51] Hearn and his Romford-based Matchroom sports management company and its stable of stars dominated snooker in the 1980s. While his protégé Steve Davis was cleaning up on the table, Hearn set about cleaning up off it by turning the players he managed into characters. It was an ethos he has been calling '*Dallas* with balls'[52] for decades. 'We were the first ones to get into the soap-opera mentality,' he tells me. 'I got the eight players I was managing in a room, and I didn't change anything, I just made them expand their own personalities to understand that this was good marketing.' Thus Willie Thorne, who liked a gamble, would constantly be giving the price on a favourite; the jovial Dennis Taylor would always be telling jokes; Welshman Terry Griffiths would sing lullabies. 'It wasn't just to make people feel good or be famous it was actually monetising their IP value. As much as I think a lot of myself, Mark McCormack really started that with Arnold Palmer, and I was a student of most things American on the basis that eventually they come over the ocean to us.'

What Hearn had learned from McCormack was that entertainment was as crucial as ability in raising a player's profile 'There's no point becoming great at something if no one knows you,' he says matter-of-factly. 'If you can become a hero, you don't even have to be that good sometimes. But if you can mould the glory of being the best with being the most famous then you've absolutely bang had it off.' Yet given the choice, Hearn says he would always choose fame over ability. 'You make more money by being famous than being good. And reality TV shows us that's true because the people on reality TV aren't good at much, but they're awfully famous and they can reach people for sponsors because of their fame.'

The tabloid circulation war of the 1980s and the resulting sensationalisation was a godsend for Hearn. 'The truest phrase that's ever been said is "No publicity is bad publicity". It gave us a huge platform of people that became aware of the sport. Alex Higgins is a great example of that because you were sat on the edge of your chair waiting for him to do something because you've heard about his reputation and that reputation was built by the tabloids. It was a period of "never mind whether it's true – just make the letters bigger", which can only be good for getting into people's mindsets.'

Higgins was the prototypical flawed genius. Wildly gifted, he was capable of pulling off spectacular, risky shots and making fast, thrilling clearances, he was also ill-disciplined on and off the green baize. An alcoholic, Higgins was prone to regular run-ins with the game's authorities and was fined for a range of offences from hurling a cue at a spectator to fighting with another player. His private life also played out on the pages of the tabloids. It was because of this persona – one Hearn says 'could not have been dreamed up' – that the Matchroom boss rebuffed the player's appeals to become part of his team. 'He turned me down point blank, saying I was impossible to manage,' wrote Higgins.[53] Yet Hearn still appreciates the value Higgins brought to the sport. 'The job on day one was to make sure everyone looked smart, like a gentleman,' says Hearn. 'Higgins did me an enormous favour by being as bad as he was, not under my control; he gave me a comparison but still gave the sport the excitement that only he could. Of my lot Jimmy White was a bit more exciting than the rest of them put together, but most of them were Steve Davis clones.'

Davis was the polar opposite of Higgins: reliable but dull. *Spitting Image* lampooned his persona by sarcastically nicknaming him Steve 'Interesting' Davis. Some thought such coverage would be detrimental, but Hearn recognised it as an opportunity: Davis became the boring character in Hearn's soap opera. He was soon the face of Minolta's 'boringly reliable' photocopiers. The next evolution was for Matchroom to start selling its own products by licensing its name, something Hearn had learned in his pre-snooker days working in the textile business. 'I'd seen people like Mary Quant getting five per cent of turnover for using her name on a range of fabrics, for example,' says Hearn. 'I thought "what a fucking cool business that is – you don't do anything, and they send you a cheque".' Soon snooker fans were able to buy everything from Matchroom cues to Matchroom aftershave, duvet covers, slippers and wallpaper.

The benefits of using a star athlete to promote products was something not lost on a range of companies. In 1985, Bladon-based computer games firm Tynesoft licensed Botham's name for a new cricket game. The home computer market had taken off five years earlier following the launch of the Sinclair ZX80. Priced at £99.55 for the ready-built model and £79.95 for the self-assembly kit, it was the first computer in the world to cost under £100. Some 50,000 were snapped up, and such was the demand the waiting list was several months long. Along with other computer companies such as Acorn and Commodore, Sinclair became a household name. Further success followed with the ZX81 and then the Spectrum, which was launched in 1982 and sold more than five million units globally. The Spectrum's success also created demand for content and within a few years some 23,000 games were available, including *Ian Botham's Test Match*. For the time, the game had a considerable amount of flexibility, allowing players to compete in either limited overs or full Test matches. When bowling, players could set their field, choose their speed and even throw down a few bouncers. Yet, despite this, the gameplay was poor even by the standards of the day and the game was not well received. The same cannot be said about a title released the previous year which kick-started the sport-computer game tie-in market: *Daley Thompson's Decathlon*.

Like Botham, Thompson was an all-rounder, demonstrating skill across ten athletics disciplines in his chosen event. Also like Botham, he bossed his sport. Thompson won gold at the Moscow Olympics in 1980 and then successfully defended the title in 1984. He also won three Commonwealth golds and two European Championship golds. When he won the inaugural decathlon world title in 1983, he became the first athlete in any athletics event to hold Olympic, World, continental and Commonwealth Games titles simultaneously. The world record he set at the 1984 Olympics remained unbroken for eight years. *Daley Thompson's Decathlon* was produced by Manchester-based company Ocean and was the first computer game to feature a named athlete. 'Brand association is something we invented by chance with Daley,' says the game's creator Paul Owens.[54] 'The fact that it sold so well certainly made us sit up and look for the next one.' At the time, adverts in computer magazines were the main avenue for selling games and Owens and his colleagues realised that if they could tie their products to someone or something recognisable that would make their adverts stand out. 'So that's what we did,' Owens says, 'we managed to attach Daley's name to the game. He was a celebrity at that point. He was appearing on TV and he was in people's minds because of the upcoming Olympics [in Los Angeles in 1984].'

Inspired in part by the arcade game *Track and Field*, players of *Daley*'s competed in ten events accruing points to determine who would win gold. Thanks to the frenetic action required to make the on-screen sprites run fast, jump high and throw long, the game was blamed for causing many broken joysticks and more than a few damaged keypads. One anomaly was the colour of the Daley Thompson figure, which was white. 'I felt guilty about that,' says Owens. 'You've only got eight colours on the Spectrum. I tried all the alternatives, but they looked really poor. Daley came into the office one day and I showed him the red and the purple and he said "no, you're right, don't worry about it", so we stuck with the white. He was more concerned about the way his figure ran, telling us he lifted his knees up more. It was something we changed in subsequent editions. But we wrote the game in six weeks, and we didn't have professional graphics artists, so you got what you got.'

The game was written quickly so it could be released just after the 1984 Olympics in Los Angeles, such a 'date-defined' launch being another innovation from Ocean. Thompson's gold-medal-winning performance in LA made *Daley*'s a bestseller and it dominated the games charts, proving a turning point for the company. Thompson has also acknowledged the game's huge success, saying that he has been asked 'tens of thousands of times'[55] – more than any other question – whether he was any good at it. Ocean would soon move away from sports to concentrate on tie-ins with international appeal, in particular movies, releasing games such as *Batman*, *RoboCop* and *Jurassic Park*. However, it was *Daley Thompson's Decathlon* that proved the benefit of such tie-ins, paving the way for a host of titles that are popular today, such as *Madden NFL*, *Tony Hawk's Pro Skater* and *FIFA*. It also demonstrated that not only sport was being commodified, so were the people who played it: the talent.

CHAPTER 3

Born in the USA

I

BY today's flat-screen standards, the television that stood in the corner of our lounge in the early 1980s was absurdly bulky. Deeper than it was wide, thanks to the cathode ray tube protruding from the back, it was encased in wood-effect plastic. It had a speaker to the right of the screen and above that a panel with buttons labelled: BBC1, BBC2 and ITV1. There was also a mysterious fourth button: ITV2. At the time, it served no meaningful purpose (it just took you to ITV), but the mere suggestion of a new TV channel was the stuff of *Tomorrow's World*.

Debate about the need for a fourth TV channel and what form it should take had been simmering since the 1960s. Various competing interest groups made a series of proposals and counterproposals, including a channel dedicated to the Open University, a third BBC channel and a second ITV channel. However, it was criticism of the BBC/ITV duopoly which drove much of the debate. To work in television, you had to work on their terms. Many programme makers felt excluded. They wanted change.

Ultimately, the Thatcher government implemented a hybrid

model. The new channel was to be publicly owned; it was to be 'innovative and experimental' and to appeal 'to tastes and interests not generally catered for'[1] (although what these tastes should be was not spelled out). At the same time, it would receive arm's length funding from the fifteen companies that comprised the ITV network. To recoup their investment, they would sell advertising on Channel 4 in their respective regions. The Independent Broadcasting Authority was to ensure it stayed editorially distinct from its funders. Lastly, in a move that chimed with the new prime minister's free-market ideals, Channel 4 would commission, not create, programming. It was hoped that this new competitive marketplace among independent producers would foster a spirit of entrepreneurship while also weakening unions in the industry.[2]

Thus, there was to be a third voice on British television and at 4.45 p.m. on Tuesday 2 November 1982 the mystery button on our television finally came into its own. The test card faded to black, the specially commissioned four-note signature tune played and animated blocks of red, green, blue, yellow and purple formed themselves into the channel's ident: a giant number '4'. The first programme shown was *Countdown*, the title music the same as it is today despite having been given a modern twist since. Just prior to that was a four-minute montage of what content viewers could expect. Sport was conspicuously absent.

Channel 4's mandate to be different and distinctive from the pre-existing channels coupled with the fact that the BBC, and to a lesser extent ITV, had the rights for the main sports and events sewn up, meant it was easy for the idea of sport on Channel 4 to be dismissed and so, initially, it was. However, there was a backlash against the decision and a pressure group, Sport on Four, was set up to try and overturn it. Derek Brandon, an independent sports programme producer, was asked by the organisation for his advice on what sports might be viable for the new channel.

About a year before Channel 4's launch, Brandon along with some members of the pressure group were granted a meeting with the new channel's chief executive Jeremy Isaacs to press their case. 'He gave us a speech saying, "the BBC has all the important sports contracts. There's nothing there for us, we're not going to get involved in a bidding war. I don't think we need sport," and so on,' Brandon explains.[3] 'I said, "if you're going to be distinctive and different, get your own sport which is distinctive and different." Jeremy asked me what sport that should be, and I said, "American football". He agreed straight away. He knew a bit about the sport, he'd been to America, he'd seen it and he just said "yes".' With the green light given and in the absence of meaningful competition from the BBC and ITV, and in the days before Sky, obtaining the rights was relatively easy. They were acquired for $87,000.[4] There was no bidding war.

II

Prior to the 1980s, most people in Britain had only a tangential experience of American football, if that. The opening credits of the US soap opera *Dallas* provided a blink-and-you-miss-it aerial shot of the Dallas Cowboys' stadium with its unfamiliar pitch markings denoting yardage. The few games that did take place in Britain were contested by teams of US Armed Forces personnel, mainly on American airbases. ITV's *World of Sport* showed a thirty-minute highlight package of the end-of-season Super Bowl, which pits the AFC and NFC divisional winners against each other, beginning with Super Bowl V in 1971, but it was presented more as a novelty than a serious sporting contest. Coverage in newspapers, was just as scant, with brief, irregular reports, again, only covering the Super Bowl.

Until Channel 4 started broadcasting the sport, the only place screening live coverage of the Super Bowl was the Odeon Leicester Square. Brandon had been to watch Super Bowl XV between the Oakland Raiders and the Philadelphia Eagles in 1981 and he took Isaacs the following year. 'It was mostly expat Americans with a hardcore of a few English people who had been to America and had seen the sport,' Brandon recalls. 'I think people flew in from around Europe as well, because there wasn't enough of a marketplace to have the live feed into Paris or Munich and other places. The Americans all wore the gear, especially if they were supporting one of the teams that was involved.' Sport on Four quickly became Cheerleader Productions after it was decided the original name made it sound as if the company was responsible for all the channel's sports output. Brandon and his colleagues set about producing an edited highlights programme that fulfilled the channel's brief to innovate and provide viewers with content they couldn't find anywhere else. 'I think if we'd got the contract to cover sport for ITV, we wouldn't have felt too motivated to do so differently from the way they and the BBC did things,' explains Brandon. 'So, it would have been a middle-aged white man in a suit and tie with a flat set behind him, which had the programme title on it, plus a glass of water and a telephone on the desk. We threw all of that away. Because Channel 4 set out to be distinctive and different and to reinvent the wheel in every other respect, there was no need for us to think boringly and traditionally.' Thus, the usual sports presenter's attire was discarded, replaced by smart casual. The desk was done away with, the hosts instead perching on barstools in front of a map of America with team helmets showing where the relevant cities were. 'It was totally alien to how sport was done on the BBC and ITV,' says Brandon, 'and of course they hated it.'

Brandon chose as the main presenter Nicky Horne, a DJ with Capital Radio, because of his presenting skills but also because he knew relatively little about the sport, and paired him with Miles Aitken, an American former basketball player who became the first black sports presenter on British television. 'I used to listen to Nicky, on Capital Radio, and he was a great broadcaster with a great voice. I thought, what we want is an Englishman who is a good broadcaster who knows nothing about American football – like the audience – so that the presenter learns the sport at the same rate, or preferably thirty seconds before the audience.' says Brandon.

'It was a stroke of genius,' Horne tells me,[5] 'because if there was something I didn't understand I would ask Miles; I was the conduit for the viewer.' To further help the audience, the programme began with a ten-minute 'idiot's guide' to the sport, explaining the rules and key terms. Some 20,000 wrote in for a printed version;[6] however, as the season progressed and viewers became better informed, the on-air guide was reduced in length until it was about two minutes long.

The footage that Channel 4 used was provided by the American networks CBS, ABC and NBC via IMG, the rights holders outside the US. Unlike coverage of football in Britain, in which four or five cameras were used, the Americans broadcasters were using as many as twenty-five. This was eye-opening for the production team, and it also enabled them to create highlights montages. Early on the decision was taken to ditch the library music used by the BBC and ITV and play these packages over songs in the charts. 'They were designed to tell the story of the week, or a particular game,' says Horne, recalling the example of the career-ending injury sustained by the Washington Redskin's legendary thirty-six-year-old quarterback Joe Thiesmann in 1985, just two years after he had led the team to victory in Super Bowl XVII. 'We agonised over whether to show it,' Horne tells me. 'The music sequence was to "Say It Ain't So, Joe" by Murray

Head. I remember there were tears in the edit suite when we put that one together.'

'No one had ever seen it before,' says Brandon, 'recognisable music, some of it funny but sometimes you'd say, "Oh shit, they're making a point". And we had little music bursts too, like Bruce Springsteen's "Born in the USA" to lead into highlights sequences. It was ground-breaking.' However, it wasn't cheap. While library music cost around £30 a minute, chart music ran into the hundreds. The very first programme included a montage set to the Rolling Stones' 'Gimme Shelter'. 'I still believe it is one of the best music sequences I've ever seen for sport,' says Brandon. 'It was full of these amazing shots of players playing in the snow and water cascading down the steps of the stadium — just the most fantastic montage. Elaine Rose made it and she ran the whole bloody song, which was about five minutes long. That would have cost Channel 4 a couple of grand. I don't know if they quite knew what they were into, but we did it and we did it every week.'

Now a standard part of sports programming, it was another revolutionary innovation and the established broadcasters, who had initially been dismissive of Channel 4's presentation, soon started copying it. 'Imitation is the sincerest form of flattery,' says Horne, 'and when we saw the BBC doing music sequences at the end of their coverage, we upped our game, so it was really good for us.' Similarly, the press, spurred on by Channel 4's coverage, quickly began to take a keen interest. Sport sections started carrying results of matches and then reports. The *Daily Telegraph* produced a weekly magazine, which had a readership of around 100,000 at the end of the 1980s[7] and a range of other sport-specific titles were launched, such as *Touchdown*, *Gridiron* and *First Down*. Very soon the Super Bowl had become part of the calendar of main events that the top sports writers would cover.

This extra media activity was driven by the huge success of

Channel 4's coverage. The first show was broadcast the Sunday after the channel launched and was introduced by a reconfigured ident. The '4' was made to look like an American footballer wearing a Stars and Stripes helmet, holding an American football and snorting steam menacingly. The programme was deliberately and strategically placed in the late afternoon 'God slot'. While BBC1 and ITV had a statutory obligation to run religious programming at that time, Channel 4 was mandated to provide something different. Just as the new channel scheduled films on Saturday afternoons to offer an alternative to *Grandstand* and *World of Sport*, so it scheduled its American football coverage as an alternative to *Songs of Praise* on BBC1 and ITV's *Highway* (BBC2 tended to broadcast *The Money Programme* or *News Review* at that time). The first show garnered 1.569 million viewers[8] and the average for the first season was 1.1 million.[9] It was regularly in Channel 4's top ten most viewed programmes and in Britain's top ten sports programmes.[10] Brandon isn't surprised by the success. 'I couldn't understand why the whole world wasn't watching it, because there was nothing else to watch at that point, with respect to people who enjoy *Songs of Praise*,' he says.

Initially the Cheerleader team planned only to provide highlights of the Super Bowl, albeit with a quicker turnaround than the usual week-long delay, but Isaacs pushed them to go further. 'Straight out he said: "No, no, we'll do that live",' Brandon tells me. 'That was most unusual for British television to be open right into the small hours doing a live event from the other side of the world.' So, less than three months after Horne had introduced the first highlights show, he found himself in the Pasadena Rose Bowl fronting live coverage of Super Bowl XVII. 'From a presentation point of view, it was thrilling, having to fill all the American commercial breaks. But it was also terrifying because you've got to be on your game for three and a half hours.' The Washington

Redskins beat the Miami Dolphins 27–17 and it was a success for Channel 4, too. Back in Britain, some two hours after the other channels had shut down, around 4.5 million people were still watching.[11]

Yet, the ratings told just part of the story and, as Horne remembers, the wider impact they were having quickly became apparent. 'We'd only been on the air for about five or six weeks, and I was walking down Oxford Street when I saw a couple of people wearing Raiders jackets. It was just like "bloody hell" there really is something going on here. We felt it very much at Cheerleader and Channel 4. That was something else about it, those oversized jerseys and those big puffer jackets with "Raiders" or "Redskins" on and there were all these great logos. There was even a kind of romance to the names: "the Chargers" and "the Packers". It's not like "Manchester City".'

Around the same time, while walking in London's Hyde Park one Sunday morning, Horne encountered some people playing American football as a result of their seeing the sport on Channel 4 and their numbers quickly grew to more than two hundred after Horne ran a story about them on Capital Radio.[12] This was the beginnings of the London Ravens. The team played their first organised competitive games in 1983 against a team from the Chicksands US Airforce base, attracting a crowd of 4,500 to Chelsea's Stamford Bridge.[13] By 1986 there were two leagues. Thirty-eight teams played in the British American Football League (BAFL) with a further seventy-two competing in the rival Budweiser League. Anheuser-Busch, the American drinks company that owned Budweiser, invested £300,000 in the sport in Britain,[14] also underwriting the production costs of the early years of Channel 4's coverage (the *Daily Telegraph* replaced them in the latter part of the 1980s). They were not alone in trying to capitalise on the sport's popularity with companies such as American Express,

Hitachi and Toshiba also sponsoring new teams. Soon the Manchester Spartans, Milton Keynes Bucks, Birmingham Bulls and Leicester Panthers were familiar names, able to attract crowds several thousand-strong to their games. In April 1986, around 13,500 people turned up to watch the Surrey Thunderbolts host the Paris Blue Angels at the Aldershot Army Arena[15] and a few months later the inaugural Budweiser Bowl attracted a sell-out crowd of 18,000 at Crystal Palace.[16]

By now Cheerleader were into their stride. The highlights show was regularly attracting in the region of six million viewers and live coverage of Super Bowl XX, in which the Chicago Bears beat the New England Patriots 46–10 at the Louisiana Superdome, attracted close to twelve million viewers.[17] In August, the razzamatazz came to Wembley when the Bears played the Dallas Cowboys in a pre-season exhibition game dubbed the America Bowl. The 82,700 tickets sold out in a week. London rolled out the red carpet for players (and their cheerleaders). However, it wasn't the teams' quarterbacks or the Bears' star running back Walter Payton who caught the public's imagination but his teammate William Perry, known as 'The Refrigerator', or 'Fridge'. Perry, a defensive linesman who acquired the nickname because of his size and eating habits, was already a media star, having appeared in *The A-Team* and *Wrestlemania*. He even had his own GI Joe action figure. Perry was the focus of much of the media's pre-game coverage which resulted in headlines like 'My Willie's Not Fat Says Mrs Fridge'[18] and an appearance on *Wogan* along with his teammate Mike Singletary.

It was no coincidence that American football's popularity arose during English football's lowest ebb. Beset by tragedy and violence at the tail end of the previous season, the sport was also subject to the TV blackout during the autumn of 1985 resulting from the dispute between the Football League and the BBC and

ITV over the cost of rights. 'There was nothing else to watch in football terms,' said ITV's then head of sport John Bromley, 'and suddenly The Refrigerator was a bigger name than Gary Lineker, the Chicago Bears better known than Arsenal among the kids. Soccer made a big mistake – you must never go off the box.'[19]

III

Channel 4's coverage of the NFL was part of a wider incursion of American-made, or American-focused, programming into British TV schedules. As a telly addict kid, I was enthralled by shows about talking cars, super-helicopters and Vietnam veterans who loved it when their plans came together (although they didn't all like flying). There were ground-breaking comedies like *Cheers*, *Moonlighting* and *The Cosby Show*, and dramas like *Magnum PI* and *Cagney and Lacey*, to name just a handful. The programmes were attractive to British broadcasters. They had high production budgets – higher than the budgets of most British-made shows – but, crucially, could be bought for less than the cost of a British-made show. And they were popular. Of all TV imports to Britain in 1977, 43 per cent came from America. By 1984, US programming made up 71 per cent of the total.[20] Horne feels that this Americanisation of British culture explained, at least in part, some of the allure of Channel 4's NFL coverage. 'I think we just hit the zeitgeist at precisely the right moment,' Horne says. 'The UK was very grey at the time and soaps like *Dallas* presented a very affluent environment, all that wealth and intrigue was great escapism. Remember, when we started, we edited out all the breaks, all the timeouts. When you edit like that and you've got time to craft the edit, it looked incredible. It looked like *Star Wars*.'

The escapism spilled over into the high street. Soap fans could

buy all manner of merchandise from the *Dallas* boardgame to
bedlinen and wallpaper, or Forever Krystle perfume, named after
the *Dynasty* character Krystle Carrington. Sales reached £210
million a year by 1985.[21] The same year, model Nick Kamen
walked into a laundrette, stripped down to a pair of crisp white
boxer shorts and socks, and made Levi jeans cool again. Once a
counter-cultural symbol in the 1960s, jeans had lost their allure
having become associated with dads (and not particularly trendy
dads). During the recession of the early part of the 1980s denim
became seen as the ideal fabric for hard-wearing work, not leisure,
clothes. There was even concern that jeans would go completely
out of fashion. Levi Strauss wanted to relaunch both their brand
and their original shrink-to-fit 501s. The TV advert starring
Kamen, created by Bartle Bogle Hegarty, was set in 1950s smalltown USA, and was infused with Americana from a GI in uniform
to a woman wearing cardboard 3D glasses with red and green
lenses. Kamen even sported an Elvis-style quiff. All this was set to
the soundtrack of Marvin Gaye's classic 'I Heard It Through the
Grapevine'. Within a year, sales of Levi 501s had soared by 800
per cent[22] and the ad had to be pulled as demand outstripped supply. Sales of boxer shorts also spiked. Even Lee Jeans, another
American company, reported a 40 per cent rise in sales, despite
not having done anything.[23] Gaye's track became a UK Top 10
hit a year after his death in 1984.

Another American company that used television advertising
effectively was McDonald's. Wimpy introduced the hamburger to
Britain in 1954. However, these were sold in a coffee-shop setting at
its Oxford Street corner house. Dining out in Britain was a mainly
middle-class habit, enjoyed at leisure in quiet, pleasant surroundings
with traditional waitress service. McDonald's was to change that.
When the company opened its first British restaurant in Woolwich,
south-east London, in October 1974, it was seen as something of a

novelty. Customers complained about the lack of butter on buns, and knives and forks to eat with. Some even doubted whether there was a viable fast-food market outside London. McDonald's set about educating its customers in this new way of eating, while also trading on its novelty factor: 'There's a difference at McDonald's you'll enjoy' was an early slogan.[24] At the same time, the company deliberately played on its American heritage. Growth was slow at first. There were just ten McDonald's in Britain, all in London, in 1977, the year in which Burger King, its closest rival in America, opened its first British outlet. However, rapid expansion followed on the back of aggressive television advertising concentrated in the geographical areas covered by the larger ITV regions, such as Granada in the North West. It was no coincidence that when McDonald's opened its 100th restaurant, in 1983, it was in Manchester. That number had more than trebled by the end of the decade.

For some, however, the Golden Arches were a symbol of everything wrong with American culture. The standardised design of the restaurants was, some claimed, homogenising British town and city centres, disregarding local identities and culture in the process. As the number of McDonald's restaurants grew in Britain, so did the level of obesity, which doubled between 1983 and 1994,[25] sparking a national conversation about the problems of fatty, nutritionally valueless 'junk food'. Campaigners criticised the environmental impact, Greenpeace launching annual protests against McDonald's in 1985.

Dallas, like McDonald's, also became a byword for what some saw as damaging American cultural imperialism. Such was the alarm about the influx of American television shows that in 1981 the government attempted to limit its incursion onto British screens by restricting the amount of programming from non-UK/EEC countries on commercial TV to just 14 per cent. Although not formally bound by the same limits, the BBC more or less followed suit. However, most of this American content was packed into primetime slots. In 1982, some 31 per cent of the BBC's output in peak viewing hours came from abroad, 26 per cent from the USA.[26] Thus, the impression was created that British viewers were being exposed to 'wall-to-wall *Dallas*', the phrase used by critics of the increasing amount of American programming. (In the 1990s, academics would coin the phrase 'Dallasification' to describe the phenomenon.[27])

In some respects, none of this was new. Concerns about the Americanisation of British culture began when Hollywood production companies started exporting their films in the 1920s. These fears were reinforced in the immediate post-war years with the growth of youth subcultures which adopted rock 'n' roll as their soundtrack of choice.[28] However, in the 1980s concerns about cultural hegemony began to coalesce with concerns about British sovereignty prompted by Margaret Thatcher's close political relationship with American president Ronald Reagan at a time of increasing Cold War tensions. In 1977, the Soviet Union installed SS20 missiles in European Russia, causing alarm among Western leaders concerned about the imbalance this created in the region. In response, the Americans deployed Pershing II and cruise missiles at bases in a range of NATO allies, including Britain, as a supposed deterrent.

For many this only made the threat of nuclear war seem greater. The sense of impending doom was made more palpable by a government advertising campaign in which every household received a pamphlet, *Protect and Survive*, with advice on 'how to make your home and your family as safe as possible under nuclear attack'. (Given this advice amounted to leaning doors against a wall and covering them with mattresses, it's debatable how useful the advice actually was.)

These fears spilled over into popular culture. Frankie Goes to

Hollywood's anti-war song 'Two Tribes' was No. 1 for nine weeks from June 1984 – a longer consecutive period than any other track during the decade. Its video began with the haunting sound of the nuclear warning siren and ended with the Earth exploding. In between, lookalikes of Reagan and his Soviet opposite number Konstantin Chernenko engaged in a no-holds-barred bare-knuckle fight. Raymond Briggs, who had delighted children (and adults) with *The Snowman* and *Fungus the Bogeyman*, delivered an altogether more harrowing vision in *When the Wind Blows* in 1982, about a retired couple dealing with the aftermath of a nuclear strike. However, this was nothing compared to the BBC drama-documentary *Threads*, which explored the full visceral horror of a nuclear attack on Sheffield and the grim, long-drawn-out after-math for survivors. When it aired on 23 September 1984, it was, some said, 'The night the country didn't sleep.'[29]

By this time there was already widespread opposition to the siting of the American missiles on British soil. CND, the Cam-paign for Nuclear Disarmament, which was formed in 1957, underwent a revival. Mass anti-nuclear demonstrations took place across Western Europe. In December 1982, around 30,000 women travelled to Greenham Common Airbase in Berkshire, where some of the missiles were to be housed, held hands and encircled the base. The following year, 70,000 protesters formed a fourteen-mile human chain from Greenham to RAF Aldermas-ton and on to Burghfield, the site of a weapons factory. The protests had been driven by various groups of women, some of whom eventually joined forces to set up peace camps. Early on it was decided these should be women-only. The protestors viewed the missiles as the pinnacle of patriarchal violence. Margaret Thatcher might have been the country's first woman prime min-ister, but when she entered Downing Street in 1979 she was one of just nineteen female MPs, the lowest number in any post-war parliament other than 1951. The political arena was a masculine domain which the protestors, camped outside the gates of Greenham Common beyond the barbed wire and armed guards, were literally and symbolically shut out of. However, their very presence was a threat to the established order, which they also challenged by weaponising traditional notions of femininity, in particular motherhood, and arguing that their protests were about protecting the future of their children.

IV

Despite the ongoing Cold War tensions and the criticism in some quarters of the close relationship between the US and the UK, American football was not the only sport from across the Atlantic that the public embraced. On the last weekend of September 1984 around 130,000 people[30] descended on Donington Park in Leicestershire to watch the Multipart Truck Grand Prix. The event was organised by Andrew Marriott, who ran a sports marketing company at the time, as a way of promoting the parts division of one of his clients, Leyland Trucks. Although Marriott had got the idea for the event after watching a similar race in Holland, the sport had originated in America in 1979.

The huge crowds at Donington were a result of publicity from the *Sun*, *Truck Magazine* and Radio 1 DJ Mike Smith, who took part in the race himself, and they were so large that they brought both the M1 and M6 motorways to a standstill.[31] 'We were overwhelmed,' says Marriott.[32] 'I don't think they all paid to get in to be honest. There was such a tailback that it went past East Midlands Airport. They couldn't get emergency vehicles in, so they had to divert some planes and leave others grounded.'

A range of drivers from other types of motor sports were invited to take part including former motorcycling world champion Barry Sheene, his Suzuki teammate Steve Parrish, Formula 1 driver Martin Brundle and Stig Blomqvist, the World Rally champion. However, they were all beaten by Duilio Ghislotti, an Italian amateur who stopped off on his way to deliver washing machines to Newcastle.[33] 'He simply unhooked his load, competed, and then continued on to the North East,' says Marriott. Another entrant was taking a break from delivering dog food.

Behind Ghislotti, in third place, was British driver Richard Walker. A rally driver and transport contractor local to Donington, the Grand Prix, he says, 'ticked all the boxes' for him.[34] His performance attracted sponsors and he went on to compete in the nascent European Championship, being crowned class champion three times. The sport, which eventually came under the control of the FIA, motorsport's world governing body, continued to be popular, regularly attracting crowds of up to 70,000 to race meetings at Donington, Brands Hatch and Silverstone and in 1989 it made its debut on *Grandstand*. As millions of viewers got their first taste of truck racing, Walker was involved in a spectacular crash. 'Luckily with my rallying experience, I managed to put the truck into the barrier sideways on. We were doing about eighty miles an hour and the barrier would have stopped me, but maybe I wouldn't have been talking to you now if I'd hit it head on,' Walker tells me matter-of-factly. 'The back axle broke free and that went pogoing down the track. I spun round three of four times and ended up in the middle of the track but luckily no one hit me. It looked quite spectacular; it was very good television, the BBC used it quite a few times. I was OK, but *Grandstand* was put off the air for an hour as they had to repair where the axle had drilled into the tarmac.' The disruption to the programme caused by the crash meant the sport never received significant national TV coverage again and

by the early 1990s it had begun to flounder. It was professional-
ised; gone were the washing machines and dog food, but so too
were the crowds and by 1994, just ten years after the first Grand
Prix at Donington, truck race meetings were attracting barely
5,000 fans at best.[35]

By the end of the 1980s, the popularity of Channel 4's American football coverage was also falling. After several seasons Horne
and Aitken left and their departures precipitated a fast turnover
of presenters. Frank Gifford, the legendary ABC commentator,
became the main host alongside John Smith, a British-born former kicker with the New England Patriots. After a season they
were replaced by the Vicious Boys (Angelo Abela and Andy
Smart). Employing the British comedians was an attempt to revert
to the ethos of the early shows, but it backfired. The audience was
now more serious about the sport and the pair were quickly
replaced by another British-born kicker, Mick Luckhurst, who
had played in the NFL for the Atlanta Falcons and the Minnesota
Vikings. The decline continued in the early 1990s, not least as a
result of the rise of Sky Sports' coverage of the Premier League.
Although they would ultimately usurp Channel 4's American
Football coverage, they would also build on its innovative legacy.

CHAPTER 4

Let's Get Physical

I

IN 1983, Britain had not yet fully shaken off the hangover of the 1970s. Margaret Thatcher, still in her first term as prime minister, was teasing the prospect of an early general election. The Falklands War had been won, but the battle with the miners lay head. So, too, was Big Bang, the deregulation of the financial markets, which would be at the heart of her legacy. Inflation had been cut from a high of 21.9 per cent in May 1980 but, as a consequence, unemployment was heading towards three million. The country was in an odd place, trying to pull away from the previous decade but still in its shadow. Its colour palette was dull: dark brown, musty orange, black. It was against this dour backdrop that on a chilly January morning Diana Moran stepped onto the nation's TV screens wearing a bright green leotard. Moran, who would become known as 'the Green Goddess', was at London's Waterloo Station. Her job: to entice people to take a break from the early morning rush to work and take part in a live aerobics session during the debut episode of the BBC's new *Breakfast Time* show. 'It was incredibly cold,' Moran remembers. 'Nothing had ever been done like this before. I think the commuters thought I'd gone absolutely mad.'[1]

Born in Bristol, Moran had begun teaching what was then called 'exercise to music' to her girlfriends in their twenties, inviting them over to sessions at her house. After a recommendation, this led to her teaching classes first at Butlin's in Minehead, and then at Pontins. 'I taught holidaymakers of all ages: mums, dads, grandparents, children, all of them at the dancefloor. They loved it,' Moran recalls. She became so popular that Butlin's soon asked her to train other instructors, rolling the sessions out in camps across the country. At the same time, she was on a programme called *Here Today*, broadcast on ITV's West Country franchise, HTV, for which she did a short exercise slot every week. 'It was the start of daytime television. It was a bit risqué at the time.' It was then that she came by the green leotard that would forever be her trademark. 'Nobody was wearing Lycra at the time. Everybody was wearing little black shorts and Aertex blouses. So HTV sent me to London to buy a leotard. I love yellow, so I bought a yellow leotard and wore that in the first week, but they said: "You can't wear that; you look like a large prancing canary." The next week I bought a coffee-coloured one and they said: "You definitely can't wear that! You look naked." They asked me what other colours there were, and I said: "Well, there's a terrible green" and they said, "Try that", and of course it was very telegenic and that was that.'

The programme was broadcast across the ITV network and that eventually brought her to the attention of *Breakfast Time*'s creator Ron Neil who asked her to front a regular exercise slot, 'Getting Britain Fit', every morning between 6.45 and 7.00. Initially Moran was hesitant about making the commitment, but Neil persuaded her to make the switch with the promise that she could record her segments for the forthcoming week at the BBC

Bristol studios on Sunday nights. However, the week before *Breakfast Time* went live, those plans changed. 'They rang me and said, "We think that it would be a good idea if we had you on Waterloo Station early in the morning with all the commuters," and that's what I did. It got huge attention from the press, and it took off from there; there was no going back.' Moran quickly became known as the Green Goddess, a nickname bestowed on her by her former employers at HTV. 'When I started with the BBC, I asked them what they wanted me to wear and they said, "Oh, your green, of course." After that first day, the national press went wild and they went back to HTV and said: "'ere, dish the dirt on this bird will you. Who is she? Where's she from?" Well, first of all, I wasn't a "bird" I was forty-three but the HTV publicity department said, "Are you talking about Diana? Our Green Goddess?" The rest is history.'

While Moran was braving the winter weather, back in the *Breakfast Time* studio were Frank Bough, who had been chosen as the show's main host due to his experience fronting three hours of live sport on *Grandstand* each week, and his co-hosts Selina Scott and Nick Ross. The programme had been created as a rival to *Good Morning Britain*, to be broadcast by TV-am. The new ITV morning franchise had been awarded in 1980 but its launch was delayed until 1983 to avoid overshadowing the launch of Channel 4 the previous November. This allowed the BBC to steal a march on their commercial rivals and go to air first. It was, as Ron Neil put it, 'the last new thing on television',[2] although Ross suggested that there were some 'cynics' who believed 'that television in the morning is sort of decadent'.[3]

The two-week head start meant that by the time *Good Morning Britain* launched, the BBC team had ironed out the glitches in their own coverage and were well into their stride. They'd been able to build viewer loyalty and set the agenda, determining what people thought television's 'last new thing' should look like. Despite its team of high-profile hosts, the so-called 'Famous Five': Anna Ford, David Frost, Robert Kee, Michael Parkinson and Angela Rippon, *Good Morning Britain*'s critics decried its overly serious and intellectual approach. In February, two-thirds of viewers chose the BBC. A month later, TV-am's CEO Peter Jay, who had defined the programme's 'mission to explain' ethos,[4] resigned. In April, Ford and Rippon were sacked and their male counterparts dropped from weekday presenting duties. By May, *Breakfast Time* was pulling in around 85 per cent of the available audience. Moran's enthusiasm and energetic routines were an important part of the mix, so much so she soon had a competitor: Mad Lizzie.

'I got my job because of the Green Goddess's popularity and the publicity she got,' says Lizzie Webb,[5] who was that competitor. An English and drama teacher, Webb was also running classes, which she called 'Funky Dance', at the Dance Centre in Covent Garden. One of the regular attendees was Jane Tatnall, and she recommended Webb to her boss, Greg Dyke, who had been brought in to rescue the ailing TV-am following Jay's departure. Tasked with getting viewing figures above a million, he set to work. Recognising that most people who watched television in the mornings were housewives and children, Dyke changed the focus of the output from hard news and current affairs to horoscopes, bingo and celebrities. He also saw the popularity of Roland Rat, a puppet with a brash, arrogant persona aimed at children during the school holidays and made him central to TV-am's output. Although the rodent superstar had made his debut before Dyke took the reins, this didn't stop the *Sun* from repeatedly referring to Dyke as 'Roland Rat's dad'.[6] While Roland, with his sidekick Kevin the Gerbil, was there to appeal to the children, Webb, who had by now been given the nickname 'Mad Lizzie' by Dyke after

Tatnall told him how fun her 'mad' routines were, was there for their mums. Within a month, ratings had doubled to 400,000.[7] Within just three months, they were reaching heights of 1.75 million, settling at just above a million when Roland was taking a break. 'Greg wanted to bring in someone that would counteract the Green Goddess's popularity,' says Webb, 'but he could also see that exercise was becoming very popular.'

II

This rise in interest had been sparked by the combination of a cultural innovation from America and a technological innovation from Japan. Jane Fonda, the Oscar-winning actress and political activist, had opened several fitness studios in California, teaching some classes herself. On the back of their success, she released the eponymous *Jane Fonda's Workout Book* in November 1981. By March 1982 it was top of the *New York Times* non-fiction list, where it stayed for six months. In April a complementary double album was released, peaking at No. 7 in the UK charts and going double platinum in the USA. A video was then rushed into production. Filmed in three days with little rehearsal, it was, like the book and album, a huge success, becoming the highest selling home video release of the early 1980s.

This was the foundation upon which Moran and Webb built their success. 'She was the initial catalyst,' says Webb. 'Without Jane Fonda "going for the burn" there possibly would never have been this explosion of interest and it wouldn't have taken off in the same way.' At the BBC, Moran and her colleagues were always conscious of what Fonda was doing. 'I crept up behind her after a few months,' she says. 'And from across the Pond, we were vying with one other. If she brought out something, I brought out something. I always had an eye on what Jane Fonda was doing. She was my sort of age and if she could do it, I could do it.'

It wasn't just the exercise industry which benefited from the success of Fonda and those who followed in her wake. The increased focus on fitness came hand in hand with a booming interest in what we were eating. In 1982, Audrey Eyton, the co-founder of *Slimming Magazine*, released *The F-Plan Diet*, which promoted high-fibre foods. With over a million copies sold, it was the year's bestseller. In its wake, demand for Bran Flakes, whole-wheat bread and pasta and baked beans all rose. The video industry also received a boost.

The first video cassette recorders (VCRs) went on sale in 1978 but at £799 they were too expensive for most people. Prices quickly fell, but while the cheapest VCR could be picked up for £172.80 in 1980, it still cost more than a fridge-freezer and nearly two and a half times as much as a standard black and white TV. Few knew whether VCRs would take off, and if so how they would develop. The wedding of Prince Charles and Lady Diana Spencer in 1981 was the first event to provide some answers. Adverts tempted people with the prospect of being able to 'rewind at any time to study the bride's dress [and] fast forward or backward to find your favourite moments'.[8] Sales doubled as a consequence, and by 1982 a fifth of all households in Britain owned a VCR. However, as Fonda acknowledged in an interview a decade after her first video was released, there was still not much you could do with one other than record your favourite TV programmes. 'Hardware was crying out for software in order to make people want to buy and use the hardware,' she said. 'I didn't realise that I was meeting a need. Not just for exercise but for something that would help build a whole home-video industry. This was the kind of product that was needed.'[9]

With cinema attendances falling from a high of 1.6 billion

admissions in 1946 to forty-three million in 1984, rental stores began to spring up on high streets and out-of-town shopping parades across the country. You could even pop to the local news-agents to borrow a video, or grab one while you were filling up your car. However, unlike cinema releases such titles were uncerti-fied. Along with buying your milk and your petrol, you could casually rent titles like *Cannibal Holocaust*, *The Driller Killer*, or *I Spit on Your Grave*, no questions asked. In response to the ensuing moral panic over these so-called 'video nasties', fuelled by headlines such as 'Rape of Our Children's Minds',[10] the powers of the British Board of Film Classification were extended to include videos in 1984, and a list of banned titles produced. Fonda's video was not among them and along with the likes of the behind-the-scenes documentary *Making Michael Jackson's Thriller*, which sold more than a million copies, it proved there was a market for so-called 'sell-through' titles (those aimed directly at consumers) as well as rentals. This in turn further increased sales of VCRs; by 1987 there was one in over half of all households, more than owned a car.

The music industry also benefited. The soundtrack for Fonda's video contained songs from a range of artists such as The Jack-sons, REO Speedwagon and Billy Ocean and soon younger artists were reinforcing the link between fitness and beauty, sport and dance. 'My first album was a total aerobics record,' said Madonna in a 1985 magazine interview. 'I make records with aer-obics in mind.'[11] Initially Moran used military-style music, because of its beat, but she was soon choosing the tracks to which she choreographed her routines from the previous week's *Top of the Pops*. At the same time, Webb was being courted by record pro-moters. 'The pop music I was using had a great influence,' she says. 'If I used the same song three or four times a week, it could get into the charts. It was really when Simon Cowell began to realise how television could be used to promote a single. He and all the record companies would send me their singles in the hope that I would use it either as an exercise piece, or I'd invite people like Sinita and Sonia on, or Black Lace when they released "Aga-doo". I've got a whole load of gold discs from people to thank me.' She even received a handwritten thank-you note and an invitation to lunch from ex-Beatle George Harrison after helping his song 'Got My Mind Set on You' reach No. 2. 'The next one,' he wrote, 'is called "When We Was Fab" – could be when we had flab!'

III

The technology might be different, YouTube and social media having replaced VCRs, and aerobics no longer featuring on breakfast TV, but both Moran and Webb can see a clear line from their daily televised exercise routines and fitness videos to the popularity today of the likes of Joe Wicks and even the exercise equipment company Peloton, whose first post-Covid lockdown ad campaign had the tagline 'There's nothing like working out from home'. Moran calls it an 'extension' while Webb calls it an 'update', also pointing to the popularity of workout DVDs fronted by reality TV stars which bridged the gap. What was different was the impact that aerobics had on women's lives. 'It stopped them just being thought of as the little woman at home, cooking, look-ing after the kids and putting the slippers out for hubby when he came back,' says Moran. 'Women became more liberated, more independent – I know because it happened to me.' A range of social factors, from the expansion of higher education to increased ownership of domestic appliances led to women taking a different attitude to their own time and their own bodies. Not only did this give them the confidence to get out of the house and begin to exercise, but it also feminised gyms, giving them a space to exercise.

'Gyms in those days were for gangsters and boxers; they were very male,' says Debbie Moore, the founder of Pineapple Dance Studios.[12] 'Pineapple West in Paddington Street had been part of the Mayfair Gymnasium, where the Kray twins used to go.' Born in Urmston, in Lancashire, Moore won a modelling competition for *Honey* magazine aged fifteen, after which she left school to become a full-time model. One of her first jobs was in New York, where she met photographer David Grant. Known as the 'Shrimpton and Bailey of the North' they married in 1966, but divorced two years later. Moore returned to London, and after she gained several stone in weight due to an under-active thyroid, a doctor recommended that she take up dance, so she joined a class run by Arlene Phillips at the Covent Garden Dance Centre, where Lizzie Webb had taught Funky Dance.

When the studio suddenly closed, Moore decided to set up her own in a nearby derelict former pineapple warehouse in the old fruit market. And so the Pineapple Dance Studio was born. 'It was all about timing,' says Moore. 'I'd left school when I was fifteen, I had been a model for eighteen years but somehow or other I had my lightbulb moment when the Dance Centre closed down and I just knew that I was driven to open this place.' Like Moran, she saw the positive impact that this new-found freedom and confidence was having on women's lives. 'In those days, men running off with their secretaries, or a younger model, was much more commonplace,' she says. 'I witnessed these women coming in a bit shy, maybe they'd let themselves go, they'd had a couple of kids, they weren't working. Suddenly they realised they could get fit, and they could get into shape. Suddenly they were losing weight and getting it together. They were transformed.'

Yet Moore had 'only discovered dance by default'; her

background was in fashion. During her career, she had also worked as a 'fit model', a sort of live mannequin. This enabled her to see how the clothes were made, and gave her an understanding of the production process. After Pineapple had opened it became increasingly obvious to her that the dancewear available was not fit for purpose. 'It was in school uniform colours like maroon, green and brown. And it was made of shiny nylon pique, I thought, "why is it all nylon? It's so sweaty." So, I went to DuPont [then the producers of innovative materials] and asked whether they could do cotton Lycra.' The company developed a range of fabrics for Moore to experiment with. At the same time, she also saw that the dancers were customising the clothes, cutting the legs higher and the backs lower. So she asked the manufacturers to do the same, and to introduce brighter colours. As sales of the new dancewear took off, she launched her own fashion label which, she says, 'took dancewear from the studio into the street'. Soon the new designs spilled over into high street fashion. Influenced by musicals like *Cats*, films like *Flashdance* and *Fame*, and Madonna's early look, women began pairing leotards with jeans. Footless tights became leggings. Legwarmers and ra-ra skirts became wardrobe staples. By 1990 an estimated £35 million was being spent on such items every year.[13]

Reebok was another British company that capitalised on the growing number of women taking part in aerobics, dance classes and other similar forms of exercise. When Fonda released her first video, women either took classes in bare feet or in shoes appropriated from other sports, such as running or tennis, not ideal as they did not allow the necessary sideways movement. So, Reebok, a Bolton-based firm looking to expand into America, developed a shoe specifically for aerobics. Made of glove leather and lined with terrycloth so they were softer than other trainers, the Freestyle was the first sports shoe designed specifically for women and it was clear there was a gap in the market. When the shoe was launched in 1982, the first 32,000 pairs sold out in weeks. The company's global sales grew from around £130,400 in 1980 to £8 million in 1983, the Freestyle accounting for around 50 per cent. By 1987, Reebok's sales had reached £875 million.[14] It helped that Fonda began wearing Freestyles, with their two distinctive Velcro straps, in her videos. Other celebrities also gave them the seal of approval, tacitly or otherwise. Paula Abdul appeared in ads for the shoes, and Mick Jagger sported a pair in the video for 'Dancing in the Street'.

IV

Nike, like Reebok, was another sports footwear manufacturer that came to prominence during the 1980s. They dismissed Reebok's innovative Freestyles, suggesting that aerobics was just 'a bunch of fat ladies dancing to music',[15] their growth instead coming on the back of another health craze: jogging. In an echo of Nike's attitude toward aerobics, Adidas, the leading sports footwear manufacturer at the time, dismissively argued that 'jogging is not a sport'.[16] In the 1960s and 1970s, few people went running for fun. Most considered it an arduous, even boring, pursuit suitable only for soldiers, boxers (who called it 'roadwork') and elite athletes. According to Brendan Foster, who won bronze for Great Britain in the 10,000 metres at the 1976 Olympics, even they were greeted with scepticism on the streets. 'Now when you see someone running in your neighbourhood, you don't bat an eyelid but when someone went running forty, or fifty years ago people would say, "Oh bloody hell! Who's he? What's he doing?" '[17]

Just days before we spoke in July 2021, Foster had been marking the fortieth anniversary of the Great North Run, with publicity activity that saw him running along the beach at South Shields, the race's traditional finishing stretch. Foster had been inspired to set up the half marathon while training in Auckland prior to the Moscow Olympics in 1980. At the time, New Zealand was experiencing something of a jogging boom thanks to track coach Arthur Lydiard. He had a novel belief that, far from being a monotonous task, running could be fun 'and from the fun will come the will to excel'.[18] He trained several New Zealand athletes to Olympic success in the 1960s but also encouraged patients at the heart hospital where he worked as a physiotherapist to undertake gentle long-distance running for its health benefits. In the process, he set up the Auckland Joggers Club and in 1972 members of the club founded the Ports of Auckland Round the Bays race.

During their stay in the city, Foster and his training partner David Moorcroft decided to enter. 'When we got to the start line there were ten thousand people there and we'd never seen anything like it,' Foster tells me. 'Robert Muldoon [the prime minister of New Zealand] was the official starter and I said to David, "this must be a big deal".' The race started in the city centre, then continued along the sea front before finishing in St Heliers Bay. 'There were people having parties on the beach,' says Foster. 'The atmosphere was great, the weather was great, the people were great fun. It was a carnival. I said, "After the Olympics, after I retire, I'm going to organise something like this in the North East of England."'

By the end of 1980, the Olympics over with, Foster met with some friends from the Gateshead Harriers and explained his vision and they set about making it a reality. Various routes were explored: north from Newcastle to Morpeth, west to Chester-le-Street, but there was only ever likely to be one outcome. 'If you're going somewhere from Newcastle, psychologically the natural thing is to follow the River Tyne,' says Foster. And so it was that the race would take place from the city centre to South Shields on the coast, a place where Foster had spent his childhood summers. Foster tells me that this also determined the race's distance, saying, 'Accidentally when you went from the city to the coast it was a half marathon.' Names such as 'The Geordie 5,000', the 'Tyne Race' and even the simple 'Newcastle–Shields Race' were considered; however, in the end, inspiration was taken from another geographically important marker: the Great North Road.

While jogging was born in New Zealand, according to Foster it was 'nourished in the USA and then exported around the world'. Running coach Bill Bowerman had been to New Zealand to see Lydiard's methods in 1962. He imported them to America and four years later he released a book simply titled *Jogging*. It was an instant hit, selling over one million copies and helping to spark a jogging craze in the country. Recognising the gap created by Adidas's disinterest, Bowerman, along with his colleague Phil Knight, set up a company to distribute running shoes, which would eventually become Nike. In 1970, the first New York Marathon was held. It attracted just 126 starters of which only fifty-five completed the course. By 1981, helped by the presence of celebrities and the media, the race attracted nearly 14,500 entrants, over 13,000 of whom finished. What had started as a small-scale event for elite athletes had become a carnival for runners of all abilities. Just like Foster in Auckland, another former Olympian, Chris Brasher, was inspired by the atmosphere when he took part in 1979. 'What really struck him,' his son Hugh Brasher says, 'was running through the five boroughs, seeing the different communities coming out to support the runners in their own way and then that the "gun crime capital city of the whole world" was uniting behind twenty thousand everyday people doing something that isn't everyday.'[19]

Chris Brasher, who died in 2003, might have stepped from the

pages of a *Boy's Own* annual. He was being considered for a second
assault on Mount Everest had Edmund Hillary failed in 1953. In
the event, Hillary's success spurred Brasher, along with Christo-
pher Chataway, to help Roger Bannister conquer the 'Everest of
the track' by acting as pacemakers when he ran his sub-four-
minute mile in Oxford in 1954. Two years later Brasher won gold
in the 3,000 metres steeplechase at the Melbourne Olympics. Initially disqualified, he was subsequently reinstated on appeal. After
celebrating with a thirsty British press pack, he took to the podium
'pissed beyond pain'.[20] By the time he took part in the New York
Marathon, he had retired from athletics, although he was still a
keen orienteer, and was working as a journalist for the *Observer*.
On his return from New York, Brasher wrote an emotional
account of the marathon with an impassioned call to arms: 'I
wonder whether London could stage such a festival? We have the
course, magnificent course, but do we have the heart and hospitality to welcome the world?'[21] With his friend and former steeplechase
teammate John Disley, he set about answering his own question.

Thus, two similar events were being simultaneously organised
at either end of England and it was Brasher's marathon that was
first across the finish line on 29 March 1981. Although the modern event had been created for the inaugural Olympics in Athens
in 1896 to commemorate the historic run of Greek soldier Phei-
dippides from Marathon to Athens in 490 BC, London had also
played a significant role in its development. The distance was only
standardised as 26 miles and 385 yards at the 1908 London Olympics. The planned course covered the twenty-six miles from
Windsor Castle to White City Stadium. The extra 385 yards was
added so the finish could take place in front of the royal box,
where Edward VII would be in attendance.

The inaugural London Marathon saw American Dick Beardsley and Norwegian Inge Simonsen cross the finish line together in

a time of 2:11:48. Joyce Smith was the first woman to finish in 2:29:56 and, just under five hours later, Marie Dominique de Groot and David Gaiman were the last to finish. Almost exactly three months later, the first Great North Run took place. Northumberland-born former Olympian Mike McLeod won in 1:03:25. Karen Goldhawk, the first female winner, finished fourteen minutes later and Alan Robinson, the first wheelchair race winner, finished a further fourteen minutes behind her. Some 12,000 other people took part, eclipsing the 7,055 who took part in the London Marathon and making it the country's largest mass-participation sporting event, something that continues to this day. Foster believes the distance is part of the appeal. 'The marathon is a bloody long way,' he says. 'A half marathon is also a long way, but it's more achievable.'

V

Today both races are synonymous with charity runners. No one bats an eyelid when they are overtaken by a Smurf or bump into Darth Vader at a water station, but this wasn't always the case. Roger Bourbon, dubbed the 'running waiter' – he ran sporting a bow tie and waistcoat and carrying a bottle of Perrier water on a silver platter – was the first, but he attracted attention because he was, at the time, unique. The link to charity grew organically. However, it perhaps shouldn't have been a surprise that it did as it was a decade in which the country embraced such events.

Children In Need was born in 1980 and, five years later, the country seemingly ground to a halt to watch a cast of global popstars come together for Live Aid. After witnessing the harrowing scenes of the famine in Ethiopia in 1984, Bob Geldof, with Midge Ure, organised the concert to build on the success of the charity record 'Do They Know It's Christmas?' Some 74,000 people packed into Wembley Stadium while another 89,000 attended at the John F. Kennedy Stadium in Philadelphia. Upwards of 1.5 billion watched around the world.

The year 1985 was marked by charity events. Comic Relief was formed (although people had to wait another three years before they were given an excuse to wear a red nose in public) and Ian Botham walked from John O'Groats to Land's End with the aim of raising £100,000 for Leukaemia & Lymphoma Research. He raised ten times that amount. Kevin Keegan, then the England captain, had taken part in the first Great North Run, diplomatically wearing a shirt that bore the colours of both leading North East football teams, Newcastle and Sunderland. He donated 50p to charity for every person who finished ahead of him. In the days before the full horrors of his crimes were revealed, the DJ and TV presenter Jimmy Savile became a regular feature of the London Marathon, raising millions for charity and helping to further popularise the event.

However, it was media support that really helped the two races gain the popularity and longevity that they have today. Interestingly, they were pre-dated by the People's Marathon, which was held in the Birmingham suburb of Chelmsley Wood in May 1980. In a bid to encourage ordinary people to take up running, the organiser John Walker decided that no one who could run the distance faster than two hours fifty minutes was allowed to enter. However, some 750 people did, and *Athletics Weekly* was moved to write: 'In years to come, when marathon fields several thousand strong will be commonplace in Britain, it will be seen that the event which triggered off the mass long-distance running movement in this country was the inaugural People's Marathon.'[22]

The race only ran for five years, in part due to the fact that the London Marathon had become established, and Hugh Brasher believes that the fact that his father was a journalist was instrumental in the event's success, enabling him to promote it to a wider audience. In an echo of Barry Hearn's comments about snooker, he also suggests that the television coverage the event received was crucial. 'You can't underestimate the power of the BBC as a broadcast partner,' he says. 'It suddenly reached people that could never have been reached previously. They looked at the six thousand people out on a rainy day taking part and they said, "Well, they're no different to me, if they can do it, so can I." People watching it got inspired by the TV coverage to then enter the next one.'

Foster moved the Great North Run from June to September, so it was not competing with the likes of Wimbledon and the British Grand Prix for national TV coverage and went as far as to suggest that BBC *Look North* and the *Newcastle Journal* were, along with him and his colleagues, founders of the race. It was when Phillip Crawley, the editor of the *Journal*, dropped by Foster's house on the night of the inaugural race with a first edition of the following day's paper that he realised what they'd achieved. 'There was a big picture on the front of runners crossing the Tyne Bridge — which is still the classic picture — and Phil said, "I think you're on to something with this". He was right, it went on from strength to strength.'

In the wake of the events, running boomed. In 1982, there were 106 marathon races in the UK, with nearly 100,000 entrants between them — more than double the number that took part the previous year. The increasing interest saw an improvement in times. In 1978, only four men in the world had run the marathon faster than two hours and eleven minutes; by the end of 1981, twelve men had bettered that time. While there is now more or less parity in the number of men and women running marathons, at the time there was a stark gender split — there were only 300 women in the 7,000 runners that started the first London

Marathon, something Hugh Brasher puts down to the sexist comments that women received while out running. Yet despite this, there was a demonstrable improvement in women's times. In 1978, only three women had gone faster than two hours forty. By 1981, twenty-nine women had done so. Three years later, in 1984, the Olympics held a women's marathon for the first time.

It wasn't just the times of the very elite athletes that were improving. At the start of the decade, only 3,000 people in Britain had recorded a time of under four hours. By the end of 1981, 10,000 had done so. Since then, each course has been completed by more than a million people and for both Foster and Brasher this is the real legacy: the fact the sport became inclusive.

VI

Among the people taking part in the first Great North Run were twenty-nine wheelchair entrants. By contrast, at the inaugural London Marathon there was no wheelchair race. Although wheelchair racers had competed in other similar events, such as the New York Marathon and the People's Marathon, Brasher was against the idea. He argued that the event was governed by international athletics rules defining it as a road running race. Furthermore, he claimed that including wheelchair racers who could reach speeds of thirty miles an hour on the downhill sections of the course alongside runners, the majority of whom would only be travelling at around six miles an hour, was a safety concern. 'That is just a formula for another accident; another person being disabled,' he told Channel 4 News.[23]

Brasher's attitude was not uncommon. Britain in the 1980s was an unwelcoming environment for disabled people. There was no law protecting them from discrimination and so employers were under no obligation to make workplace alterations to accommodate them. Pavements did not have dropped kerbs. Few buildings had disabled lifts or accessible toilets. Wheelchair users were often asked to leave cinemas and cafés because they supposedly took up too much room or created a fire risk. Those who wished to travel by train had to book several days ahead. They would then be placed in the guard's van with the postbags and other people's bikes. There was rarely any heating and at night there were often no lights. They would still have to pay full fare. Guide dogs were banned from restaurants. Until 2000, patients in mental health facilities were denied the right to vote. Many others were simply unable to cast their ballots because polling stations were inaccessible.

Furthermore, the norm was for children with significant levels of impairment to go to segregated schools. 'It was the default position, parents were actively encouraged to send their kids away,' says former Paralympian Tara Flood,[24] who, although not a thalidomide baby (the name given to children born in the late 1950s/early 1960s with often severe impairments as a result of their mothers taking an anti-morning sickness drug), was born with similar impairments. Despite the fact that her family lived in Preston in Lancashire, Flood was sent to school in East Sussex, where she stayed until her mid-teens, only going home a couple of times a year. 'That was a devastating experience for all sorts of reasons,' she recalls. 'It made me an invisible member of my family because I just wasn't present for most of the time. I had no experience of mainstream life until I left segregated school aged sixteen when I was thrown into mainstream college which at the time felt like a terrifying circus of non-disabled people of a similar age that I had nothing in common with and certainly no shared life experience.'

The school was well known for its supposedly pioneering work on finding solutions to impairment. 'What that really meant was devising gadgets that they could stick onto kids to make us appear normal. I had the full works, I had artificial legs and gas-powered artificial arms with hooks on. I look back on that with such horror. I felt like Metal Mickey at the time.' Flood has never been moved to try and find out why she was born with the impairments she has. 'I'm not interested,' she says matter-of-factly. 'I am who I am. But it took me until my mid-twenties to get to that point because of the damage of segregated education forcing me to hate the body that I was in and to not see anything positive about being a disabled person. It was then that I met some disability rights activists, and it changed my life. I discovered the social model of disability, and it was like a light switching on in my life. I realised that I wasn't the problem to be fixed or cured — that it is about disability pride.'

In 1981, Joey Deacon, who suffered from a severe form of cerebral palsy, appeared on the BBC's *Blue Peter* to help promote the programme's annual appeal. Born in 1920, Deacon had very limited fine motor skills and difficulty talking. He was admitted to a so-called 'subnormality hospital' when he was eight following the death of his mother, spending the rest of his life there. Deacon was highly intelligent. In 1974, with the support of three friends, he wrote a short autobiography called *Tongue Tied*, which was published by Mencap as part of the series *Subnormality in the Seventies*, and he was also the subject of a BBC documentary. Royalties from the book and donations that came in after the documentary enabled Deacon and his friends to move into a specially designed bungalow in the hospital grounds. For the producers of *Blue Peter*, Deacon seemed like the perfect positive showcase of disability. However, his appearance backfired. Soon the terms 'Joey', 'spaz' and 'spastic' became widely used terms of abuse among schoolchildren across the country. Consequently, The Spastic Society charity was even compelled to rebrand as Scope in 1994.

Deacon had appeared on *Blue Peter* as part of their celebration of the United Nations (UN) International Year of Disabled Persons, a precursor to the International Decade of Disabled Persons. By endorsing disability as a human rights issue, the UN created the opportunity for disabled advocacy groups to gain funding to support campaigns for anti-discrimination legislation and improved accessibility and inclusion. As the decade progressed, the disability rights movement grew. Professor Mike Oliver developed the social model of disability, arguing that disabled identity was imposed upon people with impairments and that the difficulties they faced in their day-to-day lives were not a result of those impairments but, rather, society's failure to adapt to their needs. With the right infrastructure, funding and education, such barriers could be overcome. Disabled people began to self-organise and pursue a clear set of goals. In 1968 the Race Relations Act had been passed, and the Sex Discrimination Act had followed seven years later; there needed to be anti-discrimination legislation for disabled people, too. Activists began holding disability rights demonstrations, politicising and weaponising their bodies by chaining themselves to buses and trains and forming picket lines. In an ironic twist that succinctly hammered home the protestors' message, those arrested who used wheelchairs were often either quickly de-arrested or found that their own vans were commandeered by police who didn't have accessible vehicles in which to take them to the cells.[25]

One campaigner pushing for inclusion was Tim Marshall, who had lost the use of his legs in his twenties following a climbing accident. Determined not to let his accident define him, he had taken up wheelchair racing, competing in the second People's Marathon and organising wheelchair races around Derwentwater in the Lake District. However, his main ambition was to instigate a wheelchair race in the London Marathon. In face of opposition from Brasher and Disley, he wrote to the Greater London Council

(GLC), which threatened to pull support for the event. There were concerns that the row might mean the 1983 marathon would be the last, but the GLC and the organisers reached a compromise which, like most compromises, satisfied no one. Wheelchair racers would be allowed to compete, but they had to start at the back of the field and follow a control car for the first four miles.

Despite their admission to the race, disabled participants were still marginalised. *The Times*' report on the agreement for them to compete differentiated between the 'London Marathon proper' and the wheelchair race.[26] Seventeen of the nineteen wheelchair racers who started completed the course, with Gordon Perry winning in a time of 3:20:07. The first woman to finish − there was no separate women's wheelchair race − was Denise Smith in a time of 4:29:03. Although the wheelchair racers received medals, they were not the same as those received by non-disabled competitors, which took the gloss off the achievement for some.[27] At the same time, Brasher's concerns about safety were, to a certain extent, proven valid as there were three minor collisions between wheelchair racers and runners. Two changes were made in 1984. Firstly, wheelchair athletes received the same medals as their non-disabled counterparts, and the GLC held a special ceremony for the 1983 entrants at which they received full medals. Secondly, to avoid the potential for further collisions, the wheelchair race started first, ahead of the other competitors.

Finally, the disabled competitors were out in front and soon newspapers were reporting on them seriously, and separately from their non-disabled counterparts. There was even avid speculation about when a wheelchair athlete would break the two-hour barrier. In 1985, the BBC showed pictures of the winners of all three races: the men's, women's and the wheelchair race.[28] Tanni Grey-Thompson, who would become one of Britain's most successful Paralympians, was watching at home. Then just thirteen, seeing wheelchair athletes competing on television was an inspiration. 'It was the first time that I saw international disabled athletes competing. It just showed disabled people doing sport and it wasn't patronising. I was already doing a bit of wheelchair racing, but the London Marathon definitely tipped the scales. It seemed quite exciting and fast. I thought: "I'm going to do the London Marathon one day; that's what I want to do."'[29]

Grey-Thompson was born with spina bifida and wore callipers when she was young, becoming increasingly reliant on a wheelchair from the age of seven. Unable to go to the same local secondary school as her sister, because, like many others, it did not accommodate wheelchair-bound pupils, she instead went to a comprehensive nine miles from home. Sports meant competing with non-disabled pupils or attending a nearby special school. Her parents also cultivated her interest, encouraging her to try as many different sports as possible. 'I swam, but I didn't really enjoy swimming. I played a bit of basketball, but it was hard to play that locally, whereas wheelchair racing, you could just go off and do it. I thought it was something I could enjoy and, if I tried hard, do well at.'

Many of her early sporting heroes were Welsh. Gareth Thomas, because of her mother's love of rugby union, and also Chris Hallam, a flamboyant wheelchair athlete. Known as 'Shades' because of his penchant for wearing dark glasses during races, Hallam was, like Grey-Thompson, born in Wales. A keen non-disabled athlete, he was a member of the Welsh swimming squad when at the age of seventeen his back was broken in a motorcycle accident, leaving him paralysed below the chest. In effect he had no muscles in his stomach, lower back, groin and buttocks. So, he took up weightlifting to build his upper body strength. As soon as he left hospital, he returned to the pool to compete in disabled competitions, quickly dominating his class and setting British and world records and winning gold in the 50 metres breaststroke at the 1982 World Games for disabled athletes. Looking for a new challenge, he turned to wheelchair athletics, competing in the London Marathon three times: winning and breaking the course record in 1985 and 1987 and crashing out after he hit a pothole in 1986. He also won the Great North Run wheelchair race four times. He often wore a leopard-print Lycra suit, and thanks to his moustache and bleached-blond mane he was described by *The Times* as 'Ian Botham's younger, bigger, tougher brother'.[30]

'He was the first person I saw. It was "Oh my God, look at him. This is amazing,"' says Grey-Thompson, who suggests that, without Hallam, wheelchair racing as we know it would not exist. 'He was out there, and he was quite bold in the way he behaved, with his hair and his tan; everything. He didn't allow people to patronise him. He would only be sponsored as an athlete; he wouldn't take charity money, so he just set a really important tone. He was a Marmite character, but because he didn't allow this "pat-on-the-head" stuff he helped hasten the development of the sport and the media coverage.' Grey-Thompson also believes that coverage had a wider impact, changing the perception of disabled people in general. 'In the 1980s disabled children were still locked away in institutions. There were very few disabled people in work — the statistics on that are still appalling. You didn't see many disabled people out and about because it was really hard to get out when nowhere was accessible. So that coverage had a really important role to play.' Hallam died of cancer in 2013 aged forty-nine. However, when he was at his athletic peak, he was aware that the coverage of his achievements and those of his fellow wheelchair athletes was changing the way people viewed disability. 'People no longer look at us as "cripps",' he said in an interview in 1987, 'but as well-known local sportsmen.'[31]

VII

While events like the London Marathon and the Great North Run were beginning to raise the profile of wheelchair athletes, there was very little representation of wider disabled sport in the media. In part this was due to the fact that organisation of disabled sport was disparate, with the four major disability groups: wheelchair athletes, competitors with visual impairments, those with cerebral palsy, and amputees and Les Autres (that is, people with locomotor disabilities not included in other categories) rarely competing together. Starting in 1948, events shadowing the four-year cycle of the Olympic Games were organised. From 1960 these often took place in the same country, if not the same city. However, the link was informal at best. Furthermore, in some countries disabled sportsmen and women were met with such disdain that their existence was not even acknowledged. The Soviet Union, hosts of the 1980 Moscow Olympics, refused to organise a parallel event for disabled athletes, one official bluntly claiming 'We have no disabled in the USSR.'[32]

As a consequence, the Netherlands was chosen to organise the event. So, on 21 June, Princess Margriet, the sister of Queen Beatrix, welcomed 1,973 athletes from forty-two countries at the Papendal stadium in the Veluwe woods some five miles outside Arnhem. More than half of the competitors were wheelchair athletes. However, the Games, named the Olympics for the Disabled, were a significant step forward, consolidating the four major disability groups by including cerebral palsy athletes for the first time.

Four years later while the Olympics took place in Los Angeles, the four disability groups were split: the wheelchair athletes competed in Stoke Mandeville, the rest in Nassau County, New York. 'I was only sixteen or seventeen and I'd only been out of the country once,' says Flood, who competed in the USA, 'so it was really, really exciting. I had a pretty negative sense of who I was as a disabled person, that didn't shift until much later. But what sport gave me was a really positive sense of my ability as a sports person, as a swimmer, because I was really successful.' Flood would go on to represent Great Britain at swimming in three consecutive Paralympic Games, winning gold and setting a world record in the women's 50 metres breaststroke SB2 in 1992. Her access to disability sport was, she admits, 'the only positive thing' that came out of her experience at school, which had links with the British Sports Association for the Disabled.

However, once she left and moved to London for work, her access to training facilities was limited to weekend camps organised by Les Autres. 'There weren't any disability swimming clubs and mainstream ones wouldn't entertain me. I used to work for NatWest at NatWest Tower which had a swimming pool in the basement. They let me train in that at about 5.30 in the morning. I then did a full day's work and I then trained after work. I had no sponsorship. I was competing for my country. Yet my country provided no support for me as an elite athlete. It was an outrage really.'

The New York Games were, Flood remembers, 'a bit home-spun. There were very few spectators. People who had been to other events said that '84 was much more competitive, but I had nothing to judge it against. It didn't feel hugely elite, it didn't feel hugely serious.' However, four years later in Seoul there was a marked change. It was the first time in twenty-four years that the Paralympic Games had taken place in the same city as the Olympic Games. Significantly, it was the first time they shared the same venues. 'The Koreans took it to a whole different level, it was bigger, it was more organised. It felt like it was about competition,' says Flood. The organisers brought in schoolchildren, community and church groups to fill the venues. Some 75,000 people attended the opening ceremony where South Korean president Roh Tae-woo opened the Games. It was the beginning of the modern Paralympics. The following year, the International Paralympic Committee (IPC) was established as the governing body of the Games. Since then, they have gone from strength to strength. A record 2.7 million tickets were sold for the 2012 Paralympic Games in London, in which more than 4,000 Para athletes from 164 countries competed. About 3.8 billion people from more than 100 counties tuned in, a figure surpassed in both Rio in 2016 and Tokyo in 2021.

The increased media interest also began in Seoul in 1988, when 2,368 journalists and associated personnel attended. Despite this there was very limited coverage in Britain. Flood's work colleagues had no idea of her achievements, or that she was representing her country at an elite level. Nor did her family. 'For a long time, I didn't tell anyone at home,' she says. 'I didn't think anyone wanted to know. There was nothing in the media, I didn't think people were interested.' What little coverage there was did not focus on the sport, or Flood's achievements, but her impairment. 'It was all the same old triumph over tragedy nonsense: "oh look at brave Tara, isn't she fabulous?" I hated it, but because I was still very young I didn't have the confidence or the sophistication of language to challenge that kind of crap.'

It's an attitude that Grey-Thompson says still exists in coverage today, referring to it as 'inspiration porn'. 'It's quite a patronising attitude to have towards disabled people: that we've all got to be pitied and we've all got some adversity to overcome. I hate that "overcoming adversity" phrase because some people have, and some people haven't. I didn't have much adversity in my life because my parents didn't allow it. But it's the assumption that just because I'm a wheelchair user I've got adversity. It comes from a really patronising place and thinking our lives are worth less.'

Furthermore, at the 1988 Games there was, Flood says, a hierarchy of media interest. 'It was very, very narrow in terms of who they wanted to talk to. The focus was definitely on athletes who didn't look like they had any significant level of impairment: wheelchair users and any athletes that had been involved in any of the demonstration events at the Olympics.' This hierarchy was also apparent in how events were organised. Flood was not able to compete at the Commonwealth Games where the classification system was effectively used to exclude certain competitors. 'Swimming classifications were between one and twelve,' says Flood. 'Classes nine and ten upwards included swimmers with less significant impairments. I was a class two or three, so you know where this is headed. Anyone below a five really was generally a no-go for media attention. It's shameful. What does that make you feel as an athlete?' she asks rhetorically. 'Invisible. It makes you feel invisible and devalued. Even though I know I was a fantastic and very, very successful swimmer.'

PART II:
IDENTITY

CHAPTER 5

Sisters Are Doin' It For Themselves

I

SPURRED on by the encouragement of the Green Goddess and Mad Lizzie on television and the more inclusive attitudes of gyms and private health clubs, 12 per cent of adult women were taking part in some form of keep-fit exercise, such as aerobics or yoga, by 1987.[1] The increased involvement of women in sport reflected the culmination of several significant factors which had appeared to reshape gender roles within British society. There was a female prime minister and the number of women entering the workforce accelerated during the decade. By 1990 some 68 per cent of women aged between twenty-five and fifty-four (defined as the 'prime working age') were in work, an increase of ten percentage points from 1983.[2] Most of this rise came through full-time work.

This increase was due to changes in other aspects of women's lives. Divorce rates were at a near all-time high, although they had plateaued after rising through the 1960s and 1970s. There were also fewer marriages and more children born outside marriage. Illegitimacy was gradually becoming less of a stigma and the number of abortions rose to record highs, apart from in Northern Ireland where it remained illegal. By 1984, there were nearly one

million single-parent families in the UK. The number of women
with a child who had never shared a house with a partner grew by
168 per cent between 1981 and 1991 to 430,000. The expansion of
higher education in the 1960s saw the number of female graduates
increase sixfold between 1960 and 1990.[3] In turn, this led to a growing number of women with expectations of both work and
self-fulfilment.

Yet, this belied some significant difficulties women faced in
pursuing sports, particularly those considered, by men at least, to
be bastions of masculinity. Motherhood was one. Not only did it
require women to take a break from sport, one that could lead to
retirement, particularly for those playing at an elite level, but
childcare demands also threatened participation. Despite the
increased number of women entering employment, the gender
division of household labour remained more or less unchanged.
The expectation was still that women should take responsibility
for housework, shopping and childcare. The average amount of
time women over sixteen spent on such chores had peaked at 6.78
hours per day in 1960. Despite the supposed rebalancing of gender relations, this had only fallen to 5.3 hours per day by 1984.[4]
Thus, far from being liberating and creating leisure time for
women, female employment compressed their available free time
by creating the 'double burden' of (paid) work outside the home
and (unpaid) work inside it, a burden that men, in the main, did
not have to bear.

This uneven division was reflected in the FA's 'Friends of Football' campaign in 1986. A bid to counteract the damaging effects
of football hooliganism, it was family-oriented, hoping to entice
people other than young men to start attending games. It focused
on boys who played the sport, dads who took them to games and
mums who washed their dirty kit. The campaign thus inadvert-
ently reinforced the view that while they could support their sons'

and husbands' sporting endeavours in unglamourous 'backroom' roles, there were some sports women just weren't supposed to play.

The Sex Discrimination Act, designed to outlaw discrimination on the basis of gender and marital status, had been passed in 1975. Crucially it exempted 'any sport [. . .] where the physical strength, stamina or physique of the average women puts her at a disadvantage to the average man'.[5] In the USA, Title IX, passed in 1972, was a watershed moment for women's sport, ensuring that girls had the right to equal opportunities in all sporting activities that received federal funding, such as education. By contrast in Britain the legal exemption within the Sex Discrimination Act was eagerly invoked.

In 1978, Appeal Court judge Lord Denning ruled that eleven-year-old Theresa Bennett was no longer allowed to play competitive football against boys her own age, even though she had been chosen for her team on merit. The ruling ignored medical evidence demonstrating the physical similarities between pre-pubescent boys and girls, instead sticking rigidly to the average man/average woman distinction in the act. Nine years later, two girls from the Putney Corinthians picketed the FA's AGM after they had been banned from playing for the team in the final of a London Under-11 cup competition. Labour MP Peter Hain, whose two sons also played for the team, branded the move 'sexual apartheid'.[6] Research for the English Schools Football Association (ESFA) demonstrated that by the mid-1980s the game's authorities were significantly out of step with reality. Many schools were simply ignoring the law. Girls were playing football in some 60.1 per cent of schools and a further 22 per cent reported a demand for girls to be able to play. 'We just don't like males and females playing together,' responded the FA secretary Ted Croker. 'Anyway, it's not natural.'[7] It would be another three years before the FA reluctantly bowed to the inevitable, changed its rules and allowed girls and boys under the age of eleven to play competitive football together.

In Scotland the situation was even worse. The country's FA had been the one dissenting voice when in 1971 UEFA nations voted 39–1 in favour of member countries taking control of women's football. The ban on the women's game was not lifted in the country until 1974. By then, one of the country's brightest stars, Rose Riley, had moved to France to pursue her dream of being a professional footballer. She had a glittering career, winning the League title in France with Reims. She played in Italy for ACF Milan, Catania and Lecce among other teams and won eight Serie A titles and the women's Coppa Italia four times. She twice won the Golden Boot in Italy. Despite these achievements, after ten games for Scotland, Reilly was banned by the country's FA, a decision she was not directly informed about and for which she was given no explanation. The Italians had no such qualms. Thanks to a dual passport, Reilly was eligible to play for her adopted homeland. She played a total of twenty-two times for Italy, scoring thirteen goals and captaining them to victory in the Mundialito, a forerunner of the World Cup, in 1984. In the same year, Reilly received the highest individual accolade of all, being voted the world's best female footballer.

II

Growing up in Hull, Reilly's English counterpart Carol Thomas had also been unable to play competitive football. Instead, she joined in games with her male schoolfriends (the only girl to do so). Her chance to play competitive football came in 1966, when a female neighbour who played for the BOCM ladies' team in the local works league saw Thomas playing in the street and invited her to join the team. At the time the women's game was effectively banned by the FA.

It had briefly risen to prominence during the First World War when women took on traditionally 'male' jobs, particularly in munitions factories. With the Football League suspended due to the conflict, some 150 women's teams were formed across the country,[8] playing charity games to raise money for the war effort or injured veterans. They were well organised, attracted tens of thousands of fans and, significantly, huge revenues. In short, they came to be seen as a threat to the men's game. In 1921, in a crude but effective attempt to reassert control the English Football Association determined that the game was 'unsuitable' for women. It couldn't stop them from playing so it did the next best thing, banning League- and FA-affiliated teams from allowing women's teams to use their facilities, a measure soon imposed across Britain. Limiting the women's game to parks and recreation grounds also limited its ability to attract large crowds and collect income at the gate. Any chance the women's game had of being financially independent and developing was crushed.

When women did take to the pitch, they often faced hostility. 'People were frowned upon for playing women's football,' says Thomas, who along with her teammates had to endure sexist comments from male spectators.[9] 'Today they'd probably get locked up for what they said during some of our games. It was a different era and they got away with it unfortunately.' Although most men came to watch women's football with scepticism, Thomas says a lot went away with a completely different view, being impressed by the players' technique and enthusiasm for the game.

The FA finally lifted its restrictions in 1971 and Thomas made her England debut three years later aged nineteen. Just six games after that, she was made captain. A tough tackling right back, she became an integral part of what was a rock-solid defence. England lost just five of the twenty-nine tournament matches in which Thomas was captain (two of those on penalties) conceding less than a goal a game in the process. It's hard to overstate her achievements as an international player. Not only was she the first woman to win fifty international caps for England, playing in fifty-six of England's first sixty-three internationals, but at the time of writing she is still the country's second-longest serving captain. She is also the most successful, taking on the armband at a time when an increasing number of women's tournaments, both official and unofficial, were being played.

In 1981 Thomas was the first England women's captain to lead the team outside of Europe, when they travelled to Japan for the Portopia tournament. Three years later, in 1984, they reached the final of the UEFA European Championships — the first official European tournament for women. The sixteen teams that entered were placed into four groups of four and played each other home and away, the winners progressing to the semi-finals. As there was no host, the semis and the final were two-legged affairs. Despite the seemingly progressive move from UEFA, they insisted that the women used size four balls, normally used by nine to fourteen year olds, and played only seventy-minute games. It was, says Thomas, demeaning.

England bossed their group, which included Scotland, Ireland and Northern Ireland (Wales did not enter as they did not have the funds to do so). Thomas' side won all six games, conceding just one goal in the process. Denmark were dispatched in the last four, setting up a final against Sweden. The first leg was at Gothenburg's Ullevi Stadium where just a year earlier the Aberdeen men's team had stunned Real Madrid in the Cup Winners' Cup final. A crowd of more than 5,000 witnessed a tight, hard-fought contest. Sweden dominated. Thomas kept the visitors in the game with an athletic goal-line clearance, but it was settled by a solitary goal from Pia Sundhage. Broadcast live in Sweden, there was also a strong contingent in attendance from the home side's press. By contrast, there was no coverage in England and only a few reporters turned up.

Permission from the FA to play the return leg at Wembley never arrived. Nor did any of the major London teams allow their stadia to be used. So, the game was played at Luton's Kenilworth Road on a quagmire of a pitch. Thomas was again at the heart of the action, setting up Linda Curl for the only goal of the game. England won on the day but with the aggregate score level the game headed to penalties, which the visitors won 4–3. After the trophy presentation, a disappointed Thomas was interviewed by a freelance TV crew covering the game, telling them, 'If people don't come and watch women's football after today's game, there's something wrong with them.'[10] It was clear from the emotion in her voice that this wasn't just about their disappointment on the pitch. 'Me saying what I said was frustration,' Thomas tells me. 'We put everything in. We weren't professional. We had to pay to go down to London to catch the flights. It cost us a lot of money to play for our country and we were all so proud. All we wanted was to have a bit of recognition for what we were doing.'

Her disappointment was born in part from the lack of media interest in England. 'In Sweden it was all over the papers and it was televised, whereas here there was nothing like that,' Thomas tells me. 'There were very few reporters and the clips I've got are from people who went with their own cinecameras.' The day after the final, she was interviewed by Selina Scott in the BBC *Breakfast Time* studios, becoming the first woman footballer to be interviewed on national television, but it was a fleeting moment in the sun and the FA did not build on the exposure to grow the women's game.

Later in the summer, England came third in the Mundialito tournament, won by the hosts Italy, who were captained by Reilly, the Scottish exile. For Thomas the difference in the attitude to the game in England was stark. The Italians, like the Scandinavians, took the women's game seriously and resourced it properly. Most club players were paid a salary, and had accommodation provided. Teams had a full backroom staff of coaches and medics to support them and were sponsored by major companies. When England returned to Italy the following year for the 1985 tournament, they reached the final where they faced the hosts. Two goals from Marieanne Spacey and one from Brenda Sempare were enough to see England win 3−2. It was a significant achievement, and one Thomas looks back on with pride. 'Most of the Italian ladies, if not all of them, were playing semi-professionally,' she says. 'So, to actually beat Italy on their home turf was probably one of my best achievements.'

England sustained their position at the highest levels of international competition throughout the rest of the decade. They reached the last four of the 1987 European Championships, losing to Sweden in the semi-finals. This was followed by another Mundialito victory in 1988, in an expanded tournament with two groups and semi-finals. Again, England beat the hosts Italy in the final, thanks to a brace from Linda Curl. The victory brought further recognition for England when they were named Team of the Year at the inaugural *Sunday Times* Sportswomen of the Year Awards, the brainchild of journalist Sue Mott.

By this time, Thomas was no longer part of the England team. She played one more game after the 1985 Mundialito final − her fiftieth as captain − before retiring at only thirty-one after eleven years playing for England because she was pregnant.

III

Thomas had turned down offers to play in New Zealand and Italy, but several British players moved abroad to play club football. This drain of talent was the subject of a BBC documentary, *Home and Away*, in January 1987. The programme focused on Reilly and her striking partner at AFC Despar Trani, Kerry Davis, the first black woman to play for England. Davis had impressed Italian scouts in the 1985 Mundialito and signed for Roi Lazio. That was followed by two years at Trani and a year at Napoli. Debbie Bampton, who went on to captain England after Thomas, and Marieanne Spacey, who had a lengthy career at Arsenal, also spent time playing in Italy.

Home and Away was just one of a growing number of programmes that explored and promoted women's involvement in the sport. In 1989, the ex-football reporter turned scriptwriter Stan Hey was asked by one of the emerging independent production companies pitching ideas to the nascent Channel 4 to come up with a story based around the question 'what if a woman ended up managing a men's football team?' Hey, who had written for *Auf Wiedersehen, Pet* and *The Lenny Henry Show*, proposed *The Manageress*. 'The fun was looking at football through female eyes,' says Hey.[11] 'I knew a lot of women were mad about football, but that wasn't reflected in the press or on television. It was really saying "women can like football too". That was the agenda with a small "a".' Watching the series now provides a grim reminder of football's dark years at the tail end of the 1980s; facilities for fans and players alike are terrible. Yet the series was also ahead of its time. While the initial focus was, Hey says, on practicalities like how Gabriella Benson, the eponymous manageress, would 'deal with the players swearing, being naked, farting, all that sort of thing', it very quickly began to look at how she could make a difference in the sport. She introduced yoga and aerobics to the players' training routine, unheard of at the time but now commonplace. She changed the menu in the canteen, and the team's tactics (both of which were met with consternation). She even asked them not to tackle in training but to win the ball through anticipation. Tackling, Benson argued, was a last resort. 'It was just this feminising thing I wanted to explore,' says Hey. 'It came at a time when the game was especially brutal with hooliganism and the European ban and then the unintended brutality of the stadium tragedies. It just felt like that macho stuff had sort of come to an end.'

In April 1989, Channel 4 also broadcast highlights of the WFA Cup final between Leasowe Pacific (now Everton Women) and Friends of Fulham (now AFC Wimbledon Ladies) at Old Trafford. It was the first time the women's final had received such coverage, although the programme was nearly pulled as it came just a week after the Hillsborough disaster. Following in the wake of such a tragedy was bound to make the event an emotional one, and such feelings were magnified by the fact that three of the Leasowe team – Liverpool supporters Dianne Coughlin, Cathy Gore, and Jill Salisbury – had been at the game, as had the manager's daughter, Michelle Jackson. Mercifully all four were unharmed but understandably the team cancelled their league match against St Helens the following day. After much deliberation they decided to play in the cup final, the players who had been at Hillsborough getting the final say. In what was a muted affair, both teams wore black armbands and a minute's silence was held before the game.

Fulham were favourites, boasting England players Spacey and Sempare, who had scored in the Mundialito final the year before, and future national team manager Hope Powell, but Leasowe won 3–2. More than a million people tuned in to watch the highlights and the goals were also shown on *Saint and Greavsie* the following Saturday. Co-host Jimmy Greaves was clearly conflicted. 'I'm not a chauvinist, believe me,' he assured his presenting partner Ian St John. 'I love ladies' tennis and ladies' hockey and everything but I'm not so sure whether [football] is a game for ladies.' At the same time, he couldn't deny the players' ability. 'Actually, the skill looked better than the men's,' he acknowledged. 'But we won't go into that.'[12] It was indicative of the mixed feelings of many male football fans towards the women's game. They were used to 'ladies' being restricted to 'feminine' sports and had little, if any, exposure to women playing 'masculine' sports. When they did, they continued to try to argue that women couldn't, or shouldn't, play despite the obvious evidence to the contrary.

Conversely, many in the women's game saw the coverage as a watershed, giving it much needed wider exposure, and making the players themselves think differently. Spacey, who was among the players Channel 4 had profiled prior to the final, later recalled being recognised in a McDonald's in London after returning from Old Trafford. 'It was quite a moment of realisation at how powerful television could be in getting the game out to a wider audience who didn't attend the games,' she says.[13] 'It changed our mentality – we started taking a more professional outlook, but it was also from there the game grew. That was the start of it. From there the game has become something people knew was out there happening.'

IV

Even in sports where there had been no ban, women faced familiar impediments to participation, particularly at elite level. In 1989, Tracey Edwards skippered the first all-female crew in the

Whitbread Round the World Race (now the Volvo Ocean Race), which takes in six legs over 32,000 nautical miles from England to Uruguay to Australia to New Zealand and back, with a stop in America. She had blagged her way onto a 1985 Whitbread entry as cook, much to the displeasure of the rest of the crew, who were all men. 'It's the last garden shed at the bottom of the garden, and they didn't want women in there,' says Edwards.[14] 'They made my life pretty miserable for the first couple of legs.' However, after they won a leg coming into New Zealand, their attitude began to change. 'I went from being "that bloody tart on the boat" to suddenly being our good luck charm with seventeen older brothers. So, it kind of turned around, by the time we were in the second half of the race, they were teaching me, and I was learning.' It was navigation where her ambition lay, and as she came to the end of the race, Edwards had what she calls the most profound thought of her life: 'No man will ever let me navigate on his boat in my lifetime.' To fulfil her ambition, Edwards realised she needed to assemble an all-female crew. At the age of twenty-six, that's what she set about doing, although few in the male-dominated sport believed she would succeed.

In theory there was no reason why an all-women crew could not enter the race; it was not technically a male-only sport, but barriers were still placed in their way, not least sponsorship in a sport that required a high-tech boat and the resources to last in a race spanning September to May. 'Because we were an all-female crew, we thought we would get loads of PR but because we were an all-female crew, lots of people thought we were going to die. We did have people saying to us, "This is a great PR opportunity but if you die, people will blame us for giving you the money to go and sail in the ocean."' A second-hand yacht, *Maiden*, was bought and thanks to the support of smaller sponsors and even members of the public sending them money, the crew set about making it raceworthy themselves. However, they couldn't gain what Edwards calls 'that critical mass' of funding required to compete. That eventually came from Royal Jordanian Airlines. Edwards had established an unlikely friendship with King Hussein of Jordan, who had been advising throughout the project. 'I just did not want to ask him for money,' Edwards says. 'I wanted to do it on my own but when we got to the point where we literally wouldn't be able to cross the start line, he said, "If your country won't sponsor you, mine will."'

Once it was clear *Maiden* would be able to take part, the crew were subjected to considerable media attention; however, unlike their male counterparts, they were rarely asked about the race. Instead, questions focused on their makeup, whether they were all lesbians or, conversely, whether they had entered to hook up with the male competitors. They were even asked if they all got their periods at the same time. There was also scepticism from male competitors. Grant Dalton, the skipper of one of the rival entries who went on to manage Team New Zealand, said, 'If *Maiden* gets around the world in one piece, I will run naked up Auckland high street with a pineapple up my arse.' They did, he didn't. Edwards says that the crew were treated with amusement by a wider male audience but also received 'a very aggressive, negative, vociferous reaction' that bemused her. 'I remember a guy coming up to me in the pub and literally jabbing his finger in my face and saying, "You're all going to die". It was hard to understand. When I look back, I think, "Why weren't you angrier at the way people were treating you?" Of course, we just took it because that was the time.'

The all-female crew quickly proved their mettle, winning the Route of Discovery Race from Cádiz to Santo Domingo and beating eleven other Whitbread crews that had also entered. It showed they weren't just there to make up the numbers, but there was also a backlash. 'Make no mistake, when we won that transatlantic race, and beat every other Whitbread boat that was using it as a test, there was anger,' says Edwards, who believes that the aggression they faced was a reflection of the fact they now had to be taken seriously. 'They couldn't ignore us any more,' she says. 'They were going to have to face the fact that women were in the race around the world, but most of them thought it was embarrassing they were in the same race as women.'

As *Maiden* won two legs of the Whitbread race and eventually came second in her class, this embarrassment eventually turned to respect, albeit at times perhaps grudging. The crew had initially been dismissed as 'a tin full of tarts' by *Guardian* journalist Bob Fisher. 'He definitely changed his tune as we went round,' says Edwards. 'When we sailed into New Zealand, he wrote "not just a tin full of tarts, a tin full of smart, fast tarts". We thought that was great until someone pointed out the word "tart" was still in the sentence. But it was baby steps, this was a hardened misogynist who had taken a step in the right direction.' Edwards also became the first woman to be awarded the Yachtsman of the Year trophy, its very name signifying the barriers she and her crew were breaking down.

Any doubts the crew had about the wider impact they had made were dispelled by the reception they received in Southampton at the end of the final leg. As *Maiden* made her way up the Solent, she was escorted by hundreds of boats and thousands of people throwing flowers and cheering. 'The noise was huge,' says Edwards, 'there were motorboats and people screaming.' Even more people were waiting onshore. As she recounted her memories of the welcome, Edwards was moved to tears. 'If I could relive one day of my life, that would be it.'

V

As emotional as the scenes of *Maiden*'s welcome home were, the image that dominated coverage of the crew's achievements was of them arriving at Fort Lauderdale, Florida, all wearing swimsuits. It would become the most syndicated sports photograph of 1990.[15] Edwards and her crew had decided to dress that way in part to deflect attention from the fact that they had had a poor leg, but there were also wider considerations. 'We thought we'd always looked smart coming into port and we did that on purpose because we weren't male clones. We are girls that want to sail, so that image was really important.' Edwards says she found the experience of sailing in their swimsuits hugely liberating. 'I felt like an Amazon. We knew we looked good. We knew we'd been leading to that point, we knew we'd won two legs, so we felt we'd earned the right to dress as we wanted to dress.' However, Edwards and her crew quickly began to question their decision. 'Afterwards we all had huge crises of conscience: "What will modern feminists think of us? Have we let the side down?" It bugged me for years.' It was a conversation with her daughter Mack, after the premier of a documentary about *Maiden*'s achievements, that eventually put Edwards' mind at rest. 'She said, "Mum, you're always telling me that people can't tell women what to wear; you wear what you want to wear and what feels good. That's what you did. I see it as strength."'

The response to the photograph was something that should not have been unexpected. The oversexualisation and objectification of women's bodies had been normalised throughout the 1980s not least by the publication of photographs of naked and semi-naked women which had become staple fare in the tabloids. The *Sun* led the way with the introduction of Page 3 girls in 1970 and the racier 'Starbirds' were deemed an essential ingredient in the launch of the *Daily Star* in 1978. The best-known Page 3 pin-up was Samantha Fox who first appeared in 1983. She was sixteen, making her the country's youngest professional topless model. With a 36D bra size, she set a trend for extremely young, large-breasted models, the likes of Maria Whittaker, Kathy Lloyd and others following in her wake. Fox transcended Page 3. She retired from modelling at twenty and became a celebrity in her own right, forging a successful pop career as well as having an ill-fated attempt at presenting the 1983 Brit Awards alongside Mick Fleetwood of Fleetwood Mac. Best forgotten by both.

The prurient coverage of women quickly spilled over onto the sports pages, particularly in the coverage of Wimbledon, one of the few events in one of the few sports in which women got something approaching an equal amount of coverage to their male counterparts. In 1985, Anne White wore an all-in-one catsuit and the following day found her picture on the front of five of the eight national newspapers. She was quickly and politely asked by All England Club officials not to wear it again. Although White found the request annoying, she acquiesced as she didn't 'want to make people spill their strawberries and cream'.[16] Ironically, the accepted attire was more revealing, allowing the *Sun* to run a 'Wimblebum' feature for the 'rear-watchers'. One photograph used was of Canadian player Carling Bassett bending down to tie up her shoelace. Like Fox, she was just sixteen at the time.

While Page 3's supporters argued it was harmless, if titillating, fun, not everyone agreed. Clare Short, part of the new intake of Labour MPs in 1983, introduced a bill designed to ban such content from the country's newspapers. Even the *Sun*'s former editor Larry Lamb, who had launched Page 3, expressed some concern. Although not supporting Short's call for a ban, he did acknowledge there was an element of sexploitation involved and said he was worried about the 'fiercely competitive situation in which girls in some of our national newspapers get younger and younger and more and more top-heavy'.[17] Predictably, the *Sun* retaliated. Then edited by Kelvin MacKenzie, the paper took to labelling Short 'killjoy Clare' and 'Ms Misery' and launched a 'Save our Sizzlers' campaign led by Fox.

Short's efforts were always doomed to failure due to the procedural mechanics of parliament, but they gained support from women across both the country and the political spectrum. In many respects, her campaign was an extension of a national conversation that was at its most emotive in November 1980 following the murder of Jacqueline Hill. A third-year student at Leeds University, Hill was the last known victim of Peter Sutcliffe. Dubbed 'the Yorkshire Ripper', Sutcliffe was caught seven weeks later, ending his near six-year reign of terror across the North of England. Women had long been angered by police advice to stay indoors after dark, arguing that it was men, the perpetrators of violence against women, not women, the victims of that violence, who should have their lives restricted by curfew. Groups of women took to the streets around the country in a series of 'reclaim the night' marches. These protests reached a peak after Hill's killing, when some women invaded cinemas showing the film *Dressed to Kill*, throwing red paint at the screens. Sex shops were attacked and a group of some thirty women broke into the *Sun*'s offices in Fleet Street in protest against the sexualised nature of Page 3.

It was in this environment that Erika Roe streaked topless at Twickenham during a Test between the England and Australia men's teams in January 1982. Roe had been persuaded by her sister to pull a sickie at the bookshop where she worked and go to the match. Her inhibitions diminished by several pre-match beers, Roe was further persuaded to 'do something outrageous'.[18] So, in the lull of half-time, she threw her bra and cigarettes to her friends, caution to the wind and headed onto the pitch. The mainly male crowd greeted her with huge cheers and, spurred on, Roe flung her arms up and back, an image immortalised by the pitch-side photographers and splashed across the nation's papers for days to come. She was led off the pitch, her breasts covered by a combination of policemen's helmets and the Union Flag of Ken Baily, a celebrated figure who regularly attended sporting events dressed as John Bull, and whom Roe later dismissed as 'a ridiculous man with his flag'. As this was taking place, the BBC's 'Voice of Rugby' Bill McLaren commented, 'There's a young fellow there, and he's so excited he's taken his shirt off.'[19] He wasn't being ironic. From the distance of the commentary box, he hadn't recognised Roe was a woman and had assumed she was a man. And why wouldn't he? After all, for most male rugby fans, women in the stands were a rarity, women on the pitch even more so. Yet clearly there were female rugby fans, and there were female players, too.

The first women's international rugby union match took place in 1982, between the Netherlands and France in Utrecht and the following year, the Women's Rugby Football Union (WRFU) was formed in Britain, chaired by Carol Isherwood. Isherwood had grown up in Leigh in the North West of England, where her father took her to watch rugby league. However, although she was allowed to train with the male pupils, she was not allowed to play in competitive matches. For Isherwood, the opportunity to play the game finally came when she left home for Leeds University and one summer met a player for the Sheffield women's team. After one game for Sheffield, she set up a team at Leeds, which would be one of the founder members of the WRFU. The first women's rugby team had been formed at Edinburgh University in 1962 and higher education provided the framework around which the sport initially grew. Of the twelve founder members of the WRFU, all but one was a university side, the exception being

Welsh team Magor Maidens, which was also the only team from outside England.

One of Isherwood's initial responsibilities was to produce a starter pack advising women how they could set up a team after they left university. 'You don't want to reinvent the wheel and set up your own club,' says Isherwood,[20] 'so we were knocking on the door of men's clubs and asking if we could have a women's section.' The pack told women what they needed to do, who they needed to approach and the arguments to make. The most persuasive was simple: tell the men's club that if they started a women's team, their bar takings would increase. Money talks: the women's game quickly gained a foothold as graduates dispersed around the country and set up their own teams. Within three years the number had grown from twelve to about seventy. The media started paying attention. *Rugby Post* magazine began carrying regular match reports and the BBC broadcast a documentary about the Maidens. Speaking to *The Times* in April 1985, Deborah Griffin, who was captain of Finchley women's team, said the standard was improving and was 'equivalent to good schoolboy rugby'.[21] This was in part because, unlike men, women players did not start playing at school and so had not been encouraged from a young age to play in positions that best suited their physiques. Despite the rapid growth of the sport, there was still no organised competitive rugby and still only a few hundred women playing regularly around the country. Thus, by necessity, women players 'simply [had] to slot into gaps in an existing team'.[22] Many had transferred from other sports such as hockey and netball and were still getting to grips with basic rugby skills, tactics and formations. Perhaps inevitably the response to the idea of women playing rugby was mixed although, mirroring Carol Thomas' experiences on the football pitches of Hull, that often changed once men saw them play.

The next step in the game's development was international competition. In 1985 a thirty-six-woman squad from America toured Britain, playing matches against teams from Yorkshire, the Midlands and the South of England before taking part in a rugby festival. The women's game in the US was about a decade ahead of that in Britain. It had the space to flourish alongside the men's game which was developing at a similar pace and did not have what one of the American coaches called 'the super-macho image rugby has elsewhere'.[23] There were more teams, more players and an established national championship. Thanks to Title IX, American players had access to more funding and better coaching. They were fitter, more experienced and took the game more seriously than their hosts. In the ten matches played, the Americans scored a total of 330 points without conceding a single one. Far from being embarrassed, however, it showed female players in Britain how they needed to improve. 'We saw what the standard could be and the standard we could play at, and we thought: "How do we get there?" "What do we need to do?"' says Isherwood.

Along with her colleagues on the WRFU, she set about trying to answer those questions and in April 1986 they organised the first match for a women's Great Britain side, Isherwood captaining the team against France. The group organised trials, a selection process, coaches, and the venue at Richmond. It was an indication of how limited the organisational structure of the women's game was in those early years, something reinforced when the French team landed at Gatwick; the person detailed to meet them was waiting at Heathrow. The visitors were expecting a team bus, not the Tube tickets provided, but eventually arrived at the university halls of residence in which they were billeted. The British players had to stay at friends' houses, there being no funds to cover the cost of their accommodation.

Despite two tries (a try then worth four points) from Karen

Almond, the French won 14–8, but it was another step forward for the British game. The match received considerable press and TV coverage, the overwhelming majority of which was serious and positive. It plugged the WRFU into a network of other national teams, facilitating regular international competition. It also showed that there was a depth of talent that allowed the home nations to form their own teams, the beginnings of what was then the Five Nations. Almost a year to the day after she skippered Great Britain, Isherwood achieved a notable double by also becoming the first woman to captain the England women's team, against Wales. The match at Pontypool, which England won 22–4, was both teams' first international game. Again, the lack of resources was stark. There was no team bus, the England players had to make their own way there. Accommodation was a youth hostel in Chepstow. However, it was a month of firsts. Wasps' women's team played Richmond in the club championship final at Twickenham. A curtain-raiser for the men's county championship final, it was the first full fifteen-a-side women's game played at the stadium. The game was developing apace and in 1991 Isherwood was part of the England team that reached the final of the inaugural women's world cup, losing to America at Cardiff Arms Park. Three years later, England returned the favour, beating the Americans in the final with Isherwood among the coaching staff.

VI

One of the journalists present at the ground-breaking Great Britain match at Richmond in 1986 was Sally Jones. Earlier that year, BBC *Breakfast Time* had undergone a revamp. Out went the comfy sofas and pullovers associated with its launch three years earlier in January 1983. In came desks and suits, a more sober look intended to reflect the greater focus on politics and current affairs. Out, too, went some of the presenters. Selina Scott and Nick Ross left, but Frank Bough stayed. So did Sally Magnusson, and they were joined by Jeremy Paxman and Kirsty Wark to present the news, and Bob Wilson, the former Arsenal and Scotland goalkeeper, and Jones to present the sport. A BBC trainee, Jones had been working as a news presenter for Central, the ITV franchise covering the Midlands, but her real passion was sport. An accomplished athlete, she was also doing the occasional cricket and tennis report for ITN and sometimes fronted ITV's gymnastics coverage. Jones also wrote a women's sports column for *Today* newspaper. Although she didn't know it when she accepted the offer to join to join BBC *Breakfast Time*, Jones became the channel's first female sports presenter. 'Suddenly there was this welter of publicity. It took me by surprise, people going through my dustbins and trying to find out from my neighbours if I had a boyfriend. You were considered news just because you were a woman presenting sport on the BBC.'[24]

There had been pioneering female sports journalists before Jones. Julie Welch was the first woman to write match reports for the national newspapers and Mary Raine was the first female voice heard on BBC Radio's *Sports Report*. Yet there was still a fascination with Jones' appointment. The idea of a woman entering the male bastion of the sports stadium press box saw her become the subject of numerous articles, in some of which she would be asked to pose in revealing football strips or with a variety of sports equipment such as tennis rackets or cricket bats. There was a noticeable gender split in the tone of questioning she received. Male journalists asked whether a woman could be taken seriously reporting sport and tested her knowledge. 'They would always say, "Can you explain the offside rule?",' says Jones. 'Fortunately, I could, and they always used to be terribly impressed.' By contrast, women reporters tended to be more interested in her personal life or clothes. 'Every interview would always start off with what you were wearing. Once a woman from the *Birmingham Post* came early and I'd been out running, so I was in my ancient trainers and an old tracksuit. The fact I was so informally dressed occupied the first two paragraphs of that particular feature.'

In 1988, Jones, alongside Bob Wilson, hosted the daytime coverage of the Seoul Olympics produced by BBC Sport. While Jones is quick to point out that she enjoyed much of her time at the BBC, she found a noticeable difference between BBC *Breakfast Time*, where there was a more or less even gender split among the editorial staff, and BBC Sport, which was decidedly male. 'It was almost as though I was the lone female in the bar trying to get a drink and there was a broad row of male backs between me and the barmaid,' she says. It wasn't just fellow journalists who were sceptical about the ability of women journalists to report on what was considered a male domain; some of the public also made their feelings known. 'Every time I read the rugby league results on BBC *Breakfast Time*, I used to get five pages of well-reasoned abuse written in green ink from old blokes in Wigan and Castleford saying, "What can a slip o' a lass know about rugby league?"' In reality, Jones knew as much as, if not more than, most of her male colleagues. However, their gender was enough to confer upon them the legitimacy and authority sceptics were unwilling to afford Jones. Not only did she and her female contemporaries find their ability being questioned on the basis of their gender rather than their skill or experience, they were also held to a higher standard than their male counterparts. Viewers were waiting for the tiniest of errors, as if that would justify their scepticism. 'Once Sue Barker confused Queen's Park and Queens Park Rangers because she's not a football specialist and I remember the gloating and the unpleasant letters,' says Jones. 'If some bloke had made a minor slip, people would have ignored it.'

This scrutiny was magnified by the fact that Jones felt she had a responsibility to do well for those women who would follow in her wake. 'You always felt that you were carrying the prospects of all potential women sports presenters, or reporters, on your shoulders,' she says. This created huge pressure for Jones and other women who were coming into the profession at the time, such as Barker and the late Helen Rollason, both colleagues at the BBC, and Hazel Irvine on ITV. 'My natural action was just to put an absolutely impassive face on and not let them see they were getting to me, which helped me get through it,' Jones says, 'but it probably didn't show them the damage they were doing either by ignoring me, or not being encouraging.'

As in the sports they were covering, parenting and in particular childcare were still seen as a woman's domain. Rollason was another of the few women covering the Seoul Olympics. 'I believe when she worked for Channel 4, they used to test her out the whole time saying, "You've got to bring your passport to work with you every day because we might send you off to Europe at the drop of a hat,"' says Jones. At the time Rollason was a struggling single mum. 'She did amazingly,' says Jones, 'and I was so glad she got all that recognition in later life. It was quite funny to see all those people who'd plagued her at the BBC and ITV, then turning round and giving her absolute hero-grams when she was ill and later died.'

VII

The achievements of Jones, Rollason and their female contemporaries in the media are tangible because their words were broadcast on national television or printed in the national press. In short, there is a record of what they did. By contrast, the achievements of their female sporting counterparts were often more ephemeral. Some are beginning to get wider recognition. Isherwood is in the Rugby Union Hall of Fame, and Reilly in the Scottish FA Hall of Fame. However, the absence of regular television coverage — the crucial exposure that elevated (male) darts and snooker players from the saloon bar to the chat show, and seared events like Botham's Ashes into the national consciousness — meant most people were simply unaware that women were representing their countries in traditionally 'male' sports.

Furthermore, the absence of that coverage means their triumphs, and disappointments, are no longer available to be replayed and further encoded into our shared sporting history and mythos. True, you can watch coverage of the first leg of the women's 1984 European Championship on YouTube, but the commentary is in Swedish, there is no build-up and there are no post-match interviews. Crucially, it's not replayed regularly in coverage of the contemporary women's game. The absence of footage of the second leg in Luton makes it even easier to airbrush that game from history. The legacy of Edwards' success with *Maiden* was almost forgotten until a recent documentary of the same name brought it to a wider audience. It took two years to track down the footage shot of the race.

In most sports, the achievements of female players were simply not recorded in the diligent way the achievements of their male counterparts were. The information available to us is inaccurate and incomplete. That which is not in the public domain is possibly lost forever. In 2007, the Welsh Women's Rugby Union issued an appeal for help tracking down the women who had played in the country's first game, in Pontypool, for an anniversary celebration. They had the players' names; they just didn't know what had happened to them in the twenty years since. That wouldn't happen in elite-level male sport.

Isherwood and her former colleagues are curating a list of the women who played for England in the early years of women's rugby union. It's a difficult task reliant in part on memory. In 1984, the *Rothmans Football Yearbook* found room for schools' football and university football – both worthy of record – but there was no mention of Thomas and her teammates reaching the final of the European Championship, nor of their Mundialito victory the following year. The 1980s was a golden period of success for England's women's footballers yet Thomas believes it was, and continues to be, overlooked. 'We like to think we were the pioneers after the ban got lifted. We just persevered and did our best, but a lot of people today don't think women's football started until the middle of the 1990s. Our era is completely forgotten.'

CHAPTER 6

A Little Respect

I

WHEN Major Walter Wingfield began promoting his new sport of 'lawn tennis' in 1874, he believed that women's involvement was vital for its long-term success. Early marketing materials included pictures of female players, advertised 'ladies bats' and offered discounts to female customers. Thus, while women had to wait decades to have meaningful involvement in other sports that evolved in the Victorian era, such as football and rugby, they were avid participants in tennis from its earliest days. Within a few years, the more adventurous female players had left the confines of the country house lawn to enter tournaments springing up around the country. Far from meeting with disapproval, they were encouraged, and their ability appreciated, the *Daily Telegraph* noting: 'Ladies are not banished in this case but have proved themselves in many instances no mean antagonists for the stronger sex.'[1] This culminated in 1884 when Maud Watson beat her sister Lilian in three keenly fought sets to become the first women's singles champion at Wimbledon.

A century later, as the manicured lawns of London SW19 were undergoing their final preparations before the arrival of the world's best tennis players, it was a woman who was the sport's most dominant player. John McEnroe was enjoying his best season and would obliterate Jimmy Connors in the men's final, but Martina Navratilova, another lefty, reached even more imperious heights. Going into the tournament, the defending champion was unbeaten in thirty-one consecutive matches and had lost just once in her previous eighty-six. She had won four of the last six Wimbledon singles titles and was on course for her fifth consecutive Grand Slam title. Yet throughout the fortnight she was dogged by the press, more interested in her personal life off the court than her achievements on it.

In 1981, the tabloid *New York Daily News* had outed Navratilova as bisexual in the wake of Billie Jean King also being outed in a court filing by her former lover, Marilyn Barnett, who was seeking financial support. Despite several relationships with women, Navratilova had hidden her sexuality as best she could, fearing that it might prevent her from gaining US citizenship after defecting from Czechoslovakia. In the end it did not. However, the information was, she said, 'ticking away like a timebomb'.[2] According to the notebook of journalist Steve Goldstein, in whom she had confided, Goldstein had asked Navratilova for reaction to the King story, and she had told him that cosmetics company Avon, then the chief sponsor of women's tennis, would pull out of the game if she too came out. Once her citizenship was granted, and with the legal action against King still in the news, Goldstein informed Navratilova that his employers were going to use the interview. She pleaded for them not to, but the paper printed the story anyway. Navratilova later acknowledged she had been naïve to be so open but still saw it as a breach of trust. However, the revelation gave her the freedom to live her life as she had always wanted. 'I didn't have to worry any more,' she reflected decades later. 'I didn't have to censor myself.'[3]

The story was an indication of the increased interest in the private lives of tennis players. Nowhere was this greater than in Britain and it reached a peak in 1984. Seemingly no player was able to escape the prurient questions and telephoto lenses of the tabloids. Yet it was Navratilova, an openly gay player who dominated her sport and did not hide her lovers, who received the most attention. She arrived in London having just started a relationship with a new partner, Judy Nelson, a former beauty queen the tabloids took to calling a 'blonde Texas mother of two'. The day before the tournament began, Nelson filed for divorce from her husband and when she turned up to watch Navratilova's second-round victory over Amy Holton, the paparazzi were waiting, the noise of their camera shutters all but drowning out the polite applause of the crowd. 'You guys are pathetic,' said Navratilova disdainfully.[4]

As in previous years, she rented a house in Wimbledon Village, close to the courts. The paparazzi were there again, trying to get a shot of the champion with her new lover. Throughout the fortnight and at all hours, reporters were knocking on Navratilova's door. She branded them 'scum' and refused to comment, but there was no escape. The division between the American and British press reared its head again, and although the champion tried to 'distinguish between the tennis writers and the gossip writers',[5] press conferences descended into farce. There were few questions about what had happened on court. 'You guys are really reaching,' Navratilova responded on one occasion. 'Can't we just talk about tennis, please?'[6] Her pleas fell on deaf ears.

Chris Evert, the president of the WTA, called the situation 'horrendous' and angst-ridden Wimbledon officials wrung their hands in despair at this unseemly disruption to the sanctity of the All England Club. An emergency meeting was called, and players told they could abandon press conferences if the questioning became 'provocative or repetitive'.[7] While tournament organisers condemned the media treatment of players, in their own subtle way they too denounced Navratilova by ensuring she played on Centre Court less often than a defending champion and No. 1 seed would normally expect to. None of this fazed her; if anything, it simply reinforced her determination. For the second year in a row, she powered her way to the title without dropping a set, beating perennial rival Evert in the final.

Whether by coincidence or design, within a year of the double revelation about King and Navratilova Avon no longer sponsored the WTA tour. King, too, lost sponsorship deals estimated to be worth about $1.5 million, and Navratilova was long considered 'an orphan on the endorsement front',[8] receiving far fewer than Evert. The pair were good friends off the court and intense rivals on it, playing each other eighty times over a sixteen-year period, Navratilova winning forty-three of the matches. Yet while she came to dominate their meetings in the latter years, Navratilova could never usurp Evert's position as America's sweetheart. In part, that was because, unlike Evert, she was only a naturalised American. However, it was also because of her sexuality and the fact that she did not conform to the accepted norms of femininity.[9]

These norms had become increasingly important for the sport following the disclosures about Navratilova, its dominant young star, and in particular King, who was the leading figure in the creation of what would become the WTA Tour. For many, this only seemed to confirm and reinforce the stereotypical link between lesbianism and women's sport; it was a link which had to be symbolically rejected. Thus, while Evert was lauded in *Tennis Week* for bringing 'femininity to a feminist game',[10] Navratilova, who began to take a completely different approach to training, was subject to remarks about her increasingly muscular appearance. Influenced

by basketball star Nancy Lieberman, she had started lifting
weights, running daily, playing tennis for up to four hours a day,
and employed a nutritionist, all commonplace now, but derided at
the time. Tactically, too, Navratilova's game became more aggressive; more 'masculine'. This disparaging coverage reached a nadir
when *Sunday Express* editor John Junor wrote that Judy Nelson had
been foolish to abandon the security of a heterosexual marriage
to be with Navratilova, who he shamefully labelled 'that hatchet
faced lesbian'.[11]

II

There was, of course, a flip side. If sportswomen were supposed
to be feminine, then sportsmen were supposed to be masculine
and the mere rumour that they might be gay was enough to see
them struggle to turn on-field success into off-field wealth. A little
over three weeks after Navratilova's 1984 Wimbledon triumph,
US athlete Carl Lewis won Olympic gold in the 100 metres, 200
metres, long jump and 4x100 metres relay, emulating the achievement of his hero Jesse Owens in the 1936 Berlin Games. The Los
Angeles Games were the first in America for fifty-two years and,
at the height of Reagan-era jingoism, Lewis dutifully draped himself in the star-spangled banner. He was articulate and
good-looking. In short, he had all the ingredients needed to cash
in big. Yet his relationship with Nike ended in acrimony shortly
after his quadruple success, and a long-mooted sponsorship deal
with Coca-Cola never materialised. The fact that Lewis had no
major endorsement deals despite his exalted position in athletics
was, some felt, 'eerie and mysterious'.[12]

Rumours that Lewis was gay had long swirled around the athlete, so much so that in the run-up to the LA Games he publicly

and emphatically denied them. However, that did not stop Britain's Daley Thompson turning up to a victory press conference after defending his decathlon title wearing a T-shirt emblazoned with the words 'IS THE WORLD'S 2ND GREATEST ATHLETE GAY?' After being asked who he was referring to, Thompson casually told reporters, 'The second athlete could be anybody. Carl Lewis, anybody . . . But you have to realize that in Britain, gay means happy.'[13] Few believed that either his target or message were as ambiguous as he suggested. The incident further fuelled the rumours about Lewis, as did his androgynous look and flamboyant dress sense. Four years later, in the run-up to the Seoul Olympics, *Sports Illustrated* questioned why Lewis had no major endorsement deals. Was it, author Dan Geringer pondered, 'the homosexuality rumour thing'? In response, New York sports agent Arthur Kaminsky suggested that it might well be and that although Lewis' sexual orientation was 'his private business [. . .] homosexuality does concern Madison Avenue a great deal. For the issue to be raised is as bad as if it were true.'[14] Nike executive Don Coleman put it more bluntly: 'If you're a male athlete, I think the American public wants you to look macho.'[15]

At the time, the perception of gay men in British society was equally stereotypical, not least due to the exaggerated camp personas of hugely popular TV stars such as Larry Grayson and John Inman. Building on the traditions of older comedians such as Frankie Howerd and Kenneth Williams, their shows were regularly watched by millions. Grayson, as host of *The Generation Game*, became known for catchphrases like 'what a gay day' and 'he seems like a nice boy' all delivered through pursed lips and with a hand on his hip. Inman found fame in *Are You Being Served?*, playing menswear assistant Mr Humphries. Significantly, both men hid their own sexuality and tried to distance themselves from suggestions that their on-stage personas were in any way real. Grayson told the *Daily Mirror*, 'I'm not really a queer or a homosexual. I'm just behaving like one'.[16] Inman argued that Mr Humphries' sexual preferences were never mentioned, while the show's co-creator David Croft argued that the character was 'just a mother's boy'.[17] Much of the public was willing to buy into the conceit, but such portrayals provoked ire within the gay community where the over-emphasised link between homosexuality and effeminacy was seen as highly negative and damaging. In 1977, members of the Campaign for Homosexual Equality demonstrated outside the Brighton Corn Exchange where Inman was appearing in a summer show. He was, they argued, distorting the image of gay men. In the absence of any high-profile openly homosexual men to act as a counterbalance, the template of what it meant to be gay had been set (and it would remain ingrained in the public consciousness for many years to come). It was effeminate, immature and ridiculous, in short, the unthreatening 'other' to the stereotypical heterosexual man.

In many respects, gay and bisexual men were effectively invisible in many areas of society. Although it might have been frowned upon, sex between women was not illegal; by contrast male homosexuality only became legal in Britain in 1967. However, the new law initially only came into effect in England and Wales. It was another fourteen years before Scotland decriminalised homosexuality, Northern Ireland being the last of the home nations to do so, in 1982. Yet, the change in the law did, albeit very slowly, begin to shift wider public attitudes. John Curry being named BBC Sports Personality of the Year in 1976, an award voted for by the public, was perhaps indicative of that.

When Curry won gold in the men's singles figure skating at the Olympics, earlier in the year, it was the first medal of any colour for Britain in any event at the winter games in twelve years and only the fifth since the Second World War. Just twenty-seven days earlier he had won the European title, a victory which turned him from a relative unknown in a niche sport to a national hero virtually overnight. With an Olympic medal in his sights, Curry suddenly became the focus of huge media interest and when he took to the rink at the Olympia Eisstadion in Innsbruck for the Olympic final, some twenty million were watching on television back in Britain. What they witnessed was more than just a victory; it was a paradigm shift. Curry redefined the sport, infusing his routine with balletic dance moves that challenged the sport's athletic orthodoxy. Yet the following day, when Curry faced the press, there was only one subject they wanted to ask him about: his sexuality.

It may seem odd to devote space in a book about the 1980s to an athlete who reached his competitive peak in 1976, but the reality was that during the decade gay and bisexual male sports stars were, like the demographic they came from, effectively invisible. A world-renowned, Olympic gold-medal-winning sportsman revealing that he was homosexual was unheard of. In the run-up to the Games, Curry spoke candidly to a journalist from the Associated Press (AP) and admitted that he was gay, something about which there had previously been only rumours and insinuation. The agency held the story back until his victory, after which it was syndicated around the world. 'John undoubtedly wanted it out,' says his biographer Bill Jones.[18] 'He subsequently claimed that he'd been misquoted, and his words manipulated, but his close friends and the journalist in question are in no doubt that he was savvy enough to realise that he was getting it out there through a journalist whose copy was passed on, and on, and on in a way John thought he would never have to confront.'

In an era before rolling news and social media, the story took a couple of days to have an impact. When it did, predictably it made huge headlines. In a bid to quell the media interest, a press conference was hastily arranged. Words like 'masculinity' and 'virility' were soon introduced into the conversation. The implication was clear: because Curry was gay, those characteristics could surely not apply to him; he must instead conform to the camp cliché made popular by Grayson and Inman. Eventually, exasperated, Curry asked one journalist: 'Do you think what I did yesterday was not athletic?'[19] Yet, despite the negative tone of the questioning, it was the journalists, not Curry, who seemed to be on the back foot, skirting around the issue. 'What was interesting about the press conference was that because there wasn't the language in common circulation for asking those questions, the journalists didn't really have the confidence to engage with it,' says Jones. 'John was the one who was setting the pace, although that didn't make it any easier for him at the time.' There were some progressive voices. Notably Chris Brasher, the co-founder of the London Marathon, was one of the few who dealt with the story in a considered way, writing in the *Observer*: 'When everyone had telephoned their story and discussions broke out in many languages around the bar, opinion began to emerge that it was [Curry] who was normal and that it was we who were abnormal. [. . .] However much the law has changed, the minds of most of us are full of taboos.'[20]

'It was extraordinarily brave but also incredibly destructive for him,' says Jones. 'When John got back to Britain, he found the world was divided between people who didn't give a shit, and the establishment in Fleet Street and the sport.' That division was writ large before the year was out. In December, Curry picked up the BBC Sports Personality of the Year award, beating Formula One champion James Hunt (the epitome of heterosexual masculinity) into second place. It was one of just several TV appearances that month for Curry. An hour-long special filmed in the summer for LWT was broadcast on Christmas Day. A couple of weeks earlier Curry had appeared on Michael Parkinson's chat show. The ballet dancer Rudolf Nureyev, also gay, was a guest on the same programme. Interestingly, Parkinson did not interview the two together as he did with many guests.

Curry was also invited to the Sports Journalists' Association Christmas dinner to pick up another award. He arrived late, and as he made his way to his seat through Fleet Street's finest and other assorted luminaries, the comic entertaining the guests spotted Curry, 'It's good to feel the Christmas spirit among us all,' he said, breaking into his routine. 'Here comes the fairy for the tree.'[21] For many of the assembled journalists, this was a step too far. Although a few laughed, more jeered and booed. The comedian Eric Morecambe shouted 'disgraceful'. Curry would later confide that it was 'one of the most hurtful incidents of my life'.[22] It also made up his mind: there was no place for him in Britain. 'John decided to leave because the country offered neither the privacy, the secrecy nor the liberality for him to function without feeling degraded,' says Jones. 'New York was a much easier place to hide but it also seemed much less hung up by the whole notion of gayness. The ripple of coming out began in San Francisco and moved east, but it was a big, long time before it crossed the Atlantic.' By the end of the following March, Curry had moved in the other direction.

III

In February 1980, Curry returned to the Winter Olympics, where he watched from the commentary box as Robin Cousins, eight years his junior, retained the men's singles title for Great Britain. Even if he'd wanted to, Curry was unable to compete, having forgone his amateur status, but he was invited to play a part in the closing ceremony in which he performed another routine that defied the sport's established aesthetics.

A fortnight earlier, some 3,000 miles away at Norwich City's Carrow Road, another bright sporting talent, footballer Justin Fashanu, had announced himself to the British public in unforgettable style. The Canaries' young striker scored the goal of the season, if not the goal of the decade. A wicked, swerving volley made on the turn, it was an outrageous piece of individual skill, magnified by the fact that it came against the champions, Liverpool. Watching it now, the slightly grainy quality of the footage, and the pitch browning like a worn carpet, makes the *Match of the Day* coverage seem like a museum artefact, a snapshot of another, long-ago era. Yet the goal has since been replayed so often it is encoded into the visual lexicon of the game.

Two months later Fashanu made his debut for England's Under-21s in the first leg of their European Championship semifinal against East Germany at Sheffield United's Bramall Lane. England lost 2−1, but Fashanu scored England's goal and did not look out of place in a team including full internationals Kenny Sansom and Glenn Hoddle, and others, such as Terry Butcher, who would soon graduate to the senior team. Fashanu's future seemed bright. He was in the vanguard of black players who were challenging racial stereotypes and breaking into the domestic game's top teams as well as the national side. Yet it wasn't Fashanu's colour that made him an outsider in the world of football. As with Curry, it was the fact that he was gay.

Fashanu had made his debut for Norwich against West Bromwich Albion in February 1979, a little over a month before his eighteenth birthday. By the end of the season, he'd scored five goals in sixteen appearances. The following season, the one in which he scored the wonder goal, he was the club's leading scorer in the League. The season after that, he scored nineteen goals in forty League appearances and a further three in six cup games. He was the team's top scorer again and, despite Norwich being relegated, his performances drew the attention of the country's top clubs. Manchester City, now managed by his former Norwich boss John Bond, and Liverpool, the European Cup holders, both expressed an interest, but it was Nottingham Forest, managed by the mercurial Brian Clough, that eventually prised him away from Norfolk. It was just two and a half years since Forest had made Trevor Francis the first £1 million player, and the club paid a similar fee for Fashanu, making him the first million-pound black player.

As costly as the move was for the club, it was arguably more so for the player whose form seemingly disappeared overnight. It was nine games before he scored his first League goal for Forest, against Middlesbrough in October. Another couple came towards the end of the following month, and then they dried up. By any measure the move had been a disaster. From the outside looking in, it seemed as though the young striker simply couldn't make the step up to what was then not just one of the biggest clubs in England but also in Europe.

Clough was known for keeping new signings on their toes, especially the expensive ones. Even Francis, an established England international signed with much fanfare, was given his first runout for Forest in the reserves and forced to brew the tea for pre-match meetings. Furthermore, the team that in three glorious seasons had won first the League and then back-to-back European Cups was in decline, as was Clough's relationship with Peter Taylor, his long-time assistant. At the end of Fashanu's only full season at Forest, Taylor retired on health grounds, only to become Derby County manager three months later, a move Clough considered an irredeemable act of betrayal.

Furthermore, Fashanu was not the type of player that Clough

was used to dealing with. 'Justin was not your typical footballer,' says Peter Tatchell, the human rights activist, who was close friends with Fashanu in the early 1980s.[23] 'He was very well spoken, very well informed, with a curious intellect and he was extremely gregarious. You could chat to him about almost any subject and he would usually have an intelligent, thoughtful perspective to offer. We discussed everything from football to classical music, art, politics, and history.' Fashanu was also outgoing with a penchant for fast cars and bright clothes (including a canary-yellow tuxedo), earning the name 'Fash the Flash' which, for whatever reason, also irked Clough. Frank Clark, who had joined Forest's backroom staff after finishing his playing career with the club, thinks that the manager found Fashanu's personality hard to deal with. 'It seemed as though sometimes Justin was openly defying him, and he didn't like that very much.'[24]

Fashanu thrived when his confidence was high, his biographer Nick Baker noting that his form appeared to depend on who was managing him at the time; if the relationship was good, so were the striker's performances, and vice versa. Clough relished intimidating his players. He would prowl the touchline in training sessions carrying a squash racquet, the threat that he would use it as an offensive weapon always there. Although he never did, he wasn't averse to the use of force, on one occasion slapping Fashanu on the side of the head after the player withdrew from a game forty-five minutes before kick-off claiming he wasn't fit enough to play. It is little surprise that many of the younger players were scared of Clough. Fashanu became so afraid of his manager that just talking about him made him break into a sweat and Clough even claimed that Fashanu 'used to burst into tears if I said hello to him'.[25] The manager was unable to adapt his methods, which clearly worked with many players, to accommodate Fashanu. 'I can't imagine how he'd have coped in Middlesbrough [one of

Clough's former clubs] in the 1950s,' he lamented to Duncan Hamilton, then a reporter for the *Nottingham Evening Post*.[26]

However, according to Tatchell, as far as Fashanu was concerned there was one root cause for the fractious relationship with Clough: his sexuality. 'Justin gave me the impression that it was primarily because he was gay. Clough was uncomfortable and unsympathetic with having a gay player on the team and repeatedly made that obvious to Justin.' That attitude is reflected in the uncompromising way Clough spoke about Fashanu in his autobiography, first published in 1994, in which he referred to the player as 'the "poof" Justin Fashanu'[27] and suggested that he found it difficult to accept Fashanu as 'one of us'.[28] Clough soon became aware that his new striker was visiting gay clubs and according to Viv Anderson, who played for Forest at the time, started calling Fashanu a 'poof' in training.[29] The players took this to be just an insult, not the reality, but Clough confronted Fashanu about his sexuality, or in his words 'put him to the test'.[30]

In an oft-quoted exchange, Clough asked Fashanu, 'Where do you go if you want a loaf of bread?' 'A baker's, I suppose,' came the reply. 'Where do you go if you want a leg of lamb?' Clough continued. 'A butcher's,' Fashanu responded. 'So why do you keep going to that bloody poof's club in town?' Clough demanded. Apparently, Fashanu shrugged in response. 'He knew what I meant,' wrote Clough, 'and it wasn't long before I could stand no more of him.'[31] The fractious relationship had a devastating effect on Fashanu, who spoke to Tatchell on many occasions about the difficulties he was having with Clough. 'He was clearly very emotionally and mentally thrown off-balance by it. I think that was reflected in the way his game went downhill. He would say to me things like "How can I play my best if my boss hasn't got my back?" He had quite a few discussions with Clough but got nowhere with him, there was still this constant nagging undercurrent of hostility and bigotry.'

Fashanu's confidence was shot. 'I like Nottingham, but I don't want to stay at Forest. Not with him,' he told Hamilton.[32] After just one season at the club, the striker was sent to Southampton on a month-long loan. In a more sympathetic environment, his form began to return. Fashanu scored three goals in nine games. He was also recalled to the England Under-21 squad for the two-legged European Championship final against West Germany, playing and scoring in the first game as the team went on to lift the trophy. However, his time on the south coast was short-lived, the Saints unable to afford to keep him.

On his return to the East Midlands, Fashanu was immediately told that he would be loaned to Derby County and should stay at home until the move went through. The striker refused, so Clough called the police to escort Fashanu from the training ground. It was a humiliating incident for the player and marked the end of his brief time at Forest. A cut-price move across the Trent to Notts County, managed by Howard Wilkinson, followed. The former teacher had managed Fashanu in the England Under-21 side and believed that he still had something to offer in the top flight. Fashanu's form began to return, five goals in fifteen games helping the team avoid the drop.

It seemed that Fashanu still had a bright future ahead of him when, on New Year's Eve 1983, he was involved in a seemingly innocuous challenge from Russell Osman. A cut on his knee required several stitches; however, the needle used hadn't been properly sterilised and the wound became infected. Before it could be treated it caused significant damage. Fashanu was forced to miss the rest of the season and to undergo several operations. 'I know there's a legend grown up around Justin that it was his sexuality that ruined his career,' says Clark, 'but that's not true; it was the severe knee injury that more or less ended his career. One of Justin's greatest strengths was his athleticism, but he couldn't get that back, he lost that.' At one point, doctors advised Fashanu that he might not be able to play again. It was a diagnosis the player was determined to prove wrong. Over the next twelve years he would bounce from club to club in England, Scotland, America and Canada, but he would never reach a consistent level of performance again.

Now we're used to goals being immediately clipped and shared on social media, but Fashanu's best years came just before regular TV coverage of football began. Not all matches were televised or even filmed, so there is no record of many of the games he played for Norwich. As a consequence, it's easy to reduce him to the status of a one-goal wonder, a player who fluked the spectacular and achieved little else; Clough certainly did. In his first biography, the erstwhile Forest boss suggested that when he signed Fashanu the player had 'just scored a well-publicised goal for Norwich against Liverpool'.[34] Even Duncan Hamilton, in his memoir-cum-biography of Clough, suggested that 'Fashanu made his reputation on the basis of a solitary goal'.[35] The reality was somewhat different.

'He is defined by that one goal because it was a super strike,' says Clark, 'but he contributed a lot more at Norwich, there's no doubt about that.' Some eighteen months passed between Fashanu scoring against Liverpool and Clough signing him, during which time Clough saw the player score twice in three games against Forest (then European Cup holders). Clough also spoke to Joe Royle, Fashanu's teammate at Norwich, about the player and received a ringing endorsement. Furthermore, Fashanu had proved himself to be a consistent goalscorer. He scored five times in eleven games for the England Under-21 team. Over four seasons with Norwich, he had found the net forty times in 103 appearances (thirty-five goals coming in ninety League games). To put that into perspective, it was a better goals-to-games ratio than the likes of Dwight Yorke, Teddy Sheringham and Peter Crouch ended their careers with. The idea that he was, as Clough opined, 'absolutely hopeless',[36] simply belied the facts.

IV

Nottingham is no New York. Yet just as moving across the Atlantic gave John Curry the opportunity to find himself in a way that he couldn't in 1970s Britain, so the move to the East Midlands allowed Fashanu to truly discover himself in a way he couldn't in Norwich. He was suddenly pitched into a city with a vibrant social life and, crucially, a growing gay scene. The month before he was signed by Clough, La Chic: Part Two, Britain's first licensed gay club, opened its doors on the Nottingham's Canal Street. At its peak it was the best gay club outside London. Fashanu became a regular. Initially he would discreetly enter through a side entrance. However, as he became more confident, he would drive up to the front and leave his distinctive white Toyota Supra parked outside.

It was little wonder that Clough soon found out and yet it seemed as though Fashanu wanted his secret out in the open. 'He did take some risks appearing with me in public and I suspect on a deeper unconscious level he probably wanted to be outed to end the burden of leading a secretive double life,' says Tatchell. 'Justin had a reckless streak, a daredevil, come-what-may attitude sometimes. He could be very studied, controlled, on point and then suddenly he'd do or say something that was completely unexpected and possibly quite risky.' At the time Tatchell was in the headlines as the Labour Party's candidate for the Bermondsey by-election, where he had been chosen by the local party against the wishes of leader Michael Foot. His sexuality became a touchstone issue during the campaign. The Liberal/SDP Alliance, whose candidate Simon Hughes eventually won, printed leaflets saying the election was 'A STRAIGHT choice'. The constituency was also flooded with 10,000 anonymous leaflets calling Tatchell a 'traitor' and showing a picture of him next to the queen along with the words 'Which Queen will you vote for?'[37] Offensive graffiti such as 'Tatchell is a communist poof'[38] was daubed around the constituency. The press sent young boys to his door and printed his address, precipitating death threats. He was regularly physically assaulted while out canvassing. As such, Tatchell cautioned Fashanu about the risk of taking him to public events. 'I said, "It's not going to take much for journalists to put two and two together and you're going to face a grilling." He said, "I'm prepared to make some compromises but I'm not going to compromise on this and run around hiding like a sheep."'

At the time Fashanu was deliberating about whether or not to go public about his sexuality. 'There were moments when we discussed it,' says Tatchell, 'and although I cautioned that I didn't think he was emotionally and psychologically ready, he was very seriously considering coming out in the early 1980s. He said many times to me, "I don't like skulking around in the shadows."' However, when presented with the opportunity, Fashanu backed away. In 1982 a journalist from the *Sunday People* approached him to ask if rumours he was gay were true. Fashanu issued a denial, and that was enough for the paper to run a story, under the guise of the player hitting back at the gossip. Fashanu sued and won damages. It was indicative of the fact that football, unlike the more artistic ice skating, was considered a 'man's sport', in which no one admitted they were gay. Furthermore, in the decade or so since Curry had come out, public attitudes towards homosexuality had begun to harden significantly. 'The 1980s was a very toxic period,' says Tatchell. 'There was a huge increase in gay-bashing attacks and murders, simultaneously there was a massive rise in arrests of gay and bisexual men for consenting behaviour.' Absurdly, although sex between gay men had been decriminalised, arranging to do so was not. Men could be prosecuted for exchanging telephone numbers in public or attempting to contact each other with a view to having sex. This apparent anomaly was exploited by the police and in 1989 more than 2,000 gay men were prosecuted for gross indecency, a greater number than at any time since the 1950s and nearly three times as many as in the 1960s.[39]

This was the culmination of the increasingly intolerant attitude and policies of Margaret Thatcher's government, whose moral crusade was in part a reaction to the permissiveness of the 1960s and 1970s. Thatcher had been one of the few Conservative MPs to vote in favour of the decriminalisation of homosexuality; however, twenty years later, at the start of her third term as prime minister, she delivered a significantly less sympathetic message in her party conference speech saying: 'Children who need to be taught to respect traditional moral values are being taught that they have an inalienable right to be gay. All of those children are being cheated of a sound start in life.'[40] The following year, the Local Government Act was introduced, Section 28 of which forbade local authorities from promoting gay politics, and schools from teaching the acceptability of homosexuality as a 'pretended family relationship'.

It was the first new anti-gay law in Britain for a century, yet it proved unworkable. By the time of its repeal in 2003, there had been no prosecutions under Section 28. It was, however, a symbolic totem within a hard-fought culture war. The year before Thatcher's speech, *EastEnders* became the first soap to introduce a gay character, Colin (played by Michael Cashman). The *Sun* greeted the news with a front-page 'exclusive' headlined 'IT'S

EASTBENDERS'.[41] Storylines centred on the character explored many issues affecting gay men and challenged stereotypes, but they also provided grist for the tabloid mill. When Colin shared a mouth-to-mouth kiss with his on-screen boyfriend, then-*Sun* journalist Piers Morgan described it as a 'homosexual love scene between yuppie poofs'. In the same article, Tory MP Terry Dicks decried the 'revolting scenes' and 'perverted practices' and called for the soap to be scrapped.[42]

Yet in wider popular culture homosexual stereotypes and gender norms were beginning to be challenged. The 'gender-bending' personas of singers such as Boy George, Marilyn and Annie Lennox pushed the boundaries of what it meant to look 'masculine' and 'feminine', while songs like 'Relax', by Frankie Goes to Hollywood, and 'Small Town Boy', by Bronksi Beat, were not only sung by openly gay men (Holly Johnson and Jimmy Sommerville respectively), but also addressed aspects of gay life. The artwork and lyrics of 'Relax' so outraged Radio 1 DJ Mike Read that he refused to play it, precipitating a ban by the station . . . and sending the single straight to the top of the charts. A second 'clean' version of the video also had to be filmed after the first, which had an S&M aesthetic and depicted simulated gay sex, was also banned by the BBC and MTV. 'Smalltown Boy' was by contrast less provocative, but its plaintive lyrics and emotive video were a more heartfelt articulation of the rejection and fears felt by many gay men subjected to bigotry and violence by society and even those closest to them.

Channel 4, with its remit to appeal to people not catered for by the pre-existing channels, began to produce programming for gay audiences that depicted gay lifestyles, such as the magazine show *Out on Tuesday* and the film *My Beautiful Laundrette*. The comedian Julian Clary, who sported garish bondage-inspired PVC outfits and shocked audiences with explicit jokes about gay sex, became

one of the channel's breakout stars, subverting the camp stereotype popularised by John Inman and Larry Grayson. When the
former footballer turned *Sun* 'telly pundit' Jimmy Greaves said
that Clary was 'a prancing poofter', Clary responded that he
didn't prance, he minced. Such programming was at odds with
the values of the Conservative government, something senior MP
Norman Tebbit made clear when he buttonholed Jeremy Isaacs,
the channel's chief executive, at an embassy dinner. 'You've got it
all wrong, you know, doing all these programmes for homosexuals
and such,' Tebbit said. 'Parliament never meant that sort of thing.
The different interests you are supposed to cater for are not like
that at all. Golf and sailing and fishing. Hobbies. That's what we
intended.'[43]

V

Although it's not exactly clear when or where the diagnosis was
made, by 1987 the news Curry had feared was confirmed: he was
HIV positive. Initially identified in June 1981 among gay men in
America, the sexually transmitted condition, known as human
immunodeficiency virus, would if untreated lead to acquired
immunodeficiency syndrome (AIDS). In those early days there
was little Curry could do. He knew it was only a matter of time
before the likely onset of AIDS and that would in turn be an all
but guaranteed death sentence. In the meantime, Curry had to
watch the pandemic ravage the community in which he had
finally found sexual liberation. 'Throughout John's skating career
John's lovers were skaters and the decimation of the male professional ice-skating population in the AIDS epidemic was
catastrophic,' says Jones.

The virus quickly crossed the Atlantic although initially it was

met with disinterest. Soon the first British patients had been identified, one of whom was thirty-seven-year-old Terry Higgins. He
died in July 1982 and his friends set up the Terrence Higgins Trust
dedicated to raising awareness and research funds in response to
the crisis. The charity led where initially the government failed to;
however in 1986 the Department of Health launched a £20 million awareness campaign. Leaflets titled 'Don't Die of Ignorance'
were sent to twenty-three million households encouraging people
to wear condoms when having sex and not to share needles if taking drugs. Adverts with icebergs, representing a huge hidden
danger, and tombstones with the word 'AIDS' chiselled into them,
ran on TV and in cinemas.

The information was practical, not moral, but although it did
not blame gay and bisexual men for the disease, it did little to
undermine wider homophobic attitudes, particularly in the press.
Hysteria and hostility spread through the mass-market tabloids as
homosexual men were scapegoated for causing the disease that
was devastating their community. In May 1983, a *Mail on Sunday*
headline warned of a 'gay plague'. With its biblical overtones, the
term was adopted by Fleet Street as convenient shorthand for
the virus and embedded itself in the public consciousness. Soon
AIDS was being identified in other sections of the population,
namely intravenous drug users, and haemophiliacs who had
received blood transfusions. The media's prejudice intensified;
while the latter were cast as 'innocent' victims, drug addicts and
gay men were condemned. Gay celebrities were repeatedly har-
assed at home by tabloid journalists; Jimmy Somerville, lead
singer of The Communards as well as Bronski Beat, was told by
one paper that they would print a story saying he had AIDS
unless he could present a negative test.[44] The nadir was reached
when the *Sun* quoted an anonymous psychologist suggesting that
'all homosexuals should be exterminated to stop the spread of

AIDS. It's time we stopped pussyfooting around.'[45] The broadsheets, while not overtly homophobic, were hardly any better. They did little to report the truly devastating effect on the gay community or lack of funding for gay and HIV organisations. Many of the stories they printed were inaccurate and some would not have looked out of place in their downmarket counterparts. An editorial in *The Times* claimed that 'many members of the public are tempted to see in AIDS some sort of retribution for a questionable style of life'. The paper also asked, 'Is it wise to share a bathroom or lavatory with a homosexual?'[46]

As the government's stance on homosexuality toughened, fears over AIDS grew and the media demonisation of gay men became more hostile. So, too, did public attitudes. In 1983, according to the British Social Attitudes Survey, one in two people believed that sex between members of the same sex was 'always wrong' and a further one in ten thought it was 'mostly wrong'. Just 17 per cent thought it was 'not wrong at all'. Four years later, the number of people who believed that homosexuality was 'always' or 'mostly wrong' had risen to 75 per cent, while the number who thought it was 'not wrong at all' had fallen to 11 per cent. More than half the British population did not think it was 'acceptable' for a gay or lesbian person to be a teacher and more than four in ten people did not believe gay people should hold 'a responsible position in public life'. Against this backdrop, it's hard to imagine BBC viewers acknowledging the achievements of an openly gay man by voting him Sports Personality of the Year as they had just eleven years before. It is little wonder that Fashanu and other gay sportsmen continued to shy away from publicly acknowledging their sexuality.

In 1990, Fashanu was reunited with Frank Clark, then manager of Leyton Orient. Clark and the club's physio Billy Songhurst often spoke to Fashanu about his sexuality and whether he should go public. 'We did chat to him and said, "Look, it won't be as bad as you think it will be," but that was easy for us to say. He was very unsure about it. We couldn't convince him and obviously we weren't going to force him. It was a fear of the response in general, not just the media; the crowd, the fans. He was apprehensive about that, which I could understand.' Fashanu's knee injury curtailed his stay in east London and so he moved to Canada. While there he sold his story to the *Sun*, something that shocked many people given the paper's attitude not just to homosexuality but also on racial issues. However, it seemed his hand had, at least in part, been forced. 'My understanding is that he was going to be outed by a Sunday paper,' says Tatchell. 'To pre-empt that he decided to proactively go to another newspaper to tell his story on his terms. He justified it by saying the *Sun* was the biggest mass-circulation paper; it was the paper most read by football fans and if he came out on his terms in that paper then the chances of them doing the dirty on him were much reduced.'

Fashanu's revelation, along with John Curry's fourteen years earlier, bookended the 1980s. In the intervening decade the former wrestled with his sexuality, feeling the need to hide it as best he could, while the latter all but disappeared from public view, driven to live in America where he felt more comfortable. Curry died in 1994, finally succumbing to the ravages of AIDS at the age of forty-four. That he had lived with his condition as long as he had was, doctors felt, a consequence of his supreme fitness. Four years later, Fashanu, too, was dead. He had been accused of sexually assaulting a seventeen-year-old youth in America – allegations he denied – and, fearing jail, left the country. In May 1998, he was found hanged in a lock-up garage he had broken into in Shoreditch. He was thirty-seven. In Clough's second autobiography, published five years after Fashanu's death, he expressed some regret at how he had treated Fashanu and admitted that his wife, Barbara, had criticised his handling of the situation. Yet Clough again repeated the anecdote about his disparaging confrontation with Fashanu and called him a 'fraud',[47] suggesting that the fundamental problem lay with Fashanu for hiding his sexuality. There was no acknowledgement that either societal attitudes or Clough's own approach had created an environment unconducive to a young, gay man coming out.

CHAPTER 7

People Are People

I

When Roland Butcher walked down the pavilion steps and onto the pitch at Bridgetown's Kensington Oval in March 1981 to make his Test debut, it was the stuff off boyhood dreams. An attacking middle-order batsman, his love affair with the game had begun at the stadium in Barbados' capital city when, as an eleven-year-old, he was taken to watch the West Indies play Australia. Bill Lawry and Bob Simpson became the first opening pair to score double centuries in the same game, their first-wicket stand of 382 for the visitors falling just short of the world record. From then on, the young Butcher was hooked, but when he finally stepped onto the international stage, he was not playing for the country of his birth but for England, the first black man to do so. 'Barbados was the place I was born in, where I spent my child-hood, and where my family's whole history and culture was,' Butcher says.[1] 'To be playing there and to be playing against the team that I wanted to play for as a kid made it very special. There was a great feeling of pride.'

The crowd also took pride in Butcher's achievements. He had been unsure how he would be received but the Barbadians

embraced him as one of their own and acknowledged his achievement for what it was. He received a standing ovation and play was
held up until it dissipated. 'The whole ground erupted in the sort
of noise you've never heard before,' says Butcher. 'Everywhere
that I played it was similar. I think people were generally very
happy that someone who had made it into the England team was
making their debut there.'

Butcher made seventeen as England were dispatched for a
measly 122 in less than forty-eight overs. At the close of play on
day two, the hosts led by 149 runs and still had nine second-
innings wickets in hand. Then tragedy struck when England's
assistant manager, the popular Ken Barrington, died of a heart
attack in his hotel room. The squad was devastated, but they completed the match and the tour's remaining four weeks, which
included two Tests. They had already coped with the cancellation
of the second Test after Robin Jackman, a late replacement for
the injured Bob Willis, was denied entry to Guyana due to his
ties with apartheid South Africa.

Given this disruption it was little surprise that the West Indies
were, as many expected, the dominant side, winning the series 2−0.
Even in the two drawn matches, England had been significantly
behind after the first innings and needed help from the weather to
secure a result. Butcher made seventy-one runs across his five
innings at an average of 14.20, but it should be remembered that
this was a tough baptism against one of the most fearsome pace
attacks the game has known: Colin Croft, Michael Holding, Joel
Garner and Andy Roberts operating at or near their peak. In the
aftermath, Butcher was dropped from the team and, although he
didn't know it, his international career was over. In 1983, as his
form was returning and a Test recall looked possible, he was hit in
the face as he tried to hook a delivery from Leicestershire's West
Indian fast bowler George Ferris. Butcher incurred several

fractures and required two operations. His eyesight never fully recovered. While he was able to play for Middlesex, the county for which he had made his professional debut in 1974, for another seven years, he never played for England again.

Although the significance of Butcher's achievement was not acknowledged by *Wisden*, overshadowed as it was by Barrington's death and the Jackman affair, he was acutely aware of its importance. 'After I achieved the milestone of playing for England, the reality set in that I'd become a bit of a role model,' Butcher says. 'Me playing for England helped other black players believe, "Hang on, if he can do it, I can do it too," then there's a trickle-down effect.' But Butcher was also conscious that his achievement had a wider impact. 'I became very aware after that black people in all walks of life will be believing that "if I work hard enough and do the right things, I may have a chance to make it."'

Butcher, like Justin Fashanu, was part of the wave of sports men and women – the children of immigrants, or immigrants themselves – who started to gain prominence in British sport in the 1970s and 1980s. His parents were part of the 'Windrush Generation' named after the *Empire Windrush*, a refitted former German troopship, that arrived at Tilbury dock in 1948 with 492 passengers, each of whom had paid £28 to make the 8,000-mile journey from the Caribbean to Britain. They were at the vanguard of what would become large-scale migration. By 1971, the number of settlers in Britain from the so-called 'New Commonwealth' (that is former colonial countries) had increased from 200,000 to approximately 1.2 million. The majority of these were black workers enticed by campaigns such as those of the Ministry of Health and London Transport, which opened a recruitment office in Barbados. These jobs tended to be in the relatively stagnant sectors of what was an otherwise fast-growing economy, where low pay, long hours and shift work put off British workers.

The first arrivals required no entry papers or visas to enter Britain as at the time all Commonwealth citizens were considered legitimate passport holders (something that would come back to haunt numerous families decades later during the Windrush scandal beginning in 2018). By 1961, the West Indian population in Britain had grown to 172,000 from just 15,000 ten years earlier,[2] prompting a backlash against such an influx of immigrants. In response, in 1962, the Conservative government passed the Commonwealth Immigrants Act. At face value, this defined a person's right to immigration on the basis of the authority issuing the passport. The reality was somewhat different. Those whose passports were issued by the UK authorities, citizens from the 'old', white or white-ruled Commonwealth countries – Australia, Canada, and South Africa – maintained their right of entry; those whose passports were issued by a colonial or Commonwealth authority, citizens from the 'new', or non-white Commonwealth countries – those in the Caribbean and South East Asia – lost their right of entry.

The act still allowed the dependants of migrants to join their parents in Britain, leading to a significant influx of children from the West Indies, of which Butcher was part. His parents had moved to England from Barbados in the mid-1950s, leaving Butcher and his sister Margaret with their grandmother and aunts. The youngsters made the journey in May 1967 when Butcher was thirteen. 'It was a culture shock, as you would expect,' he tells me. 'It was the first time I had travelled overseas. England is so very different to Barbados. In Barbados you have sun three hundred and sixty-five days of the year, in England you had the seasons, with one season longer than the others. The other part that was a huge culture shock was that in Barbados as a youth wherever you went cricket was being played, but in England it was football.'

In 1968, an amendment to the act further limited the right to live and work in Britain to those who had at least one parent or grandparent who was born in, or was a citizen of, the UK. The Immigration Act of 1971 restricted immigration further still, by which time some 304,000 West Indians had settled in Britain. Although immigration slowed, and the number of West Indians living in the UK who had been born outside the country plateaued, the community of Caribbean descent continued to grow. By 1981, it was an estimated 500,000 and it included, for the first time, thousands of people of Afro-Caribbean descent – many of them in their late teens and early twenties – who were either born in Britain or emigrated there when they were so young that the country was effectively the only home they knew.

As this community grew, so did the number of black men and women gaining national prominence, and the representation of black lives. In 1987 Diane Abbott became the first black female MP, having been elected alongside other ethnic minority candidates Bernie Grant, Paul Boateng and Keith Vaz, all for the Labour Party. It meant that for the first time since the 1920s there was black and Asian representation in the House of Commons. Moira Stuart and Trevor McDonald provided a calm, reassuring presence on news bulletins for the BBC and ITN respectively. In 1983 ITV's long-running soap *Coronation Street* introduced its first black character – Shirley Armitage, played by Lisa Lewis – and two years later the original cast of *EastEnders* included a black family, the Carpenters. Lenny Henry, who had burst onto the scene in 1975 as a sixteen-year-old in the talent show *New Faces*, had become an established star with his own TV series, and was the face of *Comic Relief*, which he co-founded.

Unsurprisingly given its remit, Channel 4 was the most progressive in its representation of minorities. The Black Theatre Co-operative was commissioned to write and perform the channel's first sitcom, *No Problem!* The first original comedy series to address the lives of a black British family, it ran for two series from 1983. The following year, Channel 4 imported *The Cosby Show* from America. At the time the show was a ground-breaking, non-stereotypical and positive representation of middle-class black life. Before the decade was out, the first episode of *Desmond's* was broadcast. Set in a Peckham barber shop, and starring Norman Beaton in the titular role, it became Channel 4's longest running sitcom. Also, the channel's film production arm was one of the producers of *My Beautiful Laundrette*, which told the story of an unlikely love affair between Omar (Gordon Warnecke), a young Asian man, and skinhead Johnny (Daniel Day-Lewis), a key theme being Omar's attempts to reconcile the position of his father, who despairs of their adopted country, and his uncle, who sees it as a land of opportunity.

Sport was another arena in which black men and women were coming to prominence, with increasing numbers competing at an elite level and representing national teams. The 1978/79 season saw West Bromwich Albion consistently field a trio of black players – Brendon Batson, Laurie Cunningham and Cyrille Regis – nicknamed 'the Three Degrees' after the American all-female soul group. In November 1978, Viv Anderson became the first black man to play for England at senior level, against Czechoslovakia. It was a milestone in what was the country's most popular sport and Roland Butcher believes it will have helped other players in other sports. 'I'm sure that what Viv Anderson did would have subconsciously helped me to have got where I've got,' says Butcher, 'because I will have internalised what he achieved in a sport that was not particularly friendly to people of colour. For him to make that breakthrough will have helped everybody else down the line, not just in football, to believe they could really achieve things.'

The 1980 Moscow Olympics provided the launch pad for Daley Thompson's career. Born to a Scottish mother and a Nigerian father, the twenty-one-year-old was already the world record holder but gold in the Soviet Union catapulted him to even greater levels of fame. Sprinters Beverley Goddard, Heather Hunte, and Sonia Lannaman scooped bronze in the 4x100 metres relay. Thompson won gold again in Los Angeles in 1984, and at the same Games Tessa Sanderson won gold in the javelin, making her the first British black woman to claim an Olympic gold. As well as this increased presence in football and athletics, Rosie Sykes became the first black woman to represent England at hockey, a sport which remains resolutely white – as of 2022, only two other black women have represented England and Great Britain in the sport – and Desmond Douglas established himself as Britain's top table tennis player and one of the best in the world. In 1987 he was awarded an MBE for his contribution to sport and the following year competed in the Olympics when table tennis was included for the first time, coming ninth in the doubles partnering Skylet Andrew, who won three gold medals at the 1989 Commonwealth Games.

Although Butcher was still eligible to play for the West Indies, and had dreamed of doing so as a boy, when the call came to play for England, the decision was 'a no-brainer', he says. 'I'd been in England since 1967. I was married, I had a son, it was my home. It really took the option of playing for the West Indies off the table; by doing that I would have put myself in the position of being an overseas player.' At the time, the seventeen County Championship teams were allowed to have just one overseas player within their squads. Playing for the West Indies would have significantly limited Butcher's options, not least because many teams chose a fast bowler to fill the spot. 'From my point of view, that made no sense whatsoever,' he says. 'Why would I put myself in a position where I could find myself out of work and my family having to suffer? When you get the chance to play Test cricket it doesn't matter who you play for, there's a feeling you have achieved a goal you set out to achieve all those years ago.'

II

Butcher didn't experience the overt racism that other sportsmen and women did. 'Why that is, I don't know,' he says. 'My father was the first black person in Stevenage, and when I arrived he had really established himself there. When I moved to Middlesex, I was a very private person. I was not the sort of person who wanted to be in crowds, who wanted to party. So, in many ways, I guess, I would not have come in contact with those kinds of people. I did not have the types of experiences of the guys who lived in inner-city London where everybody is in a tight squeeze.' Furthermore, when he moved to Middlesex after a stint at the MCC, he was one of five black players in the team along with Norman Cowans, Wilf Slack, Neil Williams and the West Indian Wayne Daniel, who along with Butcher were dubbed 'the Jackson Five'.[3] 'There was strength in numbers, there's no question about that,' Butcher says. 'On my own, it may have been a different experience. It would have been much easier for things to happen.'

In retrospect, however, he does feel that he was subject to discrimination, particularly when he was not picked for the Centenary Test against Australia at Lords in late August 1980, commemorating the first Test between the two countries in England. 'That was not my thought at the time. You think purely as a cricketer. But later on, I internalised that it wasn't for ability, because 1980 was a great year for me at county level, I'd played in an ODI for England and scored the fastest fifty by a debutant in history, and got picked for the overseas tour. So, it begs the question why was I not picked for this symbolic Test between two arch-rivals? Looking back now, I believe perhaps they were not ready for a black player in that type of event.'

Other black cricketers were subject to abuse. David 'Syd' Lawrence, who would in 1988 become the first British-born black man to play for England, made his county debut in 1981, aged just seventeen. 'I remember my first away game at Gloucestershire,' he said in a Sky Sports documentary in 2021. 'Somebody knocks on my door in the evening and one of my teammates has left a banana skin.'[4] Lawrence was left thinking, 'I'm a cricketer, what makes me different? Why would somebody want to do that, just because of the colour of my skin?'[5] He also suffered racial abuse from Yorkshire supporters who threw bananas at him while playing at Scarborough in 1984.[6] Phillip DeFreitas made his England debut in 1986. 'I lost count of the number of letters from the National Front saying, "If you turn up at the ground, if you play for England, we will get a sniper and shoot you and we will also kill your family,"' he said in the same documentary. 'I was receiving this two or three days before I go and play a Test match.'[7] The threats left him fearing for his life but also questioning his place in Britain. Both men told a similar story: they received little, if any, support at the time and did not speak out because they did not want to be seen as 'troublemakers'. Consequently, they suffered in silence.

While the racism in cricket tended to be insidious, suffered behind the scenes, in football, a less genteel and more tribal sport, it was pervasive. Outsiders were not welcome. Racism was the most extreme expression of that exclusionary sentiment. Consequently, some within the far-right National Front (NF) party saw the terraces as a fertile recruiting ground. Football hooligans were exactly the sort of people who could engage in the street violence against groups like the Anti-Nazi League and the immigrant community. The life experiences of these young working-class white men, many of them disaffected, made them more susceptible to right-wing, racist ideologies. As black players began breaking into the game and the England team in significant numbers in the late 1970s and early 1980s, they were seen as a metaphor for the immigrant population scapegoated for Britain's social and economic ills, perceived or otherwise.

Bulldog, the newspaper produced for the NF's youth wing, had a regular column, 'On the Football Front', and urged fans to 'join the fight for race and union'.[8] The party was particularly active at Arsenal, Chelsea, Millwall and West Ham in London, as well as Manchester United, Nottingham Forest and Leeds United,[9] distributing leaflets and selling merchandise outside their grounds. In his New Year statement in January 1981, David Lane, the chair of the Commission for Racial Equality (and, notably, a white, former Conservative MP), warned of the rising number of verbal and physical attacks on both the black and Jewish communities in their shops, places of worship and at football. The Commission called on managers and supporters to condemn such abuse and for stronger action from police and politicians at local and national level. 'These merchants of hate are still very few,' said Lane, 'but it is time for the moderate majority to ensure that their number and their menace grow no greater.'[10] Violence between Luton and Millwall fans during an FA Cup match in March 1985, which also saw police and Asian shopkeepers targeted, and between Birmingham City and Leeds United supporters a couple of months later, was blamed by some on the National Front. There was also evidence that a handful of Chelsea National Front members had been involved in the violence at the European Cup final between Liverpool and Juventus which led to thirty-nine deaths the same year.

While many of those who had a propensity to fight on the terraces also had a tendency to shout racist abuse, there was little
proof to support the notion that the far-right group was instrumental in the organisation of the terrace violence that marred the
game. The 1985 Popplewell Inquiry, which investigated the rioting between Leeds United and Birmingham City supporters, and
at the European Cup final, concluded that 'there is little to con-
nect [such groups] with organized violence', adding that 'it is right
that too much importance should not be attached to their activities'.[11] While some hooligans flaunted their membership of, or at
least sympathy for, the National Front and its fascist ideals, many
hooligan firms were multi-cultural in their make-up. Cass Pennant, whose mother emigrated from Jamaica, became a leading
member of West Ham's Inter City Firm (ICF). Riaz Khan, born
in Leicester to a Pakistani family, found sanctuary from the racism
he had suffered growing up by becoming a member of the Baby
Squad, the hooligan gang that followed the city's football team.
There is even some evidence that on at least one occasion the ICF
joined forces with the Socialist Workers Party to fight the National
Front.[12] It's undeniable, however, that one reason why the National
Front saw football as a recruiting ground was that not only those
who engaged in hooliganism, but also large sections of many
clubs' wider fanbase, frequently and openly expressed racist sentiments, many fans gaining a perverse sense of pride from the fact
that the team they supported contained no black players.

One photograph, taken during a Merseyside derby in February 1988, encapsulated this pervasive abuse and players' response
to it. It showed John Barnes, in Liverpool's famous all-red kit,
dismissively and deftly backheeling off the pitch a banana that
had been thrown at him by Everton fans. Although it had been
nine years since Viv Anderson had first played for England and
six since Justin Fashanu had moved to Nottingham Forest for a £1

million transfer fee, Barnes was the first black player to command a regular place in either Merseyside team. He had regularly experienced racism, both while he was at school and after he joined Watford at seventeen, particularly from fans of Chelsea, West Ham and Millwall, but also from opposition players who regularly called him a 'black bastard'.[13] It was by no means an uncommon experience. Biographies of players from the era are replete with stories of the abuse they suffered. Paul Canoville signed for Chelsea in December 1981, aged nineteen. When he made his debut in April the following year as a substitute against Crystal Palace at Selhurst Park he became the club's first black player. Writing about the game, he tells how, when he was sent out to warm up down the touchline, he heard 'loud individual voices through the noise: "Sit down you black cunt!", "You fucking wog – fuck off!" Over and over again. Lots of different people. I hardly dared look around. They were right behind me. I snatched a glimpse. They were all wearing blue shirts and scarves – Chelsea fans, my side's fans, faces screwed with pure hatred and anger, all directed at me . . . I felt physically sick. I was absolutely terrified.'[14] The club's owner and chairman Ken Bates received letters from supporters outraged by the abuse, but also letters castigating him for signing Canoville, one of which included the message 'No more blacks at Chelsea' and was also booby-trapped with eight razor blades that nearly sliced the fingers of the secretary who opened it.[15]

Despite this, Barnes was shocked by the response to his move to Anfield in the summer of 1987. After he signed, the walls of the stadium were daubed with racist slogans such 'Liverpool are white' and 'There's no black in the union jack'.[16] He received abusive letters from people angry that a black player should be playing for Liverpool, one of which implored him to 'go back to Africa and swing from the trees'.[17] The club received many more.

Barnes' stellar performances in his first few games for Liverpool, all away from home due to work taking place at Anfield, meant that the abuse from his own fans quickly evaporated. It was in four games against near-neighbours and rivals Everton that Barnes had what he called his 'first experience of mass racism'.[18] In a League Cup match at Anfield in late October, Everton fans spat at Barnes, threw bananas at him and chanted 'Niggerpool' and 'Everton are white'.[19] Philip Carter, the chairman of both Everton and the Football League, branded his own club's fans 'scum' and appealed for no repeat in the second match, also at Anfield, four days later. It was to no avail. It was in the third match, an FA Cup fifth-round tie at Goodison Park, that the infamous photograph of Barnes was taken. Televised, the game was watched by millions. That it pitted the First Division's two dominant teams against each other elevated its significance further. Abuse that was routine, that had been taking place every week in non-televised games, was now in the spotlight, laid bare for all to see. A month later the teams met for the fourth time, again at Goodison. This time there was little racism. 'Maybe people were embarrassed by the sight of so many bananas during the televised game,' Barnes wrote, 'maybe they became bored, maybe my refusal to respond stopped them trying.'[20]

What didn't stop were questions about his commitment to England. Barnes' first game came in an Under-21 match against Denmark at Copenhagen's Hvidovre Stadium in September 1982. Alongside Barnes, the line-up included three other black players, Paul Davis, Cyrille Regis and Chris Whyte, all of whom were subjected to racist abuse from England fans, many associated with the National Front. As the countries' senior teams were playing the following night at the city's Idrætsparken, there was also a sizable contingent of English journalists at the Under-21 match and they condemned the fans' behaviour in their reports.

Barnes' first full cap came the following year against Northern
Ireland. His first goal came in his tenth appearance in June 1984
against Brazil at the Maracanã in Rio de Janeiro. The *Seleção* had
gone unbeaten at the stadium since the 1960s, but this did not
faze Barnes. Just before half-time, he controlled a chip from Mark
Hateley with a cushioned touch off his chest just inside the Brazilian half. From his position on the left, he powered forwards, slicing
through four defenders, who seemed both drawn in and repelled
by some invisible force, inexplicably none making a meaningful
challenge. Barnes drifted towards the centre of the pitch until on
the edge of the six-yard box he deceived the keeper and slotted
home.

In the second half, Barnes returned the favour for Hateley, setting up England's second as they ran out 2−0 winners, but it was
his first-half wondergoal that grabbed the headlines. In the spiritual home of the Brazilian team, the Englishman had scored the
most Brazilian of goals. The hosts were happy to celebrate what
they had seen, one Rio-based paper referring to it as 'the greatest
goal ever seen at the Maracanã'.[21] For some England fans, it
counted for nothing. As the team flew from Rio to Santiago, they
found themselves on the same flight as a small coterie of National
Front supporters. Repeatedly abusive to Barnes and fellow black
players Viv Anderson and Mark Chamberlain, they also symbolically erased Barnes' performance, saying that England had only
won 1−0 because goals scored by black players didn't count.[22] It
was the expression of an extreme form of xenophobic nationalism, built on the idea that nationhood was exclusively white.

Despite winning another sixty-nine caps and scoring another
ten goals during the next eleven years, Barnes' Maracanã performance was for many the high point of his international career.
By his own admission, his performances for England were not
consistent; he was rarely able to replicate his club form at

international level. The reasons were varied and complex: his debut international goal set unrealistically high expectations; his club sides, especially Liverpool, gave him the freedom to operate in a way the national side simply did not; he was the type of flair player the England set-up of the 1980s just did not trust (Glenn Hoddle similarly failed to perform as well for country as for club). Many, however, questioned whether, having been born in Jamaica and moving to Britain with his family when he was thirteen, Barnes was truly committed to England. In February 1993, prior to a home World Cup qualifier against San Marino, the *Daily Mirror* printed a damaging story claiming that Barnes had told his teammates that he wanted the West Indies to beat England at cricket, and asking how he could represent the country under such circumstances. Barnes had been joking, but as a consequence he was booed throughout the match by the Wembley crowd.

The abuse on the plane, the newspaper article which grossly misrepresented dressing-room banter and the brickbats that followed in the stadium were all in their own way an articulation of the Thatcherite ethos that immigrants should assimilate British cultural norms and the belief that too few did so, a notion expressed in sporting terms by one of her most ardent supporters, Norman Tebbit. In an interview with the *Los Angeles Times* in April 1990, Tebbit argued that Britishness could be measured by whether an immigrant passed what he called the 'cricket test': that is, who did they support during a cricket match – England or the country of their birth. 'Which side do they cheer for?' he asked. 'It's an interesting test. Are you still harking back to where you came from, or where you are? And I think we've got real problems in that regard.'[23] The message was clear: you could be black, or British, but you couldn't be both.

III

As much as groups like the National Front sought to scapegoat the immigrant population for the high unemployment the country was experiencing, in reality the economic situation hit the non-white community hardest. At the start of the decade, 7 per cent of white men were unemployed with the rate among non-whites, who made up 3 per cent of the population, slightly higher at just over 10 per cent. However, while 12 per cent of whites were unemployed at the peak of the recession in 1982, the figure among non-whites leapt to nearly 30 per cent.[24] In turn, the young were disproportionately affected. Of the 1.2 million under-twenty-four-year-olds who were unemployed, more than half were aged sixteen to nineteen. Thus, while the Windrush generation had come to Britain because of the promise of work during a period of relative prosperity, their children's experience was altogether different.

These second-generation immigrants viewed sport as a viable way out of the poverty and lack of opportunity that confronted them. It was a grim echo of the story of the earliest black sportsmen in Britain, ex-slaves who gained a certain level of celebrity and wealth after being given their freedom in recognition of their achievements in bare-knuckle bouts organised by their former owners. Boxing was a sport in which black men were not only allowed to compete but also gained conspicuous success, thus it was attractive and became the first sport in which black sportsmen competed in significant numbers. There were still barriers to entry. It was not until 1948 that the British Boxing Board of Control (BBBofC), formed nineteen years earlier, abolished its rule requiring those contesting British titles to have two white parents, although still only those born in Britain could do so. In 1968, the

Board modified the rule, declaring that title challengers had to have been domiciled in Britain for ten years – five more than was required for British citizenship. Boxing's colour bar had been lowered, but only slightly.

By 1981, four out of ten British boxing titles were held by fighters of West Indian origin or descent, and one-third of the 448 professional boxers registered by the BBBofC were black. Many were inspired by Jamaican-born Bunny Sterling who became the first immigrant to win a British title, beating Mark Rowe at Wembley in 1970, and Antiguan-born Maurice Hope, who became the first black British immigrant to win a world title when he took the WBC light-middleweight belt from Rocky Mattioli in 1979. Hope, who moved to Britain in 1960 at the age of nine, saw himself as the representative of the black community and was keen to articulate the struggles that community faced. 'People like myself, and the footballers and athletes, we're black and have been pressed down. OK? But they can't keep us down forever 'cause we're going to show whites that we're better than them at their own game. We've made it, so we're showing other blacks they can make it as well.'[25]

One of the black British boxers who followed in his footsteps was Errol Christie. Christie, who died in 2017, was born in Leicester and raised in Coventry to parents who emigrated from Jamaica in the 1950s. He began boxing when he was eight years old and demonstrated prodigious talent in his amateur days, regularly winning by knockout. Captain of Team England between 1980 and 1983 – the first black man to hold the position – he earned a place in the *Guinness Book of Records* for being the only British boxer to win all ten available amateur titles. The high point came in 1982 when he was crowned the European Under-19 amateur champion. He turned professional the same year and his propensity for winning bouts decisively and early continued. Comparisons were made with the American world champion, Sugar Ray Leonard. By 1985, when he fought Mark Kaylor in a British middleweight title eliminator, Christie had lost just one of his first twenty-one professional fights, a shock first-round stoppage against the unfancied Belgian Jose Seys being his first defeat in seven years.

At twenty-four, Kaylor was a couple of years older than Christie. Born in in Canning Town in London's East End, he had also enjoyed a superb amateur career. Part of the Great Britain Olympic team at Moscow in 1980, he had lost in the quarter-finals on a split decision. After he turned professional, a run of twenty-four consecutive victories culminated with Kaylor knocking out Roy Gumbs in the fifth round of their fight for the British and Commonwealth middleweight titles in 1983, belts Kaylor would lose the following year to Tony Sibson. Christie's management team had been goading Kaylor over several months, regularly upping the cash on offer, and it seemed a matter of when, not if, they would face each other. The deal was finally struck for a fight on Bonfire Night, 5 November 1985; the purse was £82,500, a record for a non-title bout at the time. The winner would take home 60 per cent and earn the opportunity to fight Herrol 'Bomber' Graham, who by then held the British and European titles; the loser would see his career brought to a juddering halt. There was also something much more visceral at stake.

A month before the fight, Christie and Kaylor met at the Stakis Regency Casino in London's Russell Square for a press conference to announce their much-anticipated fight. Initially it played out in typical fashion. The fighters squared up to each other, fists held up in a pretence of menacing aggression for the benefit of the assembled press photographers. 'Think I came out on top there,' Christie joked after the pair separated. Kaylor, who was talking to someone else, ignored the comment at first but then his quick temper got the better of him. He turned and bent down, whispering something in his opponent's ear. Christie claimed Kaylor called him an 'ugly black bastard';[26] Kaylor subsequently denied using the word 'black'. It was enough to light Christie's own short fuse, and he jumped up from his seat. All pretence was dropped. This was no PR stunt; the pair began fighting for real.

Herrol Graham, the man who awaited the winner, was in attendance to add to the hype; he stepped in to separate the fighters but not for long. The brawl spilled out into the car park where Kaylor tried to barge Christie into a fountain. One of the press photographers captured the scene, Christie with his left hand on Kaylor's neck, Kaylor coiled to deliver a retaliatory blow. Behind them, a uniformed casino doorman, shock etched on his face, held out a hand in a futile attempt to intervene. 'You could say this was a clash of cultures that was being played out time and time again on working-class streets throughout Britain,' wrote Christie in his autobiography. 'White boot boys who wanted to put uppity niggers back in their box and black rude boys who weren't going to take their shit anymore.'[27]

'As far as Errol was concerned, he was fighting the king of the skinheads,' says Tony McMahon, who worked with Christie on his book, *No Place to Hide*.[28] 'His parents were of the generation who came off the boats to the "motherland" and felt a certain deference. Although they were treated abominably, there was a feeling that they had to behave themselves and mind their Ps & Qs,' adds McMahon. 'One of the things that changed that for Errol's generation, which came of age at the end of the 1970s, was the situation on the streets – the rise of the extreme right.'

In May 1981, while he was still a teenage amateur based in Coventry, Christie was one of around 8,000 people who joined a protest following the murder of twenty-year-old Asian student Satnam Singh Gill who was beaten, kicked and stabbed to death by a group of skinheads in broad daylight just yards from the city's main shopping precinct. Coordinated by the Coventry Committee against Racism, an umbrella organisation including thirty-seven community associations, temples and political groups, the march passed off peacefully until it reached Broadgate in the city centre and was confronted by a group of skinheads chanting 'Sieg Heil' and 'There ain't no black in the Union Jack'. Mounted police tried to keep the two factions apart but were met with a hail of glass bottles and rocks; eleven were injured and seventy-four arrests were made. The protest did nothing to prevent further racially motivated attacks in Coventry and the following month Dr Amal Dharry was stabbed in the heart by a skinhead and died ten days later. His seventeen-year-old killer had committed the crime for a bet. It was in this crucible that Christie's very public, very personal, campaign against racism was forged. It was also as a response to this that The Specials, the mixed-race 2-tone band from Coventry, released 'Ghost Town'. Written by founder of the band, Jerry Dammers, the song's haunting, nihilistic lyrics chronicled the racial tension and austerity that was spreading across the country, its slow reggae beat and accompanying Middle Eastern-style wail adding to the sense of poignancy. 'Britain was falling apart,' said Dammers years later. 'The overall sense I wanted to convey was impending doom.'[29]

IV

Given its subject matter, the release of 'Ghost Town' was eerily timed. The day before it reached No. 1 in the charts on 11 July, a series of riots broke out across the country, although there had been warning signs the previous year. In April 1980 police, some with dogs, raided the Black and White Café, in the rundown St Paul's district of Bristol, on suspicion of the illegal sale of alcohol and cannabis. The café was a meeting place for black residents and had taken on greater significance following the closure of similar establishments by the authorities, thus the raid heightened the feeling of a community under attack. The police, who subsequently claimed they thought the operation would be routine, soon found themselves in confrontation with a growing crowd outside the café. Stones and other missiles were thrown and police vehicles attending the scene overturned, one set alight. At around 7.30 p.m., the police withdrew, and the trouble petered out around midnight. Twelve people were later charged with riotous assembly, although none were found guilty. In the aftermath police and local and national politicians expressed their shock, *The Times*' journalist Fred Emery noting that 'no one at Westminster would have even shortlisted Bristol as the potential powder keg which many afterwards said it had long been'.[30] This suggested an unwillingness to recognise the concerns and growing frustrations of the black community, not least because they had been given a voice just a year before in a study of life for black people in the city by sociologist Ken Pryce, who had identified St Paul's as an area with high potential for trouble. Significantly, it was called *Endless Pressure*.

The following January, thirteen black youngsters were killed in a house fire during a sixteenth birthday party in New Cross in south-east London. The youngest, Andrew Gooding, was only fourteen; ten others were also teenagers. A fourteenth victim, Anthony Berbeck, who was never able to come to terms with the trauma of losing his friends in the blaze, later took his own life. Neither the queen nor Margaret Thatcher sent messages of condolence, something they both did when forty-eight teenagers died in a nightclub fire in Ireland five weeks later; then the victims were white. The slogan 'Thirteen dead and nothing said' became widely used as members of the local community accused police of not taking seriously their claims that the fire had been the result of a racially motivated arson attack. Other black homes in the area had been attacked and a black community centre had recently been burned down. The owner of the house in which the party took place had also received racist letters. Although an inquest later that year would record an open verdict (as would a second inquest in 2004), this perceived indifference led to the organisation of the Black People's Day of Action. Around 10,000 gathered at the burned-out house, laid flowers and then marched for seven hours through some of London's busiest streets. It was a watershed moment, signalling a collective response from the black community and an organised demand to be heard.

Yet the authorities did little to change their attitudes. In April, police launched Operation Swamp 81, during which ten squads of between five and eleven officers patrolled Brixton's streets for a week. Police questioned 943 people, of which just over 50 per cent were black, and made 118 arrests; of those seventy-five were charged but only one with a serious crime. The operation had ultimately failed as a means of targeting crime, but it heightened tensions. When officers were spotted trying to help an injured black man, their actions were misinterpreted, triggering three days of unrest that would see 82 arrested, 279 police officers and an estimated 45 members of the public injured and 145 businesses damaged. For the first time on the British mainland, petrol bombs were thrown. The destruction, while not necessarily planned, was not random. A pub where the landlord discriminated against blacks was targeted, as was a newsagent that refused to serve homosexuals, while the local law centre and an anarchist bookshop were both left untouched.

There was then six weeks of calm, until in early July skinheads heading for a concert featuring third-generation punk bands The 4-Skins and The Business in Southall's Hambrough Tavern,

which had recently been sued for barring ethnic minority customers, attacked locals, smashed windows and chanted National Front
slogans. The area had suffered racial violence in the past. In 1976,
eighteen-year-old Sikh student Gurdip Singh Chaggar had been
murdered by a gang of white youths and three years later, during
an Anti-Nazi League demonstration, New Zealander Blair Peach
died after being struck on the head 'almost certainly' by an officer
from the Met's riot squad.[31] This time local Asian youths fought
back. Some 110 people were hospitalised and the Hambrough
was burned to the ground. On the same night in Toxteth in Liverpool, police tried to arrest a black man they thought was stealing
a motorbike. It was in fact his own. A small group threw stones at
the officers in a bid to assist his escape and fighting lasted for several hours. The following day police poured into the area and the
fighting began again on a much larger scale. On the second night,
some 229 officers were hospitalised, and it was clear that the
police had lost control; in a futile effort to regain it – rioting would
last nine days in total – they deployed CS gas, another first in
mainland Britain. The same weekend there were two nights of
major rioting in Manchester's Moss Side and trouble spread to
most major cities across the country. Even in the rural market
town of Cirencester, Gloucestershire, a police car was firebombed.
There was one last riot, again in Toxteth, on 28 July, the day
before the royal wedding of Prince Charles and Lady Diana.
Then the trouble died out as quickly as it had begun.

While there was no single overarching cause and a variety of
local factors were at play, it could not be denied that in Brixton
and Toxteth the trigger had been specific police actions that local
black youths had interpreted as harassment, an issue addressed by
Lord Scarman, who had been tasked with reporting on the causes
of the Brixton riot. He identified racial prejudice among some
Metropolitan Police officers, recommending this should become

a sackable offence (a recommendation that was rejected) but determined that the force itself was not inherently racist and that '"Institutional racism" does not exist in Britain'.[32] He also highlighted the lack of ethnic minority officers (at that time the 24,000-strong force included fewer than 200 non-white officers) and argued that more should be done to recruit officers from minority backgrounds. Some felt his findings did not go far enough, but significantly for the first time it provided official acknowledgement of distrust in the police. Scarman also argued that the wider social context could not be ignored, recommending that the government looked to reduce inequalities in housing, education and employment and that in the short term this should be enacted by positive discrimination. This largely liberal tone meant Scarman's report was, according to Thatcher biographer Hugo Young, 'a rare artifact of the Thatcher years couched in pre-Thatcherite language'.[33] Ultimately, most of his recommendations about social reform were ignored, while those he made about strengthening the police were enacted.

It was thus perhaps inevitable that there would eventually be further trouble. In the space of just under four weeks in September and early October 1985, a series of riots took place in Handsworth in Birmingham, Brixton, Toxteth and the north London housing estate of Broadwater Farm, many of which seemed to have the same underlying causes as the 1981 trouble, in particular heavy-handed policing that worsened already poor relations with black residents. Trouble in Brixton was sparked by the shooting of Dorothy Groce when police burst into her house looking for her son Michael in connection with a firearms offence. Dorothy was left paralysed from the waist down, but rumours spread throughout the community that she had been killed. A group gathered outside the local police station chanting 'murderers' and demanding disciplinary action. Mild skirmishes turned into two days of rioting during which photo-journalist David Hodge died, and fifty-three other people were injured. A week later, Cynthia Jarrett died from heart failure after she had been pushed over by an officer during a police search of her home following her son's arrest. Jarrett's family led a peaceful march to Tottenham police station, again demanding justice, and although they made it clear they wanted no trouble, once more this spilled over into violence. As before, stones and petrol bombs were thrown, and cars and shops set alight. By midnight, fifty-eight policemen and twenty-four other people had been taken to hospital. Two police were shot and a third PC, Keith Blakelock, died after being set upon. He suffered forty stabbing injuries, eight of them to the head. Six men were charged with Blakelock's murder and three convicted in 1987, although those convictions were overturned four years later when it was found police had tampered with their handwritten notes of the interrogations.

It was against this backdrop, just three days after the Broadwater Farm riots, that Christie and Kaylor's photoshoot brawl took place, adding fuel to a still smouldering fire. The pair were charged with bringing the sport into disrepute by the British Boxing Board of Control, Kaylor subsequently fined £15,000 and Christie £5,000. Commander David Polkinghorne, in charge of policing the Wembley event, wrote to the BBBofC and urged them to postpone the fight, while Al Hamilton, the Jamaican-born journalist and founder of the Commonwealth Sports Awards, called on the government to ban it, warning that the crowd would be dominated by Kaylor fans, many also supporters of West Ham United, which had a large National Front contingent. There was widespread concern that the fight would become an extension of the riots. Such fears were not unwarranted; trouble at boxing was a regular occurrence, particularly when a black boxer beat a white opponent.

The most infamous incident came in September 1980 when American fighter Marvelous Marvin Hagler, who went on to dominate the middleweight division for much of the decade, took the WBA/WBC titles off Alan 'Boom Boom' Minter with a commanding, aggressive display at Wembley Arena. The fight was infused with racial tension. In the build-up, Minter was reported as saying he 'did not intend to lose to a black man', Hagler that he 'did not shake hands with white flesh'.[34] Both said they were misquoted, Minter claiming he had said 'that black man' and Hagler pointing out that he only ever shook hands with his opponents after fights. Their 'clarifications' did little to dampen the growing ill feeling. Whatever the truth, Minter, who sported Union Jack underpants at the weigh-in, became the unofficial poster boy of white English racists. On the night, the 10,000-strong crowd was drunken, boisterous, malevolent. It included a significant contingent of supporters of the National Front. Some were wearing Beefeater costumes; many were draped in Union Flags. In an ill-advised move, beer was being sold by the crate. Leigh Montville, there as a correspondent for Hagler's hometown paper the *Boston Globe*, was filled with foreboding as he stood in the lobby and watched scores of fans hoisting them onto their shoulders before heading into the arena. 'I couldn't have anticipated what was going to happen,' he said years later, 'but I remember thinking that no good was going to come of this.'[35]

The bookies had the champion down as the marginal favourite, but Hagler was never in trouble. He took to his task with brutal efficiency, quickly opening cuts over both of Minter's eyes, and then mercilessly attacking them, leaving the Englishman struggling to see through a mask of blood. The fight was over just one minute and forty-five seconds into the third round, when referee Carlos Berrocal stopped the contest. Almost immediately the arena descended into chaos. Fans disappointed at the home favourite's defeat and enraged by what they felt was an unjustified early stoppage by the referee, who was also black, vented their anger by hurling bottles and cans into the ring. Hagler was forced to flee under police escort. He later said the experience made him feel like a thief, not a new world champion. A window of his car was smashed as he left the venue and he vowed never to fight in Britain again. While Hagler had police protection, VIPs and journalists had to fend for themselves, some using their chairs as shields. ABC Sports' Howard Cossell took refuge under the ring apron, and his BBC counterpart Harry Carpenter was struck on the head by a bottle. It was the 'low point' of his time commentating. 'Wembley Arena was reeking not so much of nationalism,' Carpenter said, 'but had a decidedly rancid smell of racialism.'[36]

Five years later, that stench still hung heavy in the air but, for the promoters, calling off the Christie–Kaylor fight was unthinkable; there was too much money at stake. So, the fighters were brought back together for a conciliatory public handshake. Unlike the brawl, it was a PR stunt and did nothing to dissipate the tension over the next two and a half weeks. Like Minter, Kaylor was adopted as a totem of a constituency of white English racists. Christie was subjected to death threats and his parents warned not to attend the fight.

When the night came around, as Christie strode out from his dressing room he faced a sustained volley of racial abuse from what *Boxing News* labelled 'the extreme right-wing fascist element in Britain, an element that is represented in Kaylor's home territory of West Ham'.[37] For Christie, it was akin to a 'lynch mob'.[38] Police were guarding every entrance; they threw a protective cordon around the boxing ring. Unlike during the Hagler/Minter fight, no alcohol was on sale inside the arena. Cass Pennant had been hired by Terry Lawless, Kaylor's manager, to organise security. Pennant cherry-picked people he knew could command respect, spot troublemakers and squash any incidents of violence before they took place. They patrolled the venue in T-shirts bearing the logo 'Keep it Cool', but the atmosphere was still febrile; during the first round someone let off a firework. In the middle of all this, a boxing match took place.

The fighters began where they had left off in the casino car park, attacking each other with ferocious intensity. Both were knocked down in the first round, and the fight quickly became a battle of attrition. The winning blow came in the eighth round when Kaylor caught Christie with a long right and then a left hook, leaving his opponent face down on the canvas. Christie crawled towards his corner and tried to regain his feet; it was to no avail. Kaylor leapt onto the ropes in celebration and although Christie was booed as he left the ring, there was no repeat of the Hagler/Minter riot that many had feared. Victory for the crowd favourite, the low number of Christie supporters in attendance, the alcohol ban, the presence of the police and Pennant's security operation all helped prevent the event descending into violence.

Almost a year to the day later, Kaylor faced Graham at the same venue and lost, like Christie, in the eighth round. He would not win another title. For Christie, once so imperious, defeat became a regular occurrence: he lost six of his next twelve fights and quit boxing in 1993. A fighter who had shown so much promise and reached such heights as an amateur became defined publicly and personally by just one defeat as a professional. 'I think the Kaylor fight just switched something in his head,' says McMahon. 'For Errol it was like the coming together of his street fighting past and his boxing career. He felt his whole life had been leading up to that moment, and then he fucked up. He felt he had betrayed every black person in Britain by losing. That's a heavy cross to bear.' Christie could only characterise his loss in devastating terms, tortured by the belief he had let his community down.

It was, he felt, the end of his 'entire life's struggle'. Worse still, it had happened 'in plain view of my enemies'.[39]

V

In the 1980s, boxing became one of the weapons in the battle for TV ratings as the BBC and ITV scrambled to find sports to fill their schedules. World title bouts, those featuring the likes of Muhammad Ali and Roberto Duran, had always been televised, but in the 1980s boxing became a regular fixture in the weekend schedules. Entrepreneurial managers like Frank Warren and Micky Duff marshalled stables of fighters at all levels and all weights and, prior to his defeat to Kaylor, Christie was one of the biggest, becoming ITV's main boxing attraction. In one notable publicity photograph for the network, he stood, bare-chested in his boxing shorts, brandishing a Union Flag on a raised platform at the back of a crowd of light-entertainment stars: the likes of David Jason, Ernie Wise and Anneka Rice. Christie was the only black man in a sea of white faces. Despite this, Christie felt that he was not earning the sort of money that his white counterparts were from marketing and advertising deals. After numerous attempts to tap into this sort of revenue, it became clear to him that those in charge of such budgets thought 'black faces didn't sell products'. As a consequence, he wrote, they were 'invisible on the front of fashion magazines or TV ads'.[40]

Where Christie and most other black British boxers were unable to secure lucrative endorsement deals, one was, although it came at something of a personal cost. Despite losing the two heavyweight title bouts that he fought during the decade, against Tim Witherspoon in 1986, and Mike Tyson in 1989, Frank Bruno became one of the most popular black British celebrities of the

1980s. He was a regular on TV entertainment programmes such as *Family Fortunes*, *Comic Relief* and *The Little and Large Show*, became the face of products such as HP Sauce, performed in pantomimes and was immortalised by his own *Spitting Image* puppet. Born in Wandsworth in south London in 1961, Bruno was the youngest of six children. Expelled from school at eleven for punching a teacher, the young Bruno began channelling his energies into boxing and turned pro in 1982. Despite his imposing stature – Bruno stands at 6ft 3in. and had a fighting weight of 17 stone 12 lb – his celebrity persona was safe and unthreatening.

Bruno formed an entertaining double act with BBC boxing commentator Harry Carpenter which spawned Bruno's catchphrase 'You know what I mean, 'arry?' more often than not accompanied by a resonant, friendly chuckle. He was packaged by his management team of Duff and Terry Lawless in a way that meant he could be keenly embraced by the *Sun* and the BBC and thus become embedded in the wider public consciousness as a patriotic national symbol. This public persona was underpinned by his avowedly conservative politics. 'I am a fiercely patriotic Royalist, and consider myself a Britisher to the bone,'[41] Bruno wrote in an early biography, also declaring himself 'a dedicated fan of Maggie Thatcher'.[42]

Professor Ben Carrington argued that in the 1980s Bruno 'was given the choice [. . .] to be black *or* British, and he chose to be British',[43] passing Norman Tebbit's 'cricket test', no doubt with flying colours. It was an assimilationist version of black masculinity that was deeply problematic for many in the black community. 'Bruno was perceived as an Uncle Tom, we all thought he was a sell-out,' says Spencer Fearon, a boxing historian and commentator, who grew up in London during the 1980s.[44] 'People used to take the mickey out of him because they thought he was so dumb. He is incredibly intelligent – don't be fooled by what you see on

TV – but because he was just seen as this dumb black guy, that's why we didn't like him,' Fearon adds. 'He was a darling to white Britain; he was "Our Frank", but he had to play it safe and kinda dissociate himself from his blackness. He just thought, "I'm the one who's being accepted to this hierarchical status, so I'm just going to continue doing what I'm doing. I'm going to be friendly; I'm going to be inoffensive," and I think his inoffensiveness was offensive to black people; it was like "fuck this shit". Hence why someone like Muhammad Ali was greatly idolised. Black folks were looking for this rebel, for someone to stand up and say certain things, which we didn't get, unfortunately, from Frank Bruno.'

Bruno's unwillingness to confront racial inequality (he once wrote, 'I have never got involved in the black-white thing'[45]) was exemplified when he fought South African Gerrie Coetzee at the height of the anti-apartheid campaign, despite numerous protests against the bout and appeals for Bruno to pull out from other (black) fighters such as Maurice Hope and John Conteh.[46] Bruno won by a knockout in the first round, having argued that he had to take part as it was an eliminator to face Witherspoon, the defending WBA heavyweight champion (although some suggested Bruno could have targeted the WBC or IBF belts instead).

Bruno would fight for the world title again in 1993 against Lennox Lewis – another bout he would lose. The build-up, which took place in the aftermath of the murder of black teenager Stephen Lawrence by a gang of white youths, was infused with questions of race and national identity. Lewis, like Bruno, was born in London to Jamaican parents, but he moved to Canada aged twelve, winning gold for the country in the 1988 Olympics. Bruno played on this, claiming that his opponent was '. . . not British', adding, 'Nobody cares about Lennox Lewis in Britain.'[47] Lewis responded by questioning Bruno's blackness, referring to him as an 'Uncle Tom'.[48]

It was an accusation that cut deep. Two years later Bruno beat

Oliver McCall on points at Wembley after twelve gruelling rounds. The world title he had craved for so long was finally his. Interviewed in the ring live on Sky Sports by Ian Darke in the immediate aftermath, Bruno was close to tears. Ignoring Darke's questions, his voice breaking with emotion, the new champion declared, 'I'm not an Uncle Tom, man, no way. I love my brother, I'm not an Uncle Tom.' In the three-minute interview, he would repeat the sentiment eleven times. It was, Fearon says, a 'profound moment', the closest that Bruno came to publicly acknowledging how he was perceived. Carrington characterised it as Bruno 'coming out'; now that he had finally reached the summit of his sport, he could 'announce, publicly, the secret he had long been carrying with him, that he was in fact black British and had been for a long time'.[49] In the decades since, Fearon has come to know Bruno through his work in the sport. His opinion has changed, and he acknowledges that in the 1980s, when black cricketers were receiving death threats for playing for England, and racist abuse was commonplace in football, the choices open to Bruno might not have been as straightforward as they seemed. 'As a kid I weren't too sure on him, but where I stand now, I have a totality of love for the man,' says Fearon. 'Now that I know Frank Bruno, I know that he had to be a chameleon to survive the environment he was in at the time.'

PART III:

CONFLICT

CHAPTER 8

Where the Streets Have No Name

I

FROM the moment he appeared in the doorway of the aeroplane that had brought him to Belfast airport, his young son Blain in his arms, to the moment he made an impromptu speech on the balcony of the city's Royal Hall several hours later, Barry McGuigan was mobbed by well-wishers. Just two days earlier, on 8 June 1985, he had won the WBA world featherweight belt after a hard-fought points win over defending champion Eusebio Pedroza in London. McGuigan had intended to head straight for his family home in Clones just south of the Irish border, but after he was told that Belfast's Lord Mayor had organised a victory parade, he changed his plans. Some 70,000 lined the Royal Avenue to greet their hero as he made his way down the street on the back of a lorry. It took an hour to cover 500 yards, the scenes compared to those on VE Day. It was a great year for Northern Irish sport. The country's football team were on their way to qualifying for their second consecutive World Cup, Dennis Taylor won snooker's world championship and motorcyclist Joey Dunlop won his fourth consecutive TT Formula One world title. However, it was McGuigan who truly captured the public's imagination, lauded not only for his victory in the ring but also what it meant outside.

Dubbed 'the Clones Cyclone', McGuigan had come to prominence as a teenager in the mid-1970s. The organisation of amateur boxing on both sides of the Irish border was indicative of the island's complex history. After the foundation of the Republic in 1922, the sport continued to be run on an all-Ireland basis. However, this led to anomalous situations. McGuigan won gold for Northern Ireland at the Commonwealth Games in Edmonton in 1978. However, two years later at the Moscow Olympics, he fought for Ireland. Northern Irish boxers had no other option because there was no separate governing body for Northern Ireland, and at the Games a competitor's 'nationality' was determined by a sport's international federation, on the basis of which national organisations were affiliated to them. When he turned professional, McGuigan had a choice to make and, as he wanted to fight for the British title, he applied for British citizenship. Not everyone welcomed the decision. Graffiti labelling him 'Barry the Brit' went up on the walls of west Belfast.

From a Catholic family – his grandfather had been a captain in the IRA in the 1920s – McGuigan was married to a Protestant, his childhood sweetheart Sandra. He would later acknowledge that 'everything I did took place against the backdrop of the Troubles',[1] but McGuigan refused to take sides. Instead he used his position to promote unity and peace. He rejected the symbols that might have been seen as a show of allegiance to one side or the other, choosing to fight in blue velvet shorts with a white dove emblazoned on the leg. Before he fought, his father gave a rendition of 'Danny Boy', one of the few songs in Ireland sung by Catholics and Protestants alike. The exhortation 'Let Barry do the fighting' became well known on both sides of the border.

The fight against Pedroza, who had made nineteen successful

defences of his title over seven years and was unbeaten in more than a decade, was the pinnacle of McGuigan's career. *El Alacran* (the Scorpion) refused to fight at Belfast's King's Hall, where the atmosphere could overwhelm McGuigan's opponents, so the contest was taken to Queens Park Rangers' ground, Loftus Road, in west London. It was still effectively a home bout for McGuigan. On the morning of the fight, some 3,000 turned up for the weigh-in at the Odeon Leicester Square. The fight itself was a 27,000 sell-out. Such was the fervour for McGuigan inside that it took him twelve minutes to reach the ring from his dressing room. Some 19.5 million[2] were watching at home. McGuigan knew his ageing, but still brilliant, opponent was technically superior, so planned to fight at a pace that would tire out the Panamanian and take away that advantage. The champion had the better of the opening six rounds, but the turning point came in the seventh when McGuigan caught him with a right to the head. Pedroza survived a count to eight and the fight continued. Neither man could land a decisive blow in the remaining eight rounds, but the challenger had done enough. McGuigan was declared winner by unanimous verdict.

After his welcome in Belfast, McGuigan found thousands more were waiting in his hometown of Clones. A few days later, it was on to Dublin where 250,000 filled the streets to hail his achievement. By the end of the year he had been named the inaugural winner of the RTÉ Sportsperson of the Year award and BBC Sports Personality of the Year, the first person not born in the UK to win the award. However, while many on both sides of the sectarian divide cheered him on during his pursuit of the world title, it's hard to measure what impact he actually had. The few hours that he spent in the ring and the jubilant scenes of celebration that his victories prompted were in many respects just a brief ceasefire. As one McGuigan fan told Harry Carpenter at the time: 'Sure, while he's fighting, we're behind him as one. But when it's over and we move outside . . .'³ His sentence went unfinished, but the message was clear.

The Troubles were born of the anger many Catholics felt at the systematic discrimination they were suffering in housing and employment. Inspired by civil rights protests in America, young nationalist leaders like John Hume, Austin Currie and Bernadette Devlin began challenging the status quo. However, the response of loyalists and the British state magnified sectarian divisions. British troops returned to the streets; the IRA was rejuvenated. In 1972, the British government prorogued the parliament at Stormont, imposing direct rule. It was the worst year of what had become known as the Troubles. More than 500 people were killed, over half of them civilians. Thirteen were shot dead by the British Army on 30 January and another fourteen wounded during a peaceful march on what became known as Bloody Sunday.

In the 1980s, the IRA increasingly took their campaign onto the British mainland. In October 1981, a device planted outside Chelsea Barracks killed two people, both civilians, and injured forty others, twenty-three of whom were soldiers. The following July a bomb placed under a bandstand in Regent's Park killed seven military bandsmen. Earlier in the day, a nail bomb was detonated in Hyde Park, killing four members of the Household Cavalry. However, it was the grim pictures of the mutilated corpses of seven horses lying in pools of their own blood that shocked the nation. One of the injured horses, Sefton, was given a 50/50 chance of survival but pulled through after eight hours of surgery. Get-well messages flooded in, as did £620,000 in donations which helped fund a new surgical wing at the Royal Veterinary College. Sefton became a celebrity, appearing on numerous TV shows and being named Horse of the Year.

Given such goodwill, it was little wonder that the kidnapping of Shergar the following year gripped the nation. Owned by the

Aga Khan, the bay colt had won the 1981 Epsom Derby by ten lengths, the longest winning margin in the race's history. This was followed by victories in the Irish Derby and the King George VI and Queen Elizabeth stakes before he was retired to stud. His owner turned down offers to buy him, instead syndicating him at a value of £10 million.[4] On 8 February 1983, a group of machine-gun-toting men in balaclavas descended on the Ballymany Stud in Newbridge, Co. Kildare and bundled Shergar into a horsebox. They were widely suspected to be members of the IRA, although the group never claimed responsibility. A ransom demand of £2 million, was subsequently made. Negotiations soon broke down and Shergar was never recovered.

The year ended with another six people being killed by a bomb left in a car outside a side entrance to the department store Harrods in London. The IRA's most audacious act came in September 1984, eight months before McGuigan's fight with Pedroza, when they bombed the Grand Hotel in Brighton, in which many Conservative politicians were staying during their party conference. Not since the shooting of Spencer Perceval in 1812 had a British prime minister been assassinated, and not since the Gunpowder Plot of 1605 had there been an attempt to wipe out the entire government. The bomb, which was on a long-delay timer, had been planted by Patrick Magee three weeks earlier. Posing as a guest, he had hidden the device behind the panel of a bath of a sixth-floor room. It triggered at just before three o'clock on the final morning of the Conservative Party conference. Five people were killed, including the MP Sir Anthony Berry, and thirty-four injured, among them Thatcher's close ally Norman Tebbit, the party chairman, and his wife, Margaret, who was left permanently disabled. The chief whip John Wakeham was the last person to be pulled from the rubble alive, having been trapped for seven hours. His wife, Roberta, died.

As the country woke to news footage of the devastation – the hotel's collapsed façade eerily lit by arc lights as the fire service searched for survivors – many saw it as a huge propaganda coup for the IRA. The group claimed responsibility: 'Today we were unlucky, but remember we only have to be lucky once.'[5] Their primary target had indeed been lucky. Although Margaret Thatcher's hotel suite bathroom was destroyed, she was uninjured. Just a few hours later, she delivered a defiant speech to the conference as scheduled. 'The fact that we are gathered here now, shocked but composed and determined, is a sign not only that this attack has failed, but that all attempts to destroy democracy by terrorism will fail,' she told her audience.[6]

Thatcher's Britishness, which was in many respects an extension of Englishness, had little room to accommodate Celtic, and in particular Irish nationalist, sensitivities. The attempt on her own life, coupled with the assassination of Airey Neave, one of her closest colleagues who had been killed by a car bomb shortly before the 1979 general election, reinforced her resolve to offer no compromise to Republicans. Sinn Féin, the IRA's political wing, were locked out of talks for the rest of the decade, their voices literally being taken away by broadcasting restrictions introduced in 1988 that determined that they should be dubbed. The party had no involvement in the Anglo-Irish agreement, which was signed in November 1985 and recognised the right of the Irish government to have a say in a range of issues affecting the north, including security, the economy and even which flags could be flown.

The agreement also came as a shock to Unionists. Although it had partly been designed to improve cross-border security by removing the ability of those responsible for terrorist acts in the north to escape to the south with impunity, they did not see it that way. The month after the agreement was signed, all fifteen Unionist MPs demonstrated their opposition by resigning their seats and triggering a series of by-elections. 'British we are, British we remain,' Ian Paisley told a crowd of 100,000 who gathered outside Belfast City Hall in protest. 'Now Mrs Thatcher tells us that the Republic must have some say in our province, we say "never, never, never, never".'[7]

In this context, McGuigan's repeated pleas for peace seemed increasingly forlorn; even he accepted that although trouble abated when he fought, the peace did not last.[8] In the wake of the Anglo-Irish agreement, the brutal, attritional tit-for-tat violence escalated; a death toll that had fallen for three consecutive years between 1983 and 1985 rose steadily in the following three. Even Thatcher was later moved to acknowledge that 'Our concessions alienated the Unionists without gaining the level of security co-operation we had a right to expect.'[9] There were victims on both sides, as well as among British military personnel. The worst atrocity occurred on 8 November 1987 when an IRA bomb went off during a Remembrance Day parade in Enniskillen, Co. Fermanagh, killing eleven and injuring sixty-three, one of whom died after thirteen years in a coma. It seemed there was no escape from the relentless nature of the conflict.

II

McGuigan may have offered brief respite from the Troubles, but other sports in Ireland, where clubs were perceived as being either 'green' (Catholic) or 'orange' (Protestant), served only to reflect, or, worse, accentuate, Northern Ireland's deep divisions. Founded in 1884, the Gaelic Athletic Association (GAA) was part of a wider revival of Gaelic culture, which also included the Irish language, literature and religion, aimed at preventing the onset of widespread British cultural hegemony. Political nationalism was at the association's core, its founder Michael Cusack arguing that if Irish people continued to play British sports, in particular football and cricket, so-called 'Garrison games' due to their links with the military, then indigenous Irish culture would be destroyed. Thus, the GAA promoted what it called 'Irish native games', in particular hurling and Gaelic football, and infused them with a distinct notion of Irishness. This attitude was indicative of the link between politics and sport, between *identity* and sport. It was also a tacit acknowledgement and rejection of the key role sport played in enforcing the cultural mores of Britain throughout its empire, which was growing in wealth and power at the same time modern sport was developing. The other Celtic nations, Scotland and Wales, embraced English sports, using them as an arena in which to assert their distinct national characteristics. 'Fitba' against the auld enemy at Hampden Park and rugby at Cardiff Arms Park enabled Scottishness and Welshness to be fed by an antagonism towards, and defined in opposition to, the English.

From the outset, the GAA took a more exclusionary route. Rules were introduced excluding members of the Royal Ulster Constabulary (RUC) and the British Army from membership and also banning GAA members from playing, promoting, or attending 'foreign games' (namely football, hockey and rugby, cricket being added to the list shortly after). The latter regulation was eventually lifted in 1971, the increased ownership of televisions across the country during the 1960s, coupled with the decision of RTÉ, the national broadcaster, to screen rugby and football internationals, creating the inconsistency of people potentially being banned from watching a match in person that they could watch without censure in the comfort of their own homes.

Despite this, in the north the GAA and its associated clubs still offered nationalists an unambiguous expression of dissenting Irish identity in a state ruled by the British. The association's ethos meant it played a central role within the Catholic community, something not lost on Republican prisoners who went on hunger strike in early 1981. The strike was the culmination of a series of escalating protests aimed at regaining special category status for the campaigners who demanded to be treated not like ordinary criminals, but as political prisoners. Among other things, they wanted to be allowed to wear their own clothes, be exempt from work duties and have the right of free association with other political prisoners. These rights had been granted in 1972 (after another hunger strike) but were subsequently rescinded four years later in the wake of the Gardiner Report. Following this, a new prison complex, HMP Maze, was built on the site of the former Long Kesh Detention Centre. Referred to colloquially as 'The Maze' or 'the H Blocks' because of its eight 'H'-shaped buildings, it was where anyone convicted of a 'scheduled terrorist offence' was imprisoned after 1 March 1976. This change in policy prompted a campaign to have the rights restored. Prisoners initially refused to wear clothes, either going naked or just using a blanket for cover, then they took to smearing excrement on their cell walls and refusing to wash – the so-called 'dirty protests'. A fifty-three-day hunger strike followed, after which the prisoners claimed concessions had been granted. Margaret Thatcher rejected this assertion, saying that it was 'wholly false'.[10] A second hunger strike was all but inevitable, and so it began on 1 March 1981.

At the time, there were approximately 420 prisoners involved in the campaign, of which around a quarter were GAA members.[11] They felt it was important to gain backing from across nationalist Ireland, and along with campaigners outside jail, believed that if they could get the GAA to issue a statement of support then other cultural organisations and trades unions would follow suit. They targeted the association at all levels, writing letters, sometimes smuggled out of jail on toilet or cigarette paper, highlighting the humanitarian aspect of their campaign. This enabled the GAA, which was an avowedly 'non-party-political' organisation, to offer tacit support by determining that as long as any action by its members was peaceful, it was not in breach of its rules. This did not stop numerous displays of support both official and unofficial. Club banners were displayed at H-block marches, although it is not clear if such action had been sanctioned by the respective clubs, and there were demonstrations at GAA games. Some led to clashes between fans and the Garda; Union Jacks were burned at others. In July, during the Ulster Senior Football Championship final between Down and Armagh at Clones, about an hundred protesters carrying banners supporting the hunger strikers ran onto the pitch and formed themselves into an 'H'. Some were concerned that a heavy-handed reaction from the Garda could have caused a riot and they were persuaded not to intervene.

By then, the relationship between the National H-Block Committee, a pressure group supporting the prisoners, and the GAA had become more complex as the former had nominated Bobby Sands for the Fermanagh and South Tyrone by-election caused by the death of Frank Maguire, an independent Republican MP. Sands stood under the political affiliation 'Anti H-block'. Numerous GAA members canvassed for him throughout the brief election campaign. Various clubs in the area placed newspaper advertisements urging their members to vote for Sands and held election meetings after games. Joe Keohane, who had a celebrated Gaelic football career with Kerry in the 1930s and 1940s, spoke in support of Sands at a rally on the day before the election, his status as a GAA star being used in publicity material.[12] Apart from Harry West of the Ulster Unionist Party, all other candidates stood aside, and Sands won with 51.2 per cent of the vote. His election, and the nomination of nine other hunger strikers as candidates for the summer's general election in the south, forced the GAA's hand. Such action ran counter to its 'non-party political' ethos, and the association issued a statement saying: 'It is not possible for GAA clubs, county boards or other units to be involved in any way.'[13] There was a qualification: 'What members do as individuals will, of course, be their own business.'[14] Many clubs in the north simply ignored the directive.

Partly because of his election success, Sands became the most well-known of the hunger strikers, but his high profile was also because he was the first to die, on 5 May, after he had gone sixty-six days without food. Three more hunger strikers passed away before the month was out. Two more died in July, four more in August. Each death sparked riots, each funeral drew thousands of mourners. However, the grim reality was the campaign had achieved maximum effect in the immediate aftermath of Sands' passing and subsequently produced diminishing returns. By the time the strike was called off due to intervention of the families of the remaining strikers in October, coincidentally on the day of the All-Ireland hurling final, no concessions had been gained. Indeed, the Representation of the People Act 1981 was passed to prevent prisoners serving sentences of more than one year from standing for election to parliament and thus a repeat of Sands' victory. Thatcher suggested in her memoirs that the strike was a 'significant defeat for the IRA';[15] however, it also strengthened Sinn Féin. Although Sands had not been elected as a representative of the party, the Republican movement's political wing gained international exposure, supporting Thatcher's belief that the 'unfortunate' hunger strikers 'are of more use to them dead than alive'.[16] Sands' victory was also the start of the dual strategy of political engagement alongside armed struggle, labelled 'an Armalite in one hand and a ballot box in the other'[17] by Sinn

Féin's publicity director Danny Morrison. Two years later, Gerry Adams, the party's leader, was elected MP for the Belfast West constituency, but refused to take his seat in the House of Commons or swear loyalty to the crown, a policy followed by the party's MPs to this day.

Of the twenty-three who went on hunger strike, nine were members of the GAA. Of the ten who died, five were GAA members and two, Kevin Lynch and Kieran Doherty, were active within the association.[18] Lynch, a member of the Irish National Liberation Army (INLA), the paramilitary wing of the Irish Republican Socialist Party, who was serving a ten-year sentence for a range of firearms offences, was a member of the Dungiven hurling club and had captained Derry to victory in the All-Ireland Special Under-16 final nine years earlier. In the aftermath of his death, after seventy-one days without food, the name of the club was changed from 'St Patrick's' to 'Kevin Lynch's' in the twenty-five-year-old's honour. It was a long-standing tradition of commemorating those considered to be martyrs in the fight for Irish freedom, but it only served to reinforce the belief that the GAA was intrinsically linked to Republican terrorism. Such was the distrust and animosity among the Protestant community and in particular Loyalist paramilitaries, towards the GAA, that the Ulster Freedom Fighters issued a statement saying all the association's personnel were considered to be legitimate targets.

The all-Ireland nature of the Gaelic games meant that GAA players, supporters and officials had to make repeated journeys across the border, bringing them into regular contact with the British Army who would stop and search them. It was while making one such crossing in February 1988 that Aiden McAnespie was shot in the back by a British soldier at the Tyrone/Monaghan border while on his way to play football for his local club, Aghaloo. The twenty-three-year-old was just yards from the ground when the incident happened. By the time his teammates reached him, McAnespie was dead. 'He was just a lad going to a Gaelic match on a Sunday,' recalled his brother, Vincie.[19] The soldier claimed he had discharged his weapon accidentally, McAnespie's relatives claimed he had been repeatedly subjected to harassment and threats while he crossed the border, and his killing was often cited during the Troubles as a reason for maintaining Rule 21 prohibiting members of the security forces from playing GAA games.

McAnespie's killing was by no means an isolated incident: during the 1970s and 1980s, five members of the GAA club Naomh Éanna, known as St Enda's, in Glengormley, Co. Antrim, were killed, and its club house was burned down thirteen times.[20] Between 1973 and 1993, the St Joseph's GAA Club in Ballycran, Co. Down, was the target of seven arson attacks.[21] By contrast, Republicans targeted cricket clubs: the North of Ireland Cricket Club pavilion in Ormeau, Belfast, the Cliftonville Cricket Club in north Belfast, and the Downpatrick Cricket Club pavilion in Co. Down were all attacked at one time or another. Protestants who played the 'foreign' or 'Garrison' games, were also killed. In April 1982, Noel McCulloch was killed by an IRA bomb. He should have been on tour in the Bahamas with his rugby club, Rainey Old Boys, but he had to stay behind because the flight was over-booked. Later the same year, John Martin, a former RUC reservist, was shot at the petrol station where he worked in the centre of Armagh city centre. He had been secretary of his local cricket club, and several teammates were among the pallbearers at his funeral.[22] None of these men died because of the sports they played, but the sports they played were, no matter which side of the divide they came from, unequivocal representations of who they were and how they saw themselves within the wider context of Irish society.

III

Like the GAA, rugby was administered on an all-Ireland basis, by the Irish Rugby Football Union (IRFU). Along with cricket, another sport similarly organised, it was suburban and middle-class. However, the majority of Catholics involved were from the south, in particular Leinster and Munster. North of the border, it was essentially a Protestant sport. As the 1980s began, there were high hopes for the national team after a touring side skippered by Fergus Slattery and including the likes of Moss Keane, Willie Duggan, John O'Driscoll, Ollie Campbell, and Phil Ord won both Tests during a tour of Australia in the summer of 1979. The following year they came second in the Five Nations behind England's Grand Slam-winning side, but in 1981 success turned to failure when they earned the wooden spoon. The season ended with a defeat at Lansdowne Road against the touring Australians, a game that marked the debut of Trevor Ringland, just over a week after his twenty-second birthday. 'When I joined the team in 1981, it was coming to maturity. They were guys who were at the peak of their international career,' he tells me.[23] The following season, with their experienced pack, christened 'Dad's Army', leading from the front, Ireland turned the form book on its head to secure their first Triple Crown since 1948, outside-half Ollie Campbell kicking all twenty-one points in the definitive game against Scotland. 'It was a special time,' Ringland continues, 'the economic situation in Ireland was not very good either and you had the Troubles in Northern Ireland and sport in many ways gave a positive light to the wider society.'

Twelve months later, Ireland topped the table again, sharing the championship with the French. However, this was followed by another wooden spoon. 'That team had maybe become too mature by 1984,' says Ringland. 'In 1985 another group of young players came through who were full of energy, full of ideas and Mick Doyle was a coach who released those ideas and gave us the confidence to play with the passion and skill we knew we had.' They were champions again, a 15−15 draw, again with the French, the only blemish on their record. Almost inevitably, this was followed by their third wooden spoon in six years. Then, in 1987, Ireland beat England 17−0 at home and Wales 15−11 away, finishing second behind Grand Slam winners France, victories that gave them hope of a strong showing at the inaugural World Cup due to start in Australia and New Zealand, in May. They had been drawn in Pool 2 alongside Wales, Canada and Tonga. Thus, their first game, against the Welsh, was effectively a play-off to see which of the two sides would top the group and, in all likelihood, play England in the quarter-finals. Having only just beaten both teams, Ireland had eyes on the last four.

However, a month before the tournament began, the squad suffered a devastating blow. As they drove south from Belfast to Dublin to attend a Saturday-morning training session, Nigel Carr, David Irwin and Philip Rainey narrowly avoided death in an IRA car bombing. The target was Lord Justice Sir Maurice Gibson, Northern Ireland's second most senior judge, who was travelling in the opposite direction. He had been on the IRA's hit list since acquitting a member of the Parachute Regiment, Private Michael Williams, charged with killing twelve-year-old Majella O'Hare in 1976. (In 2011, the British government issued an unprecedented apology to Majella's family, acknowledging that Williams' courtroom explanation was 'unlikely'.[24]) This reputation was reinforced when Gibson made comments widely seen as tacitly approving a 'shoot-to-kill' policy.

On the day of the bombing, the seventy-three-year-old Gibson and his wife were returning from holiday on what was at the time the main road between the two capital cities, something that made it the site of regular IRA attacks. The Gibsons were escorted to the border by Garda officers after which they had a short drive through Killean where they would pick up an RUC escort. However, just half a mile into Northern Ireland a 400-lb bomb in an abandoned Ford Cortina was detonated by an IRA man overlooking the road. The blast left a crater 20 feet long, 10 feet wide and 6 feet deep. The couple died instantly. Their car was thrown across the road, into the path of the vehicle containing the three players at a speed estimated to be more than 120 miles an hour. Miraculously, no one else was killed although a group of nurses in a separate car also travelling south were injured.

Ringland and a number of other players were in another car on the same road about twenty minutes behind. 'We were diverted at the border. There were no mobile phones in those days, so we knew something had happened, but we didn't know what.' It was only when they arrived at the training ground that they found out their teammates had nearly been killed. Although the players were not the target of the attack, it was indicative of the circumstances in which those from Northern Ireland played. Jimmy McCoy, a serving member of the RUC, and Brian McCall, who was an army officer, would be driven to training in unmarked cars and had Garda officers stationed outside their bedrooms. Plainclothes police would mingle with the squad when they went to the pub. The deepest irony of the incident was not lost on the squad; three players from Northern Ireland who played for a team representing the whole island had nearly been killed by those pursuing reunification. 'It didn't drive a wedge through the rugby team,' says Ringland, 'it actually made us even more focused because that was in direct counter and contrast to the ideology that was uniting people by blowing them to bits.'

Irwin and Rainey both made it to the World Cup. Carr did not. He was a world-class openside flanker, but fractured ribs, a damaged spleen and a broken leg ended his international career after just eleven caps. Ireland lost the opener. As predicted, victory for the Welsh saw them top the group and play England in the quarter-finals, a game they won before they fell in the last four to New Zealand. Conversely, defeat condemned Ireland to a last-eight match against Australia in Sydney, which they lost.

As they headed to the tournament, Ireland faced the prospect of being the only participating country without an anthem. It was the consequence of a debate about which flag and anthem should be used at games, disagreement over the symbols of national identity used by different sporting organisations mirroring wider divisions in Irish society north and south of the border.

In 1926 '*Amhrán na bhFiann*' (The Soldier's Song) was adopted as the official national anthem of the Republic of Ireland. The song had been sung by those opposed to British rule, a history that presented a problem as the rugby team not only played at Lansdowne Road in Dublin but also Ravenhill in Belfast. Thus, the IRFU had determined that '*Amhrán na bhFiann*' should be played at Lansdowne Road and no anthem used at matches elsewhere.

After much discussion, it was decided to play an instrumental version of the nineteenth-century ballad 'The Rose of Tralee' prior to the match with Wales. No one had listened to the recording; the first time they heard it was over the speakers of the Wellington's Athletic Park. According to the *Irish Independent* it was 'a rather insipid decision by the Irish, hardly matching the stirring "Scotland the Brave" or the Welsh anthem. It was a sad day for the Irish.'[25]

Such was the embarrassment that Ireland played their remaining fixtures with no anthem, and the IRFU commissioned Phil Coulter, who had written Dana's Eurovision Song Contest winning 'All Kinds of Everything', to write 'Ireland's Call' specifically for the rugby team. It is now sung alongside the national anthem at home rugby Tests and on its own at away matches and the Irish cricket and hockey teams, also organised on an all-Ireland basis, have adopted it as well.

IV

Unlike rugby and cricket, football on the island of Ireland had had two separate governing bodies since independence. The original Irish Football Association (IFA) continued to govern the game in Northern Ireland, while the Football Association of Ireland (FAI), established in 1921, administered the game in the Republic. Both were recognised by the game's world governing body FIFA and its European governing body UEFA, and they ran separate leagues and cup competitions. Unlike the Gaelic games, the sport was not overtly exclusive and despite its historic link to Britain – its denunciation by the GAA as a 'foreign' sport – players from not only Protestant but also Catholic communities took part. Thus, it was one of the few areas of cultural life in which there were intra-community encounters. It also reflected the deep divisions within society, the usual symbols of the sport – flags, chants and kits – being infused with sectarianism.

It also reflected the inequalities and deep divisions within society. Like many administrative bodies in Northern Ireland, the IFA reflected the fact that the majority of the population was Protestant.[26] In 1972, the League deemed Derry City's Brandywell ground, situated in the nationalist Bogside, a no-go area after the burning of a Ballymena United team bus. The club, which was non-sectarian but drew the majority of its supporters from the Catholic community, were forced to play their home games for the rest of the season in Coleraine, some thirty miles away. It was unsustainable, and

when the League voted 6−5 to maintain the ban the following season, the club was effectively put out of existence. 'Derry were put in
an impossible position,' says former Northern Ireland international
Tony O'Doherty who began his career as a youth team player at
Derry.[27] 'Financially they couldn't play anywhere else, it's as simple
as that. Plus, the fact that they were homeless meant it was much
more difficult to attract good players.'

Although there's no evidence that the League's actions were
driven by anti-nationalism, that's how it was perceived. Martin
McGuinness, the late Sinn Féin politician and former member of
the IRA, grew up supporting the club and suggested that the
decision was 'victimisation' and that 'Derry fans felt the Irish
League were prejudiced against them for sectarian reasons'.[28] For
the next thirteen years, the club repeatedly reapplied to join the
League and each year they were turned down. Brandywell became
a ghost of its former self, hosting only junior football matches and
greyhound racing.

Then, in 1984, Terry Harkin, who along with O'Doherty,
Eamon McLaughlin and Eddie Mahon made up the 'Gang of
four' working to re-establish the club, suggested they apply to the
league in the south. 'Nobody had ever thought of that before,'
says O'Doherty. 'It took off from there.' In 1985, with special dis-
pensation from UEFA to play in another country, Derry was
reborn in the Republic of Ireland's league. In its second season
they gained promotion to the Premier Division and in 1989 won
the league, League Cup and the FAI Cup treble − still a unique
achievement. 'Derry had fans who'd been denied football for so
long and to get the treble was a vindication of everything we set
out do; the holy grail had arrived!' says O'Doherty. Some 14,000
fans made the journey for the FAI Cup final. 'From when you left
Derry in the morning until you reached Dublin, it was a sea of
red and white. Cars, vans, minibuses, lorries, buses, anything that

had four wheels was on its way to Dublin. There was a banner on the local bridge which said, "Would the last person out of Derry please turn out the lights". We all saw it.'

The following season they welcomed Portuguese champions Benfica to Brandywell for a European Cup tie. It was the biggest game in the club's history. 'For somebody like me who had been wanting a team for all those years, it was just incredible,' says O'Doherty. 'The excitement in this city was palpable for days, if not weeks. These guys that we'd only read about, or maybe fleetingly seen on our television screens, were now going to be in the flesh in front of us in our little stadium. Unbelievable.' However, the game was nearly called off after an unexploded bomb was found in a cemetery near the ground, McGuinness stepping in to help dispose of the device. 'Martin decided that for the sake of the game he better do something, so he did something and the game went ahead.'

If much of Derry City's support came from the nationalist population, then Linfield was the mirror image, its fan base having been mainly drawn from the Loyalist community since its formation in the late nineteenth century. The club's red, white and blue colours and its exclusive recruitment policy, which meant it refused to sign Catholic players, were further indications of its Unionist stance. In 1983, Linfield signed a long-term deal allowing the IFA to lease its Windsor Park ground for international home games. The ground was situated in the loyalist Village area of south Belfast, and the agreement reinforced the notion for fans on both sides of the divide that the Northern Ireland team embodied Protestant 'Ulster'.

At the time, the national side was enjoying a period of success. They won the 1979/80 British Home Championship, a round-robin tournament contested against England, Scotland and Wales. They also qualified for both the 1982 and 1986 World

Cups. They reached the zenith in 1982 when they beat the hosts Spain 1–0 in Seville on their way to the second round. It was a team led by former Gaelic footballer Martin O'Neill, who had been educated at an all-Catholic boys' school and had grown up in a house with a picture of Padraig Pearse, one of the leaders of the Easter Uprising, on the wall in the front room.[29] The winning goal against Spain was scored by another Catholic, Gerry Armstrong. Another leading player, goalkeeper Pat Jennings, was also Catholic. What little cross-community support this engendered dwindled in the wake of the deal between the IFA and Linfield. A minority of extreme fans rejected the national team's green and white colours, wearing red, white and blue instead; the songs they sung became increasingly pro-union and anti-Catholic. Active support from nationalists dwindled. 'It was never a Protestant team,' says O'Doherty, 'but it was *seen* as a Protestant team, and perception can be more powerful than reality. It's very difficult to support a team that is, if you like, almost considered part of the state apparatus. I'm sure those who ran Northern Ireland football, particularly the international team, never meant that to be the case but it was out of their control. Everything was seen through the lens of the Troubles; you couldn't escape it.'

The deal between Linfield and the IFA didn't just make Windsor Park a Loyalist redoubt, it also made it a target. The riots sparked by the death of Bobby Sands prompted the English and Welsh FAs to refuse to play in Belfast for the 1981 Home Internationals series. It was the only time other than during the two world wars that the competition had not been completed. Hector Munroe, the sports minister, criticised the decisions and others pointed out that Windsor Park was in an area of Belfast that had been trouble-free. This did not remain the case. In February 1985 England and Northern Ireland met at the stadium in a World Cup qualifier. Both would ultimately progress to the tournament,

England without losing a game and Northern Ireland losing just twice: in their opening fixture against Finland and in the home tie against England. It was a largely uneventful match, Mark Hateley scoring the only goal with thirteen minutes to play. The most significant incident occurred off the pitch an hour after the final whistle when a car bomb planted by the Irish National Liberation Army exploded nearby. There were no injuries.

The teams were paired again for the European Championship qualifiers two years later and, in April 1987, England returned to Windsor Park. It was a match bookended by bloodshed. Two days before the game, in the Divis Flats area of the city, Iain James O'Connor, a twenty-three-year-old soldier with the Queen's Lancashire Regiment, was killed after one of two blast bombs dropped from a walkway onto the Land Rover in which he was travelling fell through the vehicle's open hatch. The day after the game, Laurence Marley, a senior figure in the IRA and one of the masterminds behind a mass breakout of Republican prisoners from the Maze prison in 1983, was gunned down by the Ulster Volunteer Force on the doorstep of his home in Ardoyne.

There could have been more bloodshed at the match, but fortunately it was averted. As the players mingled on the pitch before their warm-ups, a loud bang rocked the stadium. A photograph taken in the immediate aftermath captured a plume of smoke rising in the distance above the head of a bemused looking Gary Lineker. Behind him stood Terry Butcher, and Northern Irish players Kevin Wilson, who Butcher had played with at Ipswich, and Jimmy Nicholl, with whom he now played at Glasgow Rangers. 'What the hell was that?' said Wilson. 'I think it was a twenty-five-pounder,' replied Nicholl.[30] He was right. The IRA had detonated a bomb just 100 yards from the stadium's entrance. Fortunately, no one was injured as the police, already on high alert, had received a warning just minutes beforehand and managed to clear the area in time. In their ensuing search, they found a make-shift mortar launcher, prompting fears the ground might come under attack. After the final whistle, the England team were rushed away, an ITV interview with manager Bobby Robson cut off in mid-flow by the floor manager. 'I'm sorry, Mr Robson,' he said, 'but for security reasons we have to evacuate the ground immediately.'[31] The assembled media pack had to wait a little longer. They were, according to Martin Tyler, who had been conducting the interview with Robson, 'left in Windsor Park for an uncomfortably long period before our evacuation took place, wondering whether we would leave in one piece'.[32] The incident left the notion that the sport could bridge the sectarian divide in tatters, Harry Cavan, the president of the Irish FA, lamenting: 'Until Wednesday evening I was always fairly happy that football here was a unifying force. Last night put that belief in grave doubt.'[33]

The idea that football could bring the two sides of the community together was further undermined by the treatment of Catholic player Anton Rogan on his home debut. Born in the west Belfast area of Lenadoon, Rogan was a left back, who occasionally played as a left-sided centre-half. He made his professional debut for Distillery (now Lisburn Distillery) before signing for Celtic in Glasgow in 1986, a club whose fans were traditionally Catholic. In Rogan's second season at the club, then managed by Billy McNeil, the club's 1967 European Cup-winning captain, Celtic won the league and cup double in their centenary year. Rogan's performances earned him a call-up to the Northern Irish squad. He made his debut in Sarajevo against Yugoslavia, and a few months later won his second cap, in Athens against Greece. His home debut came on 23 March 1988, two days before his twenty-second birthday.

That March was a month of grim, tit-for-tat sectarian violence. On the 6th, three IRA members, Seán Savage, Daniel McCann and Mairéad Farrell, were shot dead by the SAS in Gibraltar. The trio was almost certainly planning an attack: Semtex was later found in a car linked to them. However, the nature of the killings reinforced suspicions that the British were employing a 'shoot-to-kill' policy. Two days after the shootings, the *Daily Telegraph* printed an editorial by Max Hastings questioning the action, in which he argued, 'Unless the government wishes Britain's enemies to enjoy a propaganda bonanza, it should explain why it was necessary to shoot all three terrorists, rather than to apprehend them [. . .]'.[34] These were sentiments compounded when Thames Television broadcast the documentary *Death on the Rock*, which the government tried to have delayed, that suggested the victims had been unlawfully killed. On 16 March, the trio's joint funeral at Milltown Cemetery was attacked by Michael Stone, a loyalist sympathiser acting independently, who fired several shots and threw grenades. Three people were killed and more than sixty injured. There was further bloodshed a few days later when two off-duty soldiers were murdered. After they drove into the cortège of one of the Milltown Cemetery victims, the pair were taken to the nearby Casement Park, the main GAA stadium in Belfast, stripped, beaten and shot.

Four days later, Rogan was a substitute at Windsor Park for Northern Ireland's game against Poland. 'This was 1988 and there was still a great deal going on, so I expected it,' said Rogan;[35] 'I was aware of things when I went onto the pitch, and I knew what I was going into before I went onto the pitch,' he added.[36] The abuse began as Rogan stood on the halfway line ready to go on. 'I wasn't really surprised, because I played for Celtic [. . .] and I know that a lot of Rangers fans support Northern Ireland. That's football, but I got booed as I just ran onto the pitch.' It was the first time Rogan was jeered during an international, and it wouldn't be the last.

V

While Windsor Park was not a welcoming place for Irish nationalists in Northern Ireland, the unexpected success of the Republic
of Ireland team, which qualified for the 1988 European Championships and then the 1990 World Cup, offered a space in which
they could reject loyalist triumphalism. 'The Boys in Green', as
they were known, in effect became an all-Ireland team, which
Northern Irish Catholics felt comfortable supporting. Furthermore, it was widely embraced by the Irish diaspora who could
support a team that for the first time included players that sounded
like them.

This seemed unlikely when Jack Charlton agreed to become
manager in February 1986. Charlton, who along with his brother
Bobby was a key part of England's World Cup-winning team two
decades earlier, had been out of work since resigning as Newcastle
manager in August 1985. His appointment was a compromise
after the FAI failed to land their first choice, Bob Paisley. When
Gay Byrne, the host of the popular *Late Late Show*, announced the
news by saying: 'I have just been handed a piece of paper here
which says that Jack Charlton has been appointed manager of
Ireland − whatever that means',[37] he summed up the widespread
indifference.

Little was expected of Charlton or the team. The Republic of
Ireland had never previously qualified for an international tournament. Historically, football played second fiddle to the GAA.
Many Irish football fans followed British teams with a strong Irish
contingent among their playing staff, or a strong Irish supporter
base. The FAI struggled financially and in 1985 it was on the
brink of insolvency.[38] Charlton's tenure got off to an ignominious
start, with defeat at home to Wales. He subsequently implemented

a decidedly English 4-4-2 system coupled with physically demand-ing long-ball tactics which soon began to pay off. He also ruthlessly exploited FIFA's ancestry rule and Ireland's citizenship laws, which determined that anyone whose parent or grandparent is an Irish citizen is also entitled to Irish citizenship, to bring into the squad players with Irish heritage, such as Ray Houghton, Andy Townsend, Chris Hughton and Mick McCarthy.

By the end of the following year, the team had achieved the unthinkable, qualifying for the 1988 European Championships in Germany, topping a qualification group that included Belgium, Bulgaria, Scotland and Luxembourg. This was then surpassed with victory against England when the teams met in their opening game of the tournament. While the Irish press heaped praise on the victors, the English media couched defeat in terms of national humiliation, a telling insight into the perception many held of Ireland as an 'inferior' country. Ireland drew their next game, against the USSR, leaving them just needing to avoid defeat in their final match against Holland to progress. It was a game too far, Wim Kieft scoring the winner in the eighty-second minute. The Dutch would eventually lift the trophy, beating the USSR in the final 2−0. Ireland had acquitted themselves admirably against both finalists. England did not pick up a single point. Charlton's iconic status was confirmed. 'There was always an affinity with the Republic,' recalls Tony O'Doherty, 'but there was no massive support here. Before the Charlton era, you wouldn't have seen kids running about here wearing Republic of Ireland jerseys. That was the start of a shift; we didn't question the fact the players spoke with English accents. They were wearing the green jersey and that's all that mattered.'

Greater success was to follow, the team qualifying for their first World Cup, in Italy in 1990. Despite drawing all three of their group games, against England, the Netherlands and Egypt, they progressed to the second round where they drew again, with Bulgaria, before winning on penalties. They were then narrowly beaten by the hosts in Rome in the quarter-finals. Their achievements at Italia '90 had even greater resonance than those in Germany. The Taoiseach, Charles Haughey, was alert to the significance, joining the team on their lap of honour after their defeat (just as he had joined Stephen Roche on the podium at the Tour de France three years earlier). The huge TV audiences and the energetic celebrations, fuelled by Guinness and accompanied by chants of 'Ole! Ole!', suggested football was a major unifying spectacle.

When the team returned from Italy, 500,000 people packed the streets of Dublin to welcome them home. On the same day, Nelson Mandela, less than six months after his release from Robben Island, also touched down in the city, there to accept the freedom of Dublin, which he'd been awarded two years earlier *in absentia*. In his acceptance speech at the city's Mansion House, he congratulated the team.

It may seem ironic that this articulation of Irishness was driven off the pitch by an Englishman who had played a key role in his own country's finest footballing hour. Yet Charlton cast himself as an 'honorary Irishman'. He made much of the fact that he had bought a house on the country's west coast as a base to go fishing, writing in his biography, 'I like Ireland. I like the Irish people, I like a pint of Guinness, I like the crack.'[39] Furthermore, he was an outsider in his own country, famously having applied for the England manager's job, following the resignation of Don Revie in 1977, and not even receiving the courtesy of a reply. Charlton's incorrigibly working-class persona was embraced by the Irish, his 'marginality within Britain resonating with Ireland's marginality *to* Britain', as the academic Marcus Free put it.[40]

On the pitch, the likes of Mick McCarthy, with his broad

Yorkshire accent, and Andy Townsend with his south London twang, seemed equally incongruous, the Northern Ireland manager Billy Bingham dismissing Charlton's team as 'mercenaries',[41] and many in the British media employing the 'Plastic Paddies' trope. For others, however, this was a reclaiming and reincorporation of the Irish diaspora which ran counter to the GAA's exclusive sense of Irish identity and represented a more outward looking, global Irishness no longer constructed in opposition to British colonialism.

CHAPTER 9

Two Tribes

I

WHEN the final whistle blew on Tottenham's FA Cup semi-final against Leicester at Villa Park in April 1982, a wave of relief swept over Ossie Ardiles. Spurs, the cup holders, had booked their place in the final but the player's mind was not on the game; it was on events some 8,000 miles away.[1] When he had gone to bed the night before he had no inkling of the trouble to come. When he woke up, the country of his birth and the country he had made his home were at war, Argentinian military forces having invaded the long-disputed Falkland Islands overnight. It had an immediately devastating impact on Ardiles. He was told, wrongly as it turned out, that his house had been attacked by vandals. There was even talk that his assets in England might be frozen. 'It felt,' he wrote the following year, 'as if a bomb had dropped on my well-ordered life.'[2] Still, duty compelled him to take part in the match. His every touch was marked by chants of 'England! England!' from Leicester fans, some of whom also called him an 'Argentinian bastard'.[3] He was also jeered by some Spurs fans, but the majority supported him, singing 'Argentina! Argentina!' and 'There's only one Ardiles!'; some even held up a banner that read

'Argentina can keep the Falklands, we'll keep Ossie'. Ardiles delivered the best response a player can, setting up Garth Crooks for the first of Spurs' two goals. It had already been agreed that he would fly out to Argentina the day after the semi-final to join the Argentinian squad for their pre-World Cup preparations. The player had to be escorted to Gatwick airport by police and bodyguards. Once he arrived in his home country, he knew there could be no immediate return to England; he would not play for Spurs again for nine months.

Ardiles had joined Spurs along with his compatriot Ricardo 'Ricky' Villa in 1978, barely two weeks after starting for the victorious Argentinians in the World Cup final at the Estadio Monumental in Buenos Aires. The match against the Netherlands was memorable for the tickertape welcome the players received on the pitch and Mario Kempes' match-winning performance. Despite his breaking a toe in Argentina's first-round game against France, manager Luis Menotti stayed loyal to Ardiles, picking the 'wreck, a player with two bad ankles'[4] for the final. Villa was also in the squad but made just two substitute appearances, replacing Ardiles in one, against Brazil. Although Ardiles' injury led to his substitution at half-time in the final, he was still in many people's team of the tournament, including that of England boss Ron Greenwood, in Argentina as a pundit, his team having failed to qualify. Thus, the £750,000 double swoop by Tottenham, a team that had just won promotion back to the English First Division after unexpected relegation the season before, was a genuine transfer sensation, the *Daily Express* greeting it with the headline 'SPURS SCOOP THE WORLD'.[5]

Foreign players are now the norm at all levels of British football but in a country that was at the time just five years into its membership of the European Community (EC) and still had a tendency to look inwards, the signings of foreign players were ground-breaking. Effectively banned in 1930, the only exceptions were those who had served a two-year period of residency. UEFA had a similar rule, but in 1978 it was determined that the EC's Treaty of Rome permitted freedom of movement. This opened the door for unlimited recruitment from within EC member states, while clubs were also allowed to sign two players from anywhere else in the world. The rule changes heralded an influx of overseas stars. While Ardiles stayed at Spurs for a decade, and Villa stayed for five years, not all new arrivals enjoyed similar success. Argentina's World Cup-winning full back Alberto Tarantini signed for Birmingham City but played just twenty-three games before returning home; compatriot Claudio Marangoni played only twenty times for Sunderland before his contract was terminated. Sheffield United tried to sign an up-and-coming youngster called Diego Maradona but baulked at the £400,000 asking price for the seventeen-year-old. Alex Sabella was signed from River Plate for £160,000 instead. Following the Blades' relegation Sabella, who later managed the Argentinian national team, moved to First Division Leeds but lasted just a season. Players from other countries started plying their trade in Britain, too. Dutchman Arnold Mühren joined Ipswich, helping them win the UEFA Cup in 1981 before moving to Manchester United, where he won the FA Cup in 1983. Ipswich also signed Frans Thijssen while Ivan Golac joined Southampton from Partizan Belgrade.

The recruitment of foreign players to English clubs stalled during the 1980s as the post-Heysel ban on English clubs playing in European competition made them a less than attractive destination: indeed, several top English players went to ply their trade abroad as a consequence. In 1989, Arsenal were the last team to be crowned champions with a squad made up exclusively of players from Britain and Ireland. (Just a decade later, on Boxing Day 1999, Chelsea became the first Premier League club to field a team including no British players.) Eric Cantona on the pitch and Arsène Wenger off it are often credited with bringing a more sophisticated European ethos to the British game, but the seeds were sown in 1978. The technical and tactical ability of the foreign imports, in particular Ardiles, began the gradual change. Teams increasingly passed through midfield, instead of bypassing it with long balls forward. The balance began to shift from a focus on physical strength to a more cerebral approach.

It was thanks to a technically stunning goal in the 1981 FA Cup final replay against Manchester City that Villa weaved himself into English football folklore. He had not settled as well as Ardiles, but that was quickly forgotten under the Wembley floodlights on a Thursday night. The game had see-sawed between the two teams and with fourteen minutes to play the score was tied at 2–2. Graham Roberts won the ball outside Spurs' area. A quick pass freed Tony Galvin to make a surging run down the left before he passed inside to Villa. The Argentinian then made his way to the left-hand side of the box, before twisting back to the centre, leaving two City defenders in his wake. Sound-tracked by John Motson's excitable commentary, 'And still Ricky Villa . . . What a fantastic run . . . He's scored! Amazing goal!', Villa slotted the ball beyond the advancing keeper Joe Corrigan. It was worthy of any final and would later be voted the best goal scored at Wembley in the twentieth century.

Of the pair, it was Ardiles who made the biggest impact off the pitch, not least thanks to Spurs' FA Cup final song, 'Ossie's Dream (Spurs Are on Their Way to Wembley)', which reached No. 5 after the replay victory. Written by Cockney duo Chas 'n' Dave, it included a solo by Ardiles in which he expressed his love for 'Tottingham' and also included unfortunately prescient lyrics: 'We're marching off to war, We're sending our soldiers to Wembley, Under General Burkinshaw, We know the enemy will fear us in the battle coming up . . .' Ardiles' reputation reached even greater heights after he starred alongside Bobby Moore, Pelé, Michael Caine and Sylvester Stallone in the film *Escape to Victory*. Ardiles' character, Carlos Rey, was best remembered for executing a 'rainbow kick', done by rolling the ball up the back of his standing leg with the other foot before flicking the standing leg to propel the ball in a 'rainbow' arc over his own head, hence the name. In playgrounds across the country, school kids would, with varying degrees of success, subsequently try to replicate the trick which became known simply as 'doing an Ardiles'.

All this meant little after the outbreak of hostilities. Ardiles' departure for Argentina the day after the semi-final against Leicester was seen by some as a political statement, but it had been pre-arranged. With Ardiles gone, Villa was left to face the prospect of the FA Cup final on his own. His choice was stark; no matter what he did, he would receive criticism. When Villa told Argentinian journalist Bernardo Neustadt that he thought the war was wrong due to the loss of life, Neustadt effectively branded him a traitor and cut the interview short.[6] The image of the player shaking hands with members of the royal family and observing the British national anthem would only serve to heighten that feeling. The reception received by Ardiles in the semi-final gave a hint of the treatment Villa could expect from QPR fans if he played at Wembley, but the situation was even more febrile come the final. The Argentine ship *General Belgrano* had been sunk on 2 May and HMS *Sheffield* hit in retaliation two days later. On the day of the final, HMS *Ardent* was sunk with the loss of twenty-two lives. Villa decided not to play in the game, nor in the replay five days later.

While Villa continued to play for Spurs the following season, Ardiles had made the decision that he could not. With the north London club unwilling to sell him, a six-month loan move to Paris

Saint-Germain was agreed, the player returning to Spurs in January the following year. He set up Glen Hoddle for an equaliser in his first match against Luton. Spurs went on to finish fourth and the following season they won the UEFA Cup. His spell in Paris did not go well. 'My mind was never on the game,' Ardiles wrote later.[7] 'I did not believe I could play so badly. The war was on my mind.' By then the conflict had taken on a personal dimension for him, his cousin José having been killed during the first Argentinian bombing raid on the Falklands on 1 May.

II

When the war started, the Falkland Islands, or Islas Malvinas as they are known to the Argentines, were inhabited by around 1,800 people mostly of British descent, many of whom were farmers. Disputes about the ownership of the archipelago, situated about 300 miles off the Patagonian coast of Argentina, dated back to the 1700s with France, Spain and America all having control at some point or other, at times only for a few months. However, the islands had been part of the British Empire since 1833 following the forceable, but peaceful, removal of the then Argentinian administration. The Argentines continued to assert their claim to sovereignty and in the two years immediately prior to the Falklands War, a series of talks on the issue took place in which a range of solutions were considered. Nicholas Ridley, the junior Foreign Office minister in Thatcher's government tasked with leading the negotiations, even proposed a sale-and-lease-back solution in which Britain would cede sovereignty of the islands to Argentina and then immediately lease them back. However, this was widely rejected by islanders who shouted abuse at the MP while playing 'Rule, Britannia!' at a meeting to discuss the proposals.[8]

MPs from all parts of the political spectrum also made clear their dislike of Ridley's plans,[9] but the need for a resolution was clear. Argentina's ruling military junta, led at the time by General Leopoldo Galtieri, was pressing their claims with increasing aggression. Due to civil unrest triggered by the dictatorship's brutal regime and human rights abuses, and the country's economic decline, Galtieri saw a military campaign to recover the long-disputed Falklands as a perfect distraction.[10] On 19 March a group of Argentine salvage workers raised the country's flag on South Georgia. On 1 April, with a large invasion force approaching, the islands' governor Rex Hunt summoned majors Mike Norman and Gary Noot and told them: 'It looks like the buggers mean it.'[11] The small garrison of Royal Marines based on the Falklands supplemented by a handful of members of the territorial defence force were quickly overrun and surrendered, the Argentines taking control early on 2 April. As pictures of British soldiers lying face down in the road were flashed around the world, the news was greeted across Argentina with scenes 'akin to winning the World Cup in 1978 — when thousands of people filled the streets to chant victory slogans'.[12]

The military action by the Argentines posed an existential threat to Thatcher's leadership of the Conservatives, and the party's grip on government. The party had not held a lead over Labour with Ipsos-Mori since the day of the 1979 general election[13] and the previous year, with the country riven with inner-city rioting, Thatcher became the least popular prime minister in polling history.[14] Furthermore, the newly formed Social Democrat Party (SDP) was not just eating into the vote of the Labour Party from which its leading members had split, but also the Conservatives'. To compound these issues, a so-called 'Gang of 25' Conservative MPs were threatening to rebel against Thatcher's proposed economic policies, with some believed to be on the brink of defecting to the SDP.[15] Thus, repelling the Argentinian invasion force, either through diplomacy or preferably military force, would considerably strengthen Thatcher and her government. Lose, however, and her credibility as a strong leader − already in doubt − would be destroyed, making victory at the next general election, at the time considered highly unlikely, a near impossibility.

Thus, the decision to mobilise a task force of fifty-one warships and seventy-five auxiliary vessels to reclaim the islands was not a political gamble − Thatcher essentially had no other choice; capitulation was not an option − yet it was a significant military gamble. There were huge risks in sending 28,000 military personnel 8,000 miles into the South Atlantic winter to face an enemy already well entrenched on the ground and with effective air cover. In their book on the conflict, journalists Max Hastings and Simon Jenkins suggested there had been no detailed assessment of how the British could win such a war because, simply, no one expected one. Thus, the strength of the Argentine air force was grossly underestimated, as was the number of British losses.

If the war in the South Atlantic had been a risky affair, the battle for the hearts and minds of the British public was less so. The conflict was the last pre-satellite-TV war but also the first heavily PR-managed war. The only way for British journalists to reach the theatre of conflict was via the fleet, thus coverage was almost entirely at the mercy of the Ministry of Defence. The navy initially refused to take journalists with the task force, but after the personal intervention of the prime minister it agreed to take two camera crews, two radio reporters, two photographers and fifteen correspondents spread across three ships.[16] No equipment to transmit television pictures was embarked, thus some images were broadcast as long as twenty-three days after the events they showed had taken place, longer than it took *The Times* to report details of

the Charge of the Light Brigade from the Crimea to British readers in 1854.[17] The average delay was seventeen days, meaning the
BBC and ITV had to rely on audio from their correspondents
(Brian Hanrahan and Michael Nicholson respectively) illustrated
by still images, often just a picture of the person speaking. Only
202 photos were transmitted back to the UK during the war,[18] the
first not arriving until 18 May, some forty-seven days into the
seventy-four-day conflict. Copy that was filed was subject to a tor-
tuous censorship process first by service officers with the fleet and
then by Whitehall officials in Britain. Much was lost, much more
delayed. Reporters became used to sending their stories only to be
scooped by official briefings back in London.

Throughout the conflict, Thatcher adopted a generally
Churchillian tone, employing rhetoric that evoked the Second
World War and posed as a leader who could unite the country in
a time of crisis. A largely friendly press, which had been denied
the opportunity to report on a conflict for a generation, filled the
void in news by reflecting this. The prime minister – or 'Maggie'
in tabloid parlance – was cast as a warrior queen leading a once
great nation reawakened from its slumber in defence of the victims of tyranny. The troops – 'our boys' – and Falkland islanders
were portrayed as symbols of mythical Britain: 'WE ARE ALL
FALKLANDERS NOW' declared *The Times*.[19] Domestic
opposition was all but silenced, with debate being replaced by
appeals to strongly held nationalist feelings. The *Sun* led the way,
fervently draping itself in the Union Flag and using all the weapons of mass-circulation journalism to corner the market in
jingoistic nationalism. Readers were urged to boycott Argentinian
corned beef and submit their own 'Argie-Bargie' jokes. They were
offered £5 and a can of Fray Bentos non-Argentinian beef for
each one published.[20] In an article headlined 'THE SUN SAYS
KNICKERS TO ARGENTINA!', predictably placed on Page

3, the paper launched 'undie-cover' warfare revealing that 'thousands of women' were wearing specially made knickers embroidered with the name of the ship their husband or boyfriend was serving on.[21]

By contrast, the *Daily Mirror*, a Labour-supporting paper, was caught between its dislike of Thatcher and its abhorrence of Galtieri's regime. It adopted a significantly more measured tone than its rival, appealing for a peaceful resolution in an editorial headlined 'Might isn't right'[22] and later imploring 'The killing has got to stop'.[23] The *Sun* was dismissive of such calls, branding the *Mirror* 'Traitors in our midst' and claiming that the paper did 'not believe the British people have the stomach for a fight'.[24] The *Mirror* hit back, suggesting the *Sun* was 'to journalism what Dr Josef Goebbels was to truth'.[25] The *Sun*'s attitude to the prospect of a negotiated peace settlement was summed up simply with the first of its infamous headlines: 'STICK IT UP YOUR JUNTA'.[26] After the talks broke down the paper reworked the headline: 'STICK THIS UP YOUR JUNTA' over a story explaining how 'the first missile to hit Galtieri's gauchos will come with love from the *Sun*'.[27] It speaks volumes about the *Sun*'s coverage that when *Private Eye* parodied the paper's front page with the headline 'KILL AN ARGIE AND WIN A METRO' the paper's editor Kelvin MacKenzie exclaimed in awe: 'Fucking brilliant! Why couldn't we have thought of that, eh?'[28]

On 3 May, news came through that the Argentinian light cruiser *General Belgrano* had been hit. With the first-edition deadline fast approaching, MacKenzie responded by drawing up a front page with the simple, evocative headline 'GOTCHA!'[29] It was the logical culmination of the paper's coverage to date and it's hard to imagine it not being the gut response of many *Sun* readers – and many non-*Sun* readers – up and down the country. Yet when news started trickling through that the ship had suffered hundreds of casualties, even MacKenzie felt he had gone too far, replacing the headline with the watered-down and more uncertain 'DID 1,200 ARGIES DIE?'[30] The original headline was only printed in the early editions sent to the North East, Scotland and Northern Ireland, but it is one of the most famous newspaper headlines of the 1980s, becoming part of Britain's shared history, much like the conflict itself.

III

Ultimately, Thatcher's gamble paid off and the dispirited Argentines surrendered at Port Stanley on 14 June. Victory had come at the cost of the lives of 649 Argentinian and 255 British military personnel plus those of three islanders, all women, killed by a stray Royal Navy missile. The cost to the British taxpayer was £700 million, plus £900 million in lost ships and planes.[31] In Argentina, Galtieri resigned within days and democratic elections were held at the end of the following year. In Britain there were jubilant scenes as crowds flocked to quaysides in Southampton, Portsmouth and Plymouth to welcome back the task force, while soldiers were feted in towns and cities across the country.

Thatcher and her party rode this wave of patriotism all the way to the ballot box. The 'Falklands factor' created a huge groundswell of nationalist sentiment which helped turn her from a beleaguered prime minister facing the prospect of being a one-term loser into a triumphant three-term winner whose legacy shaped the country for decades to come. Between the start of the war and the day of the 1983 general election, the Conservatives were never behind Labour in any Ipsos-Mori opinion poll (a trend that continued until July 1984).[32] They won by a landslide, increasing their majority to 144 seats, all but ensuring Thatcher would win again in 1987, which she did. 'It is no exaggeration to say that the outcome of the Falklands War transformed the British political scene,' she wrote later. 'I could feel the impact of the victory wherever I went.'[33]

Spain also felt the impact as fans of England, Scotland and Northern Ireland travelled to the country for the 1982 football World Cup. It was the first time three home nations had qualified for the tournament since 1958. Argentina, as reigning champions, would be taking part as well. It was also the first time England had qualified for the World Cup in twelve years, but England fans had a growing reputation for trouble overseas, having been involved in major disturbances at games in Luxembourg in 1977, and Basle and Oslo in 1981. A riot in their match with Belgium in Turin at the European Championships in June 1980 led to tear gas canisters being fired into the crowd. The England fans responded by throwing them onto the pitch, causing a brief suspension in play while some players received treatment. Thirty-six arrests were made, and the FA was fined £8,000 and threatened with expulsion should there be further trouble.

Thus, in the build-up to the 1982 tournament, the possibility of one of the British teams facing the Argentines on the pitch – and, more to the point, their fans meeting on the terraces – while the countries were at war was enough to prompt significant political discussion as to whether they should take part. Matters were complicated by the long-standing cultural and political associations between Argentina and the tournament hosts, who abstained in a UN vote demanding a cessation of hostilities and an immediate withdrawal of Argentinian troops. The Spanish press greeted the invasion with some jubilation, drawing parallels with their own claims for sovereignty over Gibraltar and between 5,000 and 10,000 right-wing demonstrators marched through the streets of Madrid demanding the territory be reclaimed by force and burning Union Jacks.[34] It was enough to make Thatcher question whether Britain could repel Spanish military action in Gibraltar.[35]

On 14 May, with just over four weeks to the start of the tournament, Michael Heseltine, the Secretary of State for the Environment, who had responsibility for sport, wrote a memo for the cabinet outlining the options.[36] It was clear that FIFA had no intention of expelling Argentina – the holders – so it would be down to the British football authorities to withdraw their teams. Although they had no intention of doing so by their own volition, they had indicated that they would comply with such a request from the government. However, it was felt that the public would question why the three teams were withdrawing when Argentina, the aggressors, were not. Withdrawal could also be seen as a 'moral victory' for the Argentines and possibly as an insult to tournament hosts. Furthermore, FIFA would probably take punitive action, possibly excluding the teams from the next World Cup in 1986. Thus, Heseltine argued that no action should be taken unless the situation worsened, and public opinion changed. Indeed, Argentina was not due to face any of the British teams in the first round, could only meet Scotland in the second round and could not meet England or Northern Ireland until the final, a set of permutations dismissed as 'against the present odds' by Lord Lennox, a senior Foreign Office civil servant.[37]

Ultimately, the conflict ended the day after the tournament began with a defeat for the Argentinians at the hands of Belgium in the opening game. 'ARGIES SMASHED', sneered the *Sun* triumphantly over a story that began: 'They strutted, they cheated, and afterwards they bleated. That was the arrogant Argentinians last night. They swaggered on as world champions, and crawled off, humiliated by little Belgium.'[38] While fears that the countries might be at war during a potential meeting on the pitch dissipated, the spirit of the Falklands was still manifested in the behaviour of the England fans and the Spanish police's response to them in what at times amounted to quasi-warfare. 'Some guys who went to Spain described themselves as "the other task force",' John Williams, an associate professor at Leicester University, tells me.[39] Such sentiments were in many ways a simple reflection of wider discourses that fused the World Cup and the conflict. Prior to the tournament, England manager Ron Greenwood had drawn his own parallels between his team's 'mission' at the tournament and that of the task force,[40] while Margaret Thatcher had urged travelling fans to be 'as good representatives of this country as our armed forces have been in the South Atlantic'.[41]

At the time, Williams was a young researcher who travelled with the England fans to Spain as part of a research project into hooliganism. The behaviour he saw among many of the fans was, through its excessive patriotism, xenophobia and willingness to resort to violence, a physical manifestation of the new right ideology of the Thatcher government that had been refracted through the press – led by the *Sun*. 'The national press, particularly the tabloids, were bellicose about British nationalism and the kind of papers a lot of these guys read were incredibly racist in their expressions,' says Williams. 'I think there was a general feeling that the World Cup was an appropriate site for white young working-class guys who followed football to reassert the dominance of Britain somehow. They just wanted to be where the action was and this, in their own patriotic way, was how they could send out a message that Britain was still strong, ironically in many ways aping the messages from Thatcher's government.'

Most of the England fans were men, Williams at the time estimating that women made up less than 2 per cent of the total.[42] They were mainly employed in manual occupations, and most were aged twenty-five or younger (few were over thirty), the majority coming from the south of the country, with significant contingents of West Ham and Chelsea supporters. There was also a significant number with links to the National Front. While some fans had bought official packages through a firm called Sportsworld, which provided accommodation on campsites or in cheap hotels, many made their own way to Spain, often on what was their first trip abroad. In some cases, luggage amounted to nothing more than a plastic bag. One unemployed Arsenal fan had arrived in the country with just £1.50 in his pocket. He survived by stealing, avoiding paying rail fares and sleeping on the floors of other people's hotel rooms (the mantra of many fans was 'you never paid in bars and only mugs paid on trains'[43]). He saw just one game, England's match against Kuwait for which he had obtained a free ticket, and knew his chances of seeing other games were slim. However, he was philosophical about his situation, arguing that it was better than signing on in Islington.[44] His experience was not uncommon. 'It was an incredibly audacious ambition to go,' says Williams, 'how willing they were to accept risks to travel and to be there and to be part of this because somehow it confirmed their identities in a world that didn't really have a lot going for them.'

There were noticeable differences between the English supporters in Spain and those from Scotland and Northern Ireland. In the early 1980s, the hardcore Scottish support – the so-called 'Tartan Army' – had begun to soften their attitudes towards fans from other countries, especially when abroad. They had found that when they travelled overseas, they were often mistakenly associated with the violent reputation of English supporters. Thus the Scots began to present themselves as a 'nicer' alternative, self-policing to ensure there was no disorder. This had other benefits that the fans were quick to acknowledge; as one put it simply, 'If you are nice to people, people are nice to you. You have a better time.'[45] During the World Cup, positive comparisons were regularly drawn between the convivial attitude of the Scottish fans and the aggressive behaviour of the English. The Northern Irish fans were also different from their English counterparts. Fewer in number, they tended to be older, although some travelled with their young sons. There was no noticeable National Front presence in their ranks and the songs they sung were not confrontational.

By comparison, England fans engaged in a range of chants that could have been stripped from the pages of a red-top newspaper. 'Argentina – what's it like to lose a war?' and '*Malvinas Inglaterra*' were, along with renditions of 'Rule, Britannia!', both sung regularly.

This exceptionalism meant few fans attempted to familiarise themselves with local culture, many even refusing to learn the basic Spanish required to order a beer, instead simply pointing at what they wanted and then complaining about the 'stupidity' of the locals. 'If you go to the World Cup abroad, most fans who travel say, for example, "We are from x, this is who we are, what are you like?",' says Williams, 'whereas England fans travelled abroad at that time and said, "We're from England, this is who we are, why aren't you more like us?" They wanted to be outsiders, they wanted to be feared. They didn't want to be incorporated or be seen to be part of this festival that is the World Cup, that was not part of their agenda. They really did want to make people afraid of who they were and that was a very profound sentiment on that trip.'

In the aftermath of the tournament, Williams wrote, 'There is much hand-wringing and head-shaking at home that the image we like to think "They" have of "Us" – the stiff-upper-lip pinstripe and bowler – is being replaced abroad by that of the painted Union Jack face and the swift (televised) kick to the "silly foreigner's" balls.'[46] Williams expresses amusement when the passage is read back to him. 'Of course, we're talking about cartoon-like caricatures, but I think that was true,' he says. 'The more that people abroad experienced England football fans and English fans in a more general sense, the more that challenged these old conventions about who the English were because they saw some sections of English society that we probably didn't want them to see.'

IV

This confusion and angst about what kind of England – and what kind of Britain – the English fans represented could be seen in the debate about the England team's mascot 'Bulldog Bobby'. 'Bulldog Bobby' looked a little like the dog from the *Tom and Jerry* cartoons proudly sporting an England kit, chest puffed out, one foot on a football stamped with the words 'Football Association Approved'. At face value, he was a logical representation of Englishness. Just twelve years earlier, the England team had a real bulldog as their mascot for the 1970 World Cup. He was named Winston (for obvious reasons).

The bulldog had been defined as particular to Britain and 'remarkable for his courage' in Samuel Johnson's dictionary in the 1700s. Increasingly linked with notions of Englishness (or Britishness), by the early 1980s the bulldog had, in some people's minds at least, come to mean something else, not least because, as critics of the 1982 mascot noted, the National Front produced a newspaper called *Bulldog* and used the animal as a symbol for its youth organisation. Neil Macfarlane, then sports minister, called Bulldog Bobby 'a stupid, fat, smug, beer-bellied animal which seemed to me to epitomise everything that was bad about English hooligans'.[47] In Bulldog Bobby's defence, FA chairman Bert Millichip

invoked the notion that 'we are the bulldog breed'[48] while the FA
secretary Ted Croker suggested that 'Bulldog Bobby is meant as a
fun character'.[49] Either way, Bulldog Bobby, far from being a unifying representation of England and 'Englishness', was a symbol
to which critics were able to attribute their own negative images
of hooliganism and racism. These connotations were reinforced
when some of the England fans in Spain adopted a bastardised
version of Bobby as their own mascot. One of the most popular
T-shirts showed the animal replete with bovver boots and bottle in
hand rampaging across a map of Europe along with the slogan
'Official Hooligan – Spain '82'.[50] Others acquired Bulldog Bobby
tattoos. 'It was transformed by some people who travelled
abroad particularly in the context of what was going on in the
South Atlantic into a very bellicose, very aggressive symbol,' said
Williams.

Williams' experience in Spain was later drawn upon by Nick
Perry who consulted him while writing his play *Arrivederci Millwall*,
depicting a fictional group of the club's fans following England
during the World Cup, with one – Billy – determined to exact
violent revenge for the death of his brother in the Falklands War.
At the time, Perry was a young unknown author, and the play
received only limited exposure during its first run at the Albany
Theatre in Deptford. However, after it was named joint winner of
the Samuel Beckett Award in 1986 and the script of the play published by Faber & Faber, it gained wider attention. Four years
later, it was turned into a BBC2 drama. 'The Falklands was still
part of the culture,' Perry says.[51] 'It was relatively recent, and
there was just that coincidence of the war and the World Cup
tournament; the fans reflected that in their behaviour and attitudes. So, it seemed to me that there was a conflict that we could
base a football play on that had that political dimension built
into it.'

Perry is keen to point out that his intention was not to criticise the service personnel in the Falklands nor even the action they were taking, but the nationalist discourse built around the conflict. While he acknowledges that some critics rejected the link between the prime minister expressing nationalistic sentiments outside Downing Street and football fans being violent in Spain, Perry maintains there was a clear connection. 'What we were trying to get across is that it was no reason to "rejoice" and if you did do that, you had to take the consequences in other areas of society, such as football fans who have a propensity to fight in foreign places feeling that they're being supported by the government back home.'

If the characters portrayed in Perry's play represented the sections of society the English establishment might not have wanted others to see, a more respectable version was found on the big screen. Four days before the Falklands War began, Colin Welland accepted the Best Original Screenplay Oscar for the film *Chariots of Fire* and gave the bemused audience a 'word of warning [. . .] the British are coming'. Welland subsequently insisted he was widely misunderstood and that far from being a patriotic declaration, he was simply celebrating a reinvigorated domestic film industry.[52] Whatever his meaning, the comment, made in the run-up to hostilities, had a militaristic tone and, along with the film, became inextricably linked with the conflict.

The film did only moderately well on release in 1981, failing to make the end-of-year box office top ten.[53] However, it was well received by critics and garnered numerous awards. Nominated for the Palme d'Or at the Cannes Film Festival, *Chariots of Fire* won three Baftas, including Best Film, and four Oscars, again including Best Film. In the wake of this success it was rereleased, meaning it played at cinemas across Britain throughout the Falklands War and enjoyed a second wind at the box office. Only

Arthur, starring Dudley Moore in the titular role, did better business during 1982.[54] The 'hero's journey' narrative in *Chariots* mimicked the war, even at one point showing a newspaper hoarding declaring 'Our boys are home'. Furthermore, thanks to its celebration of British success, its articulation of 'traditional' values, such as perseverance and indomitability, and its nostalgic portrayal of Britain in the age of Empire, the film also chimed with the notion of Britishness that Thatcher was trying to revive. The film's producer David Puttnam was subsequently invited to Chequers and Thatcher and her inner circle discussed their desire for a film about the Falklands victory to be made in a similar vein.

However, this was a simplistic understanding of a film which acknowledged the high cost of conflict, for example when the Master of Caius College paid tribute to those students who 'died for England' during the First World War. Through its depiction of Liddell's pride in his Scottish roots, *Chariots* also asked what it meant to be British in a country dominated by England, much as it was in Thatcher's vision of the nation. At the same time Abrahams, a Jew of Lithuanian descent, and his coach Sam Mussabini, who was part-Italian and part-Turkish, were portrayed as outsiders treated with a disdain and racism ingrained within the establishment that was to some as recognisable in the early 1980s as it was in the early 1920s.

V

While there was no meeting between any of the three British teams and Argentina during the 1982 World Cup, four years later England played the South Americans in the quarter-finals. The teams had a long-held football rivalry. Twenty years earlier they had met at Wembley at the same stage of the 1966 World Cup.

After the game, in which Argentinian captain Antonio Rattin was sent off, the England manager Alf Ramsey had caused controversy by obliquely referring to their opponents as 'animals'.[55] The rivalry was given greater resonance by the Falklands War, not least because for most Argentinians it had been fought against England. 'Although the conflict had been between Argentina and Britain, the focus in Argentina had always been on the English,' says Argentinian football journalist Marcela Mora y Araujo.[56] 'I don't know that people in Argentina are aware of the granular nuance of the kingdom and the union, but they definitely acknowledge England as opposed to Scotland or Wales. England is the arch-enemy. If you talk about the Falklands — or the Malvinas — to anyone in Argentina, no matter what their position, they will talk about the "War against the English".'

Thus, the match in 1986 had resonance in both countries. The *Sun*'s headline on the day of the game was 'IT'S WAR, SENOR!',[57] but there were also concerted political efforts to play down such connections. Following a conversation with the Argentinian president Raúl Alfonsín, Argentina's coach Carlos Bilardo agreed with his English counterpart Bobby Robson to depoliticise the match. 'When I got the players together, I told them [. . .] not to become involved in the political aspects,' Robson wrote in his tournament diary. 'The same went for me, too. We were here to play football and I am a manager, not a politician.'[58] The Argentinians also played down the significance. When John Carlin of *The Times* asked Maradona what impact the aftermath of the Falklands might have on the game, the Argentinian captain responded testily: 'Look, mate, I play football. About politics I know nothing. Nothing, mate, nothing.'[59]

The reality was somewhat different. Many of the squad came from the same generation that made up the bulk of the conscripts undertaking *la colimba*, Argentina's mandatory military service, who were sent to the South Atlantic. Some only narrowly avoided the draft themselves. Hector Enrique avoided the conflict because his number was not picked, while Jorge Burruchaga was saved by his status as a footballer. He still had to register his availability to fight if required on a daily basis. 'After it finished,' Burruchaga later told Andrés Burgos for his book *El Partido* (The Match), 'I kept going to the barracks, and we used to ask after the other conscripts: "Do you remember so-and-so?" "He died." "And the other guy?" "Dead too."'[60]

Despite the efforts to remove tension from the game, there was still tension on the terraces. A notorious group of Argentinian hooligans, many of them Falklands veterans, called *Las Barras Bravas* (The Wild Gangs) dressed in T-shirts with '*Las Malvinas son Argentinas*' on the front and 'Pirates out of Latin America' on the back, did their best to provoke their English counterparts by setting fire to a Union Jack. Swift action from the Mexican police prevented any serious fighting. Ultimately, there was little trouble, some of the fans even shaking hands at the end of the match.[61] For once, the trouble in the stands was overshadowed by the action on the pitch.

The game exploded into life six minutes after the break when Maradona appeared to outjump Peter Shilton, England's onrushing keeper, and head home. After the briefest of hesitations to check the goal had been given, Maradona wheeled away in celebration. The England players surrounded Ali Bennaceur, the Tunisian referee, urgently tapping their arms. In the confusion, Barry Davies, commentating for the BBC, initially thought they were appealing for offside. It was only after several replays that he realised handball might be the issue. And it was. Maradona had punched the ball into the net with his left hand held just above his head. Four minutes later, with England still reeling, Maradona went from the cynical to the sublime, scoring what would later be

named FIFA's Goal of the Century. It was a glorious run that
began with the player in his own half facing towards his own goal
and ended eleven touches and 10.6 seconds later with the ball in
the England net and a trail of shellshocked opponents in his wake.
'You have to say that was magnificent,' said Davies. 'There's no
debate about that goal, that was just pure football genius.' Gary
Lineker pulled one back with ten minutes to go – ensuring he
would finish the tournament's leading scorer – but it was too little,
too late. In the immediate aftermath of the game, the first goal
was further immortalised by Maradona's post-match comment
that it had been scored 'a little with the head of Maradona and a
little with the hand of God'.[62]

Following the match, the *Sun* repurposed it's infamous *General
Belgrano* headline with the less instinctive 'OUTCHA!' splashed
across the front page. This was complemented by the subhead
'Argies get own back as England tumble out'.[63] However, the connection between the game and the conflict was overshadowed by
a focus on Maradona's performance. The player was branded a
'GENIUS – AND A CHEAT!' by the *Daily Express*,[64] the manner of his first goal reinforcing xenophobic perceptions about
Argentina and Argentinians that lingered from the conflict four
years previously and the match in 1966. There were also debates
about the suitability of the referee for such a high-profile match,
Robson's tactics and the lack of creative players in the England
team and the English game more broadly. From many there was
a simple acknowledgement that the better team, energised by the
world's best player playing at, or near, his peak, had won.

Despite his initial ambivalence, years later Maradona was
unequivocal about what the victory meant in the context of the
conflict. 'More than defeating a football team it was defeating a
country,' he wrote in his biography. 'Of course, before the match,
we said football had nothing to do with the Malvinas War, but we

knew a lot of Argentine kids had died there, shot down like little birds. This was revenge. It was like recovering a little bit of the Malvinas. In the pre-match interviews, we all said that football and politics shouldn't be confused, but that was a lie. We did nothing but think about that. Bollocks was it just another match!'[65]

CHAPTER 10

We're Living in Violent Times

I

AS THE end of 1984/85 football season approached, the sport was, wrote Stuart Jones, *The Times'* football correspondent, 'dying a slow and painful death'.[1] His diagnosis was prompted by Luton and Millwall fans fighting running battles with each other and the police during their FA Cup sixth-round replay at Kenilworth Road but it might have been delivered at several points over the previous fifteen years, a period in which the regularity and severity of such incidents was increasing. At the time, many considered football violence to be a modern phenomenon, yet it had been a feature of the game more or less since professionalism was introduced in 1888. In the twenty years prior to 1915, the FA took punitive action in relation to 116 incidents of crowd disorder.[2] Numerous others went unpunished. Fighting between rival fans, attacks on players and officials, fans forcing their way into grounds without paying, and drunken and rowdy behaviour outside stadia were all commonplace in various forms to various degrees over the ensuing decades.

It was not until the late 1960s, however, that the calculated hooligan gangs which became so prominent in the 1980s began to emerge. Initially informally organised, loose-knit alliances, these groups of young men from estates and suburbs surrounding their teams' grounds laid claim to a particular 'end' behind one of the goals as their 'territory'. They also started travelling to away games in increasingly large numbers and infiltrating the 'home' ends of their rivals. To combat the increasing level of violence between hooligan gangs, and in an attempt to keep them apart, clubs erected fences, subdividing terraces into 'pens', and police attended games in greater numbers. These measures had unintended consequences. The fences created unequivocal dividing lines, reinforcing the solidarity within the rival groups and, perhaps more significantly, clearly demarcating the territory to be defended by the home fans and 'taken' by the away fans. The increased police presence led to fighting in unpoliced environments. Violence started to spill out of stadia.

As it did, the hardcore hooligans formed highly organised, named 'firms'. The Headhunters of Chelsea, Hibernian's Capital City Service, Leicester City's Baby Squad and West Ham's Inter City Firm (ICF) all became synonymous with what from the outside looked like mindless match-day violence. Yet the hooligans, mainly unskilled and semi-skilled workers in their late teens and early twenties, were employing increasingly sophisticated strategies to plan their activities and avoid detection by the police. Chelsea's firm paid subscriptions into a building society to fund their trips[3] while the ICF adopted their name because they spurned 'football special' train services and official supporters' coaches, instead travelling on the recently launched high-speed InterCity trains. They also dispensed with club scarves and emblems so they could not be identified as football fans. In a sense, the police and the hooligans were involved in an arms race. The more measures the police took to control hooligans and eradicate violence, the more measures the hooligans took to avoid those controls so the violence could continue. As these more organised hooligan groups emerged, so the level of violence increased. It reached its grim peak in 1985.

In early March, violence during the second leg of Chelsea's League Cup semi-final against Sunderland at Stamford Bridge led to twenty injuries and 104 arrests. According to the *Daily Mirror*, the game had reached 'sickening depths of savagery'.[4] However, it was the Luton–Millwall riot ten days later that proved the tipping point. Despite the reputation of Millwall's Bushwackers hooligan firm, supporters could pay at the turnstiles to get into the match, virtually unheard of now but the way things were at the time. An unexpectedly large contingent made their way up from London, including some from other clubs, such as Chelsea and West Ham. They went on the rampage before the game, smashing shop and pub windows, leading to the closure of the town's Arndale Centre. The violence soon moved inside the ground where the vast terrace of Kenilworth Road, which had a capacity of 5,000, was soon overflowing with away fans. Before and during the game they stormed the pitch and other parts of the ground. Luton keeper Les Sealey was hit by a coin and narrowly avoided being struck by a six-inch knife.

The worst was to come after the final whistle. The hooligans ripped up the ground's new plastic seats, themselves something of a novelty, and used them as projectiles. A police officer was knocked to the ground unconscious. His colleague was kicked as he, successfully, administered the kiss of life. Forty-seven people were injured, thirty-three of whom were police officers. Some thirty-one arrests were made, leading to twenty-nine being charged; £15,000 worth of damage was done inside the stadium and £45,000 worth of damage on a train going back to London. Mercifully there were no deaths. In an era when there was, certainly by modern standards, comparatively little televised coverage of football, the events were magnified by the presence of BBC cameras filming highlights for *Sportsnight* later that evening. The footage was broadcast almost as live on the news, leaving the country aghast. Looking back nearly thirty years later, David Pleat, Luton's manager at the time of the game, said, 'That night was a bad dream. It was something we had never seen before. We had never seen people rip up seats and throw them.'[5] Margaret Thatcher demanded a report from the FA within the week and the violence started a national conversation about how to combat hooliganism.

A so-called 'war cabinet' was convened at which Thatcher and representatives from the FA and the Football League agreed a range of measures such as the stronger use of police powers inside stadia, the introduction of CCTV, a ban on taking alcohol into grounds, more all-ticket games and the introduction of membership cards.[6] Luton introduced the latter immediately, also banning away fans, while others took even more draconian measures. In response to the trouble at their League Cup game, Chelsea installed an electric fence at Stamford Bridge. Chairman Ken Bates came up with the idea while walking round his farm one morning, thinking: 'If electric fences can keep cows in, it can bloody well keep in hooligans.'[7] The idea was met with horror and the fence was never switched on. Despite these moves, the season's violence had not yet ended. The nadir had not yet been reached.

Division Two Birmingham ended the season on a high. Promotion to the First Division was guaranteed and, as the club hosted Leeds United at St Andrew's on the final day, their fans knew they would be champions if they won and leaders Oxford United lost at home to Barnsley. For their part Leeds also had a mathematical chance of promotion if they won and Manchester City, Portsmouth and Blackburn all lost.

In Northampton, Ian Hambridge's three friends were planning
to go to the match. Ian, who was fifteen, had never been to a game
before and when his mates said they were going to St Andrew's he
asked his mum if he could go too. She agreed and so, on the morning of Saturday 11 May, the four youngsters made the hour-long
train journey across the Midlands.

The match always had the potential for violence. Birmingham's
Zulu Warriors and Leeds' Service Crew were both notorious hooligan firms. Some 10,000 fans made the trip from Yorkshire,
significantly more than West Midlands Police had been expecting.
With the glory days of the Don Revie era an increasingly distant
memory, the small chance of promotion meant this was one of the
biggest matches Leeds had played since they had reached the European Cup final ten years earlier, a game that was marred by violence
and which saw the club banned from Europe for two years. It was a
grim portent of what was to come almost a decade to the day later.

The mood was ugly even before kick-off. Leeds fans making the
journey south by coach caused trouble in Burton-on-Trent, Leicestershire and Nottinghamshire. Groups of rival supporters fought
near Birmingham New Street Station. In one pub visiting supporters threw everything that wasn't nailed down out of the windows,
smashing them all in the process. The violence continued inside
the ground with the Leeds fans destroying a snack bar at the back
of the Tilton Road end. Birmingham's Martin Kuhl scored the
game's only goal three minutes before half-time. When the referee
blew for the break, trouble escalated. Fans of both teams surged
onto the pitch and pieces of advertising hoarding, masonry, wood,
even a kettle from the snack bar rained down from the visitors'
end. A thin blue line of officers equipped with only helmets and
truncheons and supported by others on horseback tried to keep the
rival hooligans apart. Leeds manager (and former player) Eddie
Gray tried to restore calm, but his own supporters pelted him with

missiles. It was around forty-five minutes before the police regained control and the players could come back out to continue the game.

When the final whistle blew at 5.17 p.m., a mass of home fans ran onto the pitch and charged the Leeds supporters. As the stadium announcer desperately pleaded over the tannoy for fans to 'go home in the name of football',[8] the police just about managed to keep the two sets of fans apart, although many were injured in the process, one after being hit in the face by a four-foot-long plank of wood. Pockets of violence continued to erupt outside the ground for another couple of hours. A children's playground was destroyed and a group of Asians returning from a wedding were attacked.[9]

Years later, a retired officer admitted it had been the most terrifying experience of his career.[10] *The Times*' Tim Austin, who was watching from the press box, wrote that it was 'by far the most serious and deplorable crowd trouble I have seen in 30 years of watching football'.[11] In his report into ground safety, Justice Popplewell described the scenes as being more like 'the Battle of Agincourt than a football match'.[12] In total 236 people were injured, but the true number is probably much higher. The St John Ambulance service tending the injured in a first aid centre beneath the main stand were so overwhelmed that they abandoned their normal recording procedures.

In the pandemonium at the end of the match Ian Hambridge had become separated from his friends. Outside the ground he took shelter in a small car park next to the line of police trying to marshal the Leeds fans on their exit. 'It's like anybody,' said PC Michael Corrigan, one of the officers in the group, years later. 'You get lost in a big crowd; you find a uniformed policeman.'[13] Inside, Corrigan's colleagues advanced towards the Leeds supporters in an effort to shepherd them out of the ground. The fans retreated to the top of the terrace but the exits to the stairwells were too narrow to accommodate them all. The pressure became huge. A free-standing wall at the back of the stand – twelve feet high but just one brick thick – collapsed, crushing those standing below.

'I heard the scream first,' recalled PC Corrigan. 'We all turned, and the next thing I know is mates of mine digging me out. I was trapped. When the wall hit me, my head was bent forward. Only my helmet saved me.'[14] Ian was not so lucky. When his friends returned to Northampton without him, the youngster's desperate parents rang the police, who said there was a young lad in Smethwick's Midland Neurological Hospital. The couple rushed to Ian's beside but arrived ten minutes too late. Their son had died from severe head and chest injuries.

In the aftermath of the tragedy, the council, the club and the police all pointed the finger at each other. While hooliganism was undeniably the root cause, there was conflicting witness testimony and so Ian's parents never found out whether the wall was pushed over, or if there was a structural fault that caused it to collapse under the sheer weight of fans leaving the ground. Had Ian's death happened on any other day it would almost certainly have been front page news; however, it was overshadowed by a greater loss of life in Bradford, where fifty-six people died in a fire at the club's Valley Parade ground. 'Ian was just another statistic,' his father Vic said, twenty years after his death, 'but our lives changed forever. He has been forgotten but we know him, and we remember him.'[15]

II

If Ian's death was overshadowed by the Bradford disaster, the Bradford disaster was in turn overshadowed by the Heysel tragedy just eighteen days later. The stadium in Brussels was the venue for a highly anticipated European Cup final between two of the Continent's best teams. The imperious Liverpool of Kenny Dalglish, Ian Rush and Bruce Grobbelaar were not only hoping to retain the trophy but also lift it for a fifth time in nine seasons. Standing in their way was the Juventus of Paolo Rossi, Michel Platini and Marco Tardelli. Nicknamed *la Vecchia Signora* (the Old Lady), Juventus were enjoying a period of domestic dominance, but this was the one trophy they had yet to get their hands on: winning it would place them in the pantheon of the greats.

The previous year Liverpool had won the European Cup against AS Roma in the Italian club's own backyard, the Stadio Olimpico, and the match had been marred by violence. 'We were under assault from the second we were there,' says author and journalist Tony Evans, present as a fan.[16] 'We were attacked on the coaches on the ring road – they were coming up to us in those soft-topped Fiats with the roofs down throwing bottles and launching flares. Before and after the match people were stabbed and slashed.' The violence got little coverage in the British press, something that angered Liverpool fans who felt that such aggression would have been condemned had it been directed at fans of other clubs. It also created a resentment that simmered for the next twelve months; when Liverpool reached the final in 1985 and found out they would meet Juventus, there was a determination that there would be no repeat of the previous year. 'We were as conscious as anyone that Turin is further from Rome than Liverpool is from London, so we had nothing against Juventus,' says Evans. 'The mood was not "let's give it to the Italians like they did to us last year", it was "no Italian will ever do that to me again; the ultras are not going to fuck with us" and that represented a very different mindset to the one we had gone abroad with previously.'

As the Liverpool fans set off into the centre of Brussels from the city's Jette station, their red and white chequered flags flying in the breeze, it looked to Evans like a medieval army on the move. Despite the sense of foreboding this gave him, and the lingering indignation from the previous year, the day started relatively peacefully. Liverpool fans soaked up the sun and the Belgian beer in the city's Grand Place. There were a few minor skirmishes; bravado but little more. Inside the stadium, Eamonn McCabe was working as a sports photographer for the *Observer*. 'It was joyous,' he remembers.[17] 'The European finals were always at the end of May which was almost like party time. I wanted to be there; as a sports photographer it was one of the highlights of my career and of course Juventus fans are so flamboyant. I know they wear black and white but to me it was colourful, exuberant. I remember the fireworks very strongly in their end and the big banners, so to me it was very exotic. It was amazing. I was like a kid in a sweetshop with these pictures.'

By now, Evans had made his way to the ground and was surprised by the lack of policing. 'There was a bloke with a fold-up table and chair taking tickets – I just walked in without giving mine.' Like others, he was also shocked by the condition of the stadium. 'You could just kick a hole in the breeze block wall. Our end was overcrowded and about an hour before kick-off one of the crush barriers in front of us went down, it was like "that's not good" but it wasn't that unusual – stadiums were death traps.' Sunburned and parched, Evans went to the back of the stand to get a drink and climbed onto the roof of a small refreshment hut. 'I was surveying the whole stadium and I thought, "This is great – we're all having a great time here,"' he says. After he climbed back down, Evans saw some people breaking into an empty neutral section between the Liverpool fans and a section of Juventus fans in Section Z. 'I thought they were climbing into it because there was loads of room – we'd been looking at it for ages because we were all crushed. I went over the chicken wire and a little charge took place. I didn't think anything of it, very few fists were thrown, it was just a little skirmish, the sort of thing you'd see regularly. I climbed back across, and I stood on the barrier looking for my mates.' Almost surprised at the ease with which they had gained entry to the closed-off area, other Liverpool fans continued on into Sector Z. Used to fighting other young working-class men, they were on this occasion confronted by what amounted to a group of tourists: Juventus fans who had travelled from all parts of Italy, and neutrals who had bought tickets intended for Belgian supporters from tour operators. Unsuspecting, and unaccustomed to such behaviour, these fathers and daughters, husbands and wives turned and ran. Some spilled onto the pitch, many others were caught in a deadly crush against a low retaining wall at the side of the terracing with a sheer drop on the other side into an access area.

McCabe, drawn by what he calls 'a red wave' washing across the far end of the stadium, had made his way around the perimeter to where the trouble was. 'Just as I got there, the wall literally broke on top of me.' With the Canon Sure Shot slung round his neck, McCabe took two quick photos. In so doing he captured one of the defining images of the horror, a black and white picture of the tangled mass of bodies trapped against the crumbling wall by the force of those behind them, arms outstretched, pleading for help. 'I knew it was horrific. I knew because I saw ten or fifteen people die and I'd never seen anyone die before. I saw them go blue and die, and I saw the medics give up on them. I knew – it's a terrible thing to say, isn't it? – I knew this was really big news.' McCabe then went into what he calls 'news photographer mode', taking pictures of the chaos unfolding around him. 'I'm shooting dead bodies, I'm shooting bodies going blue, I'm surprised I'm doing this but I'm in another gear. "I've got to get this right, because it could be really important" is what I felt at the time. It was only late at night that I realised the enormity of it.'

In Britain and across Europe millions watched the tragedy unfold on television. Only ten at the time, I was among them. I can't remember anything about the football. The record books tell me that Juventus won 1–0, the game was settled by a Michel Platini penalty after fifty-eight minutes, but it is the all-too-familiar scenes of wanton violence in the all-too-familiar surroundings of a grim, decrepit stadium that are seared into my memory. To say it looked like the aftermath of a bomb, or a report from a war zone, is not to overstate things. There was uncensored footage of dishevelled, shoeless, obviously dead bodies – something that would not be aired now – and grown men crying, a rare sight then. There was the sun-baked terrace, a mess of rubbish and discarded clothes. There was a Juventus fan with what looked like a gun (it turned out to be a starter pistol). Even in my youth I understood from the shocked expressions of the Belgian police and paramedics that they had been overwhelmed.

For a brief period it looked as if things might get even worse as Juventus fans at the other end of the pitch from the fatalities charged the Liverpool fans nearest to them. 'They began pouring out,' says Evans, 'and then the fella came out with the gun and that was like "Jesus Christ!" That's when everyone started tearing at the fences to try and get at them and I'll always remember my brother saying, "If those fences give now, football's over; there'll be hundreds dead – they've got guns."' The fences held. The riot police who had belatedly entered the stadium regained control. Sanity was restored.

In the dressing rooms in the bowels of the stadium the players were cut off from the unfolding horror (ironically it was their friends and families in the stands who were confronted by the grim reality of the tragedy). This confusion has led to conflicting stories and disagreement among players in both teams as to how much they knew. Alan Hansen wrote that the club's captain Phil Neal told the team, 'people have died out there',[18] after he had been onto the pitch to try and calm the Liverpool fans down. By contrast, Kenny Dalglish claims he was oblivious to the severity of the situation as he had 'fallen asleep and did not know there were any fatalities'.[19] One thing is certain: UEFA insisted the match go ahead, fearing that a postponement would lead to further violence and so after a ninety-minute delay the teams took to the pitch. As the game kicked off, the bodies of the dead lay in the stadium car park barely covered by flags and blankets. The German TV station ZDF refused to broadcast the game, while the Swiss station DRS terminated its coverage at half-time following viewer complaints. The BBC also received hundreds of calls but persevered, later justifying this by claiming it was in the public interest.[20]

'I've never processed the film of the game because what does a game mean?' McCabe tells me before acknowledging the tragedy changed his life. 'I walked into that stadium as a sports photographer and came back as a news photographer. I got to three Olympics and three World Cups and about ten European Cup finals. All of a sudden, I'm photographing people dying. I grew up that night.' For Evans and his friends, the fact the game went ahead and the Juventus players' celebrations after the final whistle suggested that, despite the delay, their worst fears were unwarranted. 'When the teams came out, we thought nothing bad could have happened. Platini dancing like it's one of the greatest days of his life; we thought "there can't be anything wrong – it can't be bad".' The hostile mood of the police outside suggested otherwise but still the first time Evans knew there had been fatalities was the following morning. 'My mate woke me up. I remember it being on television, but it might have been radio and they said, "forty-two dead at Heysel" and that was the first I realised there'd been any deaths, and I'd been in the section where the charge had happened.'

The death toll would eventually be revised down to thirty-nine. Thirty-two Italians had been killed as had four people from France, two Belgians and a Northern Irishman. Roberto Lorentini, a thirty-one-year-old doctor and father of two survived the first stampede but was killed in the second as he tried to give artificial respiration to an eleven-year-old boy, Andrea Casula. Andrea was the youngest victim; his father Giovanni died, too. Another victim, Patrick Radcliffe, was an archivist for the EEC in Brussels. The only British victim, he was from Belfast and wasn't even a football fan; he had gone along with a Dutch friend with a spare ticket. 'He was in the wrong place at the wrong time,' said Patrick's twin brother, George.[21] The same could be said for the other thirty-eight victims; the same could be said for Ian Hambridge.

III

Recriminations began immediately. The FA withdrew all English clubs from the following season's European competitions. This was then extended to a five-year ban, six for Liverpool. Predictably and justifiably, there was widespread outrage across Europe at the behaviour of the Liverpool fans, various newspapers labelling them 'terrorists', 'assassins' and 'worse than animals'.[22] According to Clive Gammon, writing for *Sports Illustrated* the month after the tragedy, 'through all of Europe a tower of anger raged against not merely a mob of drunken Liverpudlian hooligans [. . .] but against the whole British nation'.[23] Juventus fans burned the Union Jack in the streets of Turin. British nationals in Europe were warned to 'keep a low profile' by government officials, holidaymakers on the Venetian coast warned not to go out unaccompanied, British motorists advised to remove GB stickers from their cars.

Yet there was also an acknowledgement, particularly in the Belgian media, that the country's government was at least partially at fault. *La Dernière Heure Les Sports* suggested that the tragedy could have been avoided if there had been better segregation and the police had reacted with greater speed. In a similar vein, the Milan-based *Corriere della Sera*, at the time Italy's biggest newspaper, condemned the 'culpable impotence of the police', while the *Corriere dello Sport*, based in Rome, also cast some blame on the 'absent police'.[24] Two months after the tragedy, a Belgium parliamentary report, while holding the Liverpool fans 'who carried out the murderous charge [as] principally responsible', went on to condemn a series of Belgian 'oversights, deficiencies, and lacunae' which also contributed. The police, the Belgian FA and even UEFA were all subject to criticism while the stadium, which would later be pulled down and rebuilt, was condemned as 'dilapidated' and a 'crumbling concrete structure'.[25]

Twenty-four Liverpool fans were extradited to Belgium to face charges of involuntary manslaughter. And in 1989, following a lengthy legal process, fourteen were found guilty and sentenced to three years in prison, half of which was suspended. While their families claimed they had been scapegoated, relatives of the victims condemned the short sentences as an insult to the dead. Yet, again blame was apportioned more widely. As part of the same trial, there were also convictions for Albert Roosens, the former head of the Belgian FA, and Johan Mahieu, the police officer who had been responsible for the area of the stadium where the tragedy occurred. Both received suspended sentences for negligence and poor organisation of the match. Five other officials, including Jacques Georges, the French president of UEFA, were acquitted.

Despite the convictions of Roosens and Mahieu, it's hard to imagine that, had the Greek champions Panathinaikos beaten Liverpool in the semi-finals, the name Heysel would have become synonymous with death at a football match. Evans believes that for too long afterwards there was an unwillingness on Merseyside to accept the true extent of the Liverpool fans' culpability. 'The reality of Heysel is there's a long causal chain with a lot of links,' he says. 'If you take any one of those links out, no one dies. You can talk about the failure of the policing. You can talk about the state of the stadium. Take any one of those things out and no one dies. But our behaviour on that day as a fan group was a big link in that chain.'

As a footnote to Heysel, in April 2005 Liverpool and Juventus met for the first time since the tragedy in the quarter-finals of the Champions League, which Liverpool went on to win thanks to the 'Miracle of Istanbul' against another Italian team, AC Milan. In the first leg at Anfield, Liverpool created a mosaic of coloured cards, spelling the word '*Amicizia*' (friendship). Many Juventus fans applauded; others pointedly turned their backs. Still others held up a banner that read simply 'English, Dirty, Drunk, Infamous'.

IV

The sentiment of the Juventus fans' banner reflected the rhetoric of the British press when discussing football hooligans during the 1980s. They were dismissed with terms such as 'animals', 'lunatics', 'savages' and 'thugs'.[26] Not only did this ignore the relatively high level of organisation among football hooligan firms, but according to John Williams, who built on his research at the 1982 World Cup to become one of the foremost experts on the subject, it also pushed hooligans further to the margins of society. They became their own explanation. 'I don't think the dehumanising language of the press helped public understanding,' says Williams.[27] 'It reinforced those views that this was mindless and meaningless, and you can't have a conversation with these guys: they're just complete brutes and they're not saying something important about the human condition. Whereas my view is that they were; we just didn't want to listen too much and the way they were trying to say it was really hard for us to get to grips with.'

Ted Croker, the FA secretary in 1985, held a similar view. At the 'war cabinet' Thatcher brought together in the wake of trouble at Kenilworth Road, she asked of the football officials present: 'What are you going to do about your hooliganism?', to which Croker replied: 'Not our hooligans, Prime Minister, but yours. The products of your society.'[28] It was not the response she was expecting, and it is notable that Croker became the first FA secretary in over a century not to be knighted. Yet, as if to hammer home his point that civil unrest was not solely a football issue, the autumn of 1985 brought a series of riots across the country in Handsworth, Brixton and Tottenham. Just as fans following England abroad reflected a wider boorish jingoism, so hooliganism in the domestic game reflected wider societal divisions.

'It was a very, very violent time, and people – especially young men – were more attuned to violence than they are now,' says Evans. 'That was the world we were in. On your TV news every night you were seeing scenes of street fighting from Belfast and Derry – violence was normal.' For Evans, these incidents, and others like them, were symptomatic of an increasing level of violence in society that he feels reached a peak during the 1984/85 football season. The miners' strike ran throughout much of it, reinforcing for many the sense of a country riven by civil war, the police and government on one side, those that Thatcher branded 'the enemy within'[29] on the other.

The strike, which began in March 1984, was the result of the National Coal Board's announcement that it intended to close twenty working pits, at a cost of 20,000 jobs. The first to shut as a result of strike action was the Cortonwood colliery, near Rotherham. Soon the rest of the Yorkshire coalfield was at a standstill, as were those of traditionally militant South Wales and Scotland. However, in Nottinghamshire, miners voted against the strike, the unity that helped win previous strikes by the miners missing from the start this time. The government had long prepared for the eventuality, stockpiling coal and bringing oil-fired power stations back online. The benefit law was changed so as to deduct £15 from the dependants of those on strike to account for strike pay. Despite these pressures, the strike dragged on for twelve months, reaching its peak in June 1984 at the 'Battle of Orgreave' when some 10,000 picketing miners and members of the South Yorkshire constabulary (who would be on duty at the Hillsborough disaster five years later) fought at a coking plant in Orgreave, near Rotherham. Ninety-five miners were charged with a range of violent offences; however, all the charges were eventually withdrawn. Around a third received compensation from the South Yorkshire Police for wrongful arrest. The *Socialist Worker* drew parallels between what happened at Orgreave with the violence at Kenilworth Road, saying: 'The images of violence and of raging anger (although those witless football fans have no cause at all) lead us to question whether the fabric of society is close to collapse in Thatcher's Britain.'[30] The strike officially ended on 3 March 1985, the strikers effectively starved into surrender.

Three months later, some 600 New Age travellers including

green activists, anti-nuclear protestors and free festival-goers — others on the margins of Thatcher's Britain — were ambushed by around 1,300 police officers in a field beside the A303 in Wiltshire while heading towards Stonehenge. Dozens were injured, 537 were arrested — the largest mass arrest since the Second World War — and every one of their vehicles — their homes — was destroyed. Seven healthy dogs were also put down. Nick Davies, then a journalist working for the *Observer*, wrote of the police: 'there was no question of trying to make a lawful arrest. They crawled all over, truncheons flailing, hitting anybody they could reach. It was extremely violent and very sickening.'[31] Despite the one-sided nature of the incident, as with Orgreave it became known as a 'battle' — the 'Battle of the Beanfield'. Again, as with Orgreave the trials against those arrested collapsed. Twenty-four successfully sued for wrongful arrest. The only person convicted in relation to the incident was a police officer.

The schisms that underpinned this violence were captured and articulated by Leeds-born poet Tony Harrison in his 3,500-word poem *V*, which first appeared in the *London Review of Books* in 1985 and was subsequently broadcast on Channel 4 two years later. Inspired by Harrison's discovery that his mother and father's grave at the city's Beeston Cemetery had been vandalised, the poem imagines a conversation with the fictitious skinhead football fan Harrison believes responsible for the damage responding to the author's implied rebuke. In this context, 'V' was not just the letter that links football teams to their opponents — a recurring theme — it also stood for a much wider range of divisions within which football's problems were located.

[. . .]

These Vs are all the versuses of life
From LEEDS v. DERBY, Black/White

and (as I've known to my cost) man v. wife,
Communist v. Fascist, Left v. Right,
Class v. class as bitter as before,
the unending violence of US and THEM,
personified in 1984
by Coal Board MacGregor and the NUM,
[. . .][32]

Harrison's evocation of the struggle between different sections of society in the shadow of the Thatcher government and his indignation at the moral degeneracy of the Britain of the time were obscured by the furore, particularly when broadcast, over the profane language within the poem. The *Daily Mail* condemned it as a 'torrent of filth', while Tory MP Gerald Howarth denounced Harrison as 'another probable Bolshie seeking to impose his frustrations on the rest of us'.[33] However, right-wing polemicist Bernard Levin leapt to the author's defence, hailing *V* as 'one of the most powerful, profound and haunting long poems of modern times'.[34]

Two years after *V* was first published, Thatcher, in an interview with *Woman's Own* magazine, asked '[. . .] who is society?' before answering her own question: 'There is no such thing!'[35] Her office issued a quick clarification, but were unable to prevent the remark from becoming, at least to her critics, shorthand for an aggressively individualist worldview that prized selfishness and greed over social obligations. It also became indicative of a disintegration in class solidarities which, Williams believes, had in previous decades helped police young men more effectively, thereby limiting their excesses. 'I think that those old meanings in classed communities were becoming less influential on some young people. They were more interested in hooligan firms than where they lived.' Furthermore, belonging to a hooligan gang at a time when employment prospects were low had a certain appeal.

'Being a member of those particular firms became a ticket for a certain kind of dignity, and a certain sort of self-worth that wasn't available in other kinds of ways,' says Williams. 'For a lot of young working-class men at that time prospects looked pretty bleak. So, connecting yourself to a firm like that and having a bit of local status and having people looking afraid, or having people looking up to you in your local neighbourhood was very seductive when not much else was available.'

Evans agrees. 'In working class communities where there's not a lot of money around, how do you gain status? By being tough. People were readier with their fists than they are now. It was a much more violent world, and a lot of people didn't think twice about fighting. So, hooliganism, which became codified and mythologised in the 1980s, in its origins was just working-class young men put in confrontational situations with alcohol as a catalyst — it was as simple as that.'

But, echoing Croker, Evans says this 'wasn't just at football matches'. The year 1987 was ushered in by a series of disturbances in small cities and market towns across the country. Over the course of the following year there were some 83,000 violent offences in rural areas, a 50 per cent increase from 1980. In a memo for cabinet, Home Secretary Douglas Hurd wrote that this was seen as an 'increasing burden' by police.[36] 'There is nothing new in market town disorders,' Hurd acknowledged. 'Drunken mob violence goes back centuries; teddy boys in the '50s, mods and rockers in the '60s, punks and skinheads in the '70s inherited a long tradition. But I am concerned that the problem is getting worse.' He then went on to draw parallels between 'the rural rioter and the football hooligan'. Those in the shires were, like their urban counterparts, young men mainly aged sixteen to twenty-five years old. Being tough, which was considered 'proof of manhood', afforded them a measure of social kudos. Alcohol removed their inhibitions and pushed them over the edge. Internal and/or external restraints were few and far between. When the police arrived at the site of disturbances, both sides tended to gang up and turn on them.

Violence was also considered par for the course at many music gigs. Skinheads, goths, mods, new romantics and punks all co-existed with a deeply tribal sense of mutual suspicion, their differences accentuated by their hairstyles and the clothes they wore. Like the football grounds of the day, security at concert venues was poor, with little if any CCTV. Looking back on the era, the former *NME* journalist Paul Morley went as far as to suggest: 'The kind of music you liked was a matter of life and death. [. . .] It wasn't just about taste or lifestyle; it was really about who you were.'[37] In April 1980, a riot broke out among the 400-strong crowd at a Joy Division gig at Derby Hall in Bury after a pint glass was thrown onto the stage. In 1985, just two days after Luton and Millwall fans fought at Kenilworth Road, trouble flared at a Jesus and Mary Chain gig at the North London Polytechnic. Some in the crowd started fighting among themselves while others tried to attack the band. The PA system was pulled down, and approximately £8,000 worth of damage was caused. The release of the group's first album *Psychocandy* was still several months away but the threat (or promise) of violence at their gigs merely heightened their appeal. In September their gig at Camden's Electric Ballroom descended into similar chaotic scenes.

Yet trouble of this nature was not restricted to young working-class men. In the 1980s, two Old Etonians, David Cameron and Boris Johnson, who would both go on to become prime minister, were members of Oxford University's elite Bullingdon Club.[38] According to a female contemporary who acted as a recruiter for the club, the 'whole culture was to get extremely drunk and exert vandalism'.[39] Clad in their uniform of blue tailcoats and mustard waistcoats, members 'found it amusing if people were intimidated or frightened by their behaviour'.[40]

But none of these — the shire riots, the chaos at gigs, nor the exploits of the 'Buller' boys — was quite as public as football hooliganism. None was broadcast to aghast national television audiences like the Millwall—Luton riot and the fatal violence at Heysel. None received the same weekly headlines screaming from the pages of the newspapers. Furthermore, they tended to be relatively self-contained, while football hooliganism often spilt out of stadia and into the surrounding suburban locations, railway stations and shopping centres on Saturday afternoons. 'That whole ethos of "we only fight other lads like us", there was an element of truth in that,' says Williams, 'but it didn't mean that you weren't affected by it if you were an ordinary fan because it very often happened in the street. It wasn't in some secret and dark space late at night, so people saw it and they were frightened by it.'

V

The fear generated by the violent actions of the minority of football fans created a sense that everyone who attended a game was intrinsically nihilistic. Few leapt to supporters' defence when the *Sunday Times* dismissed them as 'slum people'[41] in the aftermath of Heysel, yet this obscured a vibrant youth subculture with a keen sense of fashion. In many respects this was an evolution of what had come before. Just as there was a long history of violence among young working-class men, so there was a long history of these gangs displaying a distinctive style. In his memoir of life growing up in Salford in the early years of the twentieth century, Robert Roberts talked of the Northern scuttlers, gangs of youths who wore clogs, bell-bottomed trousers and heavy, ornately

designed leather belts and who 'sought escape from their tedium
in bloody battles with belt and clog – street against street'.[42] The
Teddy Boys in the 1950s and the mods and rockers in the 1960s,
all mixed violence and fashion. So, too, did the punks until the
scene that had burned brightly – but only briefly – imploded with
Johnny Rotten sneering 'Ever get the feeling you've been cheated?'
to the crowd at the end of the last ever Sex Pistols gig in 1978.

Casuals, as they would ultimately become known, were there
to pick up the pieces, fans of different clubs arguing and competing over who was wearing the most on-trend clothes. 'The whole
thing about being a casual was that you wanted to look better
than everyone else,' says Terry Farley, who chronicled the movement in the fanzine *Boy's Own*.[43] 'You wanted something new.
When other people were wearing it, you were dropping it.' While
there had long been disputes about where the trend started –
Merseyside's 'Scallies', Manchester's 'Perries' (originally Fred
Perry Boys) and London's 'Chaps' all claiming to have been the
instigators – Farley, a Chelsea fan, acknowledges that Liverpool
fans were a driving force. 'People always wore trainers. Every kid
in the country had a pair of Adidas Samba in the late seventies
but no one ever thought of them as a fashion item. You have to
give it to the Scousers; the trainer craze started in Liverpool. They
definitely drove the market in this country. That obsession is
everywhere now. Every high street has one or two trainer shops
and they're still wearing the same old Adidas eighties classics.'

At the time, specialist shops sold shoes designed for running or
tennis, along with other sports clothing, but these were aimed at
serious (or semi-serious) athletes and their range was limited. The
first time British youngsters came into contact with the full pan-
oply of what Adidas and other manufacturers such as Puma had
to offer – items that are considered retro classics today – was
when they followed their teams abroad, or their friends brought

shoes back following such a trip. Liverpool's success, which saw them reach six European finals in ten seasons between 1976 and 1985, gave their supporters more opportunities to travel abroad than most others got.

Robert Wade Smith, who worked for Top Man, noticed this. In November 1982, he quit his job to set up his own business selling trainers in Liverpool. It was a no-brainer for the twenty-two-year-old. During the three years that he worked for Top Man, the Liverpool branch's Adidas concession was the country's leader, doing a third of all UK business and triple the next best.[44] However, after he set up his store, named Wade Smith, on the city's Slater Street, he encountered a problem. Adidas had over 200 designs globally, but the manufacturer assumed there would be little demand for the more expensive shoes in the UK, so only around forty were available. Wade Smith's customers didn't want them; they wanted rarer ones from abroad: Grand Slam, München, Trimm-Trab, Zelda. To meet this demand, Wade Smith withdrew all the money he had in the bank, changed it into Deutschmarks, hired a van, travelled to Germany and bought 475 pairs of Adidas shoes. His gamble paid off. Within four weeks, he'd sold out. Within two months, he'd sold £27,000-worth of Adidas trainers.[45] Wade Smith began making regular trips to Germany and Austria, where he built up a bank of contacts with retailers, regional dealers and Adidas distributors. This enabled him to bypass the manufacturer's British distribution network and stock sought-after shoes not intended for the UK market. Wade Smith expected to sell in the region of 26,000 pairs in his first year; he sold 110,000.[46] Soon his store was selling more Adidas trainers than any other shop in the world.[47] Sports shoes were no longer just functional athletics equipment, they had become fashionable leisurewear.

It wasn't just trainers. Previously unheard-of European

sportswear brands such as Diadora, Ellesse, Fila, Kappa, Lacoste and Tacchini became sought-after additions to the discerning football fan's wardrobe. As fashion journalist Robert Elms noted in his style memoir *The Way We Wore*, mocking each other's sense, or perceived lack, of style became as important a part of terrace culture as fighting. A Queens Park Rangers fan, Elms recalled a trip to Coventry City where the visitors taunted their rivals for wearing Fila which, according to the author, 'had once been the business but had gone out of fashion in London at least a month before'. With the visiting fans 'lambasting them for such gauche sartorial tardiness' the Coventry supporters' faces dropped. 'They'd been beaten, and they knew it,' said Elms. 'As the desire for a fight seeped away, they slipped away too.'[48] This brief confrontation was indicative of the numerous, constantly shifting regional variations of what was 'in' and what was 'out' – often dependent on the relative success of clubs in Europe – that were all but imperceptible to those not attuned to the latest trends. And most weren't.

'Casuals were excluded from what the magazines and the Sunday supplements were talking about,' says Farley. Football terraces were not places that the style gurus and fashion journalists of the day tended to frequent, instead their focus was on Sloane Rangers, Young Fogies and Yuppies, trends exploited, if not created, by advertisers. *The Clothes Show*, hosted by Selina Scott and Jeff Banks, was launched by the BBC with the intention of stripping fashion of its mystique and making it simply 'clothes for everyone to enjoy'.[49] It boasted an audience of some eight million and spawned a magazine and roadshow, but it did not acknowledge the organic fashion trend sweeping across the country's football stadia.

Furthermore, unlike previous youth subcultures, music was not a fundamental part of the casual scene. Liverpool band The Farm, as well as The Stone Roses, The Happy Mondays and other groups associated with 'Madchester' music, adopted aspects of casual style and attitudes. However, there was no band providing a definitive soundtrack for the trend as The Who and The Sex Pistols did for mods and punks respectively. Thus, casual fashion received limited coverage from music journalists, too. 'There was very little interest from the more mainstream press in the 1980s because it was people on the margins in Liverpool and Manchester,' says Evans. 'Even in London, it was people on the margins. We had lots of famous punks and you saw them on the telly. There were no famous casuals as such.'

The Face was the first nationally published magazine to acknowledge football-fan fashion, in 1983. Author Kevin Sampson submitted an article on the subject to the magazine in 1981 but received a rejection: 'Sounds cool, but it's a bit niche for us.'[50] Two years later, it could no longer be ignored. The magazine's editor Nick Logan contacted Sampson and asked him to update the piece. Sampson is often credited with coining the term 'casual', but it doesn't appear in his article. Instead, it is mentioned in an accompanying piece by Dave Rimmer looking at the comparative trends in London. 'They haven't got a name,' wrote Rimmer, 'though some call themselves casuals.'[51] Others rejected the term – both Evans and Farley expressed their dislike for the label – but it became a widely used catch-all for the subculture, unifying them in the minds of those on the outside.

The expensive 'designer' clothing sported by the casuals appeared to support the idea that football violence couldn't be the result of poverty, a feeling reinforced by the media's disproportionate focus on those hooligans from affluent backgrounds. 'It just confirmed them in their views that these were "too much too young guys" and we shouldn't be talking about social class and frustration and all those kinds of things,' says Williams, 'because look at what these guys could afford to buy – they're just flaunting their consumerist values.' However, this belied the reality. The overwhelming majority were young working-class men engaged in low-income, non- or partly skilled work.

Williams acknowledges the situation was nuanced, that those accounts of football hooliganism that only talked about frustration were equally simplistic and that the consumerist values the casuals were displaying were important, signifying a dissolving of old class ties. 'The idea that young men could make themselves better people by wearing more expensive clothes or waving money at supporters in more deprived parts of the country was a signature of those Thatcherite values, which were going to become a much more central part of British culture,' he says. However, as Williams points out, these clothes were often not paid for. While some fans saved up to buy them, others engaged in petty crime to get the money. Others simply stole them, the clothes becoming a badge of honour, showing rival supporters how far those wearing them had travelled to find them and thus how devoted they were. 'The fan groups I went with abroad: they didn't buy this stuff and bring it back,' says Williams. 'They wanted to steal it if they could and then bring it back and show how sophisticated they were by going somewhere else and finding stuff that no one else had. So, it was deeply competitive. It added something beyond the violence to hooligan culture, that is clearly important.'

VI

As the decade wore on casual fashion became increasingly homogenised, the once-strict regional differences dissolving and blurring into a more unified national look. Furthermore, the grim events of 1985 proved to be a watershed. Policing of games reached almost military levels, while the deaths in Belgium also caused even hard-core hooligans to pause for thought. 'It was a huge wake-up call for us all,' wrote Cass Pennant, one of the leaders of West Ham's ICF, in his autobiography. 'I've long thought the events at Heysel brought us out of that dangerous world we'd been part of for so long.'[52]

Across the country young lads who had devoted themselves to football and fashion began to look elsewhere for their thrills. Acid house provided them. Eschewing the conventional verse/chorus/verse/chorus/guitar-solo formula, house was electronic music characterised by a base line of 120 beats per minute and had few (if any) words, mostly lifted from other recordings. In an echo of punks' do-it-yourself ethos, anyone with a computer who was able to sample sounds could produce a house track, irrespective of their traditional musical skills. It gained nation-wide prominence after Danny Rampling, Paul Oakenfold and Nicky Holloway took a now near-mythical trip to Ibiza to cele-brate Oakenfold's twenty-sixth birthday in 1987. There they were inspired by the blend of breezy, summery pop music with early house tracks played by DJ Alfredo at an open-air club called Amnesia. On their return to Britain, Rampling and Oak-enfold started their own seminal Balearic club nights, Shoom and Future respectively. It provided an appealing, less insular sound and created a different attitude towards fashion, drug-taking and sexuality which challenged the mainstream, established clubs. 'I think it was very easy if you were a casual to move into acid house because it was just another gang,' says Farley, who became a leading house DJ and producer. 'But you weren't getting into trouble; your liberty wasn't at threat. I think a lot of people from that casual culture saw this was a better way forward: "I'm still getting my buzz; I'm still travelling round the country with all my mates. I can go clubbing in Leeds, I'm going to chat to those Mancs in the corner." You hadn't been able to do that before. It opened up doors, it softened edges off people.'

One of the key ingredients helping to soften the edges was the drug MDMA. Unlike alcohol, which encouraged aggression, it produced feelings of euphoria, and high levels of empathy and togetherness among its loved-up users, hence its more common soubriquet Ecstasy, shortened to 'E'. Although the drug caused some deaths, the only widespread side effect was the comedown. For many the perceived benefits far outweighed the risks and as the 'Second Summer of Love' dawned in 1988, house music exploded nationwide. Demand quickly exceeded supply. Events spilled out of small venues — Shoom had a capacity of just 300 — and unlicensed raves were organised in places like abandoned warehouses in Blackburn and across the Home Counties in empty aircraft hangars and farmers' fields, the latter easily accessible by the newly completed M25. These were the largest gatherings of young people outside football stadia and, although violence was not an issue, police saw them as a similar public order threat. On 1 July 1989, a twenty-mile section of the M4 was shut to prevent ravers from reaching an event at Membury in Berkshire. Three weeks later, similar tactics saw Heston Services in Hounslow cordoned off. Partygoers simply abandoned their cars on the hard shoulder and ran across the six-lane motorway to reach the event. In August 1989 12,000 people descended on Longwick in Buckinghamshire for a twenty-four-hour rave. Police received noise complaints from people living fourteen miles away. In July the following year, legislation was introduced threatening illegal rave organisers with penalties of six months in prison or up to £20,000 in fines. A week later, 836 people were arrested at Love Decade, an event held in Gildersome on the outskirts of Leeds.[53] The illegal rave scene had been crushed, but the party wasn't over.

The Face christened 1990 the 'Third Summer of Love'. In their

July edition, featuring a then-unknown sixteen-year-old Kate Moss in her first cover shoot, the magazine devoted twelve pages to exploring how the new youth scene had moved from the underground to the mainstream via the terraces thanks to 'football thugs with flowers'.[54] However, Farley thinks that the link between the rise in Ecstasy use and the concurrent reduction in football hooliganism was overstated; the threat of violence never disappeared. 'Ecstasy definitely put a stop to a lot of activity for a couple of years, but it didn't kill anything off. The sort of people you didn't want to be dancing next to in the club soon reverted to type.'

PART IV:

POLITICS

CHAPTER 11

Under Pressure

I

ALTHOUGH the announcement in October 1974 that the 1980 Olympics would be held in Moscow caused little interest in Britain, then recovering from a second general election within twelve months, over the following years there were calls from MPs on both sides of the political spectrum for a boycott of the Games. In 1978 the Labour cabinet considered such a move following the imprisonment of dissident Yuri Orlov, who set up and became chairman of the Moscow Helsinki Watch Committee. It was dismissed by Prime Minister James Callaghan as having 'no positive purpose',[1] although a few months later his foreign secretary David Owen argued that if British people came to believe that the Soviets were 'riding roughshod over the ethics and principles [of the Olympics, then the Games] would come under increasing pressure'.[2] Neil Kinnock, the party's future leader, was involved in the Campaign to Remove the 1980 Olympics from Moscow, which focused on the need for religious freedom.[3] This lost out to the opposing view that the policy of détente was the most effective way to reduce tensions between East and West, avoid a nuclear conflict and bring the Cold War to an end.

In response to the boycott calls, the British Olympic Association (BOA) chairman Sir Denis Follows persuaded the BOA's committee to pass a resolution committing them to attend the Games and thus allowing individual athletes to make up their own minds as to whether they wished to do likewise. This then gave the BOA a standard response they could use. It would also provide a prescient foundation for dealing with subsequent calls for a boycott after the Soviet invasion of Afghanistan on Christmas Day 1979. By then the Conservative Party had come to power and due to the amateur ethos of British sport, which meant that there was a voluntary tradition in its administration, Thatcher's government, like its predecessors, took a hands-off approach, allowing organisations like the BOA to have control over their own affairs. Consequently, just weeks before the invasion Hector Monro, Margaret Thatcher's minister for sport, dismissed calls for a boycott over human rights issues, writing: 'We believe that where and when these Games are held must remain, without interference from Governments, a matter for the International Olympic Committee (IOC) and the International Federations of the sports concerned.'[4] Thatcher herself was patron of the BOA's appeal fund to cover the costs for competing at the Games. Within a few short months that policy would be reversed.

The invasion of Afghanistan, an event Thatcher later described as 'one of those genuine watersheds which are so often predicted, which so rarely occur − and which take almost everyone by surprise when they do',[5] took place just eight months into what would become an eleven-year premiership and it was Thatcher's first significant diplomatic test as prime minister. She had long-held, stridently anti-communist feelings which began to develop during the immediate aftermath of the Second World War as the Iron Curtain descended over Europe. Although she later admitted in her biography that she could not clearly remember her political views at the time, one book she did read was Friedrich Hayek's *The Road to Serfdom*, which warned that socialism and state control of the economy would lead to tyranny. Whatever the influence, when the young Margaret Roberts spoke to the Belvedere North Conservative Club in 1949, she argued that the Cold War was as dangerous as any previous conflict and the only effective barrier to Communism was Conservatism.[6] During the following twenty-six years, as she trod the path to party leadership, her anti-communist sentiment crystallised and became a defining characteristic. By the time she became leader of the opposition, the era of détente, marked by the SALT I and SALT II arms limitation treaties in 1972 and 1979, and the West German policy of *Ostpolitik* towards their East German neighbours, was in full swing.

Thatcher was sceptical of this approach. In July 1975, less than six months after she became leader of the Conservative Party, she argued that she firmly believed the Soviet Union used détente to exploit division among Western nations and that it was failing.[7] This stance saw the Soviet army newspaper *Red Star* dub Thatcher 'the Iron Lady' the following year, a sobriquet she made her own and wore as a badge of honour.[8] Underpinning Thatcher's philosophy was her belief in a strong Anglo-American 'special relationship' which, with the British Empire crumbling in the aftermath of the Second World War, successive British governments had cultivated to bolster the country's prestige, and she took care to develop her own relationship with the USA during her four years as opposition leader.[9] Although in her first eighteen months in Downing Street the American president was not her political soulmate Ronald Reagan but Democrat Jimmy Carter, that didn't stop the strengthening of ties between the two administrations. When the Soviet Union invaded Afghanistan, Britain had only recently agreed to allow the US Air Force to station

Cruise missiles at Greenham Common and was also in discussions to purchase Trident as a replacement for Skybolt, the submarine-based nuclear weapons programme. Another motivation for offering firm support over Afghanistan was that Britain was unable to meet American requests to impose a trade embargo on Iran and freeze financial assets held by the country in London in response to the ongoing hostage crisis.[10]

Thus, the invasion of Afghanistan provided an opportune moment for Thatcher to tangibly demonstrate her commitment to the USA. It was also the first great test of her resolve to stand up to the Soviet Union since she had come to power. Would her actions speak as loud as her ardent anti-communist words? Economically the answer was, for a variety of reasons, a fairly meek 'no'. In early January, President Carter made a televised address announcing a range of sanctions, most notably the cancellation of the sale of 17 million tonnes of grain to the Soviet Union, which was struggling after a poor domestic harvest.[11] It was a unilateral move, but the American administration hoped they would get support from their European allies, not least Britain.[12] However, Britain was traditionally averse to using economic sanctions unless mandated by a UN resolution. Doing so against the USSR would set a precedent which could lead to pressure for trade sanctions to be imposed on other countries, such as apartheid South Africa. Furthermore, a government report suggested that unless British action was part of a collective campaign alongside other major trading nations the effect would be negligible. Other countries would simply fill the gap, meaning that Britain would suffer more than the Soviet Union.[13] This was something Thatcher could ill afford. The British economy was in a parlous state, hit by soaring inflation and a global economic downturn. Rising oil prices strengthened the pound and made British exports less competitive. With Thatcher's commitment to radical low-tax, low-spend monetarist policies limiting the extent to which her government could intervene to boost demand, maintaining British export sales was vital to weather the storm. Thus, the government was under pressure to maintain trading relationships, even with regimes it found unpalatable like the Soviet Union. Arguably, as a consequence, the only way to support the Americans was through the use of 'soft power'. Thatcher determined that 'the most effective thing we could do would be to prevent [the Soviet Union] using the forthcoming Moscow Olympics for propaganda purposes'.[14] However, this also put her and her government on a collision course with the BOA, the governing bodies of many sports and some of the country's top sportsmen and women.

II

In early January 1980, Thatcher met with her foreign secretary Lord Carrington and told him she felt the British team should not participate in the Games. However, she understood that for young athletes who had put in years of hard work to reach the Olympics, withdrawing at the last moment was not a palatable option. Thus, finding an alternative venue would be a better way of winning their support.[15] Carrington thought this 'impractical' and presciently suggested that the best outcome would be for the government to push for a boycott but for the athletes to attend of their own volition.[16] A couple of weeks later President Carter wrote to the United States Olympic Committee (USOC) asking them to work with other national Olympic associations to ensure the Games were moved unless the Soviet Union withdrew from Afghanistan. Thatcher supported the move, urging Sir Denis Follows, chair of the BOA, to formally request that the IOC move the Games.[17]

Follows reluctantly agreed while publicly stressing that his primary responsibility was to defend the views of sportsmen and women. Furthermore, he pointed out that no individual sport's governing body had yet declared support for moving the Games, making it all but impossible. His obvious reluctance prompted Carrington to complain that Follows was 'made of cement from the tip of his toes to the top of his head'.[18] But Follows merely reflected the views of the IOC. The body's president Lord Killanin refused to bow to political pressure, saying that the athletes must come first[19] and in early February, just as the Lake Placid Winter Olympics were about to begin (with the Soviet team in attendance), the IOC voted unanimously for the summer games to go ahead in Moscow. Any hope of the Games being moved were over, so the Thatcher administration turned its attention to pressuring the BOA to withdraw.

There was a belief that if the BOA could be brought on-side, then individual sports' governing bodies and athletes would follow suit. The organisation was conservative in outlook (Sebastian Coe described Follows as 'a classic northern Tory'[20]) and historically had close ties with government. However, in keeping with a personal style which would become the hallmark of her time in Downing Street, Thatcher's approach was highly combative and turned natural bedfellows against her, although she did not have direct dealings with the BOA. 'She never actually met us,' says Dick Palmer, the association's general secretary for twenty years from 1977.[21] 'First of all, she sent instead Lord Carrington who was the foreign secretary, and then she put together a sort of cabal of ministers. We met them the final time at the Foreign Office about four weeks before we went when they prevailed on us not to go. It included Carrington and Michael Heseltine who was a real bruiser. He said we were embarrassing Mrs Thatcher, we were embarrassing the government and we were embarrassing the country by deciding to go. Well, so be it. We had the resolution of the committee and we had determined to go.'

Thatcher herself resigned as patron of the BOA's appeal fund and the government cut off funding and logistical support. The Sports Council was directed not to cover costs not met by the BOA's own appeal nor to send staff to the Games.[22] This simply pushed Follows into the arms of Denis Howell, the former Labour sports minister, with a very simple message: 'No funds – no Olympics.'[23] Howell drew on the contacts developed when he had held the post for ten years in two separate administrations to draw financial backing from various unions and Labour councils. This in turn led to accusations in parliament of a 'disgraceful misallocation of ratepayers' money' by 'socialist-controlled' local authorities.[24] This was indicative of the tone of the wider debate, and Lord Killanin claimed a 'dirty tricks' department'[25] was operating in the British press. Follows was even convinced that his phone was being bugged and used to meet with Palmer in his Range Rover.

To counter this, Palmer contacted Pat Besford, then chair of the Sports Writers' Association of Great Britain, who agreed to call some of her colleagues from the likes of the BBC and Press Association and the *Daily Mirror* and *Daily Telegraph* to see if they would help. 'We met one night at her flat,' says Palmer. 'People like Ian Wooldridge, David Miller, John Rodda and several other quite senior journalists came along and said they would support us.' As the two sides engaged in a bitter media war for the hearts and minds of the public, Palmer began to feed a variety of stories to the BOA's newly established media contacts. 'We had an attaché appointed by the Foreign Office and they withdrew that appointment. The Irish Olympic Association offered to allow us use of their attaché, so the story was the BOA was using the Irish attaché. All sorts of stories like that began to filter through and as a result of this the perception of the British public changed from, I think it was about 60 per cent against us going to about 60 per cent wanting us to go.' Even the traditionally right-wing press criticised the inconsistency between Thatcher's 'New Right' belief in individual freedom and her government's attempts to prevent athletes from competing. Perhaps the most damning criticism came in an excoriating *Daily Mail* editorial which argued that 'it is intolerable that this government, of all governments – a government that abhors communist serfdom – should now seek to make British athletes jump to the Tories' bidding by what is no more or less than a crack of the totalitarian whip'.[26]

The government pressed on, introducing a motion to the Commons against British participation in the Games. It was hoped that strong support in parliament would create such pressure that the BOA would buckle. After a full day's debate Labour's opposition amendment condemning the Soviet invasion but against the boycott was defeated and the government's own motion passed by 345 votes to 147. Yet this was not a conclusive victory. The loyalist wing of the party fell four square behind Thatcher's drive to take action against the Soviets, but many other MPs felt that the athletes' right to compete trumped all else. Some also resented the prime minister's antagonistic handling of the situation and the treatment meted out to administrators like Follows and Palmer. Her own sports minister, Hector Monro, was not called to speak in the debate because of his disagreement with the government's position and in the end around thirty Conservative MPs defied the party whip to abstain.

It was clear that Thatcher did not yet command the full support of the party as she would come to do throughout the 1980s. As Carrington admitted, the result was 'satisfactory but perhaps not decisive enough to cause the British Olympic Association to agree to boycott the Moscow Games'.[27] So it proved. Palmer says

that the vote 'carried no real weight' and the BOA executive subsequently voted overwhelmingly by eighteen to one (with four
abstentions) to ignore parliament and accept the invitation to
compete in the USSR.[28] 'We had this clear policy which they
obviously didn't agree with,' says Palmer. 'If the BOA decided
not to go, we prevented individual athletes from having a choice –
they just couldn't go. If we decided to go then they had the choice
of whether to go or not.'

In April their American counterparts, the USOC, voted to
boycott the Games and they would eventually be joined by forty
other countries including several other major sporting nations such
as West Germany and China. The BOA held firm and the idea
that undue pressure was being placed on the British athletes was
reinforced when it was revealed that exports to the Soviet Union
had increased by 63 per cent in the first three months of the year.[29]
Such inconsistency, which seemed to single out sport, diminished
public support for the boycott. While the overwhelming majority
believed that the Soviet Union posed a military threat, they did not
speak with one voice about how, or even if, the Olympics should be
used as a sanction. A survey conducted at the end of January by
polling company Marplan for the recently launched BBC show
Newsnight found that while 40 per cent of respondents felt the
Games should be moved, 39 per cent believed they should still be
held in Moscow. More significantly, the same survey showed that if
the Games were to go ahead as planned, 58 per cent believed that
British athletes should be allowed to compete.[30]

III

Alongside the pressure on the BOA, the government exerted significant indirect pressure on sportsmen and women. Sebastian

Coe's father Peter was invited to meet Douglas Hurd, then a junior Foreign Office minister, in a bid to get him to persuade his son to withdraw. 'In the nicest possible way, they were essentially saying to my father, "Can you not keep your troublesome son quiet?",' Coe recalled years later.[31] While the government stopped short of the most extreme measures, such as withholding passports,[32] service personnel and civil servants were stripped of the paid leave to which they were usually entitled when competing at international events.[33] The athletes were still allowed to take holiday or ask for unpaid leave although managers were unofficially told to look unfavourably on such requests. Howell slammed these tactics as 'political thuggery', comparing them to the pressure placed on dissidents by communist states,[34] and the civil service unions rallied to the defence of their members.[35] For some, like Geoff Capes, it meant that in an era when many sports were still amateur, they effectively had to choose between their athletics and non-athletics careers.

In the 1980s, Capes became something of a national hero through his appearances on *The World's Strongest Man*. The international contest, a staple of the Christmas TV schedules (despite often being filmed months earlier), saw twenty or so huge men from around the world lifting rocks and large barrels or pulling trains to demonstrate their strength. Capes, who with his imposing figure and dark, shaggy beard resembled a cross between Bluto and Desperate Dan, won the contest in 1983 and 1985, trading victories with his great rival, the Icelandic Jón Páll Sigmarsson. However, Capes had begun his career in the police, following his grandfather, uncle and older brothers into the force in 1970. He was awarded the Queen's Jubilee medal for services to the community in 1977 and during the same decade he also became Britain's leading field athlete, winning Commonwealth gold for shot put in 1974 and 1978. However, his determination to go to the Moscow Olympics led to the abrupt end of both careers. 'I was told that I couldn't have leave, not by my boss, not by the chief constable, but by the government. So, I said: "I didn't train for four years only to be told that I can't go," and I quit the force,' Capes says from his home in Lincolnshire.[36] 'We were literally dismissed as part of the country. Despite all the training and all the times you've competed for your country you were told on a whim you can't go and if you do go you've got to leave your job or career.' With a young family to provide for and having lost his job in the police, Capes was forced to retire from athletics immediately after the Olympics. 'The only thing I knew was sport, so I went professional with the Highland Games* and *The World's Strongest Man.* I chose the professional career because it was there. It's always been a bit of a thorn in my side because I think I would have stayed in the police and as an athlete if I hadn't been forced into the choice. I'd spent twelve years as a policeman and could have done another twelve, and at the time I was one of the leading throwers in the world and I competed for another seventeen years. I lost all that overnight. It left a very bitter taste.'

As the reigning Commonwealth shot put champion Capes was one of the favourites for gold in Moscow, and less than three months before the Games he posted a personal best which would have ultimately been enough to win gold. However, his roles as chairman of the International Athletes Club and captain of the British athletics team, and his outspoken nature, made him a high-profile figure in the debate about the boycott and the subject of much criticism. 'I was singled out. I received a letter from Margaret Thatcher which was quite damning about my support for the Moscow Olympics,' Capes says. 'I basically told her what I

* Capes dominated the Games, winning in 1981 and five years in a row between 1983 and 1987.

thought of her and that I would not be used as a political pawn. I also received letters and phone calls threatening my family, saying they were going to kill my kids if I went to Moscow. We took them seriously and went to the police and I was given bodyguards at certain times.' Ultimately it became too much, affecting Capes' performance in Moscow, where he came a disappointing fifth. 'All that unwarranted pressure was phenomenal,' he laments. 'I didn't have a job, I was worried about where we were going to live, what I was going to do. It didn't help; I missed my chance, but you don't dwell on it.'

Capes was not alone. Allan Wells, Britain's leading sprinter at the time, was also subjected to considerable pressure not to attend. He received several letters from the government, one of which included a horrific picture of a dead girl he says he will never forget. 'Her hand was outstretched,' says Wells.[37] 'Her head was turned the other way, and three or four inches from her hand was a doll and the caption was "This is what the Russians are doing in Afghanistan". I thought it was disgusting. I just thought it was cynical the manner in which they tried to stop us from going.' It was one of several such packages received by Wells and his wife Margot, who was also his coach, in the build-up to the Games. Margot had kept the others away from Wells but on this occasion he decided to have a look. 'My curiosity in opening that letter changed the direction totally in what I was going to do,' Wells admits. Until that point, he had been unsure about whether or not to go. The correspondence made up his mind. 'It was easy to decide after I read the letter and saw the picture,' he says. 'I thought, "Right, that has given me the green light" and the next time I was asked I said, "Yeah, I'm going." I was absolutely clear and focused. By going to Moscow, I never felt we were saying, "You go to Afghanistan, you kill these people."' Wells also believes that a boycott would have ultimately been a pointless gesture. 'It wouldn't have made a ha'penny's worth of difference in Afghanistan. Bullets would have still been fired; people would have still been killed.'

Wells went on to take gold in the 100 metres and silver in the 200 metres behind Italian Pietro Mennea. He says that he knew his victory would always be devalued by some due to the non-attendance of his American rivals such as Mel Lattney, Stanley Floyd and a young Carl Lewis. 'At the end of the day you can only run against who turns up,' says Wells matter-of-factly. 'The saddest thing was I knew when I won the 100 metres that there would be criticism that I won because the Americans weren't there and that's exactly what happened. I was psychologically ready for that.' Two weeks later he took them on in a meeting at Koblenz and, despite being drained from his Olympics experience, he won, proving the doubters wrong. After the race he spoke to some of the American athletes who expressed their disappointment at not being able to compete in Moscow. 'They would have gone,' says Wells. 'I think they were dejected by it. It's a big thing for all athletes just to be picked for the Olympics and a lot of the Americans who didn't go in '80 didn't go in '84, so they missed out completely. I still feel frustrated for them.'

Calls for British athletes not to compete came not just from the government but also from what Capes called 'dissident groups' such as NOGO (National Olympic Games Objectors), co-founded by Norris McWhirter, who wrote the *Guinness Book of Records* with his twin Ross and co-hosted the related TV show *Record Breakers*, and Sir Frederic Bennett, the Conservative MP for Torbay. NOGO awarded gold medals bearing the image of five Olympic rings covered in barbed wire and carrying the motto 'honour before glory' to individual athletes who didn't attend.[38] Less than a month before the Games NOGO sent various athletes what some recipients described as a 'hate letter'.[39] The letter argued that the boycott would be more effective than economic sanctions as the former could not be hidden from the Russian public, while the latter could.[40] However, they also suggested that they did not advocate any action that might harm the British economy and it was this that Capes and many of his fellow athletes found most hypocritical. 'I wasn't any fan of the Soviet Union, and I didn't agree with the invasion of Afghanistan, but my main issue was with my own country having double standards,' says Capes. 'Businesses were still trading with Russia and my argument was if you can still trade with Russia, why are you asking us to boycott the Games? If they'd stopped trading with Russia and boycotted them financially, I would have had second thoughts about competing.'

Several governing bodies in more establishment-minded sports, namely shooting, yachting, hockey and equestrianism, did acquiesce to the government's boycott calls. Capes is dismissive of what he called the 'posh sports' whose athletes he believed did not attend because 'they were worried they might not get their MBEs'. However, at the time Killanin felt their non-attendance might have been due to the level of international support for the boycott in those sports, which would have diminished the quality of the competition.[41] Indeed, several athletes who went on to have parliamentary careers with the Conservative Party, such as Sebastian Coe, resisted pressure not to compete. Colin Moynihan coxed the British Lightweight rowing VIII, which won silver, and helped overturn the Amateur Rowing Association's initial decision not to attend. As a consequence, he was warned that his chances of becoming an MP might be harmed. Despite this he was elected to the Commons in 1983 and four years later was appointed minister for sport by Thatcher[42] before joining the House of Lords in 1997.

Britain's relationship with the Olympic movement in the

Thatcher era never fully recovered. In 1986 Birmingham made a bid to host the 1992 Olympics led by Denis Howell. Like a child caught between warring parents, the bid was effectively punished from both sides. The government refused to provide any financial support and Thatcher did not personally sign the letter of guarantee to the IOC, a symbolically damaging gesture. Despite this, Birmingham's pitch was technically excellent and when they arrived in Lausanne for the IOC vote, the bid team were confident that they would receive about twenty-two first-round votes and could pick up more as the voting progressed. Their hopes were quickly dashed when they received just eight – only Amsterdam received fewer – and they dropped out in the second round.[43] (In 1990, Manchester's bid to host the 1996 Games fared even worse. The government's support had improved from cool to lukewarm, but the bid was snubbed by the IOC. Just like Birmingham, it fell in the second round, this time with a humiliating five votes.[44])

While the immediate consequences of the boycott row were negative, the Olympic movement was grateful for the British athletes' stance. Lord Killanin was sure that their participation, along with that of other Western European countries, Australia and New Zealand, prevented the demise of the Olympics.[45] This sentiment was echoed years later by Coe, who suggested that the Olympic movement's gratitude played an important part in the success of the London bid to host the 2012 Olympics, of which he was chair. 'I don't think I would have been able to stand up in Singapore in front of the International Olympic Committee and say what I said with credibility if I had boycotted in 1980,' he said in 2006, a year after the vote. 'In hindsight it was a good decision to go for all sorts of reasons.'[46]

IV

When it became clear that the BOA would be sending a team to the Olympics, the Cold War fight moved to British television screens with the battle being fought over the interpretation of what the Games represented. The Soviet broadcaster Central Television of the USSR (CT USSR) controlled the cameras and produced the images but the BBC and the Independent Broadcasting Authority (IBA), which regulated commercial television at the time, controlled the microphones and thus – crucially – the interpretation of the images for viewers back home. During the build-up to the Games the two British TV companies announced in a joint statement that they would both cut the amount of coverage they would give to the Games by more than 75 per cent from between 170 and 180 hours each to around just forty hours each. Despite having both spent approximately £2 million on rights and setting up studios in Russia, they would no longer be treating the Olympics as an international sporting event likely to attract high viewing figures, instead treating it like a news event.[47] Despite the cutbacks on coverage, 109 British journalists still attended, a number only surpassed by the hosts, who sent 468, and East Germany, who sent 129.[48]

Two months before the Games, the National Olympic Committees (NOCs) of eighteen European countries, including Britain, issued a declaration after meeting in Rome. The NOCs stressed that their mission was to defend the Olympic principles of fraternity and universal friendship while reinforcing that it was their duty to facilitate athletes' participation in the Games. They also sought to underline 'that participation cannot in any way be taken to imply acceptance of any ideology or political behaviour'.[49] The NOCs also set out the conditions under which they agreed to take part in Moscow. These included using the Olympic flag instead of national flags and an abbreviated arrangement of the Olympic anthem instead of national anthems. 'The IOC gave permission to use their flag because they were glad we were going to the Games,' says Palmer, 'so we paraded under the IOC flag.'

The NOCs also determined to keep participation in the opening and closing ceremonies to a minimum. While some refused to have a delegation, the British decided to have one person taking part to avoid the possibility that a Soviet soldier would represent them. 'We didn't want to have an athlete in the embarrassing position of having to carry the flag,' says Palmer, 'so they said, "You're the chef de mission, Mr Palmer, so I'm afraid it's up to you." So, I carried it.' Watched by 102,000 spectators in the Lenin Stadium, and millions around the world, Palmer made his circuit of the track accompanied only by a Soviet woman carrying a blue and white name board with lettering in English and Cyrillic, introducing him as a representative not of 'Great Britain' but the 'BOA'. 'It was a very lonely, surreal experience, but it was over very quickly,' says Palmer, who has some regrets that one of Britain's leading athletes didn't have the opportunity to carry the flag as is traditional. The Soviet broadcasters did their best to minimise the impact by offering only an extreme close-up of Palmer who was on screen for less than twenty seconds. However, the Soviets couldn't hide the swathes of empty grass that offered a visible reminder that sixty-five nations were boycotting the Games, although ironically Afghanistan was not one of them. Lord Killanin alluded to the boycott in his speech, welcoming all the athletes and officials, 'especially those who have shown their complete independence to travel to compete despite many pressures placed on them'.[50]

With the official pleasantries out of the way, the sport could

begin and much of the media's focus, both in Britain and around
the world, was on two British athletes: Sebastian Coe and Steve
Ovett. If anyone was in any doubt about the attention they would
attract, some 600 journalists turned up to a pre-race press conference with Coe. Ovett had come to prominence when he won the
European junior 800 metres title in 1974. He came second in the
European Championships the same year, winning it in 1978, a
victory that saw him named BBC Sports Personality of the Year.
Coe won the award in 1979 after he broke three world records in
forty-one days – for the 800 metres, the 1,500 metres and the
mile. (It was the start of an astonishing period of dominance in
the BBC award for athletics, with Daley Thompson also winning
in 1982 and Steve Cram in 1983.) The scene was set. By the time
they reached Moscow, Coe, who was the world record holder, was
the clear favourite to win gold in the 800 metres, Ovett clear
favourite to win the 1,500 metres. He shared the world record
with Coe but, significantly, was the reigning European champion
and unbeaten in forty-five races over three years. The anticipation
was heightened by the fact that they had met in just one senior
race prior to Moscow. The prospect of seeing them race each
other twice in a matter of days was enticing.

The importance of their rivalry to the Games could not be
overstated. Ovett wrote in his biography that him and Coe withdrawing 'would have damaged the Moscow Games more seriously
than the withdrawal of many countries'.[51] It's a point on which
Pat Butcher, who was athletics correspondent for the *Financial
Times* and subsequently wrote a book about the pair's rivalry,
agrees. 'Coe and Ovett – and the Russians would admit this –
they saved the Olympics those two. I don't think you can
overemphasise the importance of Britain going to those Olympics
when the US and various other countries boycotted.'[52] This may
seem fanciful, but the American middle-distance runner Craig

Masback, who missed out because of the boycott, suggested that 'to the extent that the Moscow Games existed at all in the United States, the only significant stories related to Coe and Ovett and the 800 and 1,500. My recollection was [that] those were the only races shown on television.'[53]

In Britain, they provided just one more reason for the country to be split. As such, the pair were a godsend for the press, which made them characters in their own mini-soap opera. Thanks to his Christian name, his preppy, media-friendly demeanour and his membership of the Young Conservatives, Coe was the 'Toff'. The taciturn, aloof Ovett, who had a more rough and ready look, was the 'Tough'. 'I think Ovett contributed largely to that,' says Butcher. 'He did manifest a sort of bully boy approach to some of his opponents, taunting them by waving at the crowd and putting up a finger before he got to the finish line. Coe exhibited a sort of boy-next-door persona and was seen as a bit of a goodie-goodie.' Yet, it was Ovett who was the grammar-school boy, Coe the secondary modern pupil, and Butcher says the class differences between the pair were overstated. 'Peter Coe came from a working-class background similar to Ovett's parents, but the fact that Ovett's parents were market traders, with the sort of uncouth image that has, contributed, and the media helped push those relatively minor differences to polarise them more.' The runners were portrayed not just as rivals but as enemies. The truth was rather more sanguine. They hardly knew each other, living in different parts of the country and rarely meeting. 'We never made disparaging comments about each other in the press,' Coe would say later. 'I've spoken to Steve and we both agree it's something we are proud of. After what we'd read about each other we were led to believe we wouldn't like each other but when we met, the opposite was true.'[54]

Thus, the stage was set for a gladiatorial contest on athletics' biggest stage. As expected, the pair breezed into the 800 metres final, on the day Wells won gold in the 100 metres thanks to a photo-finish victory over Cuba's Silvio Leonard. A second gold quickly followed courtesy of Daley Thompson in the decathlon (swimmer Duncan Goodhew had also already won gold in the 100 metres breaststroke). That night, for the first time before a race Coe could not sleep. 'I just lay there listening to my heart,' he recalled later.[55] The next morning he was out of sorts, dropping a milk jug at breakfast. He had yet to regain his focus on the track where he ran a tactically naïve race, arguably the worst of his career. With 300 metres to go, commentator David Coleman was moved to say, 'Coe now has got himself in trouble right at the back.' And he had. Hanging behind with the intention of avoiding trouble and then bursting to the front near the end, Coe instead left himself too much to do when the pace quickened. By contrast, the more experienced Ovett, 'his blue eyes, like chips of ice', according to Coleman, determinedly barged his way to a position that allowed him to take gold. For Norman Fox, *The Times*' athletics correspondent, 'It asserted one important point – that [Coe] is a runner while Ovett is a racer.'[56] Coe's father had a more succinct verdict. 'You ran like a cunt,' he whispered *sotto voce* to his son in front of shocked journalists at a packed post-race press conference.[57]

For Ovett, who seemed almost bemused by his unexpected win, victory was bittersweet. As he looked to the press box he was met by grim faces: the wrong man had won. 'They were stunned,' he wrote later, 'and that upset me.'[58] Some of the journalists who had themselves been Olympic athletes took it upon themselves to give Coe some advice ahead of the 1,500 metres. Chris Brasher and Ron Clarke wrote to him outlining the best tactics and including the advice: 'The only person that can beat you is yourself.'[59] He would not lose the battle with his psyche a second time. As with the 800 metres final, the 1,500 metres final started slowly but this time Coe stayed near the head of the pack. Thus, when early leader Jürgen Straub picked up the pace with two laps to go, Coe was ready. Only he and Ovett could respond to the East German's move, but it better suited Coe, who ran the final two laps faster than anyone in history. When he crossed the line, his arms outstretched, an expression of ecstasy and relief was etched on his face. Ovett came in third, unable even to overtake Straub. In Britain some twenty million watched the race. 'So, the arguments will go on,' said Coleman in the commentary box, 'first Ovett wins and then Sebastian Coe comes home flying high.'

V

The two 'wrong' victories left the soap opera on a knife edge, but the storyline developed over the course of the following year. In Florence in June 1981, Coe shattered his own 800 metres world record by six-tenths of a second, setting a time – 1:41:73 – that would stand for sixteen years. Then, in a scintillating nine days in August, the pair swapped the mile world record three times. Coe was first, bettering Ovett's record by running 3:48.53 in Zurich on 19 August. A week later in Koblenz, Ovett claimed the record back running 3:48.40. It would last just two days. Coe won the Golden Mile in Brussels in 3:47.33, taking more than a second off Ovett's time. Despite not competing against each other in 1981, the year was the high point of the Coe–Ovett rivalry. Ovett injured his knee in a freak accident in December (crashing into some iron railings while training) and required an operation. He never truly recovered. At the Los Angeles Olympics four years after Moscow, Coe retained his 1,500 metres title – the only man ever to do so – and Ovett came third again.

For much of their careers, the pair avoided each other on the track, ultimately racing just seven times in seventeen years, yet they transformed British athletics, a sport which was still clinging to the Corinthian ethos of amateurism when they came to prominence.

Over the preceding twenty-five years the BBC's coverage of athletics became increasingly technically proficient and David Coleman emerged as the voice of the sport. But it was the Coe– Ovett rivalry that helped transform it into a major TV attraction in the 1980s. Since the 1950s athletics had been broadcast by the BBC. With the British Amateur Athletic Board (BAAB) unconvinced that the younger ITV network could do the sport justice, the BBC was able to renew its contract for the rights to athletics in 1976 at a cost of just over £250,000 for four years. By 1980 that had increased eightfold to £2 million. Bidding from ITV helped increase the price, but the BAAB remained loyal to the BBC, its long-time partner. Four years later, following another bidding war, ITV secured a five-year deal for the rights at a cost of £10 million.[60] The switch was not just motivated by the rights fees but also changes in the regulations governing commercial television that meant sponsors could advertise before, during and after an event. The BAAB was able to accrue even more millions as companies such as Pearl Insurance, Kodak and Peugot-Talbot leapt at the chance to sponsor athletics meetings.

The sport was suddenly flush with cash, and finally some of it was filtering through to the athletes. At the height of their rivalry when they were filling stadia across Europe and pulling in millions of viewers around the world, Coe and Ovett were amateurs. '[They] are two of the hottest properties in sport – comparable with Björn Borg,' wrote Chris Brasher in the *Observer*. 'Yet, unlike Borg, they are not supposed to make one penny from their talent, skill and dedication. It is ludicrous.'[61] It was also unsustainable. The challenge of Kerry Packer to cricket had alerted the athletics world to the possibility of a media entrepreneur signing up the best athletes to a professional version of the sport. In 1981, in a bid to head this off, the International Amateur Athletic Federation (IAAF) sanctioned meetings in which promoters could pay appearance money into trust funds for athletes, administered by national associations until the athlete retired. It also became possible for athletes to advertise, as long as the fee was also paid into the fund. Coe became one of the first to employ an agent – Mark McCormack's IMG – and became one of the first to advertise a product on television – the rebranded Horlicks chocolate and malt drinks. He was also able to turn down a £100,000 offer from Brut aftershave because it was 'the wrong image'. The IAAF saw this as a palatable 'soft transition' to professionalism. It would be another twenty years before the federation finally dropped the word 'Amateur' from its name. The transition was complete.

CHAPTER 12

Rebel Yell

I

PRIOR to the invasion of Afghanistan, the Moscow Organising Committee believed that the biggest boycott threat to the Games would come from African states protesting other nations' continued sporting relations with South Africa. The number of Olympic members had grown in the post-war years, particularly among African countries that had gained, or were pushing for, independence from colonial rule – many applied for IOC membership before they applied to join the United Nations. At the same time international opposition was growing to the South Africa system of apartheid. FIFA was the first major sports governing body to act, briefly suspending South Africa's membership in 1961 before reimposing the suspension two years later and expelling them fully in 1976. In 1964, the IOC voted to ban South Africa from the forthcoming Games in Tokyo. The country would not be welcomed back until the Barcelona Games in 1992.

However, South Africa's exclusion from the Olympic movement did not prevent protests and boycotts. In 1976, New Zealand's rugby union team toured South Africa, playing four Tests against the racially segregated Springboks. In response, thirty-four countries, almost all African, withdrew just hours before the opening ceremony of that year's Olympics in Montreal. The Games were the smallest since 1960, and in an attempt to prevent another damaging mass withdrawal from the Commonwealth Games in Edmonton two years later, the heads of the Commonwealth countries unanimously approved the Gleneagles Agreement in 1977 which committed them to cease sporting contact with South Africa. It was, according to the country's Olympic committee, 'the worst thing to have happened to South Africa since our expulsion from the Olympic movement',[1] a feeling seemingly shared by the white population who ranked the international sports boycott as one of the worst three consequences of apartheid.[2]

However, the Gleneagles Agreement was the result of intense negotiation and compromise to find language that suited both the black-ruled African nations and in particular New Zealand's prime minister, Robert Muldoon. Consequently, the agreement was not absolute. There was no definitive call for a ban, nor an indication of the sanctions that might be imposed on those who broke the agreement. Instead 'it was for each Government to determine in accordance with its law the methods by which it might best discharge these commitments'.[3]

II

The agreement of New Zealand and Britain was seen as a huge boost to the anti-apartheid struggle. While Muldoon took some persuading, his British counterpart James Callaghan had no such reservations, hailing it as 'a victory for all Commonwealth countries'.[4] However, within two years Callaghan had been defeated at the ballot box by Margaret Thatcher. The new government's approach to apartheid was markedly different from that of its predecessor. South Africa was a significant trading partner and seen as a useful ally in the fight against Communism. Sir John Leahy, the British ambassador to South Africa, also argued that sporting contact with the country could help end discrimination both in sport and in wider society.[5] Such softening was compounded by the traditionally *laissez-faire* approach politicians took to sport, tending to allow governing bodies to make their own decisions. Thus, when the home rugby unions invited a multiracial South African 'Barbarians' team to tour Britain in late 1979, the new government urged them to consider the wider ramifications but issued no meaningful threat of punishment.

The tour went ahead, and the lack of official resistance emboldened the four home nations to continue with a proposed British Lions tour of South Africa in 1980. In the House of Commons, the issue was split along party lines. A group of more than seventy backbench Conservative MPs signed a Commons motion calling for the government to approve the tour. In response, Labour MPs labelled them 'apartheid appeasers'[6] whose actions jeopardised Britain's place at the forthcoming Olympics. Sir Denis Follows also expressed his fears that the country would be expelled. The new prime minister's husband, Denis Thatcher, the treasurer of the London Society of Rugby Football Union Referees and a former county official himself, made his feelings clear at a society dinner. 'We are a free people, playing an amateur game,' he told his colleagues, adding, 'we have got the right to play where we like.'[7] Whitehall stayed silent on Mr Thatcher's comments, which was seen in some quarters as tacit approval.

On 17 December, the Supreme Council of Sport in Africa (SCSA), a thirty-two-member anti-apartheid body, voted to ban all British athletes and teams from competing on the African continent and to continue to push for the exclusion of Britain from the Moscow Olympics should the Lions tour go ahead.[8] A week later, the Soviet Union invaded Afghanistan. The threat of British expulsion from the Olympics (or a mass withdrawal of African countries if they weren't) was soon replaced by the threat of a wider boycott of the Moscow Games, with the British government being one of the most prominent advocates. In the first half of 1980, Thatcher wrote to Follows four times reinforcing her belief in the importance of action against the Soviet Union. In the first letter in January, she wrote: 'In an ideal world, I would share entirely the philosophy of the Olympic movement that sport should be divorced from politics. Sadly, however, this is no longer a realistic view.'[9] The government claimed that it was applying the same amount of pressure on the rugby players not to tour South Africa as it was on Olympians not to go to Moscow; however the reality was different. There were no letters from Thatcher to the home rugby unions.

Although anti-apartheid campaigners, as well as African politicians, decried the British government's hypocritical stance, the Lions tour quickly fell from the spotlight, lost in the fog of controversy surrounding the Moscow Olympics. Furthermore, the reality for British campaigners was that it was easier to disrupt events at home than stop tours abroad. Despite the efforts to dissuade them from travelling, none of the players chosen for the tour refused to go. Crucially, they also had the backing of the rugby authorities and so suffered no repercussions within the game; indeed, several went on to hold senior administrative positions. However, English winger John Carleton was sacked from his job as a teacher by the Labour-controlled Wigan Council. 'I was only twenty-three. I was disillusioned with teaching and felt I was educated enough to find another career, but I knew I might have only one shot at playing for the Lions. It was not a difficult decision,' he said years later.[10] Many, like Carleton, made the choice purely on rugby terms, something made easier by the fact that other sportsmen were in South Africa at the same time, notably the then Manchester United manager Dave Sexton who was there coaching football along with Liverpool's Steve Heighway and Viv Anderson of Nottingham Forest.[11]

The Lions tour is clearly fondly remembered by many of those who took part. It was the amateur era and most played as hard off the pitch as they did on it. 'You wouldn't swap those memories or tours for anything,' reflected one more than forty years later.[12] Not everyone approved. According to Scottish forward John Beattie, 'It was remarkably self-destructive and amateur. I couldn't believe the drinking that went on − I still can't believe it. If you weren't in the Saturday team, you got pissed on the Friday night, and if you weren't in the Wednesday team you got pissed on the Tuesday night − it was crazy.'[13] Perhaps unsurprisingly, the squad was hit by an unusually high number of injuries with eight of the original thirty players having to be replaced during the ten-week tour. The team won all fourteen of their non-international games but lost three of the four Tests, only gaining a consolation win in the final match. The comprehensive series victory for the home side provided white South Africans with a distraction from the tensions within the country. 'For three months people could and did talk about nothing but rugby: other things were relegated to the inside pages of the press,' reported the British ambassador to Foreign Secretary Peter Carrington.[14]

For the touring players, it was all but impossible to escape the shadow of apartheid. The team visited schools and hospitals in townships; however, looking back years later, scrum-half John Robbie admitted he had come to realise this was 'very stage-managed'.[15] The segregation that marred the country was also prevalent on the pitch. The Lions played against some inter-racial teams, but the Springboks were a resolutely white team and an indelible symbol of Afrikaner nationalism and politics. Some small sections of the stadia were reserved for 'blacks only' and within them red shirts were prominent, adopted by black fans to show their opposition to the segregated South African side.

The Lions' squad met opposition, too. Members of a black football team staying in the same hotel as the Lions expressed their disappointment that the tourists had broken the apartheid ban to Robbie and tour captain Bill Beaumont. Within hours the footballers had been moved out.[16] Several of the Lions players came to regret, or at least question, their decision during the tour. Andy Irvine, whose understanding of the situation developed through conversations with Robbie, later said that he 'came back thinking, "Maybe that wasn't the right thing to do" '.[17] Beattie was even more certain he'd made a mistake. 'I hated it. I'd gone amid a barrage of criticism from MPs who had written me letters, and many members of the public had joined them in trying to persuade me not to go. Midway through the tour I really wished I hadn't.'[18]

III

South Africa had become a sporting pariah. Its teams could no longer play abroad, its athletes were banned from international competition. In the months following the Lions tour, the United Nations Special Committee Against Apartheid (UNSCAA) drew up a 'blacklist' of sportsmen and women who had flouted the ban. It gave many prospective tourists reason to reconsider. In their attempts to counteract this, the South African authorities focused on two sports much loved by the ruling class: rugby and cricket. The former was, in the words of journalist Frank Keating, 'the mother's milk, the lifeblood, the elixir that fuels [Afrikaner] arrogance'.[19] The latter held a similarly exalted position in the lives of white South Africans. The cancellation of the 1970 tour to England had cast the country's cricket team into the wilderness just after a dominant 4–0 series win against Australia. The Springboks, with the likes of Barry Richards and Mike Procter in their ranks, had a strong claim to be the best team in the world. There was a thirst to see the country's top players tested by the best of the rest.

Yet that team was all-white. As in other areas of South African society, cricket was split between the predominantly white South African Cricket Union (SACU) and the South African Cricket Board (SACB). There had been some moves towards integration, but the SACB argued that their white counterparts were not truly motivated 'by the desire to organize non-racial society but to return to international cricket'.[20] Attempts at reintegration into the international fold were repeatedly thwarted by India, Pakistan and the West Indies who made it clear that the issue was bigger than cricket: South Africa would only be welcomed back once apartheid was no more. Following a meeting at Lord's with Doug Insole, the chair of the Test and County Cricket Board (TCCB), Ali Bacher of the SACU was left in no doubt: 'We can forget about getting back into cricket through the front door,' he reported to colleagues on his return to South Africa. 'We're really on our own.'[21]

The back door had been left ajar several years earlier by Kerry Packer whose World Series Cricket had given players a greater appreciation of their worth, at the same time loosening ties with their national governing bodies. It also suggested that any controversy would die down. The threats to ban players who took the TV mogul's cash had ultimately come to little; there was life after Packer. Thus, when the white South African cricket authorities set about organising a 'rebel' England tour there were players willing to sign up.

During England's tour of the West Indies in the winter of 1980/81, six players – Ian Botham, Geoff Boycott, Graham Dilley, John Emburey, Graham Gooch and David Gower – were approached and signed a letter expressing interest in a 'quiet, private' tour.[22] A few days later, England's Robin Jackman, a late replacement for the injured Bob Willis, was refused admission into Guyana because of his links with South Africa. Jackman had spent several winters in the country, coaching, and playing for Western Province and Rhodesia. His name was on the UN blacklist. England argued that the Gleneagles Agreement did not apply as Jackman had gone as a private individual. Both sides refused to back down and the Test at Bourda was cancelled.

The incident shone a light on the problematic language of the Gleneagles Agreement, which led many to argue that while teams were banned from travelling to South Africa, individuals were merely discouraged. (Others, like UN representative James Beho, took a hardline opposing view, arguing that anyone who even played against a South African should be banned, a move that would have included all county cricketers.[23]) Whichever side of the argument you were on, it was clear that there was little chance a tour of South Africa could remain either quiet or private, let alone both.

This notion was reinforced the following winter when England's tour to India was nearly cancelled due to the inclusion of Boycott and Geoff Cook, both of whom were on the UN blacklist because of their links with South Africa.[24] Consequently, the Indian government was unwilling to allow them entry. In response, the TCCB said it was unwilling to exclude them, and the players said they were unwilling to voluntarily withdraw as it would seem like an admission of guilt. The implications of this Mexican stand-off were seismic. There were fears that, had the tour not gone ahead, the international game would have been split between white and black countries, something which might well have seen South Africa welcomed back into a white-only version of the sport. Ultimately a compromise was reached. The TCCB reiterated that it did not approve of tours to South Africa and that anyone who took part in one would not be considered for selection. The players also restated their opposition to apartheid. Four months after the tour ended, Geoffrey Boycott landed in South Africa with a squad of boycott-busting England rebels.

Much of the final negotiation had taken place during the fifteen weeks England were in India and Sri Lanka. The likelihood that a rebel squad could be brought together ebbed and flowed as various players were courted, gave tentative agreement, withdrew, and then changed their minds again. Yet, by the time the team returned to Gatwick enough had signed up for the tour, sponsored by South African Breweries, to get the green light. Although there was no official backing from the South African government, there was tacit support; the organisers benefited from huge tax concessions. In a sense it was sportswashing decades before the term entered our lexicon; an attempt to legitimise a repressive regime on the field of play albeit by circumventing an international boycott. Yet according to Matthew Engel, who covered the tour for the *Guardian* and went on to edit the *Wisden Cricketers' Almanack*, few involved in county cricket would have criticised the rebels. 'At around that time, I said to a very good friend of mine within the game who was of fairly liberal-minded disposition, "I think I know of only five people within cricket who wouldn't have gone to South Africa". He replied, "Well, I'd go like a shot!" I said, "Oh fuck; it's four . . .". That was how they saw it.' [25]

Those in the rebel squad were either players who were at the end of their careers, for whom this was one final payday, or those who had a grievance with the game. Wayne Larkins fell into the latter category. A twenty-eight-year-old opening batsman, he'd played six Tests since making his debut for England in 1980, the most recent being the last Test of Botham's Ashes, at The Oval. He was approached by the organisers out of the blue at his home at around the same time as Northants teammate Peter Willey. After the initial meetings, the pair were then invited to a secret location in London. 'We walked through the door and there was Gooch, Boycott, [Dennis] Amiss, [Alan] Knott, [Derek] Underwood, [Mike] Hendrick, John Lever,' Larkins tells me.[26] 'We couldn't believe all these people were involved. We sat down and they gave us a spiel about what it was all about, and they gave us another two or three weeks to make up our minds. Virtually everyone said, "Yes, let's do it."'

Larkins is open about his reasons for going on the tour. He had become disillusioned – 'cheesed off' as he put it – with the way he had been treated by the England selectors. He'd never been given a consistent run in the team, he'd been left out of the winter tours to India and Sri Lanka without explanation, despite playing in the final Ashes Test the previous summer in which he scored a half-century. The money settled the issue. 'If you got picked on a tour, or for two or three Test matches in the summer, that would be great,' says Larkins, 'but there was never a guarantee. If you played one Test match you were always thinking, "Am I going to play the next Test match?"' At the time cricketers earned around £9,000 for the county season. Those who played for England would see their income boosted by around £1,500 per Test. Those picked for a winter tour could earn in the region of £8,500 more. Only a select few could be sure of a winter call-up, and, even then, injury could strike anyone at any time. It was a precarious living. Those not picked for the winter tours would have to find other work, perhaps coaching or playing in the southern hemisphere, or even sign on the dole. Thus, the offer of anywhere between £40,000 and £60,000 for a month's work was appealing.

'It was twenty Test matches' worth of money,' says Larkins, 'you've got to think twice about it.'

Someone who had thought twice and decided to decline was Botham. Since the initial meeting in the Trinidad Hilton, he had become England's, if not the sport's, biggest star thanks to his exploits in the summer of 1981 against the Australians. He later acknowledged that he was initially interested enough to give the proposals consideration but that he ultimately declined to take part, claiming to have turned down a double-your-money offer of £85,000.[27] After the tour had started, he publicly distanced himself in his column in the *Sun*, saying he 'could never have looked my mate Viv Richards in the eye' had he gone, adding, 'I didn't want to risk my Test career, and quite frankly I'm surprised that certain others have chosen to do just that.'[28] His statement was met with disdain. Boycott countered that 'the suggestion that he opted out of the tour on moral grounds was unnecessary and puke-making'[29] and said he would probably never be able to trust Botham again. Gooch wrote that Botham had told him he had decided to withdraw because it was not financially worth his while to go, a decision Gooch respected; however, subsequently he 'could not understand why [Botham] didn't come out with the whole story'.[30] The rebels believed that, just as they had done, Botham's advisers had made a simple financial calculation, but for their client it made more sense not to travel; for 'Brand Botham' to remain untarnished by involvement with apartheid. Whatever the truth, Botham's earnings thanks to deals with the likes of Shredded Wheat, Volvo and bat makers Duncan Fearnley dwarfed those of even the highest paid rebels.

Despite Botham's non-involvement, the tour initially still caused shockwaves. 'There was a point where they appeared to be invincible and they could do anything and break world cricket,' says Engel. 'It was a terrible, terrible shock. A huge shock to the game and to the administrators, who were terrified.' From the original six, Gower and Dilley had also dropped out. Others such as Mike Gatting and Bob Willis had expressed an interest that came to nothing.[31] Boycott, then the all-time leading Test run scorer, and Gooch, who would become the team's reluctant captain, were the star attractions. Yet, while the touring team was not a weak side it could not really be called a first-choice England XI. Of the twelve players in the initial squad, eleven had played for England but only four had been involved with the most recent tour to Sri Lanka. The squad lacked balance and strength in depth, particularly in the batting line-up. Additions were regularly promised with the implication that a big star would join. 'All kinds of names were bandied about,' says Engel, 'and it turned out to be Jeff Humpage.' An able middle-order batsman with Warwickshire, Humpage had played three one-day games for England and had scored more runs than any of the other tourists in the 1981 county season, but he was no star. 'After that their credibility began to drain away a little,' says Engel. 'Once Humpage had appeared, a little bit of the fizz went out of the bottle.'

After initial interest from fans (who were overwhelmingly white) and the South African media, the series lost some of its allure. It was a one-sided contest, the home side winning the three-Test series 1−0 and the one-day series 3−0. It was a tight, demanding schedule with seven non-playing days in a twenty-seven-day tour. It was on their days off that the level of segregation in South Africa hit home. 'We had a couple of days off and we went to the beach,' says Larkins. 'All the lovely golden sandy bits were "whites only" and the rocky bits were "blacks only". That did knock me back when I first saw that. That did upset me. It made me realise what the hell was going on.' Despite this, there was no point at which Larkins felt the squad should not have gone, 'I thought I was doing something good; I really did. We all did because we were all in that mindset of trying to talk to people and trying to help the situation.'

In South Africa protests such as those which might have disrupted a Test series in England were illegal and thus non-existent, but the reaction elsewhere was fierce. Those in the squad not already on the UN blacklist were added to it. The team was labelled 'the Dirty Dozen' in parliament by Labour MP Gerald Kaufman, who accused the players of selling themselves for 'blood-covered Krugerrands'.[32] The *Daily Mirror* suggested that 'Every run they score will be a blow to someone else's freedom'. *The Times* highlighted the hypocrisy of Boycott following the statements he had made to dispel the controversy prior to England's tour of India, suggesting his 'words have now been made to appear as no more than a gesture of convenience'.[33] Tony Lewis, the former England skipper turned BBC commentator, labelled them 'the richest, loneliest men in cricket'.

The clandestine nature of the tour's organisation suggests that the organisers and the players were not unaware of the reaction it would provoke, but in the days before global 24/7 news and sports channels, easy access to internet headlines and social media campaigns, the tourists were effectively operating in a media-free bubble. The only people who could burst it were the travelling journalists, with whom Gooch resolutely refused to engage about anything other than on-field issues. 'They saw nothing but friendly faces and so they felt very comfortable,' says Engel. 'The press were the enemy because the press were the only enemy they could see, going around asking difficult questions.' The players' attitude was summed up by a conversation Engel had with John Emburey, albeit one that took place on the second England rebel tour in 1990. 'I walked into the hotel where they were staying and he said, "Hello, what are you doing here?" and I said, "Oh, just making a living", which wasn't the cleverest reply.

He said, "So what's the difference between you coming here to make a living and me coming here to make a living?". I hadn't got an answer to that,' says Engel. 'A long time later I thought what I should have said is, "The South African government wants you to be here, but it doesn't want me to be here." That would have been my best answer, but I didn't have it at the time.'

The squad still had some measure of the opprobrium back at home thanks to telephone calls and telegrams received by Gooch and Boycott. 'We knew it wasn't going down too well,' says Larkins, 'but we made our bed and we had to lie in it and take the consequences.' The true extent of those consequences became clear when the TCCB passed judgement, issuing a three-year ban. It was not entirely unexpected. The previous summer, the Board had written to all first-class players warning them that their chances of playing for England would be jeopardised if they toured South Africa, but the length of the ban was still a shock for the players. Larkins says he had expected a year-long ban at worst. It effectively ended the international careers of the older men such as Boycott, Underwood and Knott but it had the biggest ramifications for Gooch. He was twenty-eight and had missed just two of England's forty-three Tests before the South Africa tour. The ban, he wrote later, 'struck home like a thunderbolt'.[34]

IV

Seven of the fifteen rebels would go on to play at least one Test for England after their bans were served. Larkins played seven more times, four under the captaincy of Gooch and three under that of his former Northants teammate, South African-born Alan Lamb, who had moved to England to pursue a cricket career. Because both his parents had been born in the country, Lamb was eligible

to play for England as soon as he'd fulfilled the residence requirements. By coincidence he made his Test debut in the summer of
1982, just months after the rebel tour.

The irony was not lost on Larkins. 'It was another fly in the
ointment,' he tells me. 'When I got back it became a very difficult
situation, not just for me but for Lamby as well. He'd just been
selected for England and me and Peter [Willey] were saying,
"Well, hang on a minute, you've just banned us for three years for
playing out there and now you're selecting a bloke who's still got
a property out there and who's got a maid, his mum and dad've
got maids." It was difficult for me, and it was difficult for Peter to
come to terms with all that. It was just as difficult for Lamby to be
in that position.'

Lamb was just one of many sportsmen and women who had
trodden the path from South Africa to Britain, but few elicited
as much controversy as middle-distance running sensation Zola
Budd. The 5ft 2in. seventeen-year-old was a recognised talent in
her home country, having been named South African woman
athlete of the year, cross-country athlete of the year and South
African junior athlete of the year in 1983. She strode to international recognition in January 1984, shattering the women's
world 5,000 metres record at a meeting at Stellenbosch. She beat
the previous best set by America's Mary Decker by 6.45 seconds.
The feat was all the more astonishing because Budd had achieved
it barefoot, her preferred running style. However, the international
sporting boycott meant her achievement was not recognised by
the International Amateur Athletic Federation, the sport's governing body. It also ruled out the possibility of what would have
been a hotly anticipated match up against Decker on the track at
the summer's Los Angeles Olympics.

Almost immediately, a variety of interested parties began competing to sign up the young athlete. The sports agency IMG was

among the first to move and Budd also received offers of scholar-
ships from several US universities. They were soon overtaken by
the *Daily Mail* in what the paper called 'The race to win a waif
called Zola'.[35] When sportswriter Ian Wooldridge discovered that
Budd had a British grandfather, his editor David English declared
bullishly: 'Brilliant. [. . .] She shall run for us.'[36] It was unashamed
journalistic opportunism. 'By "us" he meant the *Daily Mail* first
and Britain second,' wrote Wooldridge years later.[37] Reporters
Neil Wilson and Brian Vine were dispatched to the Budd family
farm in Bloemfontein to strike a deal. As Budd was under eighteen, they negotiated with her father Frank who signed over
exclusive rights to Budd's story for £100,000, a rent-free house in
England and the promise of support getting her a British passport
so that she could compete for Britain in Los Angeles.

Accompanying the journalists was athletics photographer
Mark Shearman who snapped a famous image of Budd running
alongside a flock of ostriches. It evocatively captured the isolated
but idyllic rural environment the youngster had been brought up
in. It was one Budd told those closest to her she did not want to
leave. She also told them she did not want to run in the upcoming
Olympics. She was ignored. Instead, her father essentially sold
her for financial gain, while the *Mail* effectively bought her to
increase circulation. She had been used as 'a saleable commod-
ity',[38] and turned 'into some kind of circus animal',[39] Budd would
write several years later. Randall Northam, who was an athletics
writer at the time, agrees. 'If the *Daily Mail* were looking out for
her and not the front page, they would have waited until 1985,
got her assimilated in this country for three years and then
launched her on the Seoul Olympics but they didn't, they wanted
the headlines,'[40] he tells me.

On 23 March, barely twelve weeks after her record-breaking
run, the diminutive athlete, her father and mother, Tossie, were

heading to Johannesburg's Jan Smuts International Airport in a black Mercedes. There they boarded a flight to Amsterdam. Upon arrival they transferred to a private plane for the short trip to Southampton. They were then whisked to a secluded house in the New Forest, tucked away from the prying eyes of the *Daily Mail*'s rivals. Thirteen days later, on 5 April, Budd was a British citizen. Her application had taken just ten days from start to finish. The average time for such a process was twenty-one months.

English, knighted by Thatcher in 1982, had exploited his personal friendship with Leon Brittan, imploring the home secretary to use his discretionary powers to grant Budd citizenship and to ensure the application was fast-tracked in time for the Olympic trials. The foreign secretary Geoffrey Howe expressed his reservations privately, Denis Howell, the former Labour sports minister, expressed his unequivocal condemnation publicly. 'It is beyond question that the procedures of the Home Office have been prostituted at the behest of the *Daily Mail*,'[41] he told the Commons in a debate on the matter. The British athletics authorities were caught by surprise; they had not been consulted. Athletes, too, were furious. Wendy Sly, Britain's leading 3,000 metres runner, boycotted the Olympic trials in protest. The BOA still selected her for the team.

The controversy around Budd went further than that surrounding the rugby players and cricketers. Unlike them, she was not just seen as an athlete breaking the boycott; rather, Budd was seen as a direct beneficiary of the Thatcher government's immigration laws which demonstrably favoured white migrants and were widely decried as racist. For decades, the Conservative Party had built its electoral success not by presenting itself as a party of class, but as a party of nation, yet the concept of the nation and what it meant to be British was not static. It was constantly being redefined to reflect the ethos of the party and social mores of the time. One of the ways the Thatcher government articulated its definition of Britishness was through legislation, in particular the British Nationality Act, passed in 1981. The act came into force on 1 January 1983 and abolished the principle of *jus soli*. Instead, it determined that to gain citizenship, not only must a person be born in the country but one of their parents must also be a British citizen.

The act reflected the central values of neo-Conservative popularism but was anathema to those on the left. Along with apartheid it became a battlefield in the 1980s culture war. The overlap between anti-Thatcher activists and anti-apartheid campaigners was growing. Black and Asian political activists, left-wing politicians, students, trades unionists, community organisers and religious leaders joined forces to transform the Anti-Apartheid Movement from a small but vocal pressure group into a mass movement. Increasingly they focused on campaigning for the release of ANC leader Nelson Mandela, who had been jailed in 1964. He was granted the freedom of several cities across the country. Hundreds of parks, streets and buildings were renamed in his honour. At the other end of the political spectrum, the Federation of Conservative Students notoriously wore 'Hang Mandela' stickers, action that contributed to the group being wound up by party chairman Norman Tebbit. Their chair at the time was John Bercow, later Speaker of the House of Commons, who has since said that he never took part in such activities.[42] However, the group were far from outliers. Senior conservative MP Teddy Taylor said Mandela 'should be shot' (he later claimed he was joking) and in 1987 Thatcher dismissed the African National Congress (ANC) as 'a typical terrorist organisation'.[43]

In April 1986 anti-apartheid protestors began a protest outside South Africa House, home of the South African High Commission, in London's Trafalgar Square. Despite numerous arrests and unsuccessful attempts to have the protest banned in the courts, it lasted forty-six months until Mandela's release in February 1990. Global awareness of Mandela's imprisonment was generated by the Nelson Mandela 70th Birthday Tribute Concert (also known as the Free Nelson Mandela Concert) at Wembley in June 1988. Conceived by producer Tony Hollingsworth after a conversation with Jerry Dammers of The Specials, who had written the song 'Free Nelson Mandela' in 1984 and founded Artists Against Apartheid the following year, the concert was broadcast to an audience of 600 million in sixty-seven countries. It was, wrote music critic Robin Denselow, the 'biggest and most spectacular pop-political event of all time, a more political version of Live Aid with the aim of raising consciousness rather than just money'.[44] By presenting the concert as a positive musical – not political – event, Hollingsworth was able to persuade broadcasters to give it significant airtime and, just as crucially, stop referring to Mandela as a 'black terrorist leader'.

V

Throughout this period, Budd remained a totem of the Thatcher government, its pro-Pretoria foreign policy and its intransigence to sanctions against South Africa, and thus a lightning rod for the protests of the Anti-Apartheid Movement. The Greater London Council led by Ken Livingstone, or 'Red Ken' as he was labelled by the tabloids, and other Labour-controlled district councils which had declared themselves 'Apartheid Free Zones' tried to prevent Budd from competing in pre-Olympic meetings. When she was able to race, she was repeatedly subjected to shouts of 'racist scum' and 'fascist bitch'.[45] These reached their most vitriolic pitch at a meeting at the Crystal Palace National Sports

Centre. Prior to the race, two protesters ('black hooligans' according to the *Sun*[46]) confronted Budd and remonstrated with her. During the race, the crowd chants of 'South African white trash', 'You're better off dead' and 'Get out of England'[47] poured down from the stands. Despite being visibly upset, Budd won the race in a British record time.

There was an understandable desire from campaigners to hear Budd condemn apartheid, but she remained resolutely silent, a silence interpreted as tacit approval of the South African government. Yet it's easy to forget that at the centre of the furore was a shy seventeen-year-old, taken out of her home and thrust into the international spotlight against her will. She has since unequivocally condemned apartheid, but also defended her younger self saying she did not feel knowledgeable enough to speak out about politics. 'Until I got to London in 1984, I never knew Nelson Mandela existed,' Budd said in 2002. 'All I knew was the white side expressed in South African newspapers — that if we had no apartheid, our whole economy would collapse. Only much later did I realize I'd been lied to by the state.'[48] Furthermore, although she could speak and understand English, Budd did not feel comfortable doing so; Afrikaans was her mother tongue. Perhaps ill-advisedly, the more she was pressed on the matter, the more stubborn she became, questioning why she had to speak out when 'Wendy Sly isn't asked if she voted Labour or Conservative; [. . .] and Carl Lewis is not required to express his view on the Contra arms scandal.'[49] What Budd wanted, she said, was 'the right to pursue my chosen discipline in peace'.[50] Northam feels she may have had different motives for not speaking out. 'All she had to say is "Anything that discriminates against another person is reprehensible"; that would have solved it,' he says. 'But my feeling is that she knew that if she condemned apartheid she would have been in trouble in South Africa and she wanted to go back.'

If Budd had hoped that the Los Angeles Games would bring her the peace she craved, she was to be disappointed. The 3,000 metres final pitted her against Decker, the woman whose world record she had obliterated barely eight months earlier. Like the Coe–Ovett showdown in Moscow, it was a sporting drama perfectly scripted for a global TV audience. America's Golden Girl on home soil versus the young pretender who idolised her. It was also, many believed, Decker's last shot at Olympic gold. She had missed the 1976 Games through injury and those of 1980 due to the US boycott. In the background, Romania's Maricica Puică, the runner some believed was the real favourite, quietly went about her business, breaking the Olympic record in the heats.

Decker set the early pace. Budd was in the chasing pack along with Puică and Wendy Sly. At about the 1,700-metre mark Budd picked up the pace, overtaking Decker then cutting towards the inside of the track. The pair clashed legs. Decker caught Budd's heel with her spikes before stumbling and falling to the side of the track, ripping the number off Budd's back in the process. Budd kept running. The LA Coliseum rang out with boos and jeers from a partisan crowd which believed Budd had tried to sabotage Decker, or at least cost her through inexperience. Budd faded, eventually finishing seventh. 'The main concern was if I win a medal I'd have to stand on the winner's podium, and I didn't want to do that,' she said later.[51] Decker pointed the finger of blame at Budd in a post-race press conference. So, too, did the officials who disqualified her before reviewing the tape, after which Budd was absolved of blame and reinstated. Thanks to the prolonged media post-mortem, which included all available camera angles of the crucial moment being repeated ad nauseum, most people could be forgiven for forgetting the race was actually completed; Puică won gold and Sly took silver.

On her return to Britain, Budd was subjected to death threats and had to be smuggled through Heathrow airport under the protection of armed police. She was soon back in South Africa for an extended stay. Speculation grew that she would not return and the day after her contract with the *Daily Mail* expired in November, Budd seemed to confirm that. 'All I want is to be happy and among my people,' she said.[52] For some, however, this reinforced the notion that she had been running under a 'flag of convenience'. A SANROC spokesman accused Budd of committing 'an international fraud with the help of the British Government'.[53] Eventually, Budd was persuaded not to race in South Africa – which would have seen her banned from international competition. Against a backdrop of anti-apartheid protests and opposition to her representing Great Britain, Budd continued to demonstrate her prodigious talent, winning the world cross-country championships in 1985 and 1986, and setting world records for the 5,000 metres and indoor 3,000 metres. Her selection to compete in the 1986 Commonwealth Games in Edinburgh seemed assured.

Despite Thatcher's landslide general election victory in 1983, Scotland was a Labour stronghold. The party controlled Edinburgh's council, which was one of nearly thirty across the country that had declared their opposition to apartheid and banned South African goods. Budd's inclusion was an opportunity for the local authority to take its protest to a wider audience. At an athletics meeting at the council-owned Meadowbank Stadium in July 1985, a large sign was displayed prominently below the scoreboard reading simply 'Edinburgh – Against Apartheid'. Channel 4, which was due to broadcast coverage of the event, cancelled transmission, citing the Independent Broadcasting Authority's prohibition on political advertising.[54] Budd won the mile race, but it was hindered by an anti-apartheid protestor who tried to impede her on the track. The Commonwealth Games were already beset by organisational problems. Thatcher had insisted there would be no government support, instead imposing a funding model similar to the Los Angeles Olympics, which relied on income from sponsorship. Not enough was forthcoming. The *Daily Mirror*'s owner Robert Maxwell stepped in purportedly to bail them out, with a pledge of £2 million, although it was later shown he had injected just £250,000.[55] In an effort to prevent further disruption of the sort experienced at Meadowbank, and to head off a threatened boycott and the resulting loss of revenue that would incur, the Commonwealth Games Federation (CGF) banned Budd along with swimmer Annette Cowley, another South African-born athlete with a British passport. It did not have the desired effect. Countries debated their participation right up until the opening ceremony, with some even withdrawing during the Games. Ultimately, of the fifty-nine eligible nations, only twenty-six took part, the smallest number since 1950. The organisers were left with a £4.3 million deficit.

Boycott threats followed Budd to the Seoul Olympics two years later. She had been accused of competing in a race in South Africa. While she acknowledged she had attended the race, Budd denied competing; she had been nothing more than a spectator. The IAAF accepted this version of events but extended its definition of 'taking part' to the broadest possible interpretation and demanded her suspension for a year. The British Amateur Athletic Board resisted. The matter dragged on for months. Eventually, Budd broke under the relentless pressure, withdrew from the team and quit competitive athletics.

VI

During the five years following the cricket tour led by Gooch and Boycott, a series of other 'rebel' teams from Sri Lanka, Australia (twice) and the West Indies (also twice) toured South Africa. The Sri Lankans were a fledgling Test nation, but that did not dim the criticism of the players who received lifetime bans from the Board of Control for Cricket in Sri Lanka. The first Australian side travelled to South Africa on the eve of an Ashes series and contained several Test players. They were labelled 'traitors' by the country's prime minister Bob Hawke[56] in what was seen by many as 'one of the most painful and traumatic moments in Australian cricket history'.[57] After the first West Indian tour the Jamaican prime minister Michael Manley wrote that the 'betrayal is extreme' before adding 'apartheid points like a dagger at the throat of black self-worth in every corner occupied by the descendants of Africa'.[58] Several of the players were socially ostracised on their return to the West Indies, some falling into drug addiction after being unable to get work of any kind.

In 1990, a second team of English rebels made the trip south. It was the most ill-timed of the lot. The apartheid regime was crumbling, South Africa was on a knife edge. Cricket was secondary to politics before the team had even left. Their plane was delayed at Heathrow due to a bomb scare and a peaceful anti-apartheid demonstration at Jan Smuts airport in Johannesburg was dispersed by police using tear gas and dogs. The tone of the tour was set. Some 2,000 protestors marched on the team's first game in the old mining town of Kimberley, but they were stopped by police about half a mile from the ground. After a four-hour stand-off with police the crowd went on the rampage through the town smashing shop windows and damaging cars.[59] In an indication of how out of touch the tourists were, captain Mike Gatting dismissed the protests as 'a few people singing and dancing'.[60] The South African government was more concerned, suggesting that the level of protest the tour was attracting could lead to a delay in Mandela's release.[61] England lost the first Test in three

days. Mandela was released on what would have been the scheduled fourth day. The day after that a bomb exploded outside
Newlands, the venue for the second Test. It was quickly announced
that the game had been cancelled and replaced by four one-day
matches, and that the tour would be shortened by a fortnight. 'I
understand a lot more about apartheid now,' said Gatting after
the news was announced.[62] After that, the protests subsided. As
with the 1982 tour, the players were banned and, as with that tour,
several (including Emburey again) would be welcomed back into
the fold and play at least one more Test for England. Some also
went on to hold senior positions in the game's establishment.
Within seven years, David Graveney, the tour's player-manager,
was appointed chairman of selectors. Gatting later became president of the MCC.

CHAPTER 13

Money For Nothing

I

'CAN you move back? We can't see Debbie.' So came the shout from the press pack crammed into the gallery above the trading floor of the London Stock Exchange. They were clamouring for a view of Debbie Moore, the founder and owner of Pineapple. 'I was surrounded by all these men,' says Moore.[1] 'So, they moved back and there I was in my ra-ra skirt, and my jazz shoes, and my leg warmers; just wearing what I wore in the office. I hadn't got dressed up specially, I didn't even know I was going to get any publicity; I didn't even think about it.' The date was 5 November 1982 and Moore had just become the first woman to take a company public.

Moore was also only the second woman allowed onto the trading floor of the Stock Exchange, the first being Queen Elizabeth The Queen Mother just a few weeks before her. Having opened the first Pineapple dance studio in 1979, by the end of 1981 Moore had opened a second and had a burgeoning clothing business. Her profits were doubling each year.[2] 'I wanted to expand because we had a cash-and-carry business at the back of our shop and lots of little shops used to come and buy leggings and leg warmers from us. Then it started to grow, and they started wiping out the stock for my own shop.' So popular was her innovative dancewear that Moore had to set up a proper wholesale business with proper manufacturing; she needed £200,000 to fund her plans. 'I had to go big time, but I needed to raise the money to fund that business plan.'

Pineapple was floated on the Unlisted Securities Market (USM), which launched in 1980 and was designed for smaller firms with a limited trading record. The shares were initially pitched at 52p. One million were issued and 400,000 (or 40 per cent of the company) were put up for sale. By the end of the first day, their price had risen to 96p. Within two months they were trading as high as £1.55. In February 1984, Moore was invited to a Downing Street 'reception for success', one of just three women among the thirty-seven guests. The following month she was named Businesswoman of the Year. Pineapple became Europe's largest retail dancewear store. The range was being sold in Bloomingdale's and Macey's in New York where Moore opened a new dance studio complex. It was the largest in the world and Bianca Jagger, Cher and Madonna were regular visitors.

At the time, Moore lamented the widespread perception that 'an ex-model had just opened a dance studio and made a million overnight'.[3] It belied the effort she had put into building the business prior to the flotation and the innovative clothing she had created, and she is adamant it simply wasn't the case: 'The money was not to take home in my handbag but to put into the business.' Pineapple's success spurred a host of others to enter the market. However, just as the aerobics business was becoming more competitive, Moore was unable to give Pineapple her full attention due to her daughter's ill health. She did her best to carry on as normal, conscious that with the company now public, the loss of its chairwoman could have a damaging effect on share prices. 'In the City,' she wrote later, 'being the mother of a child who was seriously ill would have been seen as a weakness – something, I suspect, that wouldn't have happened to a man in the same situation.'[4] In a bid to recover ground and deliver profit for the shareholders, the company started to diversify away from its original core business, becoming a marketing services group operating in areas such as sales promotions, exhibition and consumer goods. The original business was being swamped. The board even began to discuss disposing of the fashion and dance studio elements.

This prompted Moore to buy back the core businesses and the Pineapple name, for a nominal £1 in 1988. Speaking to *The Times*, she said, 'It soon became obvious that it was difficult to deliver the sort of money the City wanted out of dance, so we decided that I should privatise and concentrate on fashion and fitness, where my heart lies.'[5] Turning the company public had stifled Moore's entrepreneurial spirit; buying it back allowed her to develop the business she loved in the way that she wanted. 'I couldn't be doing with all these quarterly reports,' she says. 'You have an idea, and you have to do a presentation to the shareholders and by the time they've decided, you've gone off the idea. You can't possibly work at the speed you want to work at.'

Although Pineapple lasted just six years on the stock market, Moore had been a pioneer. Other businesswomen soon followed in her footsteps. Anita Roddick took the Body Shop public in 1984. The Ryman Group headed by Jennifer d'Abo floated two years later. In 1987 it was the turn of Sophie Mirman and the Sock Shop. However, Moore's gender was not the only pioneering aspect of the flotation. 'Pineapple was the first so-called "glamour stock". After I went public, so did Andrew Lloyd Webber, with the Really Useful Company, and then Richard Branson, with Virgin.' Companies in the fields of entertainment, fashion and marketing, which had once been dubbed too frivolous for the City, were now in demand by a market that wanted some sparkle to brighten things up.

II

Pineapple was also at the forefront of the privatisation boom that gripped the country, particularly in the second part of the eighties, and which was part of a wider financial revolution. There had been little indication of quite how seismic the change would be when the Conservatives came to power in 1979. Little changed in Margaret Thatcher's first term, but following her re-election in 1983, she appointed Cecil Parkinson as secretary of the newly merged Trade and Industry department, and he set about trying to end a seven-year dispute between the government and the London Stock Exchange which was heading for the courts following an Office of Fair Trading (OFT) inquiry into anti-competitive practices. The Stock Exchange was still operating under rules created in the 1700s, with clear demarcations between the brokers, who handled business with outside clients and were more often than not public school-educated, and 'jobbers', who bought and sold shares on the Stock Exchange floor and were mostly from working-class backgrounds. Brokers could not be jobbers and vice versa and strict rules determined the commission brokers could charge their clients. Merchant banks and foreign investors were also shut out. It was, in effect, a cosy gentlemen's club which looked antiquated compared to other global markets. Parkinson offered Sir Nicholas Goodison, the Stock Exchange chairman, a deal: the legal action would be called off if the Exchange agreed to fundamental reform. Restrictions were to end, and the market would be opened up to British merchant banks and foreign

investment banks. To ensure this complex process was done properly, it would be implemented gradually. The 'Big Bang', as it
became known, was three years in the making. When it arrived on
27 October 1986, the only real overnight change, or 'bang', was
the way trading was done. Out went the frenetic face-to-face
activity of the jobbers. Now traders could watch prices fluctuate
on a bank of computer screens and buy and sell on the telephone
(computer trading would come later). Money flooded in, creating
a bull market. Less than a year later, 'Black Monday' saw nearly
25 per cent of the market's value wiped off within forty-eight
hours. It was a salutary lesson, but the panic passed quickly.
Recovery was soon underway.

The twin forces of deregulation and improved technology also
facilitated everyday financial transactions and made consumer
credit easier to come by. In 1981, 44 per cent of the working
population, some 10.3 million people, were still paid in cash and
39 per cent of the population did not have a bank account.[6] Only
about a quarter of the population had a credit card and 93 per
cent of all transactions were still made using coins or notes. Just
five so-called 'clearing banks' – Barclays, Lloyds, Midland,
National Westminster and the Royal Bank of Scotland – issued
account holders with cheque books. They offered no interest on
these accounts, so savings tended to be held with building societies, which offered a rate of return. In turn the building societies
used this money to fund mortgages to their customers. The deregulation of the financial markets and relaxation of lending criteria
changed this, creating a more competitive market. Building societies issued cheque books; banks started offering mortgages, which
were easier to come by and, in a bid to attract customers, the
amount people could borrow relative to their salary and the value
of the property increased, fuelling a house-price boom. Banks
also began to allow people to extend their mortgage borrowing

for reasons other than home improvements. As house prices rose, people added to their mortgage debt to extend consumer spending. 'Hole-in-the-wall' ATMs enabled people to get cash without having to queue up in a bank.

Increases in house prices were further fuelled by the government's right-to-buy scheme, introduced via the Housing Act 1980. A prominent policy in the party's 1979 general election manifesto, it enshrined the statutory right of anyone who had been a council tenant for three years or more to buy their property (previously such sales had been made at the discretion of the local authority). Purchasers were also offered a discount of between 33 and 50 per cent of the value of the property depending on the length of time they had been renting, and the policy further ensured that 100 per cent mortgages were available. These were extremely generous terms. Sales peaked in Northern Ireland in 1981, and in England and Wales in 1982. There were regional variations. Take-up in England was greatest in London, the South East and the South West, and slowest in the North. Scotland lagged behind the rest of the UK and did not reach its highest annual figure until 1989,[7] prompting some analysts to suggest the Scots were sales-resistant.[8] There were also variations in who purchased their properties. Buyers were disproportionately aged forty to fifty. Most were in full-time either skilled manual or white-collar work and had more than one wage-earner in the household. Single-parent families – often the mother – and those with no, or low-paid, unskilled jobs were less likely to buy. Those with the least resources to buy also had the least incentive to do so: they lived in less desirable high-rise flats on less desirable estates.

Privatisation was the economic policy that came to characterise Thatcherism. There was no mention of it in the 1979 Conservative manifesto and in Thatcher's first term the government approached it in piecemeal fashion. The small UK medical diagnostics business Amersham International was sold, as were parts of state-owned businesses such as Cable & Wireless, British Aerospace and Britoil. The latter was an unqualified failure, being 70 per cent undersubscribed (the six merchant banks which underwrote the sale ensured the government still raised its £548 million target).[9] Thus, going into Thatcher's second term there was no sense that privatisation would become a long-term success. Nor was it the accepted orthodoxy. In a leader in the build-up to the Britoil sale, *The Times* questioned the wisdom of 'selling assets at a discount [. . .] and transferring ownership from twenty million taxpayers to a few hundred thousand shareholders, simply to raise a relatively small amount of money [. . .]'.[10] The Treasury gained £1.4 billion from privatisations during Thatcher's first term, a figure dwarfed by the £3.9 billion made from the sale of British Telecom in 1984. It was the biggest privatisation the world had ever seen; however, following the Britoil setback there was widespread fear that the BT sale would also be a disappointment. In the end it was five times oversubscribed, the share price doubling within hours of dealing starting.

The success of the sale invigorated Thatcher's belief in the shareholder economy. In January 1985, she made her philosophy clear: 'We don't think that politicians are the best people to run businesses. So, in the coming year we shall remove still more industries from state control and build on the success of British Telecom where instead of one giant shareholder, there are now millions of owners.'[11] The privatisation of British Gas followed in 1986. The flotation was supported by a popular marketing campaign imploring people to tell Sid, the archetypal private investor invented to promote the sale. If they saw him, that was. It was a huge success, bringing in £5.4 billion for the Treasury. Before the end of the decade, British Airways, Rolls-Royce, Jaguar Cars, the British Airports Authority and the regional water authorities were

all sold. Thatcherism was at its peak, but it wasn't without its critics. In a speech to the Tory Reform Group, former Conservative
prime minister Harold Macmillan likened the sale of state assets
to those by country house owners who were short of funds: 'First
all of the Georgian silver goes and then all that nice furniture that
used to be in the saloon. Then the Canalettos go.'[12]

For many, though, the raft of privatisations was seen as an
opportunity to make a small profit. As with the right-to-buy
scheme, incentives such as loyalty bonuses and discounts on utility
bills were created to make the sales attractive to small investors.
Often the offer price was below the market value, ensuring an
almost instant profit for investors (but also short-changing them as
taxpayers). Although, also as with the right-to-buy scheme, those
without disposable funds were effectively excluded from the process, the percentage of adults holding shares still rose from around
7 per cent to 25 per cent – approximately twelve million people –
during the decade.[13] In 1987, research showed that around 20 per
cent of the *Sun*'s readers had bought shares for the first time in the
previous twelve months. To meet this interest, the paper started
including a money page, claiming that when it had launched in
1969 'only toffs and the super-rich had stocks and shares'.[14] The
Daily Mirror already had a weekly four-page money section, and
the *Daily Star* started printing a range of share prices. *The Times*,
many of whose readers were the sort of 'toffs' who had been buying shares when the *Sun* launched, created a stock exchange game
called Portfolio, promoted by the comedian Mel Smith sporting a
bowler hat. Readers were given a personal 'share card' containing
a unique series of eight numbers. They had to record their daily
Portfolio total (which could rise or fall) before adding them up to
determine their weekly Portfolio total. If that matched the paper's
weekly 'dividend' figure, the reader would win or share the weekly
cash prize of £20,000. It was a very thinly disguised, more

upmarket version of bingo, which had captured the public's imagination while also fuelling the three-way tabloid circulation war. In 1989, the *Sunday Times* launched its inaugural annual Rich List. Topped by the Queen, who was sitting on a fortune of £5.25 billion, it was dominated by Old Etonians and those with inherited wealth. Of the country's 200 richest people, only eighty-six had made their own fortunes. By comparison, there were 11 dukes, 6 marquises, 14 earls and 9 viscounts.[15] However, an entrepreneurial spirit had been unleashed. Twenty-five years later, nearly 80 per cent of those listed were self-made, many of whom would perhaps have read the early lists and been motivated to join their ranks.[16]

III

The small business ethic was represented in television shows like *Only Fools and Horses*. Del Boy Trotter, played by David Jason, endeared himself to the audience thanks to his hopefully expressed but ultimately forlorn belief that 'this time next year we'll be millionaires'. The BBC show regularly pulled in more than eighteen million viewers, becoming one of the most popular sitcoms of the decade. ITV's comedy *Minder* enjoyed similar popularity. Produced by Thames Television, it portrayed a similar character in Arthur Daley (George Cole) who was always on the lookout for 'a nice little earner'. These were gently mocking but ultimately affectionate portrayals; neither of the two central characters did much more than sell stolen or faulty goods to gullible punters, the comedy value coming from the repeated failure of their efforts.

A more cynical depiction was that of the Harry Enfield character Loadsamoney, a boorish Cockney plasterer whose cash-in-hand business enabled him to earn 'loadsamoney'. Enfield first tried out his new creation on his flatmate Paul Whitehouse, before taking it to the Tunnel Club in south London, considered a rite of passage for young comedians at the time. After that, Loadsamoney found mainstream success on Channel 4's *Friday Night Live*, hosted by Ben Elton. Each week, Loadsamoney swaggered on stage, shouting: 'Shut your marf and look at my wad', while waving a handful of money at the audience. The character became so popular that he released a record, which reached No. 4 in the charts, and made an appearance on *Top of the Pops*. It is insightful that a corresponding character Buggerallmoney, a Geordie who waved an empty hand at the audience — 'soft southern bastards' — while rationalising the fact he had no cash with the rhetorical question 'So what? At least I'm not a shandy-drinking Cockney' was not a success. Enfield, who said he thought Loadsamoney was 'a complete bastard',[17] was disappointed that instead of becoming a hate figure, Loadsamoney was adopted as a figurehead by those he was supposed to be satirising. After the *Sun* used the character to advertise its bingo competition, Enfield told the paper through his solicitor that he wanted to make it clear that Loadsamoney had nothing to do with the competition. The paper responded by warning Enfield to 'Shut your mouff and look at OUR wad' before advising him to buy a sense of humour.[18] Enfield quickly realised that action was futile, and so following a skit during Comic Relief in 1989 which saw the character killed off, he stopped performing him. It was fitting that he had got the idea for Loadsamoney while observing Tottenham Hotspur fans taunting followers of clubs from the economically depressed North by waving £10 notes at them. Spurs were among the first to embrace the spirit of Thatcherism.

In the 1980s, the business of football in Britain was, in many respects, like the stock market: an old boys' club governed by antiquated rules that looked increasingly anachronistic. Club boards were dominated by local businessmen and worthies affording them status within the local community. They had often held the position for decades, or inherited it from their father. They were often stuck in their ways. Prior to 1982, directors could not receive a salary, and there were strict limits on the dividends that could be paid to shareholders. Tottenham's articles of association, in particular Article 14, gave the club's board the power to veto the registration of shares to anyone they did not approve of, with no reason given. In effect, it prevented dealing in the club's shares, making Tottenham's board, led by seventy-six-year-old Arthur Richardson, a closed shop.

The door was forced open in the early 1980s by a young businessman, Irving Scholar. He was the antithesis of the stereotypical football club board member, having followed Spurs since childhood. Over time, he graduated from the Shelf, the terrace where hardcore fans stood, to the executive boxes, a journey that mirrored his progression from being a sixteen-year-old school leaver working for an estate agent, to a becoming a self-made millionaire. He was also only thirty-three. It was through his experience as a property developer that Scholar became concerned that the proposed plans to develop White Hart Lane's West Stand had not been costed properly and could leave the club in significant debt. When his offer to help oversee the project was rebuffed by Richardson, Scholar became determined, along with Paul Bobroff, a fellow property developer and fan of the club, to wrest control of the club away from him.

They sought to circumvent the restrictions of Article 14 by initially purchasing not the shares but the proxy votes of the shareholders. Many were widows or elderly daughters of the now-deceased original owners, only too keen to cash in on shares that, somewhat ironically, most had considered to be worthless due to Article 14. In just nine months, Scholar and Bobroff hoovered up

51 per cent between them for just £600,000. After a brief period of boardroom wrangling, the old guard moved aside. The club was in new hands. As Scholar, the largest shareholder and the driving force behind the move, was still living in Monte Carlo as a tax exile, Douglas Alexiou was made chairman. It was, however, clear who was in real control.

The first significant task was to get a handle on the club's financial position. The secrecy of Scholar and Bobroff's efforts to take over meant they were unable to do the due diligence that would have preceded a more conventional takeover. What they found astonished them. VAT records had not been kept; one of Scholar's first acts was to fend off a court summons for non-payment. Accounts showed £52,000 missing from the ticket office.[19] There was no suggestion of fraud, just poor accounting. Cash was found strewn across the floor and stuffed down the back of filing cabinets at White Hart Lane.[20] Scholar was left bemused that fans could not purchase tickets using a credit card as a theatregoer might.

Initially, the only real measure of Tottenham's financial position was its bank balance, which was parlous; gate receipts were not enough to cover the club's annual costs. The transfer of Alan Brazil, the first player bought under the new regime, could only be funded after Scholar and Bobroff personally underwrote the bank loan. The club had also overspent by £1 million on the West Stand redevelopment; it was heavily in debt. None of this was unique to Spurs, for at the time 90 per cent of the ninety-two clubs in the League were losing money.[21] However, Tottenham were in trouble to an eye-watering degree. Once they had got a proper handle on the situation, the new owners found the club was actually £5.5 million in the red. It was what Scholar called 'the biggest debt in football'.[22]

For Scholar, there was one answer to the problem. 'Scholar's view was that the stock market had all sorts of companies that were listed, including leisure companies, so why shouldn't a football company be listed?' says Alex Fynn, who, as a Saatchi & Saatchi executive, worked with Scholar.[23] 'At his instigation Tottenham floated.' At the time Football League rules not only limited dividend payouts, but also determined that if a club went bust its assets would become the property of the League. Few serious investors were willing to put money into an organisation they would not fully control, which effectively prevented a stock market flotation. Again, Scholar needed to come up with a way of circumventing the regulations. 'What Tottenham did,' says Fynn, 'was set up a public company, Tottenham Hotspur plc, which owned the football club. As it was a public company it was free from some of the regulations – the restrictions – that the Football League had previously applied to the club.'

On 13 October 1983, Spurs became the first sports club in the world to issues shares, when 3.8 million priced at £1 were made available. The issue was four times oversubscribed. When trading in the shares began on the 13th, they opened at £1.06 before quickly falling to 94p, then rallying to £1.01 by the end of the first day's trading. As a flotation, it had not been an overwhelming success. 'It didn't matter,' says Fynn, 'because the people who were subscribing weren't doing it as an investment but primarily out of love and commitment to the club.' For Scholar, it achieved the aim of wiping out the club's debts.

The prospectus for the flotation also spoke to Scholar's bigger plans for the club. It was to be a 'broadly-based leisure group' focused on 'the promotion of goods and services associated with the Spurs name'.[24] It became too much for manager Keith Burkinshaw who resigned in 1984 due to the growing corporate influence at the club, his last match in charge being the second leg of their triumphant UEFA Cup final victory against Anderlecht.

Burkinshaw was widely quoted as saying 'There used to be a football club over there,' as he left White Hart Lane for the last time. The words had in fact been written and attributed to him by the journalist Ken Jones, who had in turn been inspired by the melancholy Frank Sinatra song 'There Used to Be a Ballpark', a lament on the demise of the Brooklyn Dodgers baseball team. However, they succinctly captured Burkinshaw's feelings about the way the game was going. 'Where the team was all, the centre of everything that went on at a football club,' he said, 'it has become just a part of a marketing formula.'[25]

Like Pineapple, Spurs diversified away from its core business in the search of greater revenue. The company developed White Hart Lane's restaurant and conference facilities and the ground was the venue of Frank Bruno's 1987 fight against Joe Bugner. The same year, two companies, Martex and Stumps, were added to the portfolio, the former an import agent for the latter's distribution of women's clothing and sportswear. There was a travel agency, Spurs Travel, and even a publishing wing. Tottenham Hotspur plc also became the UK distributor of Hummel, the Danish kit manufacturer. It was a disastrous partnership; kits were often not delivered on time and even Spurs themselves experienced problems. During the 1987 FA Cup final, five of the club's players walked out wearing shirts emblazoned with the name of new sponsors Holsten, and six walked out wearing shirts with no sponsor at all. The fiasco exemplified the growing burden that the non-football businesses placed on the club.

The diversification which stretched the club was compounded by a fall in revenue caused by wider problems. The game was marred by hooliganism; Spurs missed out on two seasons of European football and the associated revenue they would have brought, due to the ban imposed on English clubs following the Heysel disaster. Rising player costs and the outlay needed to convert White

Hart Lane to an all-seater stadium following the Hillsborough disaster in 1989 increased the pressure on revenue streams. However, the key problem was that the revenue Scholar had anticipated the club would receive from television was not forthcoming.

IV

The TV rights deal which saw Tottenham host the first live televised League game since the 1960s in 1983, had been done prior to Scholar taking control of the club and had come in the wake of a threatened 'Super League'. The so-called Big Five clubs – Manchester United, Liverpool, Everton, Arsenal and Spurs – had begun meeting informally in 1981, united by their mutual dislike at how the League was structured. The following year they threatened to break away from the rest of the clubs and negotiate their own TV deal. In response, the League agreed that teams could keep all their own gate receipts, instead of sharing them with their visitors, an immediate increase in income for the larger clubs, and for a limited number of games to be broadcast live on Sunday afternoons. But the BBC and ITV, effectively operating as a cartel, were able to suppress the costs and the bigger clubs, like Manchester United and Spurs, would receive the same share of the revenue as the lower division clubs. It represented less than 1 per cent of their income.[26]

The arrival on the scene of Scholar, and David Dein at Arsenal, provided fresh impetus. Like Scholar, Dein was another young entrepreneur who defied conventional wisdom by indulging his passion and investing in the football club he supported. Another self-made millionaire, in 1983 he paid £292,000 for 16 per cent of Arsenal. At the time, Peter Hill-Wood, who had followed in the footsteps of both his grandfather and father to become the club's chairman, said: 'I think he's crazy. To all intents and purposes, it's dead money.'[27] Dein, like Scholar, saw things differently. He would quickly become vice-chairman at Arsenal and, influenced by the coverage of NFL and baseball that he saw on regular visits to the USA, he believed strongly that the true value of football in England was not being realised.

This belief was reinforced by the TV rights negotiations in 1985. As discussed in Chapter One, the BBC and ITV effectively bid as one to keep the price down. They offered a four-year deal worth £3.8 million in the first year, rising over the course of the deal. In return they wanted the rights to show nineteen live games: sixteen League matches plus two League Cup semi-finals and the League Cup final plus an option to show matches on a regional basis. Robert Maxwell, the owner of Oxford United, argued that the rights were worth significantly more. As the owner of Mirror Newspapers and the main shareholder in MTV Europe, his was a persuasive voice, and the League rejected the TV companies' offer. Yet they were in no position to negotiate, their hand weakened by the catalogue of violence and tragedy that beset the game as the negotiations were taking place and the fact that millions stayed up past midnight to watch Dennis Taylor beat Steve Davis in the World Snooker Championships final – other sports were growing into more enticing TV events. The TV companies refused to budge and by the end of the year, the League agreed a £1.5 million deal for the rest of the season, and the following year agreed a two-year deal for £3.1 million. Once again, it had been a humiliating capitulation.

This experience prompted Scholar to commission Saatchi & Saatchi to analyse the true value of football to the TV companies. Alex Fynn produced a report, *Football and Television: Its Influence on Programme Costs and Advertisement*, in which he concluded that the rights were worth between £6 million and £8 million a year – the increased value of the advertising that ITV could sell during such broadcasts, or the cost of generating similar viewing figures for the BBC. 'Irving Scholar was the only man in football who really understood the commercial aspects of football,' says Fynn, 'he was the first to appreciate television and the fees thereof and merchandising and how you might grade matches according to their importance.'

But Fynn, who the *Sunday Times* would later christen 'the spiritual godfather of the Premier League', didn't just have a clear idea of what he considered to be the true value of football; he also had some radical ideas about how the game should be restructured. 'We looked at the value of television, but we also wrote documents about how football could be overhauled. We wrote several documents running through a whole gamut of possibilities: a Super League of ten clubs; a Super League with two divisions of forty clubs; a Super League of twenty clubs.'

Their resolve strengthened by this information, the Big Five plus representatives of Newcastle, Manchester City and Southampton met in September 1985 to again discuss a possible breakaway league, which would enable clubs to negotiate their own TV deals. With negotiations between the rebels and the rest of the League at an impasse, Scholar, Martin Edwards, the chairman of Manchester United, and Philip Carter of Everton, met with representatives of Rangers and Celtic who suggested that they and four other Scottish Premier League clubs would be willing to join a breakaway league.[28] As in 1982, the threat was quashed when the rest of the English League acquiesced to the First Division clubs' demands. There would be a reduction in the number of clubs in the top division, a change in the League's voting structure and 50 per cent of all TV and sponsorship money would go to the top division. The seeds of the Premier League had been sown.

The value of football was still depressed by the lack of competition in the marketplace. Only a third player to rival the BBC and ITV would improve that situation. That came in 1988 with the launch of British Satellite Broadcasting (BSB), a conglomerate that included names like Granada, Virgin, Reed International and the French media company Chargeurs. The American experience showed that exclusive sports rights were a key driver in the success of pay TV, so in May 1988 BSB offered the Football League a ten-year deal with a guaranteed payment of £9 million a year rising to more than £25 million a year. The League issued a press release triumphantly proclaiming 'FOOTBALL PROPOSES NEW TV DEAL FOR NINETIES' that would 'net football a minimum of £200 million over the next ten years'.

Greg Dyke, ITV's new chairman of sport, realised that if he could prise the rights out of BSB's hands he could undermine the new rival before they'd even started broadcasting. He met representatives from the Big Five clubs and revealed he wanted to sign for the exclusive rights to broadcast football. He immediately won their trust by admitting, when questioned by Scholar, that ITV and BBC had effectively operated a cartel in the past. 'If there are seminal moments that change everything,' wrote the Spurs chairman, 'then this was one of them.'[29] Dyke's offer was £750,000 each to the Big Five plus another £2 million split between another five clubs which would ultimately be Aston Villa, Newcastle, Nottingham Forest, Sheffield Wednesday and West Ham; a neat geographical coverage of the ITV regions. Dyke's final offer was £11 million for eighteen League games, two League Cup semifinals and the League Cup final, but before it and the BSB deal could be put to the League for a vote BSB withdrew their offer. 'I got flack inside ITV for paying too much,' Dyke tells me. 'That's funny now.'

Neither the ITV deal in 1988 nor the formation of the

Premier League and the TV deal with Sky TV that followed in 1992 came soon enough for Scholar and Spurs. The fans began to voice their dissatisfaction with the chairman due to rising ticket prices which were not accompanied by silverware. In 1990, he was forced to resign from the board of the plc although he remained chairman of the football club. By January 1991, the club was £12 million in debt and faced being wound up by Midland, its main banker.[30] 'Scholar was a true visionary in football,' says Fynn. 'He saw the value of commercialism, and of television rights. At the time, football was a very outmoded industry, and he just applied the common sense and the business acumen that he'd built up as a successful property entrepreneur to Tottenham Hotspur, initially to their benefit but ultimately to his downfall. He just moved too far and too fast for the times.'

In 1989, Millwall raised £5 million via a share issue which helped the club move to a new stadium. They were only the second club to go public. Had Martin Edwards' plans for Manchester United come to fruition they would have been the third. Edwards became chairman of Manchester United following the death of his father, Louis, in 1980. As with Tottenham, there were shares in the club, but these were owned by a few hundred supporters who had invested mainly for sentimental reasons. Anyone wanting to buy had to wait until someone else wanted to sell, and all transactions had to be undertaken by a limited number of Manchester stockbrokers. In effect, the shares did not reflect the club's true value and there was no proper market on which to trade them. The club had considered floating on the Unlisted Securities Market — the same market Pineapple was listed on — in 1981, but this had been rejected as too costly. Following the Spurs share issue, Edwards decided to explore a full flotation, like the north London club. At the time, United was not the global behemoth it would become. Three FA Cup wins could not hide the fact that the club had not won the title since 1967, twenty-two long years that included an ignominious relegation in 1974. With envious eyes cast along the M62 to Liverpool's success, attendances had fallen to their lowest in twenty-seven years. Old Trafford needed investment to renovate the Stretford End and complete the cantilever roof that covered the other three sides of the ground. Before the plans came to fruition, Robert Maxwell tried to buy the club for a sum reported to be in the region of £10 million. The figure was probably less than that, and the deal ultimately collapsed. Five years later, Edwards came even closer to selling the club, agreeing to offload his 50.2 per cent stake to property developer Michael Knighton, who also promised to invest £10 million into Old Trafford.

The imminent sale was revealed on the Thursday before the start of the 1989/90 season by ITV's *News at Ten*. The following day, Knighton was unveiled to the media at a press conference. The son of a baker, he was a former teacher who had made his fortune through property speculation, but he was not a high-profile businessman; Edwards introduced him to the media as Michael Whetton – the name of the club's catering manager.[31] *The Times* spoke for many when it pointed out that 'No one seems to know where the wealth of this 37-year-old had come from [. . .].'[32] Knighton responded to such questions by saying, 'This is the age of the enterprise culture and I have been lucky.'[33] Like Scholar and Dein, he was a self-made man who recognised the untapped potential in football. He saw United as a brand, and had a well-researched strategic vision for the commercial side of the club that he had developed prior to making his bid. Knighton proposed among other things the creation of a range of club merchandise, the extent of which could be 'almost endless'; a superstore at Old Trafford; a club museum and stadium tours;

and a club TV channel. He recognised that United needed a more sophisticated approach to attracting sponsorship from major global companies, and Knighton also identified that satellite television, then in its infancy and dismissed by many in the game, had the potential to make TV rights worth billions, not millions. Much of this is standard stuff now but at the time it was met with scepticism.

The day after the press conference, scepticism turned to ridicule. About half an hour before kick-off in United's opening League game against champions Arsenal, Knighton introduced himself to the Old Trafford crowd in ostentatious fashion. Clad in full United training kit he ran onto a lush green pitch bathed in August sunshine, juggled the ball on his head, shoulder and knees before turning to the Stretford End and striking it into the net. Chants of 'Fergie, Fergie sign him up!' rang from the terraces as Knighton blew kisses to the crowd. He had intended it as a way of bridging the disconnect between the club's fans and its board. Those watching from the director's box saw it as a crass act of hubris. Alex Ferguson's team demolished the Gunners 4–1 and, briefly, it seemed like a new dawn for the club. Yet within a matter of months, the deal had fallen through. Knighton's initial financial backers withdrew and, as he sought to secure replacement finance, his exploits on the pitch became a stick to beat him with; he was portrayed as an Arthur Daley character; a superficial chancer who had been found out. This was unfair. Knighton did ultimately raise the required finance in time (and later won libel damages against *The Sunday Times Illustrated History of Football*, which suggested he hadn't[34]), but by then the club's board and supporters had turned against him. On one occasion when Knighton visited his solicitor, a group of fans vandalised a Rolls-Royce parked outside in the mistaken belief that it belonged to him.[35] It would have been unrealistic for him to become chairman in such an atmosphere, so he cancelled his agreement to buy the club and settled for a place on the board.

In the wake of Knighton's abortive takeover attempt, investment was still required to complete the work on the Stretford End and the decision was taken to float the club on the London Stock Exchange. For some board members this was also seen as a way of protecting the club from an asset stripper who could sell off the best players and the Old Trafford ground. 'I don't think any one person should have charge of United,' said Bobby Charlton, 'and the best safeguard is for the club to be floated on the market.'[36] Like Tottenham, United bypassed the FA's rules by forming a holding company, Manchester United plc. In May 1991, just over two and a half million shares were sold at £3.85 each. Edwards maintained his majority holding. Many of Knighton's ideas were included in the flotation documentation and would be implemented by the club. Several years later, Michael Edelson, the longest serving board member at United, would acknowledge this, saying, 'Knighton did something good for me and for United. Because we pretty much followed the plan that he'd laid down but didn't have the money to execute.'[37]

In 1989 Knighton predicted that United would be a £150 million business within fifteen years. Like his ideas for the club, the figure was met with scepticism, but it proved to be an underestimate. Just nine years later Rupert Murdoch made a £625 million bid for the club. As Knighton had suggested, the Premier League's relationship with Murdoch's BSkyB had revolutionised the game. The initial five-year TV rights deal in 1992 was worth £304 million. This was followed by a four-year deal worth £670 million. It was widely believed that when that expired clubs would negotiate with media companies on an individual basis for the rights to broadcast their home games. A host of such companies began jockeying for position. Granada bought 22 per cent of

Liverpool and spent £47 million on just 5 per cent of Arsenal shares. The cable TV company NTL spent hundreds of millions between 1998 and 2000 buying stakes in Aston Villa, Leicester, Middlesbrough and Newcastle, and Celtic and Rangers in Scotland. Amid widespread opposition Murdoch's takeover bid was referred to the Monopolies and Mergers Commission who ruled it was anti-competitive due to BSkyB's already pre-eminent position in the broadcasting of the Premier League. It was a short-lived victory. In 2005, again in the face of widespread opposition, the US-based Glazer family bought the club, borrowing £525 million secured against United's assets to fund the deal. It was just sixteen years since Knighton had tried to buy Manchester United for £10 million, and the club was valued at £790 million. In May 2021 that valuation had reached £4.2 billion.[38]

V

Within just a few months of Knighton's Old Trafford juggling act, many Manchester United fans had run out of patience with Ferguson. The opening day victory against the champions appeared to be the high point of the season and quickly faded from memory. Their next four games saw United accrue just one point. A 5–1 win at home against Millwall in mid-September was followed a week later by a 5–1 defeat away against Manchester City. The club's fanzine *Red News* printed a 'crisis' edition calling for Ferguson to resign or be sacked. During a home defeat at the hands of Crystal Palace, one fan held up a banner reading: '3 YEARS OF EXCUSES AND IT'S STILL CRAP . . . TA RA FERGIE'.[39] In early January, United were anchored in fifteenth place in the League, without a win in eight games. They were two points off the relegation zone and eighteen behind the leaders Liverpool.

An early exit from the League Cup meant the FA Cup was the club's last hope of silverware. They would start their campaign away at Nottingham Forest, who had lost in the previous season's semi-finals. It was a tough draw for United made harder by the absence of several key players through injury. It was also widely believed that defeat would see Ferguson sacked. The press scented blood. Yet, thanks to a second-half goal from twenty-year-old striker Mark Robbins, United won 1−0. Ferguson earned a reprieve, and despite continued mediocre League form, the team went on to lift the FA Cup at Wembley in May following a replay against Crystal Palace. The following year they won the European Cup Winners' Cup against Barcelona. The cycle of success that saw Ferguson's team dominate English football for the next twenty years had begun.

It shouldn't have really been a surprise. Before he was appointed by Manchester United in 1986, Ferguson had enjoyed seven gilded seasons with Aberdeen, leading them to ten trophies including three Premier Division titles, four Scottish Cups, the European Cup Winners' Cup and the European Super Cup. The first League success came in 1980, the Dons being the first team from outside Glasgow to win the title since Kilmarnock fifteen years earlier. When Celtic won the title in the following two seasons, it seemed that order had been restored. In 1982, Aberdeen lifted the Scottish Cup. Although they didn't know it at the time, it in turn led to the greatest night in the club's history as it secured qualification for the Cup Winners' Cup. They beat Bayern Munich in the quarter-finals thanks to a memorable 3−2 second-leg win at Pittodrie. And after securing a place in the final, an armada of fans made the eighteen-hour journey across the North Sea, some in the specially chartered P&O ferry *St Clair*, others in fishing boats, to see them beat Real Madrid in Gothenburg.

That was the last time a Scottish team lifted a European trophy and over the years it has come to overshadow the fact that Dundee United won the Scottish title for the first time in the same season. Jim McLean's side secured the points they needed to win the title on the final day of the season at city rivals Dundee. For Gerry Hassan, an academic and commentator, who grew up in Dundee and is a United fan, this spell of success was transformative. 'Dundee was a city that was patronised or just forgotten about until Dundee United came along. For somebody like me growing up in the city, it gave me an alternative take on Scotland. It was not just about a narrow politics, not just about the central belt with Glasgow as this dominant city culturally, and to an extent economically. There was an alternative comedy scene, there was an alternative music scene and there was this world of football. It was an uplifting story. It gave us a different version of Scotland from the one where we were all oppressed by Thatcherism.'[40]

The title success secured the Tangerines a place in the European Cup in which they reached the semi-finals against Roma. United overwhelmed their opponents at Tannadice to secure a 2−0 first-leg lead but lost the return leg at a febrile Stadio Olimpico 3−0. In the same season, Aberdeen reached the last four of the Cup Winners' Cup, where they lost to Porto. Despite the double disappointment, it was a landmark achievement. Two Scottish teams had reached the semi-final stage of European competitions and neither was from Glasgow. The 'New Firm', as Aberdeen and Dundee United became known, had established themselves as a force to be reckoned with both home and abroad. Dundee United went on to a UEFA Cup final, three Scottish Cup finals and a Scottish League Cup final, but would not add to their trophy haul during the 1980s. Aberdeen continued to dominate domestically, winning the League and Cup double in 1984 and retaining the title again the following season.

The significance of this period shouldn't be understated. It was

the first (and to date only) time in the history of the Scottish
League that there had been a three-season spell in which neither
Celtic nor Rangers won the title. The shift in the on-pitch balance
of power from Glasgow to the east coast of Scotland reflected a
cultural and economic shift that was taking place off the pitch.
While London and the Home Counties were reaping the financial
benefits of the stock market Big Bang, the north-east of Scotland
was benefiting from a windfall of a different kind. In 1969 Britain
struck oil in the North Sea and within six years the first pipeline
bringing black gold ashore had been switched on. Aberdeen,
dubbed the 'Houston of the North',[41] was a significant beneficiary. The city's harbour, once the country's busiest fishing port,
was transformed into the primary port in Europe servicing the oil
industry. Industrial parks opened in the hills around the city. Aberdeen's airport became the busiest civilian heliport in the world.
There were more flights to oil platforms in the North Sea – the
'Foggy Forties' – than there were to Glasgow or Edinburgh. There
were as many to Stavanger, Aberdeen's Norwegian oil-industry
twin, as to London. In an area with a population of 250,000,
around 30,000 new jobs were created.[42] Salaries increased. Typic-
ally, the roustabouts worked two weeks on the rigs and then had
two weeks off. When they returned to shore, they made sure they
enjoyed themselves. The city's night-time economy boomed. Burger restaurants and cocktail bars sprang up. Shops that had long
stood empty were packed with customers; hotels did great business. 'This wasn't our oil industry or oil expertise; it was something
done to Scotland by foreign-owned multi-nationals,' says Hassan.
'But it had an impact in Aberdeen because of the jobs and the
skills base that was built up.' He believes that the discovery of oil
also changed how the country understood itself. 'Scotland's identity has always been nebulous. Scotland was shifting from the
1960s with the decline of the west and the rise of the east coast,

both in terms of the population balance, and in terms of industries and economic growth. Clearly in a small way the oil discovery aided all that. Looking back, you now realise that a large part of it was due to what Glasgow was going through, and the weakness for nearly a decade of Glasgow Rangers.'

It was not until 1981 that Britain became a net exporter of oil. While the Labour Party under Harold Wilson and Jim Callaghan was unable to reap the benefits of this geological good fortune, Margaret Thatcher was. UK government revenues from oil and gas jumped from virtually nothing in the 1968/69 tax year to £565 million a decade later. By 1979/80 the figure had risen to £2.3 billion and by 1984/85 it was more than £12 billion.[43] For the Treasury, it was the equivalent of a seven pence rise in the rate of income tax. Without that revenue and that accrued from the privatisation of various state industries, the Thatcher government would have been unable to cut the top rate of income tax from 83 to 40 per cent and also meet its public spending commitments. While health and education budgets were cut, mass unemployment and the associated benefits payments meant total expenditure remained high. In his critique of Thatcher's economic policies in 1985, her predecessor Harold Macmillan didn't just lament the selling of the country's silver and Canalettos, he also warned against the over-reliance on North Sea oil revenues. 'In the ordinary working of the economy, we are practically bankrupt save for oil,' he argued. 'We are the Abu Dhabi of today.'[44] Two years later, the young Labour politician Tony Blair offered a similar critique, suggesting that 'oil has been utterly essential to Mrs Thatcher's electoral success'.[45]

As the oil revenues were sent south to the Treasury, the economic benefit was spread throughout Britain. Beyond Aberdeen and the surrounding Grampian region, little benefit was felt in Scotland. Sterling became a petrocurrency, its value artificially increased. This in turn made British exports more expensive, which somewhat ironically placed further pressure on the country's already deteriorating manufacturing industry. Scotland, like the North of England, where many of those jobs were located, was hit hard. The Clyde Valley, which stretched from Glasgow, through Paisley, Renfrew and out to Greenock, and which once thrummed to the sound of shipyards, foundries, factories, mills and brickworks, lay silent. The deprivation was captured by the *Observer Magazine*. On the cover, over a picture of an elderly woman pictured through the broken windows of the block of flats in which she lived, ran the headline 'HOME, ROTTEN HOME, what it's like to live in the worst corner of Britain'. Inside, above a photo essay of the deprivation, Glasgow was labelled 'The Ghetto City of the Poor'.[46] For Aberdeen fans, the wealth brought in by the oil industry enabled them to follow their club on its forays into Europe. They were at the forefront of casual culture in Scotland, indulging a passion for designer sportswear. This reputation was immortalised by the Italian footwear company Diadora which released a trainer named the 'Aberdeen'. It was, like the city's famous buildings, granite-grey.

CHAPTER 14

There Is a Light That Never Goes Out

I

On the morning of 11 May 1985, as Birmingham City fans were starting their promotion party, some 130 miles away in Bradford another one was starting and it, too, would end in tragedy. The previous Monday, Bradford had secured the Third Division title with a 2−0 win at Bolton. The players were set to receive the trophy ahead of the club's final game of the season at home to Lincoln − Bradford's first silverware for fifty-six years. Average attendance for the season had been a little over 6,600, but it was anticipated close to double that would turn up on the final day to join in the celebrations. Although hooliganism at the ground was rare, there had been serious disorder earlier in the season when Derby County fans got into the main stand, tore out some of the new plastic seats and started throwing them. Thus, as with many matches, police prepared for trouble and this time 144 officers were on duty in and around the ground. Their pre-match briefing focused on maintaining public order, not specifically on ensuring public safety.

None of this dampened the carnival atmosphere. The result had no relevance to either side. Prior to kick-off, Bradford manager Trevor Cherry received the Manager of the Year award. The Bradford players duly paraded the Third Division trophy and displayed messages of thanks to the fans for their support. A team of majorettes performed on the pitch. 'This was a very rare occurrence for Bradford,' says Mike Harrison, editor of Bradford fanzine *The City Gent* since 2004, who was at the match.[1] 'We got given the trophy before kick-off, which was odd because you usually get the trophy after the game. But it was just as well because you had this dichotomy that everything was happy and lovely beforehand, and no one knew that forty-five minutes later there'd be utter carnage.'

The first hint there was a problem came just before half-time. A small commotion developed in the main stand. One fan, Leslie Brownlie, noticed the smell of burning paper and heat coming from below his seat. He turned to his uncle, Eric Bennett, and exclaimed, 'Hell, it's warm down there'.[2] When the pair looked through the gap in the wooden floorboards, they saw what looked like a piece of paper on fire, but they were not unduly concerned. It was small and they felt it could be easily dealt with, Brownlie even poured a cup of coffee on the flames to try to put them out.

On the opposite side of the ground in the far corner, Harrison became aware of the disturbance. 'The first thing I thought was "There can't be any fighting, surely, it's not that sort of day." Then I saw the first whiffs of smoke.' In the Main Stand, Bennett had gone in search of a fire extinguisher, not knowing that there was no such equipment in the stand; it was kept in the clubhouse at the far end so it couldn't be used as a missile by hooligans. Instead, he alerted three police officers and one, PC Adrian Lyles, went with him to take a look. Lyles was similarly unconcerned, later saying, 'It appeared to me to be a minor incident'.[3] Still, he called to some of his colleagues on the touchline for an extinguisher.

Due to the noise of the crowd, they misheard him thinking he wanted them to contact the fire brigade, which they did.

That first call to the emergency services was made just after 3.41 p.m. Firemen were on the scene within five minutes. By then it was already too late. The entire stand had been engulfed in flames. It was in effect a tinder box. It was made almost entirely of wood and gaps under the seating facilitated the accumulation of rubbish over decades. In the aftermath, a copy of the local newspaper, the *Bradford Evening Telegraph and Argus*, from November 1968 was found along with sweet wrappers from the pre-decimal era; the club's apprentices regularly swept rubbish into the gaps beneath the seats when they were cleaning up after games. As the flames grew upwards from the seat of the fire, the low roof caused them to spread horizontally along the stand, reaching for more oxygen. A rare northerly wind accelerated their progress. Also made of wood, the roof was covered in tarpaulin and sealed with asphalt, which added further fuel to the fire which spread 'faster than a man can run'.[4]

Initially, people were slow to react. Fans in the paddock area chanted, 'Piss on it, piss on it, piss on it!' and 'Bradford's burning, fetch the engines ... fire fire, fire fire'.[5] There was no malice intended: it was simply the case that few fully understood the enormity of what was unfolding. One witness told the inquiry that after being asked to move by the police he contemplated whether to join the queue for the snack bar, instead choosing to go to the lavatory. Even when he came back out into the stand and saw smoke, he still took the time to see what was happening on the pitch.[6] Over the next minute or so the small white cloud of smoke expanded. Slowly, the crowd began to realise that they needed to get out. Despite the exhortations of the police, many of those in the seating areas made their way to the back of the stand. It was the logical thing to do: exit the way they had come in. However, as was normal, so as to stop people gaining free entry after kick-off, many of the doors were locked; bolted or padlocked. Others were boarded up. This left people trapped in the corridor at the top of the stand, exactly where the thick, acrid smoke and flames were at their worst. The bodies of twenty-seven victims were found clustered around these doors.

Those who went in the other direction, towards the pitch, were confronted by a complicated exit route akin to an obstacle course. 'There were two sections of seating,' says Harrison. 'The seating in the back was essentially just benches and in front of that were more modern tip-up seats. You'd have to climb over a wall to get into the area with the tip-up seats, then you'd have to climb over another wall to get into a paddock area where people would stand in front of those seats. Then there was another wall before you could get onto the pitch. If you were in those wooden seats at the back, you had three walls to get over.' All those who died at the front of the stand were aged seventy or over, the effort to make it over the last chest-high hurdle simply too much.

Yorkshire TV, there to capture the celebrations, instead witnessed the full scale of the tragedy: the speed with which the fire took hold; the panic of people scrambling over the wall at the front of the paddock; the acts of heroism as fans and police alike braved the intense heat to pull people to safety; the horror of one man calmly walking from the stand fully ablaze, others desperately attempting to put him out. Along with the commentary of an audibly shocked John Helm, these images were broadcast in real time to stunned viewers of ITV's *World of Sport*. In an era before rolling twenty-four-hour news channels it was one of the first incidents to get such treatment in the UK.

Helm was in a TV gantry on the opposite side of the pitch to the fire but most of the journalists were in the press box in the Main Stand. Among them was Pennine Radio sports editor Tony

Delahunty, known as 'the voice of Bradford City'. His increasingly agitated commentary gave a real sense of the desperation of those caught in the fast-approaching inferno. 'We're on fire here at Valley Parade; the whole end of the stand on one side here is in flames ... They're running out of the ground from that far end ... All the time, people are spilling onto the pitch. We can see the flames going up into the air there ... Let's get all those people out of there ... Just don't rush, watch for the kiddies ... You can hear the heat; there's smoke coming everywhere ... We are going to have to disconnect very shortly ...' The commentary is still used by fire brigades all over the world to show how quickly a blaze can develop from something seemingly innocuous like a puff of smoke to a roaring inferno. 'It was one minute eleven seconds from when my commentary broke into what was happening to when I had to leave my position,' says Delahunty.[7] 'I was the last person from that side of the stand to go down the front and out successfully apart from an old man who was struggling near to me. It was lunacy to stay as long as I did. I don't know what was going through my mind, it certainly wasn't bravery.'

The Yorkshire TV footage and the commentaries of Helm and Delahunty communicated the unfolding chaos and terror, but one thing they couldn't illustrate was the heat. Delahunty made it out of the stand but not before one of his trouser legs had started to smoke. 'We were in the stand on the opposite side of the pitch and there were thousands of people between us and the fire and yet the heat was incredible,' says Harrison. 'It was like being too close to your log burner at home.' It is estimated the temperature may have reached 900°C. Those who ran up to the stand to rescue others spoke of being unable to breathe, the flames soaking up the available oxygen. Many of the injured had not come into direct contact with the flames, some hadn't even been in the Main Stand: their clothes and hair simply caught fire from the sheer heat. People who looked unscathed from the front suffered horrific burns on their backs as they ran from the blaze. Many received injuries to the backs of their hands after they raised them to protect their heads from the fire and melting asphalt dropping from the roof.

Eventually the horror of what he was witnessing became too much for Harrison. 'Directly opposite us was the guy walking out of the stand not realising he was on fire,' he says. 'When the smoke cleared a little bit, I could see there were two people just sitting there, they never left their seats. It got to the stage where I couldn't watch any more, and I just stood with my back to the pitch.' Despite what he'd seen, when Harrison eventually left the ground he tried to convince himself that no one had died. 'So many people poured out onto the pitch I wanted to think everybody would have made it out. I was in denial. I knew they hadn't.'

II

In total, the bodies of fifty-two people were removed from the burned-out stand. Four more people died of their injuries in hospital, bringing the final death toll to fifty-six. More than 260 others were injured. The majority of victims were either over sixty-five or under eighteen. It's also notable how many had the same surnames; this was a tragedy that decimated families. 'The whole city was in shock,' says Harrison. 'People didn't know what to say. You hear about people dying in disasters and it's just numbers. It's when you see the personal tragedy, when they started putting faces and names to people, and these people are sons, daughters, mothers and fathers, it really does hit you.'

Within forty-eight hours of the fire, the Bradford Disaster Appeal fund was set up. Hundreds of fundraising events were organised, the most prominent being a charity football match at Leeds United's Elland Road between the England and West Germany 1966 World Cup final teams (England won 6−4). Gerry Marsden of Gerry and the Pacemakers organised a rerecording of the group's 1963 hit 'You'll Never Walk Alone'. Sung by The Crowd, a group made up of pop stars and TV personalities, it topped the charts for four weeks and helped raise more than £3.5 million for the fund. 'One thing I remember about the whole summer was there was a lot of love from all over the world sent to Bradford. I just found it really heartening,' says Harrison. 'The disaster fund became a very positive thing for people to do during that summertime while we all tried to somehow get our heads around what we'd heard about, or watched on the TV, or witnessed first hand.'

Despite the goodwill from around the world, it was indicative of the era that for some time afterwards the likelihood that the fire had been started by hooligans, and in particular a smoke bomb thrown by a fan, was widely considered. One of the first to float the idea was Bradford's chairman Stafford Heginbotham. In an interview with John Helm on the pitch, the stand still burning behind him, Heginbotham claimed that the 'impression in [the] directors' box was it was somebody letting off a smoke bomb, a flare, or something'.[8] The *Daily Star* went further. In a front page 'splash', headlined 'I SAW KILLER SMOKE BOMB and man who threw it is alive and free',[9] the paper's reporter Ian Trueman claimed: 'A smoke bomb caused the tragic Bradford football fire, I am convinced of it [. . .].'[10] There was no evidence to support these claims. Trueman, like Heginbotham, had been some fifty metres from the seat of the blaze and High Court judge Oliver Popplewell, who led the inquiry into the tragedy, was dismissive. 'I think the fairest thing I can say about Mr Trueman's evidence is that it is not reliable,' he wrote.[11] Yet, for several days

West Yorkshire Police refused to rule out the possibility. Further controversy was caused by the fact that Popplewell was also tasked with investigating the hooliganism at Birmingham on the same day, the link between crowd control and crowd safety made explicit by Home Secretary Leon Brittan in the House of Commons.[12]

Popplewell's inquiry took place with considerable haste. It was described by West Yorkshire Police as a 'seat-of-the-pants affair'.[13] Held three and a half weeks after the fire, when many survivors were not able to give evidence, it lasted just five days. Delahunty believes this was indicative of a widespread lack of appetite for investigating the fire fully, even from the government. 'They didn't want problems; nobody wants problems,' he says. 'Finger pointing was going in different directions at this time and it's not long before someone points fingers and says, "As the people who run our country, shouldn't you make sure these stands are safer and shouldn't you have done it sooner?" No government wants to be under too much pressure.'

Popplewell concluded that the fire was caused by a lit match, or a cigarette, being discarded onto the debris beneath the floorboards of the stand, and he went out of his way not to apportion blame. 'It is quite impossible to determine who caused the fire to start; indeed, it would be grossly unfair to point the finger at any one person.'[14] Similarly, the coroner, James Turnbull, reminded the inquest jury that they 'must not seek to imply any particular person was responsible civilly or criminally for this event' and that their verdict should 'not be couched in such a way as to imply any criticism suggesting that any particular person should be criminally liable or liable to civil proceedings'.[15] Thus directed, they returned verdicts of death by misadventure. There would be no criminal prosecutions.

For many Bradford fans this seemed to reconfirm that they had simply been the victims of misfortune – that the fire could have happened anywhere – and there was little desire to attribute blame. The issue of *The City Gent* produced immediately after the tragedy mentioned the fire just once. 'It's almost like it was too big a subject to cover,' says Harrison. 'We became very protective about the city of Bradford and the football club. The report concluded that it was a discarded match, or a discarded cigarette, and I don't think anybody would want to try and find that person and say, "You caused this fire, you caused all this." I think as with all these disasters they only happen because there's a dozen things that all coalesce at the same time.' Not everyone held the same view. Martin Fletcher was twelve when he escaped the fire. His younger brother, father, uncle and grandfather all died. Thirty years after the tragedy, Fletcher wrote a book about his experiences. During his extensive research, he discovered that in the eighteen years prior to the fire, eight businesses that the club's chairman Stafford Heginbotham had owned or been closely involved in were destroyed in fire. Valley Parade was the ninth. 'Could any man really be as unlucky as Heginbotham had been?' he asked.[16]

The fire may have been an accident, but it was certainly one that could – perhaps should – have been avoided. The Health and Safety Executive had written to Bradford twice in 1981 raising concerns about the wooden structure of the Main Stand and reminding them that fans should be able to exit it in two and a half minutes.[17] Furthermore, in July 1984, a mere ten months before the fire, the now defunct West Yorkshire Metropolitan County Council had also written to the club warning them that the wooden construction of the stand was a fire risk, particularly due to the rubbish accumulated underneath, and that a carelessly discarded cigarette could lead to a blaze. They also made the point that fans should be able to get out in two and a half minutes.[18] The year after the fire, in a civil case brought by Fletcher's mother Susan, the club was found two-thirds liable for ignoring the warnings that had been issued to them and West Yorkshire Metropolitan County Council one-third liable for not following up on the warning it had issued.

Perhaps the most significant conclusion of the Popplewell Inquiry was that, had the Safety of Sports Grounds Act and its guidance, the so-called 'Green Code', applied at Bradford, as it did to grounds in England's top two divisions and Scotland's Premier Division, the fire would probably not have started. Either the stand would have been closed or its design modified to prevent the accumulation of litter underneath the seats. In the event of a fire, the act, if complied with, would have ensured a clear route to the pitch. There would have been stewards at the back of the stand, able to open the exit gates in an emergency. Following the Valley Parade tragedy, the government extended the act to thirty-six Third and Fourth Division clubs plus twenty-two rugby league grounds. All other grounds were subject to strict safety checks by local councils. It quickly became clear that the failings at Bradford were shockingly commonplace. Twenty-seven clubs in England plus three in Scotland were forced to start the 1985/86 season with stands or terraces closed or significantly reduced in capacity. Fifteen played most of the season with one whole stand shut.[19] Wolverhampton Wanderers' Molineux had two stands shut. The wooden stand, the flammable roof, the locked gates, the lack of fire extinguishers, the poor evacuation routes were all symbolic of the widespread mismanagement of the game by its authorities. Fans, it seemed, were a troublesome inconvenience.

If there was one saving grace at Valley Parade, it was that there had been no fencing at the front of the paddock preventing people from getting onto the pitch (there was, however, fencing in front of the other stands). It was a fact not lost on Delahunty who tells me, 'If Bradford had been fenced in, you and I may not be talking now.' It was also a point not lost on those who had misgivings about the government's overt linking of safety and security, such as Geoff Lawler, the Conservative MP for Bradford North. 'I think that the view of Bradford supporters is that it is all very well hemming in a minority of hooligans,' he said in the House of Commons two days after the fire, 'but that at the same time a potential death trap might be created for thousands of decent supporters.'[20]

III

Football grounds were rarely built with the comfort of fans in mind; the Main Stand at Valley Parade − the 'best' part of the ground with the most expensive tickets − had no toilet facilities for women. Terraces were constructed the way they were because it was cheap to do so, and they enabled clubs to pack in as many fans as possible. Safety was an afterthought. The first fatality recorded at a British ground was in 1888 at a rugby match, coincidentally at Bradford. More followed at Glasgow Rangers' Ibrox in 1902 when twenty-five people died after a stand collapsed; Burnden Park in Bolton in 1946, when thirty-three people died in a crush; Dunfermline in 1968, when one fan died also in a crush; Ibrox again in 1971, when sixty-six died in yet another crush. There were also many more near misses. In all prior to the Hillsborough tragedy in 1989, thirty-five serious incidents leading to at least 4,000 injuries were recorded at twenty-nine grounds.[21] The overwhelming majority of these occurred in and around terracing. No less than *eight* official reports into crowd safety and behaviour were produced between 1924 and 1985. Lessons were learned slowly, if at all. Throughout the 1960s and into the 1970s, fans' safety was compromised, in particular through the introduction of pens and perimeter fences. The latter were installed to prevent pitch invasions, but actually they resulted in limited emergency access to the pitch. Had there been perimeter fencing at Burnden Park, the death toll would have been much higher.

Sheffield Wednesday's Hillsborough stadium was considered among the best in England. One of four League grounds to host a knock-out match during the 1966 World Cup, it was also a regular FA Cup semi-final venue during the 1980s. Like other grounds, it had seen a series of modifications. In 1977, perimeter fences were erected as an anti-hooligan measure. In 1981, thirty-eight fans were injured in a crush on the terrace at the Leppings Lane End during an FA Cup semi-final between Wolves and Spurs. Fatalities were avoided by opening the gates at the front of the fencing. The club responded by dividing the terrace into three separate 'pens' to restrict sideways movement. In 1984, the terrace was further subdivided into seven pens. The stated capacity of the stadium was never altered to acknowledge the changes and thus its safety certificate was invalidated.

As Liverpool fans headed to the ground for their FA Cup semi-final against Nottingham Forest on 15 April 1989, the sort of death trap Geoff Lawler had warned of in the aftermath of the Bradford fire less than four years earlier awaited them. Liverpool had been allocated the Leppings Lane End and the North Stand, Forest the Kop End and the South Stand. By 2.35 p.m., the central two pens on the Leppings Lane End, Pens 3 and 4, which were directly behind the goal that Liverpool would defend in an abandoned first half, were badly congested. Running along the front of them was a seven-foot-high fence with an overhang at the top; the crush at the front was so tight, some fans tried to escape. The gates between the pens were at the back of the terrace, the six-foot-high spiked fences that had been erected between them to restrict lateral movement made it all but impossible to switch.

Some 10,100 fans had tickets for that end of the ground. There were just seven turnstiles through which they could enter. Outside, congestion had been increasing since 2.15 p.m. that afternoon. Half an hour later, there were still more than 4,000 fans with tickets yet to make their way through the bottleneck and into the ground. Congestion outside was on a par with congestion inside. At 2.47 p.m., Superintendent Roger Marshall, fearful of fatalities, requested that Gate C be opened to alleviate the crush. The match commander was Chief Superintendent David Duckenfield. He had never been responsible for policing a football game before, let alone one of such importance with both sets of fans coming from outside the city. Marshall had to repeat his request twice. The third time, he said that if the gate was not opened, someone would be killed. Finally, at 2.52 p.m., with kick-off eight minutes away, Duckenfield gave the order to open the gate. In five minutes some 2,000 fans poured through. While this relieved the pressure outside the ground, no effort was made to direct those entering away from the already overcrowded central pens, the entrance to which was directly in front of them. When the teams came out at 2.54 p.m., they were greeted by a usual surge as people strained to see them. Four minutes into the game, Peter Beardsley struck the crossbar at the Kop End with a looping volley. There was another surge in Pen 3. At some point, most likely when this near miss occurred, two crush barriers, designed to prevent the crowd from compressing all the way down the terrace, collapsed. The horror of previous stadia tragedies was repeating itself, only this time there was a perimeter fence to magnify the tragedy. For those at the front hemmed in by that fencing, its few, narrow exit gates firmly shut, the pressure became vice-like. Many were crushed breathless, weakened to the point of collapse but held upright by the mass of people around them. Four minutes in that situation would lead to irreversible brain damage, any longer to almost certain death.

In a bid to escape, fans started climbing over the side fences into Pens 2 and 5, and over the fence at the front. Duckenfield was watching the unfolding events from the raised police control box at the side of the terrace barely half the width of the pitch from Pens 3 and 4. Conditioned to see football supporters only through the lens of hooliganism and thus as a law and order problem, he called up reserve officers waiting in the stadium's gymnasium and directed them to quell a pitch invasion. A request was made for dog handlers. With Liverpool fans spilling onto the pitch, the police moved to prevent a response from the Nottingham Forest fans and formed a line across the pitch. Few police in the ground appeared to understand the enormity of what was happening. Most either followed their orders, such as they were, or froze. At one point the gate in the front of Pen 3 sprang open and at least one fan was forced out by the pressure of the crowd behind him. A police officer, conditioned like his superiors to expect trouble, grabbed him, pushed him back into the mass of bodies and shut the gate.[22] Tony Evans had come through Gate C, his ticket unchecked, and made his way to his seat in the North Stand, more or less opposite where Duckenfield was, but slightly closer to the halfway line and slightly further back. It quickly became apparent to him that those scrambling out of the terraces to his right weren't bent on violence. The police reaction was, he feels, an allegory for how the country saw football fans. 'How blinded to your preconceptions of people do you have to be to not see that the crush is killing them when you're yards away?' he asks rhetorically. 'The blinkers were so strong they couldn't see any humanity and they couldn't see people dying in front of their eyes. The most frightening thing was, with very few exceptions, they stood by and watched people die. The one thing I'll never comprehend is the lines of policemen just standing there.'[23]

It was later established that the first fatalities occurred as early as 2.57 p.m., three minutes before kick-off. By the end of the day ninety-four people were dead, the eldest sixty-seven-year-old Gerard Baron, the youngest ten-year-old Jon-Paul Gilhooley and another thirty-six were teenagers. Lee Nicol, aged fourteen, died of his injuries two days later. In 1993, Anthony Bland, who had been in a persistent vegetative state since the disaster, became the ninety-sixth victim when his life-support system was switched off. In 2021 Andrew Devine died from fatal aspiration pneumonia. It was result of the brain injury he suffered at Hillsborough. The death toll had reached ninety-seven.

Forty-two ambulances attended the scene after the police finally called for them at 3.07 p.m. Only three made it into the ground, the rest were held outside by the police, again conditioned to expect trouble. Tony Edwards, who was part of the crew of the first ambulance to reach the terrace, later recalled how they were initially told by a police officer, 'You can't go on the pitch, they're still fighting.'[24] Rescue efforts were chaotic at best. Some survivors were left for dead, with no record of what happened to them until it was realised they were alive and needed emergency treatment. In one case, that was not until 5 p.m. when the person concerned was admitted to intensive care. 'That's really significant,' says Phil Scraton, who was the primary author of the Hillsborough Independent Panel's report and spent months investigating the circumstances of all the victims, 'because it demonstrated there were people who lived significantly longer than the coroner at the first inquests estimated, which was five to ten minutes maximum after they had been crushed. Through our work on the Panel, we concluded that at least forty-one people might have lived had they received immediate and appropriate medical intervention. In other words, a significant number did not die in the pens, but were alive when they were pulled out.'[25]

Only fourteen of those who did die were taken to hospital; the rest were pronounced dead at the ground, placed in body bags and laid out on the floor of the Hillsborough gymnasium awaiting identification. Bereaved families had to wait outside. They were then taken in one by one and asked to look through Polaroid photographs of all the victims' faces – many unrecognisable due to the trauma they had suffered – to see if their loved ones were among them. If they thought they were, the body was brought to the entrance of the gym for formal identification. The nightmare the victim's relatives were enduring then became worse as police officers, directed by the coroner Stefan Popper, began to question them about the drinking habits of their loved ones – all of whom had their blood-alcohol levels taken, even the children – and whether they had criminal records. 'They were treated appallingly,' says Scraton. 'All families who identified loved ones in the immediate aftermath were subjected to what was, in effect, interrogation procedures. Their treatment was accusatory: sceptical, doubting, putting words in their mouths, changing their statements.'

IV

At most disasters the media arrive in the aftermath. At Hillsborough, as with Bradford, they were there from the start, *Grandstand* cutting from the calm of the opening day of the World Snooker Championships at Sheffield's Crucible Theatre to the unfolding horror just four miles across the city. In Merseyside, anguish spread. Many had friends or relatives at the game. People gathered round shop radios and the windows of electrical stores. It soon became clear that once again the nation was watching football fans die in real time. Once again, Liverpool was involved. As at Bradford, there was a rush to blame the fans. Unlike at Bradford, that narrative took root. At 3.13 p.m. on the day of the game John Motson, commentating for *Match of the Day*, was able to tell his producer he had 'a line'.[26] According to his information a gate had been broken and people without tickets had rushed into the ground. It was just twenty-six minutes after Chief Superintendent Duckenfield had given the order to open Gate C and seven minutes after the game had been stopped. With the dead and dying in plain sight, Duckenfield, the man in charge of policing the game and whose decision had led to their deaths, informed Graham Kelly, then chief executive of the FA, that Liverpool fans had forced their way into the ground through an exit gate causing an 'inrush' onto the already packed terraces. At 3.40 p.m., Alan Green, commentating on the game for the BBC's *Sport on Two*, told his listeners there were 'unconfirmed reports that a door was broken down at the end that was holding Liverpool supporters'.[27] At 4.15 p.m. Green firmed up the story with information from Graham Mackrell, the secretary of Sheffield Wednesday, who'd spoken to the officer in charge. 'There was a surge of [. . .] about 500 Liverpool fans and police say a gate was forced and that led to a crush in the terracing area.'[28]

While the journalists at the scene were, albeit unwittingly in the chaos, the first to disseminate the police's lies they also gave a voice to fans and others, who painted a very different picture. Glynn Phillips, a GP based in East Kilbride in Scotland, was interviewed by Green after escaping the terrace and going on the pitch to help. 'Police allowed the fans to fill the middle terracing section to the point they were crammed in like sardines. Conversely the two outside portions of the terracing were left virtually empty,' he said. 'I stood and watched police allowing this to happen. It got to a point where they lost control completely.' Presciently, Phillips added: 'Unfortunately Liverpool fans are probably going to get stuck with this again.'[29] By 4.50 p.m. even Kelly was casting doubt on Duckenfield's story and hinting at police failings. In an interview with Gerald Sinstadt on *Grandstand*, he said there were two versions of events: the first that a gate had been forced, the second that a gate had been opened by police. 'Whatever it was,' Kelly added, 'there was a lack of proper control at that end of the ground.' He continued: 'I've not heard anybody suggest there was aggravation; that there was fighting; that there was trouble of that nature. [. . .] If people were allowed to go in without having their tickets checked, they were allowed in by someone in authority.'[30] Later that night a sombre Des Lynam introduced footage of the tragedy on *Match of the Day*, emphasising that 'there was no violence of any kind'.[31] The report included Liverpool fans dismissing suggestions the overcrowding was their fault by showing their full tickets. Journalist Peter Marshall, who had started the day as a Liverpool fan, ended it reporting on the tragedy on the BBC's *Ten O'Clock News*. He spoke of the lack of policing outside the Leppings Lane End which led to the crush outside, in turn leading to the police opening the gate.[32]

The Sunday papers shifted an extra 500,000 copies between them on the back of coverage of the tragedy and, spurred on by this, the dailies also devoted innumerable pages to the disaster. It's indicative of the confusion created by police allegations that in the same issue the *Independent* could talk of how 'a mob of thousands, many without tickets, thought it was alright to try and push into the ground'; but also run a piece headlined 'Key to fans' deaths lies in policing', which clearly identified the lack of organisation inside and outside the ground.[33] Soon, the narrative began to take a much darker tone. 'What is clear from the evidence is that from the outset, the South Yorkshire Police, the Police

Federation and right-wing politicians purposefully manipulated the media,' says Scraton. 'How can I state this with such certainty? I accessed contemporaneous faxes demonstrating that they released statements through an intermediary. This was a local news agency, Whites in Sheffield, a family firm. They became a conduit for the "official version" then passed on to national news outlets.'

Initially published in the final edition of the *Sheffield Star* on the Tuesday after the tragedy, under the headline 'FANS IN DRUNKEN ATTACKS ON POLICE', this story claimed that 'yobs [. . .] attacked an ambulance man, threatened firemen and punched and urinated on policemen as they gave the kiss of life to stricken victims'.[34] The allegations were repeated on the ITV's evening news bulletin in an interview with Irvine Patnick, then Conservative MP for Sheffield Hallam. The BBC also ran a lengthy piece focused on the allegations of drunkenness. The following day the national press gave full vent to the story. The now-defunct *Today* splashed on it, as did *The Times*, *Daily Telegraph* and the *Daily Express*, which reported on the 'sick spectacle of the pilfering from the dead'.[35] The *Daily Mail* quoted police saying: 'Vile fans fought us as we tried to help dying',[36] while the *Daily Star* claimed: 'DEAD FANS ROBBED BY DRUNK THUGS' with the caveat: 'WHAT COPS SAY ABOUT HILLSBORO'.[37]

The *Sun* went in the hardest. There was no qualification on their front page. As far as they were concerned the story was simply 'THE TRUTH', the headline accompanied by subheads which said: 'Some fans picked pockets of victims. Some fans urinated on the brave cops. Some fans beat up PC giving kiss of life.'[38] The page was designed by editor Kelvin MacKenzie who had initially considered the headline 'YOU SCUM', but the one he chose still caused huge outrage on Merseyside. 'That was the screw being turned within days of the disaster,' says Scraton. 'What had been straightforward reporting of the tragedy at the weekend, transformed into a narrative that fans had arrived late, many without tickets, were drunk and aggressive and attempted to force entry. That they, through their reckless and violent behaviour, were responsible for the deaths. It was a false narrative purposefully constructed to deflect responsibility from the stadium owners, the Football Association, the local authority responsible for stadium inspection and, most significantly, the South Yorkshire Police.'

People across Merseyside reacted by ripping up or burning copies of the *Sun*. Pubs banned it and sales fell through the floor with some newsagents slashing orders of the paper by as much as 80 per cent. To this day, it has never recovered its circulation on Merseyside. Over the years that infamous front page has been repeatedly held up not just as an example of the worst excesses of the Hillsborough coverage but also of tabloid journalism more generally. However, the reality is that the rest of the media coverage was little better and had been building to that point over previous three days, something that is rarely acknowledged.

The police allegations gained currency not only because they played on the negative perceptions of football fans at the time but also because of those of Liverpool and Liverpudlians. 'Liverpool fans were vilified,' says Scraton, 'and this plumbed into a broader context of condemnation directed towards the city itself and its people. It was a decade into Thatcherism. The attack − the constant attack − on Liverpool as a city was the outcome of how the uprising of the black community in 1981, and again in 1985, had been portrayed as "lawless riots" and "wanton destruction". This negative portrayal was compounded by issues around "militant" trades unionism in the city during that period. The punitive vote-winning agenda directed by Margaret Thatcher and her cabinet

was to attack trades unionism, welfarism and social housing and
the prime target in her sights was Liverpool and its strong socialist
tradition.'

Merseyside had been hit harder than most by recession. As
Britain turned increasingly to Europe for trade, Liverpool's docks,
anchored on the wrong side of the country, fell into decline. In
two decades prior to 1985, the city lost 65,000 jobs, mainly in the
docks and manufacturing. Tensions boiled over in riots in Toxteth
in 1981 and 1985, a year in which unemployment in Liverpool
was four times the national average. Merseyside became symbolic
of the urban and industrial decline afflicting the North. It also
became symbolic of the battles between the government and
Labour-run councils, and also the leadership of the Labour Party
and its left wing. Speaking to the 1922 Committee in July 1984,
the prime minister drew parallels between striking miners and the
Falklands conflict. The 'enemy without' beaten, her attention was
now focused on the 'enemy within'. Although no recording or
transcript of the speech survives, the handwritten notes Thatcher
used show a list that included 'Liverpool and some local
authorities'.[39]

Her ire was sparked by the determination of several Labour-
run councils to fund their budget deficits by increasing rates, as
opposed to cutting services. In response, the government introduced legislation to set a legal rate 'cap'. The eighteen councils,
which included the Greater London Council, Islington, Lambeth
and Sheffield, agreed a common tactic – to set no rate at all.
Soon, Derek Hatton, the deputy leader of Liverpool's Labour
council and a member of the Trotskyite Militant group, became
the councils' *de facto* figurehead and main media hate figure. It was
a loose grouping and one by one they caved in, setting rates within
the legal limit. In Liverpool, the council set a rate much lower
than they were allowed, a new tactic designed to ensure

bankruptcy and provoke a confrontation with the government. The long-term strategic benefit of this was unclear but it led to redundancy notices being sent out to all the council's 31,000 employees. This was a step too far for the party's national leader, Neil Kinnock, who issued an excoriating denunciation of Militant at the party conference in 1985. Within a year, a series of expulsions from Labour ended the dominance of Militant in Liverpool. It also effectively cemented the dominance of the centre-right within the party, at least for the next thirty years.

The episode reinforced negative perceptions of the city, which were bolstered by its representation in popular culture. Alan Bleasdale's 1980 television play, *Boys from the Blackstuff*, which focused on a gang of labourers from Liverpool working in Middlesbrough, offered a bleak portrayal of life in the North. The most arresting character was Yosser Hughes, played by Bernard Hill, who with his plaintive, and much-repeated, request 'Gizza job' seemed to speak for many in the country. The sitcom *Bread*, created by Carla Lane and first broadcast in 1986, was more light-hearted but its depiction of a Liverpudlian family who took pride in exploiting the benefits system perpetuated the image of a city full of scroungers. Following Hillsborough, the twin themes of a declining city riven with unemployment but also work-shy fecklessness, were coupled with wider antipathy towards football fans and all tied together by the 'Heysel factor', an easy truncheon to beat Liverpool fans with. The weekend after the tragedy a Gallup poll for the *Sunday Telegraph* found that already 25 per cent of people blamed the fans, with 22 per cent blaming police and 27 per cent saying they didn't know who was responsible.[40]

In his final report into the tragedy, published in 1990, Lord Justice Taylor paved the way for all-seater stadia, a fundamental change in the football-fan experience. He realised that: '[. . .] clubs may well wish to charge somewhat more for seats than for standing', but argued that 'it should be possible to plan a price structure which suits the cheapest seats to the pockets of those presently paying to stand'.[41] His advice was not heeded: ticket prices increased exponentially, working-class fans were priced out and the game was gentrified.

Five months earlier, in August 1989, Taylor delivered his interim findings. They were unequivocal. Taylor found no evidence to support the claims made to Whites and printed in the national media, writing that 'those who made them, and those who disseminated them, would have done better to hold their peace'.[42] The fundamental cause of the tragedy, Taylor determined, was a failure to stop fans entering the central pens once Gate C had been opened. This 'blunder of the first magnitude'[43] was compounded when Duckenfield failed to take any control once the disaster began. Taylor emphatically dismissed police allegations that an unexpectedly large number of Liverpool fans turned up with no, or forged, tickets in a deliberate attempt to force entry. He emphatically dismissed police allegations that alcohol was to blame, pointing out that the majority of fans weren't drunk and the few that were played no part in the tragedy. Taylor emphatically dismissed further police allegations that fans were uncooperative. 'How could they be?' he asked rhetorically, adding: 'In that crush most people had no control over their movements at all.'[44] Even on the issue of fans supposedly turning up late, Taylor pointed out that they were only required to be inside the ground fifteen minutes before kick-off and so it was to be expected that many would turn up, as they did, between 2.30 and 2.40 p.m. In short, every single allegation levelled against Liverpool fans by the police was rejected by Taylor less than four months after the disaster. The truth – the *real* truth – was obvious from the start, but not until the publication of the Hillsborough Independent Panel report in 2012, following years of campaigning by the families of the victims and survivors, would that truth be widely acknowledged. The report led to the accidental death verdicts recorded by Popper at the original inquests in 1991 being quashed by the High Court and new two-year-long inquests recording verdicts of unlawful killing in 2016. Three years later, Duckenfield was acquitted of ninety-five charges of manslaughter.

While the crudest version of the 'drink and violence' narrative blaming the fans was articulated by the tabloids, it wasn't limited to journalists and filtered out beyond the press. Brian Clough, Nottingham Forest's manager on the day, blamed Liverpool fans who he claimed – wrongly – had been disorderly and turned up late without tickets. 'Many mistakes were made at Hillsborough,' he wrote in his 1994 biography, 'but I will always remain convinced that those Liverpool fans who died were killed by Liverpool people.'[45] It did not go unnoticed that the book was ghost-written by a *Sun* journalist, John Sadler. The same year, in the revised second edition of his well-regarded history of football *The People's Game*, academic James Walvin wrote: 'Both at Hillsborough and Heysel [. . .] crowd disturbances had bedeviled the game. Football had become synonymous with hooliganism.'[46] It was an astonishing misrepresentation of the events in Sheffield coming as it did five years after Taylor's Interim Report had unequivocally demonstrated that the fans' behaviour, let alone hooliganism, had played no part at all in the tragedy. Walvin wasn't alone; many other academics either directly or indirectly linked Hillsborough to hooliganism, thus building on and further legitimising the police's false claims. In *Fever Pitch*, the book that played a vital role in laundering football's reputation at the start of the 1990s, thus making it acceptable for a mass middle-class audience, Nick Hornby wrote of Hillsborough that 'though it's clear that the police messed up badly that afternoon, it would be terribly vengeful to accuse them of anything more than incompetence'.[47] It is a simplistic view at best. In 2012, the Independent Hillsborough Inquiry showed that, far from just having 'messed up badly', members of the South Yorkshire Police force had also been guilty of a decades-long cover-up designed to hide their own culpability. Irrespective of what Hornby might think, there was nothing at all 'vengeful' about the accusations that the police had done so. They were demonstrably true.

V

Yet is it any wonder that this was the discourse that developed around Hillsborough? The alternative begged some serious questions about the state of the country's infrastructure at the time. Between 1966, when 144 people died − 116 of whom were schoolchildren − following the collapse of a colliery spoil tip at Aberfan in Wales and 1999, when thirty-one people were killed in the Ladbroke Grove Rail crash in London, there were fifteen disasters in the UK with a death toll higher than thirty. Of those, nine took place in little more than four years between May 1985 and August 1989. The Bradford disaster was the first, Hillsborough the eighth.

Just three months after fire ripped through Valley Parade, a British Airways jet taxiing on the runway of Manchester Airport burst into flames after an engine failure led to a ruptured fuel tank. It was filled with holidaymakers heading for Corfu. The similarities with Bradford were stark: the speed of the fire, inadequate exits due to densely packed seating and toxic fumes from combustible materials within the cabins contributed to the deaths of fifty-five of the 131 passengers and crew on board. In November 1987, a fire at King's Cross underground station claimed the lives of thirty-one people. Again, there were stark reminders of Bradford: a lit match dropped on a wooden escalator ignited grease and litter accumulated beneath it. This smouldered for some time before igniting into a devastating fireball. It wasn't the worst tragedy of the year. In March, the *Herald of Free Enterprise*, a roll-on-roll-off ferry owned by Townsend Thoresen, capsized just twenty-three minutes after leaving the Belgian port of Zeebrugge heading for Dover. The crew had set sail with a bow door still open, allowing water to flood in and destabilise the vessel. The death toll was 193; many of whom had taken advantage of an offer in the *Sun* for a day return fare of just £1.

The following year, 167 lives were lost following an explosion on the Piper Alpha oil rig in the North Sea 120 miles north-east of Aberdeen. Thirty-five people were also killed when signal failure led to the collision of three trains at Clapham Junction. While Hillsborough is perhaps the most infamous disaster to occur in 1989, it was neither the first nor the last. In January, engine failure led to a passenger plane on route from Heathrow to Belfast crash-landing on the embankment of the M1 motorway near the village of Kegworth in Leicestershire; forty-seven died. The final entry on the grim list was made in August when the pleasure steamer *Marchioness* and the dredger *Bowbelle* collided on the River Thames near Cannon Street railway bridge. Within thirty seconds the *Marchioness* had sunk, claiming the lives of fifty-one of the 131 people on board for a birthday party.

The sense of horror these tragedies prompted was only heightened by a series of others. In August 1987, Michael Ryan went on a shooting spree in the Wiltshire market town of Hungerford, killing sixteen and wounding fifteen others before turning the gun on himself. No motive has ever been established but Ryan's murderous rampage led to the tightening of gun controls. Two months later, eighteen people died when Britain was battered by the worst storms since 1703. Four days before Christmas 1988, PanAm Flight 103 was destroyed by a terrorist bomb twenty-seven minutes after departure from Heathrow, killing all 259 people on board. A significant amount of the debris landed on the Scottish town of Lockerbie, killing another eleven people.

This litany of tragedy, compressed as it was into such a relatively short period of time, had a profound impact on the national psyche, leading the Mass Observation Project to ask respondents to consider 'the succession of public disasters over the last few years' which 'cannot be ignored in the history of the 1980s'.[48] Even Margaret Thatcher later noted the 'appalling disasters that seemed to plague us at this time'.[49] Like many, she appeared to see them as a series of isolated, unconnected events. Not everyone agreed. In the aftermath of Hillsborough, Edward Greenspon, the European business correspondent of Toronto's *Globe and Mail* newspaper, pointed to common themes identified at the inquiries into other recent tragedies. There was, he wrote, a 'rampant disregard for safety in private and public services; poor communications once disasters occur; inadequately trained and overworked staff and, especially, dilapidated public services'.[50] James Tye, the director-general of the British Safety Council, echoed these comments following the *Marchioness* disaster four months later. 'It is no use putting these accidents down to acts of God. Why does God always pick on badly managed places with sloppy practices? He does not seem to pick on well managed places.'[51]

These comments were indicative of a shift in post-disaster discourse which increasingly reflected wider political debates. The contradiction between the government's commitment to the free market and deregulation and its traditional responsibility to ensure public safety when private organisations failed to do so was increasingly called into question. In 1989, the fourth consecutive year in which there was at least one fatal crash on Britain's rail network, opposition MPs suggested that a lack of government investment directly correlated with the rise in accident numbers and fatalities. Following the Belgrove rail accident in March 1989, which led to two deaths, Labour MP Michael Martin, within whose Glasgow Springburn constituency the incident occurred, accused the government of trying 'to get safety on the cheap on the railways'.[52] This view was supported by Desmond Fennell's inquiry into the King's Cross fire which found that 'whereas financial matters, namely productivity and budgeting, were strictly monitored safety was not [. . .]'.[53]

While the injustices of tragedies in previous decades quickly slipped from public view, in the 1980s such was their frequency and severity that there was a greater clamour to understand *why* they were happening, and *who* was responsible. Relatives of victims, and survivors, set up pressure groups, their campaigns to unearth the truth and pursue justice ensuring that the issues stayed in the spotlight for years, sometimes decades. Many of these, including survivors of the Hillsborough tragedy and relatives of the victims, came together in an umbrella organisation, Disaster Action, founded in 1991, whose work contributed to the Corporate Manslaughter and Corporate Homicide Act being enacted seventeen years later. The reality was that Hillsborough, like Bradford, was never a football issue. Nor was it a Liverpool issue. Hillsborough was a public safety issue.

EPILOGUE

World in Motion

I

WHEN Sheffield Wednesday striker David Hirst woke up on New Year's Day 1990, it is unlikely he will have guessed how the first day of the new decade would pan out for him. The Owls were hosting Manchester City in the First Division and Hirst opened the scoring with an easy header after twelve minutes. So far, so normal. However, with half an hour left, Wednesday keeper Kevin Pressman was carried off with damaged cruciate knee ligaments. Hirst went in goal and saved from both Steve Redmond and Colin Hendry as the hosts won 2−0. It was a commendable performance, but only those in the ground witnessed it: there were no cameras present. The game was the last in the English top flight not to be filmed.

The country's relationship with sport was changing, or at least how we consumed it. Two years later, twenty-two teams quit the Football League to join the Premier League, a significant motivation being the desire to tap into the riches offered by Rupert Murdoch's Sky Sports. Regular live League football, a relatively new phenomenon that people were still getting used to, was suddenly gone from free-to-air television, available only to those with a satellite dish and a sports subscription. At the time, people in Britain did not pay for TV beyond the mandatory licence fee, but Murdoch used football as a lead offering, or 'battering ram', to break into the market, agreeing a five-year rights deal worth £191 million. Football, which just fifteen years earlier received virtually no coverage from TV companies that preferred to train their cameras on cricket, darts and snooker, was now unassailably number one. It was, as Sky Sports' marketing suggested, 'a whole new ball game'.

Other factors also played a part in laundering the sport's reputation. In 1990, England, along with Scotland and the Republic of Ireland, headed to Italy for the World Cup. It was just five years since Italian fans had died at Heysel, and a decade after England and Italy fans fought during the European Championships in Belgium. Many feared the worst. Sports minister Colin Moynihan had tried to get England to withdraw. When they did not, the team was effectively banished to Sardinia to play its group games, the team's fans all but imprisoned. Yet, despite a few minor skirmishes, their behaviour was widely praised, the fans having been marshalled by the Football Supporters' Association which for the first time created fan embassies.

On the pitch, England unexpectedly reached the semi-finals, providing a surprisingly positive story, albeit one that was a slow burn. Their tournament began with an uninspiring 1−1 draw against the Republic of Ireland. A creditable 0−0 against the Netherlands − the European Champions − followed, giving a hint of what would follow, and then a 1−0 win against Egypt in the final group game was enough for Bobby Robson's team to top their group and qualify for the knockout stages. David Platt's last-gasp, balletic pirouetting volley secured an extra-time win against Belgium in the round of sixteen. A brace of penalties from Gary Lineker in the quarter-finals against Cameroon set up the last-four clash with West Germany.

'People who sneered at the game, accustomed to seeing only ugliness, found themselves unexpectedly swept along,'[1] wrote the journalist Amy Lawrence years later. And swept along they were. Approximately 26.2 million people tuned in to watch the semi-final. Some 70,000 were packed into Wembley for a Rolling Stones concert; many had brought pocket radios, some even portable TVs, so they could keep track of the game. Mick Jagger even apologised for the scheduling clash. As news of Andreas Brehme's fifty-ninth-minute opener for West Germany filtered through to the audience, there was a collective groan. When Lineker equalised in the eighty-first minute, there was − mid-song − a huge cheer. The game went to extra time and on into a penalty shootout ... The most memorable moment came when Paul Gascoigne, England's breakout star, received a yellow card that would have ruled him out of the final. His bottom lip began to wobble, his eyes welled up. Almost unnoticed by those in the stadium, his show of emotion was beamed to the millions watching at home. It gave people a different version of masculinity to identify with, humanising footballers and football for many non-fans.

Days after the World Cup final, UEFA agreed to re-admit English clubs into European competition (except for Liverpool, who would have to wait another season). Yet, despite the received wisdom, Gascoigne's tears did not change the game, nor did the tournament in which they were shed; they were, however, a useful visual metaphor for changes that had begun in the 1980s. The anti-hooligan measures introduced following the Luton−Millwall riot in 1985 − CCTV and stronger police powers inside stadia, more all-ticket matches and a ban on taking alcohol into grounds − all changed the nature of going to watch a match, something magnified by the post-Hillsborough recommendation in the Taylor Report that football stadia should become all-seater. New grounds were built; others were significantly improved. Terraces were eradicated, literally changing the way people watched the game. Football had been sanitised and repackaged for a television audience.

As if to acknowledge this, in 1992 UEFA selected England to host the 1996 European Championships. Symbolically, football would be coming home. The tournament was sound-tracked by Britpop and the anthemic 'Three Lions', sung by David Baddiel, Frank Skinner and The Lightning Seeds. When the tournament kicked off with a 1−1 draw between England and Switzerland at Wembley, football was almost unrecognisable from the sport that had been fatally riddled with hooliganism just eleven years earlier.

Yet the game was still prone to violent impulses. England's defeat to Germany, in the semi-final, again on penalties, was marked by a wave of violence across Britain. In Brighton, a seventeen-year-old Russian was stabbed five times by a gang who thought he was German. In London's Trafalgar Square, police in riot gear fought an estimated 2,000 drunken hooligans. Cars were overturned and set alight and shop windows smashed. More than 200 people were arrested and sixty-six injured. Significantly, the authorities were quick to dissociate the sport from the violence. 'I don't think by any stretch of the imagination you could call the people who took part in those disturbances genuine football fans,' said Commander John Purnell, the man in charge of policing the tournament in London. 'Genuine football supporters were the people you saw at Wembley. What we saw in Trafalgar Square were yobs − hooligans bent on destruction and causing trouble.'[2]

These sentiments were indicative of the fact that football was no longer a pariah sport seen by politicians as a law-and-order problem; instead, it was to be embraced. In October 1995, the prime minister, John Major (a Chelsea fan) took a tour of New-castle's revamped St James Park. A few weeks later, Tony Blair, the young New Labour leader, played head tennis with the Magpies' manager Kevin Keegan in front of the assembled media at the party's conference. At the same event a year later, and just four months after Euro '96 had ended, Blair, by then widely seen as the prime-minster-in-waiting, reworked the lyrics of Baddiel and Skinner's tournament anthem, telling the assembled delegates (and those watching on television), 'Labour's come home to you, so come home to us. Labour's coming home. Seventeen years of hurt never stopped us dreaming, Labour's coming home.'[3]

II

A week after their exit from Euro '96, the England squad reconvened at Hanbury Manor Hotel in Hertfordshire for Gascoigne's wedding to Sheryl Failes. Her pale pink tulle wedding dress with hand-beaded French lace and salmon-coloured netting had been designed by Isabell Kristensen. Gazza, who arrived sipping champagne, in a white Cadillac stretch limousine, wore a gold brocade frock coat by top Piccadilly outfitters Favourbrook. Security was tight, not least because *Hello!* magazine had paid £150,000 for the rights to photographs of the nuptials. The issue sold a then record 645,000 copies.

Gascoigne came to prominence as Ian Botham's star was waning. Beefy would have one last hurrah at the World Cup in early 1992, helping England reach the final where they lost to Pakistan, before his international career petered out over the course of the following summer. Had Gascoigne played a decade earlier, his exploits, like those of Frank McAvennie, would in all likelihood have been heard of, but not seen, overshadowed by those of the stars of more widely televised sports, such as Botham, Alex Higgins and Bobby George. A decade later, and Gascoigne would have quite possibly become a global celebrity, his image more carefully managed, his misdemeanours better hidden. As it was, he came to prominence at the dawn of the 'post-modern' football world of blanket coverage in the press, twenty-four-hour news channels (and latterly social media), but he did not moderate his behaviour to account for this. In the build-up to the 1998 World Cup in France, he was photographed enjoying a kebab at the end of a night out in Soho with TV stars Danny Baker and Chris Evans. It led to him being dumped from the England squad by then manager Glenn Hoddle. Gascoigne never played for England again.

His celebrity star was already being eclipsed, a young David Beckham having announced himself to the football world with a goal scored from the halfway line against Wimbledon on the first day of the 1996/97 Premier League season. Nine months later, he had helped Manchester United secure the League title and earned his first England call-up. By then he was also in a relationship with Victoria 'Posh Spice' Adams of the Spice Girls. When the pair married in 1999, *OK!* magazine paid £1 million for the photo rights. It was a significant increase from what the Gascoignes had earned. Beckham was able to leverage his on-field talent to accumulate off-field wealth. Employing a strategy similar to that which Barry Hearn had used with his Matchroom stable of snooker stars, Beckham licensed his name and image to become a brand. It set a template. Every high-profile elite athlete is now, in some way, a brand. So are sports. So are leagues.

And yet . . .

When you start to consider what sport – that mirror of wider society – reflects back at us, what it tells us about our culture, attitudes and politics, well, there change is less obvious.

Russia became a sporting outcast following its invasion of Ukraine in early 2022, outrage at this military action being

articulated through a series of sporting bans. The Russian Paralympic team was sent home on the eve of the event while governing
bodies in most sports have banned Russian teams. Just like in the
1980s, there are anomalies. In tennis, the WTA and ITP cancelled events in Russia but will allow Russian players to continue
to compete. However, Wimbledon did not, meaning Daniil Med-
vedev, the world number one, was absent from the 2022 men's
tournament. Somewhat ironically, the women's tournament was
won by Russian-born Elena Rybakina, who had become a Kazak
citizen in 2018.

In 2021, Saudi Arabia's sovereign wealth fund became
majority owners of Newcastle United and in 2022 they bank-
rolled the breakaway LIV Golf tour. Jeddah is now a stop on
the annual Formula One calendar. Amnesty International has
labelled this as sportswashing, an attempt to use sport to laun-
der the country's reputation given its woeful human rights
record. It has echoes of the discourse around South Africa in
the 1980s and begs questions about whether athletes should be
free to play wherever they want against whomsoever they want
and what, if any, responsibilities they have to speak out about
such issues.

Domestic politics has also found a voice in the sporting arena.
At the 2016 European Football Championships, which coincided
with the culmination of the torrid Brexit referendum campaign,
England fans were heard singing 'Fuck off, Europe – we're all
voting out'.[4] It was, just as at the World Cup in 1982 some thirty-
four years earlier, a crude articulation of the xenophobic anti-EU
narratives articulated by the tabloid press in the run-up to the
vote. The result, in which 52 per cent voted to leave, highlighted
the divisions in society, divisions that bled out into other issues.
When, following the murder of George Floyd, a black man, at the
hands of white police officers in the USA, England players began

to take a knee in support of the Black Lives Matter movement, some fans responded by booing.

This should not have come as a surprise. Prior to the Coronavirus pandemic, during which fans were excluded from stadia, the number of racial abuse cases within the game was increasing, prompting Troy Townsend, the head of player engagement for the anti-racism charity Kick It Out, to say: 'Hate is still alive and well within football.'[5] Just one example of this came in 2018 when Cyrus Christie scored an own goal for the Republic of Ireland and a 'fan' (the word is used in the loosest possible sense) set up a Twitter poll asking whether he should be lynched. Another social media post Christie received had a picture of four black men hanging from a tree with the words 'you're next'.[6] It had been thirty-three years since his uncle, Errol, had fought Mark Kaylor, and it was a chilling echo of Errol's description of the baying crowd that greeted him on his ring walk − overwhelmingly supporting Kaylor, overwhelmingly white − as 'a lynch mob'.[7]

Cricket's reckoning with racism also began in 2018 when Azeem Rafiq, who captained England at Under-19 level, alleged that he had been subjected to repeated racist abuse during his two spells with Yorkshire. The club was slow to respond, only launching an independent inquiry in 2020, which upheld seven of Rafiq's forty-three allegations, including that he had repeatedly been called 'Paki'. Although Yorkshire apologised, the club also concluded that the incidents in question were 'friendly banter' and that it was 'not reasonable for Azeem to have been offended'.[8] Unsurprisingly, this shocking response provoked widespread criticism. Within a matter of months, the club's chair and entire coaching staff had left. Tom Harrison, the chief executive of the England and Wales Cricket Board, described the scandal as 'an earthquake'.[9] The aftershocks were felt throughout the game. Numerous allegations were made by players of other clubs. In

2022, the entire Cricket Scotland board resigned prior to the publication of a devastating report that detailed 448 examples of institutional racism and concluded that the organisation failed in twenty-nine of thirty-one indicators of good practice, fully satisfying none.[10]

In the same year, Great Britain's Lewis Gibson was one of nine openly gay ice skaters at the Beijing Winter Olympics, of whom eight were men and one, Timothy LeDuc, was non-binary. Also in 2022, Jake Daniels, a seventeen-year-old Blackpool player, became the first openly gay male professional footballer since Justin Fashanu. It was a seminal moment which passed with no controversy, an indication that attitudes have changed at least to some degree. Fashanu had been inducted into the National Football Museum Hall of Fame in 2020. At the same time, the museum launched an exhibition exploring the hidden history of LGBT+ involvement in the game. *And yet*, openly gay male athletes are still the exception, not the norm. In 2021, former England player Rio Ferdinand told a parliamentary select committee that he had encouraged a current footballer to come out, but the player had been advised not to by their lawyer. Also in 2021, the Olympic gold-medal-winning diver Tom Daley revealed that his management team had advised him not to come out in 2013.

III

On an August afternoon in 2022, football finally came home when England's women's team beat Germany 2−1 in the final of the European Championships. Excitement and interest had been building throughout the tournament. The 1984 final between England and Sweden was celebrated along with the other achievements of previous generations of Lionesses, reminding people that, actually, women hadn't just started playing the sport. Carol Thomas received (long overdue) recognition with a British Empire Medal. Some 17.4 million people tuned into the match, making it the most watched TV broadcast of the year and a record for a women's game. The image of Chloe Kelly in a sports bra twirling her shirt above her head, after she had scored the winning goal in the final, became the tournament's iconic image. It was reminiscent of Tracy Edwards and the crew of *Maiden* as they sailed into Fort Lauderdale in their swimsuits: a non-sexualised, unselfconscious celebration of sporting achievement.

And yet, in the immediate aftermath of the victory, a report commissioned by the English Football Association showed that just 63 per cent of schools provided equal access to football coaching for both boys and girls, with the number falling to just 44 per cent in secondary schools. The notion that girls don't — or can't, or shouldn't — play football remains stubbornly entrenched, nowhere more so than in the national curriculum which does not require schools to provide access to football for girls, just 'comparable activities', such as netball, rounders, tennis and badminton.[11]

Off the pitch, there are more, and more high-profile, women sports journalists than when Sally Jones became the BBC's first female sports reporter. The coverage of the first Premier League football match broadcast by Amazon in 2019 was presented by a woman, Eilidh Barbour. *And yet*, it remains the case that there are still relatively few female sportswriters in the UK. Worldwide, sports journalism is still a male-dominated profession. Female sports journalists are paid less than their male counterparts, they are still subject to sexist behaviour. In 2022, Barbour was one of several female journalists who walked out of the Scottish Football Writers' Association annual dinner in response to a string of sexist and misogynistic jokes from one of the speakers. She later said she had 'never felt so unwelcome in the industry I work in'.[12]

The final of the women's Euros was watched by a sell-out crowd at Wembley. Demolished in 2002 and reconstructed at a cost of £798 million, the new Wembley which re-opened in 2007 was light years away from the decrepit stadium that hosted England internationals, FA Cup finals and Live Aid in the 1980s. It was a reminder of the huge changes in stadia safety and the match-day experience. *And yet*, we're still living in the long shadow of Hillsborough. No one who watched as French police teargassed innocent Liverpool fans prior to the 2022 Champions League final should be in any doubt of that. The brutality to which the fans were subjected was compounded when UEFA and the French authorities blamed Liverpool fans for causing the problems, accusing them of turning up en masse late and without tickets. The narrative did not stick for long. Unlike Hillsborough, the events unfolded live on Twitter as fans and journalists alike photographed and filmed what was going on. This did not prevent supporters of other clubs being quick to use it as an excuse to dust off the tropes about Liverpool fans' supposed self-pitying victim complex.

There were also echoes of Hillsborough in 2017 when seventy-two people lost their lives when a fire ripped through Grenfell Tower, a twenty-four-storey block of flats in North Kensington, west London. In the immediate aftermath, the similarities between the two tragedies were stark. Just as the victims of Hillsborough were a marginalised section of society – football fans, who only a few years earlier had been dismissed by the *Sunday Times* as 'slum people', forced to watch the game they loved in unsafe stadia – so the victims of Grenfell were also marginalised. They were social housing tenants; they were immigrants and asylum-seekers. Forty-one per cent of the victims were disabled; 85 per cent were from black or minority ethnic backgrounds.[13] The demonisation of those on benefits as 'shirkers' and 'work-shy', the tone of the

Brexit debate, the racist, dog-whistle reactions to desperate immigrants crossing the English Channel in search of a better life all
suggest that there are more people in Britain than might care to
admit that they thought Grenfell residents were 'slum people',
and that it didn't really matter if they were forced to live in an
unsafe tower block.

In October 2019, Sir Martin Moore-Bick, the chair of the
Grenfell Tower Inquiry, released his Phase 1 Report. Again, the
similarities with Hillsborough were stark. The shortcomings were,
he wrote, 'systemic' with 'both personnel and systems [. . .] overwhelmed by the scale of the disaster'.[14] Those initially in charge
were not properly prepared and failed to grasp the enormity of
the tragedy that was unfolding. Moore-Bick also concluded that
the refurbishment of the tower that took place between 2014 and
2016, and which saw it covered in cladding that accelerated the
spread of the fire, breached building regulations.[15] It was a grim
reflection of the modifications at Hillsborough which rendered
the ground's safety certificate invalid.

There is a lot we can learn if we look at sport closely enough.
There is a lot we can learn if we look at the 1980s closely enough.
It's vital that we don't turn away just because we don't like what
we see.

BIBLIOGRAPHY

80sCasuals, Wade Smith – The Beginning. Available at: https://www.80scasuals.co.uk/blog/2016/1/8/wade-smith-the-beginning (2016)

Anderson, V., *First Among Equals: The Autobiography* (Fullback Media, 2010)

Ardiles, O., *Ossie: My Life in Football* (Sidgwick & Jackson, 1983)

Arlott, J., 'J. M. Brearley – Success Through Perceptiveness', in J. Woodcock (ed.) *Wisden Cricketers' Almanack* (1983)

Baistow, T., *Fourth-rate Estate: Anatomy of Fleet Street* (Law Book Co. of Australasia, 1985)

Baker, N., *Forbidden Forward: The Justin Fashanu Story* (Reid Publishing, 2013)

Baker, S., *Picturing the Beast: Animals, Identity, and Representation* (University of Illinois Press, 2001)

Ball Handlers (2021): David 'Syd' Lawrence | West Indies Concussion, Racial Abuse & Becoming a Bodybuilder [podcast]. Available at: https://www.buzzsprout.com/1061851/4496516

Barker, P., 'The Hidden Legacies of Moscow '80: Changes in Ceremonial and Attitudes', in *Journal of Olympic History*, Vol. 18, No. 2, pp. 32–7 (2010)

Barnes, J., *John Barnes: The Autobiography* (Headline Publishing, 2000)

Bateman, D. and Douglas, D., *Unfriendly Games, Boycotted and Broke: The Inside Story of the 1986 Commonwealth Games* (Mainstream Publishing, 1986)

BBC (date unknown): *EastEnders* First Episode. Available at: https://www.bbc.com/historyofthebbc/anniversaries/february/eastenders-first-episode [accessed 1 May 2021]

BBC (2001): Echoes of Who Shot JR, http://news.bbc.co.uk/1/hi/entertainment/1261931.stm

BBC (2004): The BBC Guide to Comedy: Bread http://www.bbc.co.uk/comedy/guide/articles/b/bread_1299000416.shtml

BBC (2005): Pot Black Returns. Available at: http://news.bbc.co.uk/sport1/hi/other_sports/snooker/4382776.stm

BBC Sport (date unknown): Football Focus: How women's football has risen since 50-year ban. Available at: https://www.bbc.co.uk/sport/av/football/58446519 [Accessed 13 October 2021]

Beattie, J. (2014), 2 Days in 1. Available at: https://www.bbc.co.uk/radioscotland/dayslikethis/stories/2_days_in_1.shtml [Accessed 14 October 2021]

Berry, D., *A People's History of Tennis* (Pluto Press, 2020)

Bevins, A. (1996), 'Nelson Mandela: From terrorist; to tea with the Queen', in the *Independent*. Available at: https://www.independent.co.uk/news/world/from-terrorist-to-tea-with-the-queen-1327902.html [Accessed 11 November 2021]

Bingham, A. and Conboy, M., *Tabloid Century: The Popular Press in Britain, 1896 to the Present* (Peter Lang, 2015)

Bolton, P., *Education: Historical statistics, House of Commons Library Standard Note* SN/SG/4252, 27 November 2012

Bonner, P. and Aston, L., *Independent Television in Britain*, Vol. 6: *New Developments in Independent Television 1981–92: Channel 4, TV-am, Cable and Satellite* (Palgrave, 2003)

Booth, D., 'Hitting Apartheid for Six? The Politics of the South African Sports Boycott', in *Journal of Contemporary History*, Vol. 38, No. 3, pp. 477–93 (2003)

Botham, I., *Botham's Century: My 100 Great Cricketing Characters* (HarperCollins, 2002)

Botham, I., *Head On: Botham the Autobiography* (Ebury Press, 2008)

Boycott, G., *Boycott: The Autobiography* (MacMillan, 1987)

Bristow, E., *The Crafty Cockney: Eric Bristow, The Autobiography* (Arrow Books, 2010)

Brown, M., *A Licence to be Different: The Story of Channel 4* (British Film Institute, 2007)

Brown, R. (2012), Double Olympic gold medallist Daley Thompson on resurrecting his legendary Decathlon game. Available at: https://www.pocketgamer.com/articles/045990/double-olympic-gold-medallist-daley-thompson-on-resurrecting-his-legendary-decathlon-game/ [Accessed 6 May 2021]

Bruno, F., *Eye of the Tiger* (Orion, 1992)

Bruno, F., *From Hero to Zero* (André Deutsch, 1996)

Bryant, J., *Chris Brasher: The Man Who Made the London Marathon* (Aurum Press, 2012)

Budd, Z., *Zola: Autobiography of Zola Budd* (Partridge Press, 1989)

Bunce, S., *Bunce's Big Fat Short History of British Boxing* (Bantam Press, 2017)

Burn, G., *Pocket Money: Britain's Boom-time Snooker* (Faber & Faber, 2020)

Burns, J. *Maradona: The Hand of God* (Bloomsbury, 2021)

Butcher, P., *The Perfect Distance: Ovett & Coe: The Record-Breaking Rivalry* (Phoenix Sport, 2005)

Byrne, P., *Football Association of Ireland: 75 Years* (Sportsworld, 1996)

Campaign (2005) Superbrands case studies: Lucozade. https://www.campaignlive.co.uk/article/superbrands-case-studies-lucozade/232378

Canoville, P., *Black and Blue: How Racism, Drugs and Cancer Almost Destroyed Me* (Headline, 2008)

Carpenter, H., *Where's Harry? My Story* (Pelham Books, 1992)

Carrington, B., *Race, Sport and Politics: The Sporting Black Diaspora* (Sage, 2010)

Carter, J. (1980), Speech on Afghanistan. Available at: https://millercenter.org/the-presidency/presidential-speeches/january-4-1980-speech-afghanistan [Accessed 16 November 2021]

Cashmore, E., *Black Sportsmen* (Routledge and Kegan Paul, 1982)

Central Council of Physical Recreation, *Committee of enquiry into sports sponsorship 'The Howell Report'*, (London, Central Council of Physical Recreation, 1983)

Chambers, I., *Popular Culture: The Metropolitan Experience* (Routledge, 1986)

Chandler, J., 'Bolts from the blue', in *Gridiron UK*, August 1986, Issue 26, 1986

Charlton, J., *Jack Charlton: The Autobiography* (Partridge Press, 1996)

Chippendale, P. and Horrie, C., *Stick It Up Your Punter! The Uncut Story of The Sun Newspaper* (Simon & Schuster, 1999)

Christie, E. and McMahon, T., *No Place to Hide: How I Put the Black in the Union Jack* (Aurum Press, 2010)

Closer (date unknown), Television ownership in private domestic households. Available at: https://www.closer.ac.uk/data/television-ownership-in-domestic-households/

Clough, B., *Clough: The Autobiography* (Corgi Books, 1995)

Clough, B., *Cloughie: Walking on Water* (Headline, 2003)

Coleman (2021), Battle of Britain. Available at: https://talksport.com/sport/boxing/874059/frank-bruno-lennox-lewis-tyson-fury-anthony-joshua/

Coleman, S., Jemphrey, A., Scraton, P. and Skidmore, P., *Hillsborough and after: The Liverpool experience.* Hillsborough Project, First Report (Liverpool City Council, 1990)

Collins, R., 'Wall-to-Wall "Dallas"? The US–UK Trade in Television', *Screen*, 27(3–4), pp. 66–77 (1986)

Commonwealth of Nations, The Gleneagles Agreement on Sporting Contacts with South Africa, 1977 (Commonwealth, 1977). Available at:

http://thecommonwealth.org/sites/default/files/inline/GleneaglesA-greement.pdf [Accessed 13 October 2021]

Conn, D., *The Football Business: Fair Game in the '90s?* (Mainstream Publishing, 1997)

Cooper, J., 'The Foreign Politics of Opposition: Margaret Thatcher and the Transatlantic Relationship before Power', in *Contemporary British History*, Vol. 24, No. 1, pp. 23–42 (2010)

Crick, M. and Smith, D., *Manchester United: The Betrayal of a Legend* (Pan Books, 1990)

Culley, J. (1995), 'Where Are They Now?', in the *Independent*. Available at: https://www.independent.co.uk/sport/where-are-they-now-1620778.html?r=3318 [Accessed 20 October 2021]

D'Agati, P. A., *The Cold War and the 1984 Olympic Games: A Soviet–American Surrogate War* (New York: Palgrave MacMillan, 2013)

Davis, L., 'From a pub game to a sporting spectacle: the professionalisation of British Darts, 1970–1997', *Sport in History*, 38:4, pp. 507–33 (2018)

Dalglish, K. with Winter, H., *Dalglish: My Autobiography* (Coronet Books, 1997)

De Bens, Els, Mary Kelly and Marit Bakke (1992) 'Television Content: Dallasification of Culture?', pp. 73–100, in K. Siune and W. Truetzschler (eds), *Dynamics of Media Politics* (Sage, 1992)

Deford, F., 'Talk about Strokes of Genius', in *Sports Illustrated*, 16 July 1984

Demissie, S. (2014), The World Cup: considering a boycott in 1982. Available at:https://blog.nationalarchives.gov.uk/world-cup-considering-boycott-1982/ [Accessed 20 November 2021]

Disability Rights (2021): Grenfell Tower fire is 'a landmark act of discrimination against disabled and vulnerable people'. Available at: https://www.disabilityrightsuk.org/news/2021/april/grenfell-tower-fire-'-landmark-act-discrimination-against-disabled-and-vulnerable [accessed 13 December 2022]

Dunk, P. (ed.), *Rothmans Football Yearbook 1986–87* (Queen Anne Press, 1986)

Dunlop, M. (2017), My Aunt Rose Reilly: A World Cup winner with Italy. Available at: https://www.gentlemanultra.com/2017/02/11/my-aunt-rose-reilly-a-world-cup-winner-with-italy-by-martin-dunlop/ [Accessed 13 October 2021]

Dunning, E.; Murphy, P. and Williams, J., *The Roots of Football Hooliganism: An Historical and Sociological Study* (Routledge & Kegan Paul, 1989)

Dyke, G., *Inside Story* (Harper Perennial, 2005)

Edwards, R. (2015), England's 'rebel' tour of South Africa 1990: 'I thought Mike Gatting might get killed out there'. In the *Independent*. Available at: https://www.independent.co.uk/sport/cricket/england-s-rebel-tour-south-africa-1990-i-thought-mike-gatting-might-get-killed-out-there-9996444.html [Accessed 27 October 2021]

Edwards, T., *Living Every Second* (Hodder & Stoughton, 2001)

Edwards, T. and Madge, T., *Maiden* (Simon & Schuster, 1991)

Elman, P. (date unknown), Tony Hollingsworth: Nelson Mandela 70th Birthday Tribute. In tonyhollingsworth.com. Available at: https://tony-hollingsworth.com/?q=content/nelson-mandela-70th-birthday-tribute [Accessed 31 October 2021]

Elms, R., *The Way We Wore: A Life in Threads* (Lume Books, 2020)

English, T., *No Borders: Playing Rugby for Ireland* (Arena Sport, 2018)

ESPN (2004): What happened to the black cricketer? Available at: https://www.espncricinfo.com/wcm/content/story/134939.html

Everton, C., *Black Farce and Cue Ball Wizards* [Kindle DX version] (Mainstream Digital, 2011)

Feitlowitz, M., *A Lexicon of Terror: Argentina and the Legacies of Torture* (Oxford University Press, 1998)

Fennell, D., *Investigation into the King's Cross Underground Fire*. Cmnd 499 (HMSO, 1988)

Firth, P., *Four Minutes to Hell: The Story of the Bradford City Fire* (Parrs Wood Press, 2005)

Fisher, M. '"Iron Lady": How a Moscow Propagandist Gave Margaret Thatcher Her Famous Nickname', *Washington Post*, 8 April 2013

Fletcher, M., *56: The Story of the Bradford Fire* (Bloomsbury, 2015)

Foot, D., *Wally Hammond: The Reasons Why* (Robson Books, 1998)

Fowler, E., *Home Management* (George Newnes Publishing, 1954)

Fox, N. (1992), Norman Fox on the administrator with the courage to stand up to Mrs Thatcher. Available at: https://www.independent.co.uk/sport/football-ted-croker-success-at-fa-norman-fox-on-the-administrator-with-the-courage-to-stand-up-to-mrs-thatcher-1565489.html

Free, M., 'Keeping Them Under Pressure: Masculinity, Narratives of National Regeneration and the Republic of Ireland Soccer Team', in *Sport in History*, Vol. 25, No. 2, pp. 265–88 (2005)

Friedman, S. (2018), 'Zola Budd: After the Fall'. In *Runners World*. Available at: https://www.runnersworld.com/runners-stories/a21751547/zola-budd-after-the-fall/ [Accessed 26 October 2021]

Futterman, M. (2021), Martina Navratilova: Living as an openly gay superstar set me free. Available at: https://www.irishtimes.com/life-and-style/people/martina-navratilova-living-as-an-openly-gay-superstar-set-me-free-1.4587439 [Accessed 4 October 2021]

Gabriel, T. (1992), 'The Runner Stumbles'. In *New York Times Magazine*. Available at: *https://www.nytimes.com/1992/07/19/magazine/the-runner-stumbles.html* [Accessed 4 October 2021]

Garfield, S., *The Wrestling* (Faber & Faber, 2007)

Garry, T. (2021), 'We won the FA Cup a week after escaping the Hillsborough disaster'. Available at https://www.telegraph.co.uk/football/2021/04/15/won-fa-cup-week-escaping-hillsborough-disaster/ [Accessed 7 October 2021]

George, B., *Bobby Dazzler: My Story* (Orion, 2006)

Gemmell, J., *The Politics of South African Cricket* (Routledge, 2004)

Giulianotti, R. (2005), 'The sociability of sport: Scotland football supporters as interpreted through the sociology of Georg Simmel', *International Review for the Sociology of Sport*, 40(3), pp. 289–306

Glick, S. M. (1981), 'Silencing the disabled: Only the state may help the disabled; others who try are repressed', in *Index on Censorship*, 10(5): 32–3 (1981)

Goal.com (date unknown), 'This was our revenge' – when Maradona went to war with England. Available at: https://www.goal.com/en/news/1717/editorial/2016/06/22/3890864/this-was-our-revenge-when-maradona-went-to-war-with-england [Accessed 21 November 2021]

Goldberg, A. and Frank, G. (2015), A time when gigs were violent. Available at: https://www.bbc.co.uk/news/magazine-34184563

Gooch, G., *Out of the Wilderness* (HarperCollins, 1986)

Gray, J., 'Sixty Years of the Bolshoi', *Dancing Times*, 19 July 2016

Grose, R., *The Sun-Sation: Behind the Scenes at Britain's Bestselling Daily Newspaper* (Angus & Robertson, 1989)

Gurney, C., ' "A Great Cause": The Origins of the Anti-Apartheid Movement, June 1959–March 1960', *Journal of Southern African Studies*, 26(1), pp.123–44 (2000)

Hain, P. and Odendaal, A., *Pitch Battles: Sport, Racism and Resistance* (Rowman & Littlefield, 2021)

Hamilton, D., *Provided You Don't Kiss Me: 20 Years with Brian Clough* (Fourth Estate, 2009)

Hansard, House of Commons Debate archives (HC Deb)

Hansen, A., *A Matter of Opinion* (Transworld Publishers, 2000)

Harman, J (2008), The Sex, Drugs & Rock 'n' Roll Tour: England in New Zealand, 1984. Available at: https://wisden.com/stories/long-room/sex-drugs-rock-n-roll-tour-england-new-zealand-1984 [Accessed 2 May 2021]

Harris, N. (2009), 'Great Sporting Moments: Dennis Taylor defeats Steve Davis 18−17 at the Crucible', in the *Independent*. Available at: https://www.independent.co.uk/sport/general/others/great-sporting-moments-dennis-taylor-defeats-steve-davis-1817-at-the-crucible-1741225.html

Harris, R., *Gotcha! The Media, The Government and the Falklands Crisis* (Faber & Faber, 1983)

Harrison, T., 'V.', in *London Review of Books*, Vol. 7, No. 1, 24 January 1985

Hartman, R., *Ali: The Life of Ali Bacher* (Viking, 2004)

Hassan, D., 'A People Apart: Soccer, Identity and Irish Nationalists in Northern Ireland', in *Soccer & Society*, Vol. 3, No. 3, pp. 65−83 (2002)

Hastings, M., *Editor: An Inside Story of Newspapers* (Pan Books, 2003)

Hastings, M. and Jenkins, S., *The Battle for the Falklands* (Book Club Associates, 1983)

Henning, A. and Krieger, J., 'Dropping the Amateur: The International Association of Athletics Federations and the Turn Toward Professionalism', *Sport History Review*, 51(1), pp. 64−83 (2020)

Herman, M. (2020), How Maradona's 'Hand of God' quote went round the world. Available at: https://www.reuters.com/article/soccer-argentina-maradona-reuters-idUSKBN2853CL [Accessed 21 November 2021]

Hewitson, D., *The Liverpool Boys are in Town 1978/82: Where D'ya Get Yer Trainees From?* (Self-published, 2004)

Hibbert, T., *Best of Q Who the Hell . . . ?* (Virgin Books, 1994)

Higgins, A., *Alex Through the Looking Glass* (Pelham Books, 1986)

Hill, C. R., 'The politics of Manchester's Olympic bid', *Parliamentary Affairs*, 47(3), pp. 338−55 (1994)

HMRC, Statistics of Government revenues from UK oil and gas production (Her Majesty's Revenue and Customs, 2014)

HMSO, Sexual Discrimination Act (Home Office 1975

Hobson, D., *Channel 4: The Early Years and the Jeremy Isaacs Legacy* (I. B. Tauris, 2008)

Holt, R. and Mason, T., *Sport in Britain 1945−2000* (Blackwell Publishers, 2000)

Horell, S., 'The Household and the Labour Market', in Crafts, N., Gazeley, I. and Newell, A., *Work and Pay in 20th Century Britain* (Oxford University Press, 2007)

Hornby, N., *Fever Pitch* (Penguin Books, 2000)

Horne, N., *Nicky Horne's Viewer's Guide to American Football* (Robson Books, 1986)

Horrie, C., *Sick as a Parrot: The Inside Story of the Spurs Fiasco* (Virgin Books, 1992)

Horrie, C., *Premiership: Lifting the Lid on a National Obsession* (Pocket Books, 2002)

Horrie, C. and Clarke, S., *Citizen Greg: The Extraordinary Story of Greg Dyke and How He Captured the BBC* (Simon & Schuster, 2000)

Howell, D., *Made in Birmingham: The Memoirs of Denis Howell* (MacDonald Queen Anne Press, 1990)

Ingle, S. (2020): Sebastian Coe: 'I was prepared to die with blood in my boots for the 1500m'. Available at: https://www.theguardian.com/sport/2020/jul/24/sebastian-coe-steve-ovett-rivalry-forty-years-on-moscow-olympics-interview [Accessed 12 November 2021]

Ingle, S. (2021): 'I didn't just want to nibble at records': 40 years on from Coe's stunning 1981. Available at: https://www.theguardian.com/sport/2021/jun/05/i-didnt-just-want-to-nibble-at-records-40-years-on-from-coes-stunning-1981 [Accessed 12 November 2021]

Inglis, S., *Football Grounds of Great Britain* (Collins Willow, 1987)

Inglis, S., *Football Grounds of Britain* (Collins Willow, 1996)

Ipsos (date unknown), Voting Intentions in Great Britain 1976–1987. Available at https://www.ipsos.com/ipsos-mori/en-uk/voting-intentions-great-britain-1976-1987 [Accessed 21 November 2021]

Isaacs, J., *Storm Over 4: A Personal Account* (Weidenfeld & Nicolson, 1989)

Ivey, J. A., 'Double Standards: South Africa, British Rugby, and the Moscow Olympics', in *International Journal of the History of Sport*, 36:1, 104–21 (2019)

Jameson, D., *Touched by Angels* (Penguin Books, 1989)

Jefferys, K., 'Britain and the Boycott of the 1980 Moscow Olympics', in *Sport in History*, 32:2, 279–301 (2012)

Jones, B., *Alone: The Triumph and Tragedy of John Curry* (Bloomsbury, 2015)

Jones, I. (2012), Morning Glory: A History of Breakfast Television [Online], Kelly Publications. Available at https://www.amazon.co.uk/Morning-Glory-History-Breakfast-Television-ebook/dp/B009Q5O6J6 [Accessed 1 September 2021].

Jones, C. and Murie, A., *The Right to Buy: Analysis and Evaluation of a Housing Policy* (John Wiley & Sons, 2008)

Keating, F., *High, Wide and Handsome* (Collins Willow, 1986)

Kelleher, W. (2020), The apartheid tour: 40 years on, former Lions stars recall defying the protests, shock at white-only beaches and being cult heroes to black fans. In Mail Online. Available at: https://www.dailymail.co.uk/sport/rugbyunion/article-8305645/The-apartheid-tour-40-years-former-Lions-stars-recall.html [Accessed 20 October 2021]

Killanin, L., *My Olympic Years* (Secker & Warburg, 1983)

Lamb, L., *Sunrise: The Remarkable Rise and Rise of the Best Selling Soaraway Sun* (Papermac, 1989)

Litherhead, B., *Wrestling in Britain* (Routledge, 2018)

Llewellyn, M. P. and Rider, T. C., 'Sport, Thatcher and Apartheid Politics: The Zola Budd Affair', *Journal of Southern African Studies*, 44:4, 575–92 (2018)

Lowe, J., *Old Stoneface: My Autobiography* (John Blake, 2009)

Lynch, D., *Days of Heaven: Italia '90 and the Charlton Years* (Gill Books, 2010)

Macfarlane, N., with Herd, M., *Sport and Politics. A World Divided* (Willow Books, 1986)

MacNeill, M., 'Sex, Lies and Videotape', in Rail, G. (ed.), *Sport and Postmodern Times* (State University of New York Press, 1998)

McDowell, M. L. and Skillen, F., 'The 1986 Commonwealth Games: Scotland, South Africa, sporting boycotts, and the former British Empire', in *Sport in Society*, 20:3, 384–97 (2107)

McGuigan, B., *The Untold Story* (Arrow Books, 1991)

McGuigan, B., *Cyclone: My Story* (Virgin Books, 2012)

McKittrick, D., Kelters, S., Feeney, B. and Thornton, C., *Lost Lives* (Mainstream Publishing, 1999)

McLean, I. and Johnes, M., *Government & Disasters* (Welsh Academic Press, 2000)

McMahon, J. (2020), 'The secret is it's a good song': How Italia '90 and 'World in Motion' started football's love affair with music. Available at: https://www.independent.co.uk/arts-entertainment/music/features/italia-90-world-in-motion-england-football-new-order-peter-hook-keith-allen-pete-hooton-the-farm-interview-a9561466.html

Maguire, J., 'More than a sporting touchdown: The making of American football in England 1982–1990', *Sociology of Sport Journal*, 7(3), pp. 213–37 (1990)

Mair, J., Chesterton, F. and Reeves, I., eds, *What Price Channel 4? Would Privatisation be a disaster, an Opportunity or a Rebirth?* (abramis academic publishing, 2016)

Major, J., *John Major: The Autobiography* (Harper Collins, 2000)

Manley, M., *A History of West Indies Cricket* (André Deutsch, 2002)

Maradona, D., *El Diego: The Autobiography* (Yellow Jersey, 2005)

Marshall, T., *Wheelchairs, Perjury and the London Marathon* (Clink Street, 2017)

Martin, A. (2017), Colour Television: 50 Years On. Available at: https://www.bbc.co.uk/blogs/genome/entries/bee96f81-0c42-4466-9f06-9d548ab79610

Mass Observation Archive (University of Sussex), Spring Directive (1989)

May, P., *The Rebel Tours: Cricket's Crisis of Conscience* (Sports Books, 2009)

Moore, D., *The Pineapple Dance Book* (Pavilion, 1983)

Moore, D., *When a Woman Means Business* (Fontana/Collins, 1990)

Moore-Bick, M., *Grenfell Tower Inquiry: Phase 1 Report* (Crown Copyright, 2019)

Mullen, T. (2015), Heysel disaster: English football's forgotten tragedy? Available at: https://www.bbc.co.uk/news/uk-england-merseyside-32898612

Murphy, P., Williams, J. and Dunning, E., *Football on Trial: Spectator Violence and Development in the Football World* (Routledge & Kegan Paul, 1990)

Nauright, J. and Chandler, T., *Making Men: Rugby and Masculine Identity* (Routledge, 1996)

Navratilova, M., *Martina* (Alfred A. Knopf, 1985)

Nixon, R., 'Apartheid on the run: The South African sports boycott', *Transition*, 58, pp.68-88 (1992)

Norridge, J., *Can We Have Our Balls Back, Please? How the British Invented Sport* (Penguin Books, 2012)

Northam, R. (2008), When the waif of the Veldt had Fleet St on the run. Available at: https://www.sportsjournalists.co.uk/sja-news/sja-1948-2008/how-veldt-waif-had-fleet-st-on-the-run/ [Accessed 26 October 2021]

O'Hagan, S. (2009), Punch-up that made Press history. In the *Independent*. Available at: https://www.independent.co.uk/news/media/punch-made-press-history-6096465.html [Accessed 1 November 2021]

O'Hare, M. (2020), The biggest sporting duel on the planet: Sebastian Coe vs Steve Ovett. Available at: https://www.independent.co.uk/independentpremium/long-reads/olympics-1980-running-sebastian-coe-steve-ovett-a9505711.html?r=1586 [Accessed 12 November 2020]

Oglanby, E., *Black Ice: The Life and Death of John Curry* (Victor Gollancz, 1995)

Open to Questions, BBC One Television, 20 October 1986

Orders, M. (2021), 'This is madness!' The 1980s Lions tour that was very different as players drank and smoked, in *WalesOnline*. Available at:

https://www.walesonline.co.uk/sport/rugby/rugby-news/this-madness-1980s-lions-tour-21249237 [Accessed 20 October 2021]

Organising Committee of the Games of the XXII Olympiad: *Official Report*, Moscow (1980)

Osbourne, C. (2013), FA Cup: Luton v Millwall and the scar of the Kenilworth Road riot. Available at: https://www.bbc.co.uk/sport/football/21446176

Ovett, S., *Ovett: An Autobiography* (Collins Willow, 1984)

Parrish, S., *Parrish Times: My Life as a Racer* (Weidenfeld & Nicolson, 2019)

Parsons, M., 'Representing the Falklands Conflict in Words and Pictures', in *French Journal of British Studies*, 15:4, pp. 1–8 (2010)

Peach, C. (1986): 'Patterns of Afro-Caribbean Migration and Settlement in Great Britain: 1945– 1981', in Brock, C., *The Caribbean in Europe: Aspects of the West Indian Experience in Britain, France and the Netherlands* (Frank Cass & Co., 1986)

Pennant, C., *Congratulations, You've Just Met the ICF* (John Blake, 2003)

Petridis, A. (2010), Misunderstood or hateful? Oi!'s rise and fall. Available at:https://www.theguardian.com/music/2010/mar/18/oi-cockney-rejects-garry-bushell-interview

Plunkett, J. (2013), Radio 4 courts controversy with broadcast of Tony Harrison's *V.* Available at: https://www.theguardian.com/media/2013/jan/14/radio-4-controversy-tony-harrison-v

Popplewell, O., *Committee of Inquiry into Crowd Safety and Control at Sports Grounds*: Interim Report. Cmnd. 9585 (HMSO, 1985)

Purnell, S., *Just Boris: A Tale of Blonde Ambition* (Aurum Press, 2012)

Read, J., *Justin Fashanu: The Biography* (DB Publishing, 2012)

Reynolds, M., *The Gaelic Athletic Association and the H-Blocks Crisis, 1976–1981* (2015, unpublished)

Rider, T. C., *Cold War Games: Propaganda, the Olympics, and U.S. Foreign Policy* (University of Illinois Press, 2016)

Rider, T. C. and Llewellyn, M. P., 'For Profit or For Country? The Daily Mail and the Zola Budd affair', in J. Carvalho (ed.), *Sports Media History: Culture, Technology, Identity* (Taylor & Francis, 2020)

Roantree, B., and Vira, K., The Rise and Rise of Women's Employment in the UK (Institute for Fiscal Studies, Briefing Note, 234. 2018)

Roberts, R., *The Classic Slum: Salford Life in the First Quarter of the Century* (Penguin Books, 1990)

Robson, B., *So Near and Yet So Far: Bobby Robson's World Cup Diary* (Collins Willow, 1986)

Roebuck, P., *It Sort of Clicks: Ian Botham Talking to Peter Roebuck* (Collins Willow, 1986)

Rouse, P., *Sport & Ireland: A History* (Oxford University Press, 2015)

Rowing Story (date unknown): 1980 Olympic Games Rowing. Available at: https://rowingstory.com/year-by-year/1980-olympics-games-rowing/ [accessed 13 December 2022]

Rutherford, A. (2015), Remembering Belfast man Patrick Radcliffe who died in Heysel tragedy. Available at: https://www.belfasttelegraph.co.uk/news/northern-ireland/remembering-belfast-man-patrick-radcliffe-who-died-in-heysel-tragedy-31262076.html

Sampson, K. (2019), This is young, urban, male Britain – modern as hell, and how? Available at: https://theface.com/archive/ellesse-pringle-fila-nike-tacchini-lacoste

Schlosser, E., *Fast Food: The Dark Side of the All-American Meal* (Perennial, 2020)

Scholar, I. with Bose, M., *Behind Closed Doors: Dreams and Nightmares at Spurs* (André Deutsch, 1992)

Scraton, P., *Hillsborough: The Truth* (Mainstream Publications, 1999)

Searcey, I. (2012), Paralympics archive: the marathon debate (1983), viewed 15 June 2021, https://www.channel4.com/news/paralympics-archive-the-marathon-debate-1983

Sherwood, H. (2019), Sexism, vandalism and bullying: inside the Boris Johnson-era Bullingdon Club. Available at: https://www.theguardian.com/politics/2019/jul/07/oxford-bullingdon-club-boris-johnson-sexism-violence-bullying-culture

SkySports (2021), You Guys Are History: Phillip DeFreitas, Monte Lynch and more open up on racism they faced. Available at: https://www.skysports.com/cricket/news/12123/12398353/you-guys-are-history-phillip-defreitas-monte-lynch-and-more-open-up-on-racism-they-faced

Slegg, C. and Gregory, P., *A History of the Women's FA Cup Final* (The History Press, 2021)

Smit, B., *Pitch Invasion: Adidas, Puma and the Making of Modern Sport* (Penguin 2007)

Smith, G. (1984), 'I Do What I Want to Do', *Sports Illustrated*, 18 July 1988

Solarz, S. J., *Journeys to War and Peace: A Congressional Memoir* (Brandeis University Press, 2011)

Sparks, C. & Tulloch, J., *Tabloid Tales: Global Debates Over Media Standards* (Rowman & Littlefield, 2000)

Spencer, N., '"America's Sweetheart" and "Czech-mate": A Discursive Analysis of the Evert-Navratilova Rivalry', in *Journal of Sport and Social Issues*, 27(1), pp.18–37 (2003)

Sports Council, *Digest of sports statistics for the UK* (3rd edn, 1991)

Spurling, J., 'Working Class Heroes', in *When Saturday Comes*, Issue 268, June 2009. Available at: https://www.wsc.co.uk/the-archive/working-class-heroes/

Stacey, A. (2015), St Andrew's wall collapse tragedy: Policeman remembers horror at Birmingham City match. Available at: https://www.birming-hammail.co.uk/news/midlands-news/st-andrews-wall-collapse-tragedy-9166824

Stephenson, H. and Bromley, M. (eds), *Sex Lies and Democracy: The Press and the Public* (Routledge, 1998)

Storey, D. (2020), Rose Reilly: The lost superstar of women's football. Availableat:https://inews.co.uk/sport/football/womens-football/rose-reilly-scotland-fa-football-reims-milan-lecce-best-womens-player-411226 [Accessed 13 October 2021]

Stott, R., *Dogs and Lampposts* (Metro, 2002)

Strinati, D. and Wagg, S. (eds), *Come On Down? Popular Media Culture in Post-war Britain* (Routledge, 1992)

Tatchell, P., *The Battle for Bermondsey* (Heretic Books, 1983)

Taylor, I., 'English Football in the 1990s: Taking Hillsborough Seriously'. In Williams, J. and Wagg, S. (eds): *British football and social change: Getting into Europe.* (Leicester University Press 1991)

Taylor, Rt. Hon. Lord Justice, The Hillsborough Stadium Disaster 15 April 1989: Final Report (Home Office, Cmnd 962, H.M.S.O., 1990)

Thatcher, M., *The Downing Street Years* (HarperCollins, 1993)

The Age (2005): Rebels – the '85 South Africa tour. Available at: https://www.theage.com.au/sport/cricket/rebels-the-85-south-africa-tour-20051210-ge1ekr.html [Accessed 27 October 2021]

thecommonwealth.org (2016): From the Archive: Gleneagles Agreement on Sport. Available at: https://thecommonwealth.org/media/news/archive-gleneagles-agreement-sport [Accessed 11 November 2021]

The National Archive Cabinet Papers (TNA CAB)

The National Archive Prime Minister's Office records (TNA PREM19)

Thompson, B. (1996), The Interview: Barry Hearn. In the *Independent.* Available at: https://www.independent.co.uk/life-style/the-interview-barry-hearn-1303579.html [Accessed 3 May 2021]

Thompson, T. (2005), Twenty years after, mystery still clouds Battle of the Beanfield. Available at: https://www.theguardian.com/uk/2005/jun/12/ukcrime.tonythompson

Titford, R., 'Boxing Clever', in *When Saturday Comes*, edition 291 (2011)

Turner, T., *The Sports Shoe: A History from Field to Fashion* (Bloomsbury, 2019)

UPI (1981), Mrs. Thatcher called Britain's most unpopular leader since WW II. Available at: https://www.upi.com/Archives/1981/12/18/Mrs-Thatcher-called-Britains-most-unpopular-leader-since-WW-II/7728377499600/ [Accessed 21 November 2021]

UPI (1990), Demonstrators rampage against cricket tour. Available at: https://www.upi.com/Archives/1990/01/26/Demonstrators-rampage-against-cricket-tour/5303630308030/ [Accessed 31 October 2021]

Vahed, G., 'Cultural Confrontation: Race, Politics and Cricket in South Africa in the 1970s and 1980s', *Sport in Society*, 5:2, 79–108 (2002)

Villa, R., *And Still Ricky Villa* (Vision Sports Publishing, 2010)

Vine, P., *Visionary: Manchester United, Michael Knighton and the Football Revolution 1989–2019* (Pitch Publishing, 2019)

Waddell, S., *Bellies and Bullseyes: The Outrageous True Story of Darts* (Ebury Press, 2007)

Walvin, J., *The People's Game: The History of Football Revisited* (Mainstream Publishing, 1994)

Wertheim, J., *Glory Days: The Summer of 1984 and the 90 Days That Changed Sports and Culture Forever* (Mariner Books, 2021)

Whannel, G., *The Head to Head That Had to Happen: A Case Study of Television Sport and Entrepreneurship* (1986)

Whannel, G., *Fields in Vision: Television Sport and Cultural Transformation* (Routledge, 1992)

Wheeler, B. (2009), The John Bercow story. Available at: http://news.bbc.co.uk/1/hi/uk_politics/8114399.stm [Accessed 11 November 2021]

Wilde, S., *Ian Botham: The Power and the Glory* (Simon & Schuster, 2011)

Williams, J.; Dunning, E. and Murphy, P., *Hooligans Abroad: The Behaviour and Control of English Fans in Continental Europe* (Routledge & Kegan Paul, 1984)

Williams, J., 'White Riots', in Tomlinson, A. and Whannel, G. (eds), *Off the Ball: The Football World Cup* (Pluto Press, 1986)

Williams, J., *Cricket and Broadcasting* (Manchester University Press, 2011)

Williams, J. (2017), Women, Sport and The First World War. Available at: https://www.wlv.ac.uk/research/institutes-and-centres/centre-for-

historical-research/football-and-war-network/football-and-war-blog/
2017/june-to-december-2017/women-sport-and-the-first-world-war/
women-sport-and-the-first-world-war.php [Accessed 13 October 2021]

Williams, K., *The Kenneth Williams Diaries* (HarperCollins, 1993)

Williamson, M. (2008), Gandhi's Gleneagles stand-off. In *ESPN CricInfo*.
Available at: https://www.espncricinfo.com/story/gandhi-s-gleneagles-
stand-off-378325 [Accessed 25 October 2021]

Woodcock, J. (ed.), *Wisden Cricketers' Almanack 1982* (1982)

Woodcock, J. (ed.), *Wisden Cricketers' Almanack 1983* (1983)

Woolnough, B., *Ken Bates: My Chelsea Dream* (Virgin Books, 1998)

Young, H., *One of Us* (MacMillan, 1989)

Young, H. and Sloman, A., *The Thatcher Phenomenon* (BBC Books, 1986)

Yule, A., *David Puttnam − The Story So Far* (Sphere Books, 1989)

DOCUMENTARIES AND TELEVISION PROGRAMMES

Blood on the Carpet − The Split in Darts (2001). Directed by N. Mirsky. BBC
Two.

Casuals: The Story of the Legendary Terrace Fashion (2011). Directed by M. Kelly.
Urban Edge Films.

Gods of Snooker - Episode 1 (2021). Directed by M. Fuller. BBC Two.

Gods of Snooker - Episode 2 (2021). Directed by E. McGown. BBC Two.

Gods of Snooker - Episode 3 (2021). Directed by B. Lomax. BBC Two.

Hillsborough − how they Buried the Truth (2013). BBC One.

Maiden (2018) Directed by A. Holmes. New Black Films.

Moscow 1980: The Cold War Olympics (2013). Directed by G. Cook & S. Lyle.
BBC Two.

The Big Match - Live (1983). ITV.

NOTES

INTRODUCTION

1 Major (2000), p. 403.

PART I. CULTURE

Chapter 1. The Sun Always Shines on TV

1 Interview, 14 May 2021.
2 Harris (2009).
3 Closer (date unknown).
4 Holt and Mason (2000), p. 104.
5 *Radio Times*, 24 January 1980.
6 Martin (2017).
7 Quoted in *Guardian*, 9 November 2018.
8 BBC, 2005.
9 *Sun*, 3 May 1980.
10 Everton (2011), p. 91.
11 *The Times*, 4 May 2007
12 Central Council of Physical Recreation, 1983.
13 Whannel (1992), p. 71.
14 Burn (2020), p. 37.
15 *The Times*, 16 July 1983.
16 ITV (1984)
17 Quoted in Titford (2011).
18 *Sunday Times*, 19 May 1985.
19 Dunk (1986), p. 432.
20 Interview, 27 January 2021.
21 *The Times*, 2 February 1980.
22 *Guardian*, 9 September 2002.

23 Davis (2018), p. 521.
24 *Newcastle Chronicle*, 16 December 2007.
25 *The Times*, 25 September 1987.
26 Interview, 22 November 2021.
27 *The Times*, 29 August 1988.
28 *Blood on the Carpet*, BBC2, 2001.
29 Lowe (2009), p. 160.
30 *Sun*, 13 February 1985.

Chapter 2. When Will I Be Famous?

1 *Daily Mail*, 8 February 2016.
2 *Irish Post*, 3 August 2018.
3 *The Times*, 29 August 1977.
4 Williams (2011), p.199.
5 Quoted in Arlott in Woodcock (ed.) (1983), p. 87.
6 Woodcock (ed.) (1982), p. 323.
7 Quoted in Botham (2008), p. 158.
8 *Guardian*, 24 April 2011.
9 *Yorkshire Post*, 13 July 1981.
10 Woodcock (ed.) (1983), p. 326.
11 Foot (1998), pp. 18–22, 196.
12 Sparks and Tulloch (eds) (2000), p. 99.
13 Ibid., p. 103.
14 *Daily Star*, 2 November 1978.
15 Jameson (1989), p. 11.
16 Chippendale and Horrie (1999), p. 84.
17 Ibid., p. 111.
18 Ibid., p. 372.
19 Baistow (1985), p. 42.
20 PressGazette.co.uk, 11 October 2006.
21 Chippendale and Horrie (1999), p. 181.
22 BBC (date unknown).
23 *Independent*, 2 April 1997.
24 Turner (2013), p. 296.
25 *The Times*, 9 January 1987.
26 Hibbert (1994), p. xiv.
27 Quoted in Bingham and Conboy (2015), p. 124.
28 *The Times*, 3 July 1981.

29 Interview, 10 November 2021.
30 Quoted in *Washington Post*, 1 July 1981.
31 O'Hagan (2011).
32 Roebuck (1986), p. 129.
33 Interview, 11 March 2021
34 Lamb (1989), pp. 143–4.
35 Chippendale and Horrie (1999), p. 113.
36 Grose (1989), p. 88.
37 Botham (2008), p. 188.
38 Ibid., p. 194.
39 Harman (2018).
40 Botham (2008), p. 204.
41 Wilde (2011), p. 270.
42 Botham (2008), p. 241.
43 Chippendale and Horrie (1999), pp. 294–5.
44 Wilde (2011), pp. 272–3.
45 Ibid., p. 273.
46 Roebuck (1986), p. 135.
47 *Open to Question* (1986).
48 Botham (2008), p. 207.
49 Quoted in Botham (2008), p. 229.
50 Botham (2008), p. 206.
51 Interview, 17 May 2021.
52 Quoted in Thompson (1996).
53 Higgins (1986), p. 117.
54 Interview, 1 March 2021.
55 Quoted in Brown (2012).

Chapter 3. Born in the USA

1 Hobson (2008), p. vii.
2 Brown (2007), p. 27.
3 Interview, 4 August 2021.
4 Bonner and Aston (2003), p. 53.
5 Interview, 9 August 2021.
6 *Sports Illustrated*, 21 November 1983.
7 Maguire (1990), p. 221.
8 Horne (1986), p. 11.
9 Maguire (1990), p. 219.

10 *The Times*, 20 January 1984.
11 Ibid.
12 Interview, 25 August 2021.
13 http://www.britballnow.co.uk/History/Ravens/History.htm
14 http://www.britballnow.co.uk/history-index/complete-history-of-the/
    1983-to-1987---boom-time/
15 Chandler (1986), p. 36.
16 Maguire (1990), p. 223.
17 Horne (1986), p. 11.
18 *Daily Mirror*, 21 October 2011.
19 http://www.offthetelly.co.uk/oldott/www.offthetelly.co.uk/index22d6.
    html?page_id=1255
20 Collins (1986), p. 70.
21 *The Times*, 20 November 1985.
22 https://www.marketingweek.com/levis-laundrette-sales-boost/
23 *Guardian*, 10 April 1986.
24 https://www.campaignlive.co.uk/article/mcdonalds-conquered-
    uk/59278?src_site=marketingmagazine
25 Schlosser (2002), p. 361.
26 Collins (1986), p. 69.
27 De Bens et al. (1992).
28 Chambers (1986), pp. 152–8.
29 *Guardian*, 8 January 2019.
30 Parrish (2019), p. 126.
31 Ibid.
32 Interview, 20 July 2021.
33 *Independent*, 31 July 1994.
34 Interview, 14 July 2021.
35 *Independent*, 31 July 1994.

Chapter 4. Let's Get Physical

1 Interview, 8 July 2021.
2 Jones (2012)
3 BBC, 17 January 1983.
4 Horrie and Clarke (2000), p. 68.
5 Interview, 18 June 2021.
6 Dyke (2005), p. 81.
7 *Guardian*, 30 January 1999.

8 *Daily Express*, 28 July 2018.

9 As quoted in MacNeil (1998), p. 166.

10 *Daily Mail*, 30 June 1983.

11 *Spin*, May 1985.

12 Interview, 14 July 2021.

13 Sports Council (1991), p. 72.

14 Smit (2006), p. 221.

15 Quoted in Smit (2007), p. 221.

16 Ibid., p. 213.

17 Interview, 1 July 2021.

18 https://www.si.com/track-and-field/2020/05/21/jim-fixx-legacy-running-coronavirus

19 Interview, 11 August 2021.

20 Bryant (2012), p. 104.

21 Quoted in Bryant (2012), p. 198.

22 Quoted In Bourke (2017), https://www.birminghammail.co.uk/special-features/birmingham-international-marathon-john-walker-12567856

23 Searcey (2012).

24 Interview, 1 July 2021.

25 Rose (2015), https://www.bbc.co.uk/news/disability-34732084 and https://disabilityarts.online/magazine/opinion/sue-elsegood-a-life-of-campaigning/

26 *The Times*, 8 April 1983.

27 Marshall (2017), pp. 164–5.

28 Ibid., p. 172.

29 Interview, 21 June 2021.

30 *The Times*, 5 May 1987.

31 Ibid.

32 Quoted in Glick (1981), p. 32.

PART II. IDENTITY

Chapter 5. Sisters Are Doin' It For Themselves

1 Mason and Holt (2000), p. 10.

2 Roantree and Vira (2018), p. 3.

3 Bolton (2012), p. 20.

4 Horrell (2007), p. 129.
5 HMSO (1975), p. 12.
6 *Guardian*, 6 April 1987.
7 *The Times*, 26 August 1988.
8 Williams (2017).
9 Interview, 14 September 2021.
10 BBC Sport (date unknown).
11 Interview, 13 June 2013.
12 Quoted in Slegg and Gregory (2021), pp. 136, 137.
13 Interview, 5 July 2013.
14 Interview, 28 September 2021.
15 *Maiden* (2018).
16 *LA Times*, 29 June 1985.
17 Lamb (1989), p. 110.
18 *Daily Express*, 4 January 1982.
19 *Irish Independent*, 2 January 2010.
20 Interview, 12 October 2021.
21 *The Times*, 10 April 1985.
22 Ibid.
23 *New York Times*, 27 November 1985.
24 Interview, 8 October 2021.

Chapter 6. A Little Respect

1 Quoted in Berry (2020), p. 28.
2 Navratilova (1985), p. 205.
3 Futterman (2021).
4 Wertheim (2021), p. 151.
5 Navratilova (1985), p. 277.
6 *Washington Post*, 4 July 1984.
7 Quoted in *Sports Illustrated*, 16 July 1984.
8 *New York Times*, 21 January 1994.
9 Quoted in Spencer (2003), p. 26.
10 Ibid., p. 30.
11 Quoted in *Gay Times*, August 1984.
12 *Sports Illustrated*, 14 September 1988.
13 Ibid.
14 Ibid.

15 Gabriel (1992).
16 *Daily Mirror*, 8 January 1972.
17 *Guardian*, 8 March 2007.
18 Interview, 21 September 2021.
19 Jones (2015), p. 147.
20 Ibid.
21 Ibid., p. 176
22 Ibid.
23 Interview, 13 September 2021.
24 Interview, 28 September 2021.
25 Hamilton (2009), p. 160.
26 Ibid.
27 Clough (1995), p. 221.
28 Ibid., p. 232
29 Anderson (2010), p. 98.
30 Clough (1995), p. 232.
31 Ibid.
32 Baker (2013), p. 143.
33 Clough (1995), p. 231.
34 Hamilton (2009), p. 65.
35 Clough (2003), p. 234.
36 Tatchell (1983), p. 139.
37 Ibid., p. 134.
38 *Observer*, 24 June 2007.
39 margaretthatcher.org/document/106941
40 *Sun*, 13 August 1986.
41 Ibid., 25 January 1989.
42 Isaacs (1989), p. 65.
43 *Guardian*, 10 February 2021.
44 Chippendale and Horrie (1999), p. 217.
45 *The Times*, 23 November 1984.
46 Clough (2003), p. 238.

Chapter 7. People Are People

1 Interview, 10 September 2021.
2 Peach (1986).
3 ESPN (2004).

4 Sky Sports, 2021.

5 *Guardian*, 4 September 2021.

6 Ball Handlers (2021).

7 *Guardian*, 4 September 2021.

8 Dunning, Murphy and Williams (1989), p. 182.

9 *The Times*, 14 February 1981.

10 Ibid., 2 January 1981.

11 Popplewell (1985), p. 7.

12 Dunning, Murphy and Williams (1989), p. 182.

13 Barnes (2000), p. 116.

14 Canoville (2008), p. 4.

15 Woolnough (1998), p. 53.

16 Barnes (2000), p. 116.

17 Ibid.

18 Ibid., p. 120.

19 Ibid.

20 Ibid., p. 122.

21 Ibid., p. 77.

22 Ibid., p. 83.

23 *Los Angeles Times*, 19 April 1990.

24 https://www.runnymedetrust.org/blog/ethnic-unemployment-in-britain

25 Cashmore (1982), p. 40.

26 Bunce (2017), p. 177.

27 Christie and McMahon (2010), p. 209.

28 Interview, 9 February 2022

29 *Independent*, 3 July 2011.

30 *The Times*, 5 April 1980.

31 *Guardian*, 27 April 2010.

32 Quoted in *The Times*, 26 November 1981.

33 Young (1989), p. 234.

34 *The Times*, 19 September 1980.

35 Quoted in *Boston Herald*, 2 November 2008.

36 Quoted in *Daily Telegraph*, 10 September 2020.

37 Quoted in *Guardian*, 12 May 2010.

38 Christie and McMahon (2010), p. xiii.

39 Ibid., p. 219.

40 Ibid., p. 154.

41 Bruno (1992), p. 140.

42 Ibid.
43 Carrington (2010), p. 110.
44 Interview, 25 March 2022.
45 Bruno (1996), p. 5.
46 *The Times*, 22 January 1986; *The Times*, 4 February 1986; *The Times*, 19
    February 1986.
47 Quoted in Coleman (2021).
48 *The Times*, 30 September 1993.
49 Carrington (2010), p. 110.

PART III. CONFLICT

Chapter 8. Where the Streets Have No Name

1 McGuigan (2012), p. 112.
2 Ibid., p. 158.
3 Carpenter (1992), p. 152.
4 *Irish Times*, 12 May 2020.
5 *The Times*, 13 October 1984.
6 Thatcher (1993), p. 382.
7 *The Times*, 25 November 1985.
8 McGuigan (1992), p. 277.
9 Thatcher (1993), p. 382.
10 Ibid., p. 390.
11 Reynolds (2015), p. 78.
12 Ibid., p. 93
13 Quoted in *Irish Times*, 18 April 2021.
14 Ibid.
15 Thatcher (1993), p. 393.
16 margaretthatcher.org/document/121629.
17 Quoted in *Belfast Telegraph*, 28 August 2019.
18 Reynolds (2015), p. 78.
19 *Irish Times*, 4 September 2021.
20 Ibid., 4 September 2021.
21 Rouse (2015), p. 304.
22 McKittrick et al. (1999), p. 926.
23 Interview, 30 May 2022.
24 *Guardian*, 28 March 2011.

25 *Irish Independent*, 12 March 2017.
26 Hassan (2002), p. 68.
27 Interview, 7 June 2022.
28 *Guardian*, 8 April 2001.
29 *The 42*, 4 November 2013.
30 Quoted in *Guardian*, 7 September 2005.
31 Quoted in BelfastLive, 19 May 2020.
32 Ibid.
33 *The Times*, 3 April 1987.
34 As quoted in Hastings (2003), p. 135.
35 Quoted in *Belfast Telegraph*, 25 October 2010.
36 Ibid.
37 Lynch (2010), p. 41.
38 Byrne (1996), p. 131.
39 Charlton (1996), p. 232.
40 Free (2005), p. 272.
41 *Irish Times*, 1 December 2001.

Chapter 9. Two Tribes

1 Ardiles (1983), p. 140.
2 Ibid., p. 142.
3 Ibid.
4 Ibid., p. 43.
5 *Daily Express*, 11 July 1978.
6 Villa (2010), p. 186.
7 *Guardian*, 25 February 2002.
8 *The Times*, 1 December 1980.
9 Ibid., 3 December 1980.
10 Feitlowitz (1998), p. 14.
11 Hastings and Jenkins (1983), p. 72.
12 *Guardian*, 3 April 1982.
13 Ipsos (date unknown).
14 UPI (1981).
15 margaretthatcher.org/document/114228.
16 Hastings and Jenkins (1983), p. 331.
17 Harris (1983), p. 56.
18 Parsons (2010), p. 9.
19 *The Times*, 5 April 1982.

20 Chippendale and Horrie (1999), p. 136.
21 *Sun*, 16 April 1982.
22 *Daily Mirror*, 5 April 1982.
23 Ibid., 6 May 1982.
24 *Sun*, 7 May 1982.
25 *Daily Mirror*, 8 May 1982.
26 *Sun*, 20 April 1982.
27 Chippendale and Horrie (1999), p. 138.
28 Ibid., p. 151.
29 *Sun*, 4 May 1982.
30 Ibid.
31 Hastings and Jenkins (1983), p. 317.
32 Ipsos (date unknown).
33 Thatcher (1993), p. 264.
34 TNA PREM19/620 f161.
35 TNA PREM19/770 f166.
36 TNA CAB129/214 f547.
37 Demissie (2014).
38 Chippendale and Horrie (1999), p. 150.
39 Interview, 29 November 2021.
40 Quoted in Williams et al. (1984), p. 37.
41 *Hansard*, vol. 25, col. 1084, 17 June 1982.
42 Williams et al. (1984), p. 49.
43 Ibid., p. 65.
44 Ibid., p. 94.
45 Quoted in Giulianotti (2005), p. 292.
46 Williams (1986), p. 6.
47 MacFarlane (1986), p. 15.
48 Quoted in Baker (2001), p. 52.
49 Ibid., p. 54.
50 Williams et al. (1984), p. 27.
51 Interview, 6 December 2021.
52 Quoted in Yule (1989), p. 12.
53 *The Times*, 31 December 1981.
54 Ibid., 18 December 1982.
55 Ibid., 26 July 1966.
56 Interview, 14 January 2022.
57 *Sun*, 22 June 1986.
58 Robson (1986), p. 194.

59 *The Times*, 20 June 1986.

60 Quoted in Goal.com (date unknown).

61 *The Times*, 23 June 1986.

62 Herman (2020).

63 *Sun*, 23 June 1986.

64 *Daily Express*, 23 June 1986.

65 Maradona (2005), pp.127−8.

Chapter 10. We're Living in Violent Times

1   *The Times*, 15 March 1985.

2   Dunning, Murphy and Williams (1989), p. 48.

3   Murphy, Williams and Dunning (1990), p. 91.

4   *Daily Mirror*, 5 March 1985.

5   Osbourne (2013).

6   margaretthatcher.org/document/229417.

7   Woolnough (1998), p. 55.

8   Stacey (2015).

9   Popplewell (1985), p. 34.

10 *Birmingham Mail*, 11 May 2017.

11 *The Times*, 13 May 1985.

12 Popplewell (1985), p. 34.

13 *Sunday Mercury*, 3 May 2015.

14 Ibid.

15 *Northampton Chronicle & Echo*, 16 May 2005.

16 Interview, 15 November 2021.

17 Interview, 12 November 2022.

18 Hansen (2000), p. 274.

19 Dalglish (1997), p. 124.

20 *The Times*, 31 May 1985.

21 Rutherford (2015).

22 *The Times*, 21 May 1985.

23 *Sports Illustrated*, 10 June 1985.

24 *The Times*, 31 May 1985.

25 Ibid., 8 July 1985.

26 Dunning, Murphy and Williams (1989), p. 8.

27 Interview, 29 November 2021.

28 Fox (1992).

29 margaretthatcher.org/document/105563.

30 Quoted in Spurling (2009).

31 Thompson (2005).

32 Harrison (1985).

33 Plunkett (2013).

34 *The Times*, 19 October 1987.

35 margaretthatcher.org/document/106689.

36 TNA CAB 129/225/1.

37 Quoted in Goldberg and Frank (2015).

38 Purnell (2012), p. 63.

39 Quoted in Sherwood (2019).

40 Quoted in Sherwood (2019).

41 *Sunday Times*, 19 May 1985.

42 Roberts (1990), p. 225.

43 Interview, 6 January 2022.

44 Quoted in 80scasuals (2016).

45 Turner (2019), p. 200.

46 Hewitson (2004), page unknown.

47 *Casuals* (2011).

48 Elms (2020), Location 3420.

49 *The Times*, 19 January 1988.

50 Sampson (2019).

51 *The Face*, July 1983.

52 Pennant (2003), p. 386.

53 *The Times*, 23 July 1990.

54 *The Face*, July 1990.

PART IV. POLITICS

Chapter 11. Under Pressure

1 Cabinet Conclusions, 18 May 1978, TNA CAB 128/63/19.

2 *Jewish Chronicle*, 1 September 1978.

3 *The Times*, 19 September 1978.

4 Quoted in Jefferys (2012), p. 282

5 Thatcher (1993), p. 87.

6 margaretthatcher.org/document/100824.

7 margaretthatcher.org/document/102750.

8 Fisher (2013).

9 Cooper (2010).

10 Thatcher (1993), p. 88, and margaretthatcher.org/document/113764.

11 Carter (1980).

12 margaretthatcher.org/document/118179.

13 Cabinet minutes 10 January 1980, TNA CAB 130/1137.

14 Thatcher (1993), p. 88.

15 margaretthatcher.org/document/118179.

16 margaretthatcher.org/document/118173.

17 margaretthatcher.org/document/104294.

18 Solarz (2011), p. 9.

19 *The Times*, 3 January 1980.

20 *Guardian*, 24 February 2006.

21 Interview, 12 November 2021.

22 *The Times*, 11 March 1980.

23 Howell (1990), p. 294.

24 *Hansard* HC Deb (2 July 1980), vol. 987, col. 1505.

25 Killanin (1983), p. 200.

26 *Daily Mail*,14 March 1980.

27 margaretthatcher.org/document/113774.

28 *The Times*, 26 March 1980.

29 Howell (1990), p. 302.

30 *The Times*, 29 January 1980.

31 Quoted in *Guardian*, 24 February 2006.

32 margaretthatcher.org/document/113767.

33 *Hansard* HC Deb (17 March 1980), vol. 981, cols. 41.

34 *The Times*, 16 June 1980.

35 *The Times*, 14 March 1980.

36 Interview, 17 July 2018.

37 Interview, 8 Nov 2021.

38 *The Times*, 2 June 1980.

39 Rowing Story (date unknown).

40 Ibid.

41 Killanin (1983), pp. 195 and 209.

42 *Independent on Sunday*, 4 September 1994.

43 Howell (1990), pp. 315–16.

44 Hill (1994), p. 338.

45 Killanin (1983), p. 221.

46 Quoted in *Guardian*, 24 February 2006.
47 *Guardian*, 6 June 1980, and *The Times*, 6 June 1980.
48 Organising Committee of the Games of the **XXII** Olympiad (1980), p. 378.
49 Quoted in Barker (2010), p. 33.
50 Ibid., p. 34.
51 Ovett (1984), p. 77.
52 Interview, 4 August 2018.
53 Quoted in Butcher (2005), p. 159.
54 Quoted in O'Hare (2020).
55 Ibid.
56 *The Times*, 28 July 1980.
57 Butcher (2005), p. 171.
58 Ovett (1984), p. 91.
59 Quoted in Ingle (2020).
60 Whannel (1986), p. 18.
61 Quoted in Ingle (2021).

Chapter 12. Rebel Yell

1 Quoted in Hain and Odendaal (2021), p. 218.
2 Nixon (1992), p. 75.
3 Commonwealth of Nations (1977).
4 thecommonwealth.org (2016).
5 Ivey (2019).
6 *The Times*, 8 December 1979.
7 Ibid.
8 Ibid., 21 December 1979.
9 www.margaretthatcher.org/document/104294.
10 Culley (1995).
11 *Weekend Argus*, 19 June 2010.
12 Orders (2021).
13 Ibid.
14 Quoted in Ivey (2019).
15 Kelleher (2020).
16 Ibid.
17 Ibid.
18 Beattie (2014).

19 Quoted in Nauright and Chandler (1996), p. 185.
20 Vahed (2002), p. 96.
21 Hartman (2004), p. 176.
22 May (2009), p. 57.
23 *The Times*, 27 October 1981.
24 Williamson (2008).
25 Interview, 26 October 2021.
26 Interview, 25 October 2021.
27 Botham (2008), p. 180.
28 Quoted in May (2009), p. 78.
29 Boycott (1987), pp. 230–31.
30 Gooch (1986), p. 22.
31 May (2009), p. 61.
32 *Hansard* HC Deb, vol. 19, col. 22, 1 March 1982.
33 *The Times*, 2 March 1982.
34 Gooch (1986), p. 67.
35 *Daily Mail*, 6 March 1984.
36 Ibid., 9 April 2003.
37 Ibid.
38 Budd (1989), p. 4.
39 Ibid., p. 2.
40 Interview, 10 November 2021.
41 *Hansard* HC Deb, vol. 58, col. 485, 11 April 1984.
42 Wheeler (2009).
43 Bevins (1996).
44 Elman (date unknown).
45 Budd (1989), p. 59.
46 Quoted in Llewellyn and Rider (2018), p. 588.
47 *Daily Telegraph*, 27 April 1984.
48 Friedman (2018).
49 Budd (1989), p. 174
50 Ibid.
51 Friedman (2018).
52 *The Times*, 2 November 1984.
53 Ibid.
54 *The Times*, 24 July 1985.
55 Bateman and Douglas (1986), p. 111.
56 *The Age* (2005).
57 Ibid.

58 Manley (2002), pp. 304–5.

59 UPI (1990).

60 Edwards (2015).

61 *The Times*, 2 February 1990.

62 Ibid., 14 February 1990.

Chapter 13. Money for Nothing

1 Interview, 14 July 2021.

2 Moore (1990), p. 174.

3 Ibid., p. 186.

4 Ibid., p. 198.

5 *The Times*, 2 December 1987.

6 *Bank of England Quarterly Bulletin*, December 1982.

7 Jones and Murie (2008), p. 55.

8 Ibid., p. 58.

9 *The Times*, 20 November 1982.

10 Ibid., 28 October 1982.

11 margaretthatcher.org/document/105823.

12 *The Times*, 9 November 1985.

13 *Telegraph*, 11 April 2013.

14 Quoted in Chippendale and Horrie (1999), p. 267.

15 BBC.com, 18 April 2013.

16 *Management Today*, 24 April 2016.

17 *The Times*, 25 April 1988.

18 Quoted in Chippendale and Horrie (1999), p. 286.

19 Scholar (1992), p. 35.

20 Ibid., p. 42.

21 *The Times*, 10 June 1983.

22 Scholar (1992), p. 45.

23 Interview, 19 January 2022.

24 Quoted in Horrie (1992), p. 53.

25 *Independent*, 3 April 2003.

26 Horrie (2002), p. 43.

27 *Independent*, 3 June 2006.

28 Scholar (1992), p. 159.

29 Ibid.

30 *The Times*, 17 January 1991.

31 Crick and Smith (1990), p. 278.

32 *The Times*, 21 August 1989.

33 Crick and Smith (1990), p. 298.

34 Conn (1997), p. 39

35 Crick and Smith (1990), p. 292.

36 Ibid., p. 278.

37 *Daily Telegraph*, 30 May 2004.

38 *Forbes*, 7 May 2021.

39 *Guardian*, 5 November 2011.

40 Interview, 25 January 2022.

41 *Washington Post*, 15 June 1980.

42 Ibid.

43 HMRC Table 11-11.

44 *The Times*, 9 November 1985.

45 *London Review of Books*, 29 October 1987.

46 *Observer*, 22 January 1978.

Chapter 14. There Is a Light That Never Goes Out

1 Interview, 6 January 2022.

2 Popplewell (1985), p. 5.

3 Ibid., p. 7.

4 Ibid.

5 Fletcher (2015), p. 40.

6 Firth (2005), p. 40.

7 Interview, 11 January 2022.

8 Quoted in Fletcher (2015), p. 114.

9 *Daily Star*, 13 May 1985.

10 Ibid.

11 Popplewell (1985), p. 5.

12 margaretthatcher.org/document/229429.

13 Fletcher (2015), p. 156.

14 Popplewell (1985), p. 6.

15 Fletcher (2015), p. 105.

16 Ibid., p. 139.

17 Popplewell (1985), p. 23.

18 Ibid., p. 19.

19 Inglis (1987), p. 37.

20 margaretthatcher.org/document/229429.

21 Inglis (1996), p. 9.
22 Scraton (1999), p. 59.
23 Interview, 15 November 2021.
24 *Observer*, 15 March 2009.
25 Interview, 2 February 2022.
26 BBC 2013.
27 Quoted in Coleman et al. (1990), p. 111.
28 Ibid.
29 BBC Radio 4 ,15 April 1989.
30 *Grandstand*, 15 April 1989.
31 *Match of the Day*, 15 April 1989.
32 BBC News, 15 April 1989.
33 *Independent*, 17 April 1989.
34 *Sheffield Star*, 18 April 1989.
35 *Daily Express*, 19 April 1989.
36 *Daily Mail*, 19 April 1989.
37 *Daily Star*, 19 April 1989.
38 *Sun*, 19 April 1989.
39 margaretthatcher.org/document/105563.
40 Quoted in Coleman et al. (1990), p. 172.
41 Taylor (1990), p. 13.
42 Ibid., p. 44.
43 Ibid., p. 40.
44 Ibid., p. 34.
45 Clough (1995), p. 258.
46 Walvin (1994), p. 192.
47 Hornby (2000), p. 209.
48 Mass Observation Archive (1989).
49 Thatcher (1993), p. 756.
50 Quoted in Taylor (1991), p. 11.
51 *Guardian*, 22 August 1989.
52 *Hansard* HC Deb, vol. 148, col. 758, 7 March 1989.
53 Fennell (1988), p. 27.

Epilogue. World In Motion

1 *Guardian*, 15 June 2015.
2 *Independent*, 27 June 1996.

3 http://www.britishpoliticalspeech.org/speech-archive.htm?speech=202
4 *Guardian*, 11 June 2016.
5 *Independent*, 16 May 2022.
6 *Inews*, 13 February 2020.
7 Christie and McMahon (2010), p. xiii.
8 ESPN, 1 November 2021.
9 *Guardian*, 26 November 2021.
10 Ibid., 25 July 2022.
11 *Inews*, 28 July 2022.
12 Quoted in *Guardian*, 14 May 2022.
13 Disability Rights (2021).
14 Moore-Bick (2019), p. 7.
15 Ibid., pp. 583–4.

ACKNOWLEDGEMENTS

I'm hugely grateful to everybody who took the time to talk to me and help me bring the 1980s to life through their insights and contributions. I can only apologise if I have misconstrued anything that they said. I'd also like to thank everyone who helped source and arrange those interviews: Jumoke Abdullahi, Ali Betson, Christine Bower, Philippa Brock, Tony Fitzpatrick, Marie George, Matt Jackson, Emily Lewis, Lara Masters, Helen Mitchinson, Josephine Turley, Michelle Wassell and Jonathan Wilson. I'm sorry if I missed anyone off the list.

Thanks are also due to Graham Shaw and Neil Holloway for reading and commenting on drafts of early chapters and I owe a particular debt to Sarah Bowman, Daragh Minogue, Jon O'Malley and Johnny Walker for their continuing support and encouragement.

I'm grateful to my agent Jon Wood for helping me knock my initial ideas into shape and everyone at Yellow Jersey Press, in particular my editors Joe Pickering and Ellie Steel.

Durham, 2023

INDEX

Coronavirus pandemic, 388
Corporate Manslaughter and
    Homicide Act (2007), 380
Corriere della Sera, 258
Corriere dello Sport, 258
Corrigan, Joseph, 224
Corrigan, Michael, 250–51
Cosby Show, The, 69, 163
Cosford, Shropshire, 14
Cossell, Howard, 184
Cottee, Antony 'Tony', 34
Coughlin, Dianne, 116
Coulter, Philip, 209
Countdown, 25, 61
County Championship (cricket), 164
Covent Garden Dance Centre,
    London, 85
Coventry, West Midlands, 174, 176–7
Coventry City FC, 269
Covid-19 pandemic, 84
Cowans, Norman, 165
Cowell, Simon, 83–4
Cowley, Annette, 322
Crabtree, Shirley, 30–31, 32
Cram, Stephen, 294
cricket, 13, 14, 35–42, 49–54, 56,
    158–61, 163
  in Ireland, 205
  racism and, 164–6, 172, 189,
    388–9
  in South Africa, 305–14, 322–4
'cricket test', 172, 187
Crimean War (1853–6), 229
Croft, Colin, 159
Croft, David, 139
Croft, Oliver, 29
Croker, Edgar 'Ted', 109, 238,
    260, 264
Crouch, Peter, 149

Crucible Theatre, Sheffield, 11–12,
    15, 16, 368
Cruise missiles, 279–80
Crystal Palace, London, 68, 318–19
Crystal Palace FC, 169, 347, 348
culture wars, 4, 317
Cunningham, Laurence, 163
Curl, Linda, 113, 114
Currie, Austin, 196
Curry, John, 139–43, 149, 153, 156
Cusack, Michael, 200
Czechoslovakia, 134, 163

D'Abo, Jennifer, 327
D'Oliveira, Basil, 53
Daily Express, 243, 371
Daily Herald, 44
Daily Mail, 263, 284, 315–16, 321, 371
Daily Mirror, 43–4, 49, 139, 172, 230,
    247, 283, 312, 322, 332
Daily Star, 44, 46, 51, 121–2, 332,
    359, 371
Daily Telegraph, 65, 67, 216, 283, 371
Daley Thompson's Decathlon (1984
    game), 57–9
Daley, Thomas, 389
Dalglish, Kenneth, 34, 252, 256
Dallas Cowboys, 62, 68
Dallas, 45, 54, 62, 69–70, 71–2
Dalton, Grant, 119
Dammers, Jeremy 'Jerry', 177, 318
Dana, 209
dancewear, 86, 325–6
'Dancing in the Street' (Bowie and
    Jagger), 87
Daniel, Wayne, 165
Daniels, Jake, 389
'Danny Boy', 194
Darke, Ian, 189

penguin.co.uk/vintage